Data Communications and Networking
Volume II

Edited by **Michelle Vine**

CLANRYE INTERNATIONAL

New Jersey

Published by Clanrye International,
55 Van Reypen Street,
Jersey City, NJ 07306, USA
www.clanryeinternational.com

Data Communications and Networking: Volume II
Edited by Michelle Vine

International Standard Book Number: 978-1-63240-134-2 (Hardback)

Printed in the United States of America.

Contents

	Preface	VII
Chapter 1	**Spectrum-Efficient Cognitive Radio Transceiver Using Multiwavelet Filters** Manju Mathew, A. B. Premkumar and A. S. Madhu kumar	1
Chapter 2	**Improved Handset Antenna Performance via an Electrically Extended Ground Plane** Shirook M. Ali, Huanhuan Gu, Kelce Wilson and James Warden	14
Chapter 3	**A Three-Tier Architecture for User-Centric Ubiquitous Networked Sensing** Jin Nakazawa and Hideyuki Tokuda	21
Chapter 4	**Joint MMSE Transceiver Designs and Performance Benchmark for CoMP Transmission and Reception** Jialing Li, Enoch Lu and I-Tai Lu	32
Chapter 5	**Evolution of Signaling Information Transmission** Jasmina Baraković Husić, Himzo Bajrić and Sabina Baraković	53
Chapter 6	**Game Theoretic Modeling of NGANs: Impact of Retail and Wholesale Services Price Variation** João Paulo R. Pereira and Pedro Ferreira	62
Chapter 7	**A Joint Channel-Network Coding Based on Product Codes for The Multiple-Access Relay Channel** Tafzeel ur Rehman Ahsin and Slimane Ben Slimane	71
Chapter 8	**Approximate Core Allocation for Large Cooperative Security Games** Saman Zonouz and Parisa Haghani	84
Chapter 9	**Optimizing Virtual Private Network Design Using a New Heuristic Optimization Method** Hongbing Lian and András Faragó	92
Chapter 10	**An Overview of Algorithms for Network Survivability** F. A. Kuipers	101
Chapter 11	**Gain Improvement of Dual Band Antenna Based on Complementary Rectangular Split-Ring Resonator** Noelia Ortiz, Francisco Falcone and Mario Sorolla	120

Chapter 12   **Experimental Performance Evaluation of POBICOS Middleware**
For Wireless Sensor Networks   129
Jouni Hiltunen, Mikko Ala-Louko and Markus Taumberger

Chapter 13   **A Reliable and Efficient Highway Multihop Vehicular**
Broadcast Model   139
Deng Chuan and Wang Jian

Chapter 14   **A Radon Slantlet Transforms Based OFDM System Design and**
Performance Simulation under Different Channel Conditions   147
Abbas Hasan Kattoush

Chapter 15   **Antenna Optimization Using Multiobjective Algorithms**   155
X. L. Travassos, D. A. G. Vieira and A. C. Lisboa

Chapter 16   **Project and Realization of a Wide-Range High-Frequency RFID**
Gate Allowing Omnidirectional Detection of Transponders   163
Giuliano Benelli, Stefano Parrino and Alessandro Pozzebon

Chapter 17   **A Transmission Power Self-Optimization Technique for Wireless**
Sensor Networks   174
F. Lavratti, A. Ceratti, D. Prestes, A. R. Pinto, L. Bolzani, F. Vargas,
C. Montez, F. Hernandez, E. Gatti and C. Silva

Permissions

List of Contributors

Preface

The idea that a person can talk to another and convey feelings and ideas is one that never fails to amaze. In today's modern world, this idea has taken on a life of its own and is no longer restricted to face to face information flow. Words and ideas bounce around the world in seconds, while only in the last century it often took days and months for people to be able to communicate with the forms of communication and networking available. A person in Sydney talks to someone in the UK with ease and with no time lag. With the advent of networking and communications in the past few decades, life has gotten much easier and progress is faster than ever. So many advances have been made in this field but most of the research has culminated towards the internet and the phone, two things which embody the tenets of communications and networking at its core. Communication is at its core, the act of conveying information through feelings, words and now, technology. It is the foundation of the advances of human civilization, something which has brought humanity closer than ever before. Nothing embodies the idea of networking better than the internet itself. The concept of linking the world electronically might have seemed outlandish once, but we see it being made into reality every day.

Such ideas and concepts, beginning from its inception to its hopeful destination are collated here and I am grateful to those who made this book a success.

Editor

Spectrum-Efficient Cognitive Radio Transceiver Using Multiwavelet Filters

Manju Mathew, A. B. Premkumar, and A. S. Madhukumar

Centre for Multimedia and Network Technology, School of Computer Engineering, Nanyang Technological University, 50 Nanyang Avenue, Singapore 639798

Correspondence should be addressed to Manju Mathew, manj0001@ntu.edu.sg

Academic Editors: H. Ikeda and C. Yang

Cognitive radio (CR) transceiver that can offer adequate data rate and multiuser support for future wireless networks is a promising technology for reliable and spectrum-efficient mobile communication. Orthogonal frequency division multiplexing (OFDM) and scalar wavelet based schemes have been proposed as physical layer techniques for CR. This paper proposes multiwavelet packet-based multicarrier multiple-access scheme as an equally promising candidate for multi-user CR networks and using existing orthonormal multiwavelets, the performance of the proposed system is evaluated. It is shown that the error performance of the proposed system under frequency and phase offset conditions is comparable with existing schemes.

1. Introduction

With the ability to learn from and adapt to both radio environment and user needs, CR promotes viable communication and optimizes the use of radio frequency (RF) spectrum [1]. Even though OFDM-based systems have been proposed to be the most promising candidate for CR transmission [2–6], recent research work propose wavelet-based schemes to be an alternative modulation technique in terms of flexibility, adaptivity, and spectrum efficiency [7]. The efficacy of scalar wavelet packets for CR-based systems has been explored, and various results are discussed in [8–13]. Both analytical and experimental results show that scalar wavelet-based schemes insures better flexibility, sidelobe suppression, and reconfigurability at moderate complexity. Wavelet theory has been enriched by the introduction of multiwavelets, and it has been proved that they incorporate more degrees of freedom and additional advantages than scalar wavelets [14]. Hence the vector extension of scalar wavelet packet called multiwavelet packet is explored in this work for multi-user CR applications. Multiwavelet packet-based multi carrier multiple-access scheme (MWP-MC-MA) for CR applications is proposed for the first time in the literature. The uplink and downlink system model and signal

model are described in detail, and necessary equations are discussed.

The rest of the paper is organized as follows. In Section 2 a brief review on multiwavelets is given, and its communication-based applications available in the literature are highlighted. Proposed spectrum sensing method is outlined in Section 3. The system model and signal model of single user and multi-user CR environment are described in Sections 4 and 5. The performance analysis of the proposed system is portrayed in Section 6. Conclusions and future directions are given in Section 7.

2. A Brief Review on Multiwavelets and Their Advantages

To clearly investigate the characteristics of multiwavelets and to emphasize the motivation behind this proposal, a brief review on multiwavelets and their unique advantages is described in this section.

2.1. Multiwavelets and Multifilters. Multiwavelets are the generalization of multiresolution analysis (MRA) [14]. The two-scale relations lead to scaling functions and wavelet functions similar to that in scalar wavelets. But the equations are two-scale matrix equations and can be given as

$$\Phi(t) = \sum_n H(n)\Phi(2t - n),$$

$$\Psi(t) = \sum_n G(n)\Psi(2t - n), \tag{1}$$

where $\Phi(t) = [\phi_1(t)\phi_2(t)\cdots\phi_r(t)]^T$ and $\Psi(t) = [\psi_1(t) \psi_2(t)\cdots\psi_r(t)]^T$ form the set of scaling functions and corresponding wavelets. The suffix r denotes the number of wavelets and is dubbed as multiplicity. Each $H(n)$ and $G(n)$ are square matrices of size $r \times r$ and are termed as multifilters [14]. The matrix structure of the filter bank provides more degrees of freedom for multiwavelets. Unlike scalar wavelets, multiwavelet system can simultaneously provide perfect reconstruction while preserving length (orthogonality), good performance at the boundaries (linear-phase symmetry), and a high order of approximation (vanishing moments) together with short support [15]. Hence superior performance is expected from multiwavelets in signal and image processing applications compared to scalar wavelets. To exploit the communication aspects of multiwavelets for multicarrier modulation, it is required to prove the existence of orthogonal multiwavelet packet subspaces and this is discussed in [16]. Unlike scalar wavelets, high-pass filter coefficients of the multifilter cannot be obtained by alternating flip of the low-pass filter but have to be designed [17]. Design of various orthogonal multifilter banks is described in [18–21]. Application of multiwavelet packets for digital communications was first proposed by You and Ilow [22]. They have proposed the vector extension of Mallat's algorithm to implement multiwavelet packet modulation (MWPM) and have proved that spectrum efficiency will be increased r times compared to OFDM and scalar WPM. Besides, additional results are presented in [23] to verify the adaptability of MWPM to mitigate strong narrow-band interference with its flexible time frequency tiling. The symbol-overlapped multiwavelet OFDM for system capacity improvement is discussed in [24]. A simpler method to obtain direct and inverse multiwavelet transform using toeplitz matrix formation is described in [25]. All the research results prove that multifilter banks can bring enormous advantages in next-generation wireless networks. But the use of multiwavelet filter banks to implement a spectrum-efficient and adaptive modulation scheme within CR context is still to be explored. The multiple-access capability of MWPM has not been addressed so far in the literature. Performance evaluation of multiwavelets in the literature is limited to the filter banks proposed in [18, 19], and hence a fair comparison among different orthogonal multiwavelets in terms of error performance is yet unavailable. These issues are tried to address in the following sections and are the main contributions of this work.

2.2. Advantages of MWPM for CR. Features of orthonormal multiwavelet packets that make them suitable for CR applications are listed below.

(i) In the case of multiwavelets, each filter coefficient is an $r \times r$ matrix, and hence larger number of subcarriers are possible for a given bandwidth. For a transform size of N and multiplicity r, there can be as many as $r2^N$ orthogonal subbands and hence r times bandwidth efficiency. This helps allocating more subbands among different users compared to scalar wavelets and OFDM.

(ii) The discrete multiwavelet packet transform (DMWPT) implemented for data reception can be used for spectrum sensing at no additional cost. As multiwavelets provide better results in feature extraction and signal denoising compared to scalar wavelets, the multiwavelet spectrum estimator can outperform scalar wavelet-based spectrum detector described in [26].

(iii) Multiwavelets maintain orthogonality even with certain integer shifts. If the support length of multiwavelet base is $(0, L)$, the orthogonality condition is satisfied for integer shifts of the wavelet base up to L. These shifted waveforms can be used to modulate different data of the same user. Thus the capacity of the system can be improved L times for a given transform size, or the number of subcarriers can be reduced for a given data rate [24]. Thus multiwavelet-based system offers high degree of flexibility and adaptivity in terms of data rate, modulation, and number of subcarriers. OFDM subcarriers overlap only in frequency domain, and hence this kind of flexibility cannot be achieved in OFDM-based systems.

3. Spectrum Sensing with Multifilters

Spectrum sensing is the major task of CR as it is restricted to operate in unused bands. This is not common in any conventional system and hence its successful implementation is a crucial task [27]. Considerable research has been done in this area and numerous algorithms and architectures are available in literature [26–37]. The existing research results prove that spectrum sensing can be implemented in two stages—preliminary or coarse sensing at the physical layer and fine sensing at the MAC layer [28]. Energy or power detector is suggested as the preliminary sensing technique as its algorithm does not require prior knowledge of the signal characteristics. In this work, multifilter banks are exploited to calculate energy of the given spectrum and thus to locate the vacant bands. The related work, motivation, and the proposed sensing algorithm are given in the subsequent subsections.

3.1. Related Work and Motivation. Locating the vacant bands using filter banks is already addressed in the literature [29], and the merits and demerits are discussed. It has been shown that if the filter banks that can be employed for multicarrier communication of CR networks are utilized for spectrum sensing, the sensing circuit can be implemented at no additional cost [29]. The detailed performance analysis of various filter-bank-based spectrum sensing is presented in [29]. Wavelet filter bank-based-sensing is discussed in [26, 30]. A wavelet packet-based energy detector using infinite Impulse Response (IIR) scalar wavelet filters is described in [30]. IIR filters are used for sensing purpose to reduce the complexity of the sensing circuit. But this demands additional circuitry in the CR transceiver for sensing the spectrum. The use of finite impulse response (FIR) wavelet filter bank for spectrum sensing is outlined in [26] and it has been shown that the results are comparable with existing power estimation techniques. Since the sensing circuit proposed in [26], uses scalar wavelet FIR filters, its implementation is possible by utilizing wavelet-based CR receiver (demodulator) at no additional hardware circuitry. Multiwavelet FIR filter-bank-based spectrum sensing is proposed in this section which has not been addressed in the previous works. The motivation behind this proposal is the added advantage of multifilter-based spectrum sensing compared to existing filter bank-based-sensing and is listed below.

(i) Reliable feature extraction. In multiwavelet filter banks, each filter coefficient is a square matrix of size $r \times r$. Hence the filtering operation using multiwavelets involves matrix convolution. This demands r input rows in multifilter based operations. The additional input rows are obtained by repeated row preprocessing which increases the reliability of feature extraction [14].

(ii) Lower number of iterations. Even though each step of multiwavelet transform is computationally complex than scalar wavelet transform, the required frequency (time) resolution can be achieved with reduced number of iterations (at lower transform size). Hence the overall complexity of multiwavelet transform will be equivalent to scalar wavelet transform. That is, for multiwavelets of multiplicity r. Each iteration generates $r \cdot 2^j$ subbands where j is the iteration level. If r is a power of 2, $(N - a)$ iterations are sufficient to generate 2^N subbands where $r = 2^a$.

(iii) Lower number of filter taps. According to [30] the complexity of wavelet filter-bank-based spectrum sensing is $L \cdot N \log_2 N$ where L is the filter length and N is the transform size. Multiwavelet FIR filters have lower number of filter coefficients compared to scalar FIR filters within the same support length. Hence the complexity of sensing is comparable to that of IIR filter-based spectrum sensing and is lower than that of FIR filter-based scalar wavelet spectrum sensing.

3.2. Multifilter-Based Sensing Methodology and Algorithm. The spectrum analysis and data transmission proposed in this work are limited to multifilter banks of multiplicity two. Since multiplicity is two, spectrum sensing circuit needs two input rows which can be easily obtained by single repetition of the signal stream under consideration. Generating the multiwavelet coefficients of the signal stream is shown in Figure 1. The input stream is repeated, and the 2×2 matrix filters operate on both streams to generate four output

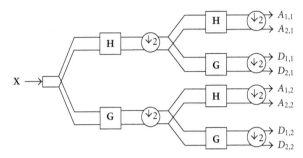

FIGURE 1: Signal decomposition using multifilters.

streams which are downsampled by a factor of 2. The decomposition process is repeated until the desired level of frequency-time resolution is achieved. Each row of the multifilter is a combination of two ordinary filters, one operating on the first data stream and the other operating on the second stream. For a given transform size, the output of the DMWPT will contain $2 \cdot 2^N$ multiwavelet packet coefficients. It is shown that at level two iteration, there are eight wavelet packet coefficients or eight frequency subbands. The coefficients corresponding to low-pass filtering and downsampling are termed as $A_{i,j}$ where A denotes approximation, i represents corresponding row, and j represents the continuous array sequence. Similarly, high-pass filtered coefficients are represented as $D_{i,j}$. Successive iterations of filtering and downsampling can also be obtained using toeplitz matrix [14]. Let $\mathbf{H[0]}$, $\mathbf{H[1]}$, and $\mathbf{H[2]}$ be the low-pass filter coefficients. The doubly infinite toeplitz matrix corresponding to low-pass filter will be

$$\begin{bmatrix} \mathbf{H[2]} & \mathbf{H[1]} & \mathbf{H[0]} & \mathbf{0} & \mathbf{0} & \mathbf{0} & \mathbf{0} & \cdots \\ \mathbf{0} & \mathbf{0} & \mathbf{H[2]} & \mathbf{H[1]} & \mathbf{H[0]} & \mathbf{0} & \mathbf{0} & \cdots \\ \vdots & \vdots & \vdots & \vdots & \vdots & \vdots & \vdots & \ddots \\ \mathbf{0} & \mathbf{0} & \mathbf{0} & \mathbf{0} & \cdots & \mathbf{H[2]} & \mathbf{H[1]} & \mathbf{H[0]} \end{bmatrix}, \quad (2)$$

where each element in the matrix is a 2×2 matrix. In practical, the size of the toeplitz matrix depends on the length of the signal sequence under consideration. In a similar manner, the toeplitz matrix can be obtained for high-pass filter. Thus the calculation of wavelet packet coefficients in each level of the signal stream can be done by simple matrix multiplication and is given as

$$\mathbf{C}_L^{(j)} = \mathbf{T}_L^{(j)} \mathbf{X}^{(j)}, \quad (3)$$

where $\mathbf{C}_L^{(j)}$ are the multiwavelet coefficients, $\mathbf{T}_L^{(j)}$ is the low pass filter toeplitz matrix, and $\mathbf{X}^{(j)}$ is the input vector at level j. It is important to note that each element of $\mathbf{C}_L^{(j)}$ and $\mathbf{X}$ is a vector instead of scalar with size 2×1. Hence $\mathbf{C}_L^{(j)}$ corresponds to coefficient value of two subbands. Similarly $\mathbf{C}_H^{(j)}$ can also be calculated corresponding to high-pass filter and thus completes the process of obtaining coefficients of level j. Once the multiwavelet packet coefficients are obtained, the energy contained in a certain band can be found from the inner product of coefficient array of the corresponding band with itself. The relationship between the energy E_{MWP} and

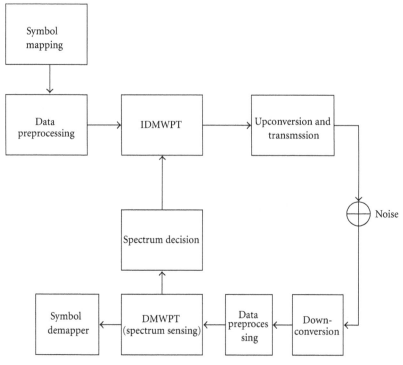

FIGURE 2: Multifilter based CR transceiver.

1: The iteration parameter j is initialized to zero. The input signal is converted into a matrix of two rows by repeating the signal.
2: The low pass and high pass filter toeplitz matrices of the corresponding iteration are calculated.
3: The Multiwavelet packet coefficients are obtained.
4: Check whether the required iteration level is achieved. If yes go to next step. Otherwise increase the iteration parameter and repeat step 2 and 3.
5: If the required iteration level is reached the wavelet packet coefficients are saved and energy of the subbands are calculated.
6: The power spectral density is obtained and is compared with the predefined threshold.
7: Preliminary decision on vacant spectrum is taken based on step 6.

ALGORITHM 1

---

power P_{MWP} for a node m and total number of samples K_{sample} is given as [26]

$$P_{\text{MWP}}^{(m)} = \frac{E_{\text{MWP}}^{(m)}}{K_{\text{sample}}}. \tag{4}$$

Power spectral density (PSD) of each subband can be calculated using the relation

$$\text{PSD}_{\text{MWP}}^{(m)} = \frac{P_{\text{MWP}}^{(m)}}{f_{\text{MWP}}^{(m)}}, \tag{5}$$

where $f_{\text{MWP}}^{(m)}$ denotes the frequency range of a single subband. The PSD calculated for each subband can be compared with a predefined threshold to determine vacant bands. A simple algorithm for spectrum sensing using multiwavelets is given in Algorithm 1.

4. MWPM in a Single-User CR Environment

Multiwavelet filter banks can be used in both single-user and multiuser CR environments. As a preliminary work, the system model and signal model of a single-user CR transceiver are outlined in this section.

4.1. System Model. The CR transceiver for adaptive spectrum sharing using multiwavelet filter bank is shown in Figure 2. The system model is similar to scalar wavelet-based CR transceiver with the replacement of multiwavelet packet transform instead of scalar wavelet transform. The vacant spectrum identification is done by measuring the power at the subbands of the demodulator output. That is, preliminary spectrum sensing is performed using discrete multiwavelet packet transform (DMWPT) as detailed in the previous section. Spectrum sensing requires vector input, and hence the signal stream under consideration is repeated based on multiplicity. Data preprocessing does signal repetition and serial-to-parallel conversion. The information from the preliminary spectrum sensing circuit is input to spectrum decision block. The spectrum decision block is a cross-layer approach which involves fine spectrum sensing at physical and MAC layers. Fine sensing at the physical layer incorporates feature extraction techniques to verify the presence of primary user (PU). Finally MAC layer takes the decision after considering certain link layer characteristics of the scanned frequency band and generates a binary information vector regarding spectrum occupancy. Once the free band is chosen by the spectrum decision block, the data symbols are mapped onto that spectrum. Similar to other transmultiplexers, inverse transform of multiwavelets is used for transmission. Due to the matrix structure of multifilters, multiwavelet-based transformation requires vectors instead of scalars. Preprocessing of data results in scalar-to-vector transformation and serial-to-parallel conversion. Inverse discrete multiwavelet transform (IDMWPT) is performed on the parallel data stream using vector extension of Mallat's algorithm by using transpose of the low-pass and high-pass matrices H and G. The process involved in IDMWPT block is shown in Figure 4. Each data symbol $\mathbf{X}[\mathbf{0}]$, $\mathbf{X}[\mathbf{1}]$, and so forth are $r \times 1$ vector points where r is the multiplicity [22]. $\mathbf{H}$ and $\mathbf{G}$ correspond to low-pass and high-pass multiwavelet filters. From Figure 4 it is evident that $r \cdot 2^2$ data symbols can be transformed into a serial stream by two levels of iteration. Successive iterations of upsampling and filtering operation can also be done by multiplication with corresponding toeplitz matrix. The details of single level multiwavelet packet transform and inverse transform using toeplitz matrix are discussed in [25]. The conditions to obtain error-free transmission under noiseless condition with multifilters are as follows.

(1) Each filter coefficient matrix should be a square matrix.

(2) For perfect reconstruction, the toeplitz matrix formed using filter coefficient matrices should be an orthogonal matrix.

At the receiver, the signal is downconverted and processed again to convert the serial stream into parallel vector symbols. DMWPT block demodulates the signal and then data is retrieved using symbol demapper.

4.2. The Signal Model. The signal transmitted from the CR node is given by

$$\mathbf{s}_{\mathrm{MWP}}(k) = \frac{1}{\sqrt{r2^D}} \sum_{i=1}^{r} \sum_{n=0}^{2^D-1} \mathbf{d}_{n,i} \Phi_{n,i}(k), \qquad (6)$$

where $\mathbf{d}$ is the vector representation of the data stream, D is the number of iterations, r is the multiplicity, and $\Phi_{n,i}(k)$ is the multiwavelet packet synthesis waveform. For ease of understanding, this expression can be represented with matrices. Let $\mathbf{X}$ denote the complete data matrix and $\mathbf{W}$ the transformation matrix or the corresponding toeplitz

matrix. The signal transmitted from the node can now be written as

$$\mathbf{s}_{\mathrm{MWP}}(k) = \mathbf{W}^T(k)\mathbf{X}(k), \qquad (7)$$

where $\mathbf{W}^T(k)$ is the transpose of the toeplitz matrix. At the receiver multiwavelet analysis is performed, and upon perfect synchronization and zero noise the demodulated signal is

$$\widetilde{\mathbf{s}}_{\mathrm{MWP}}(k) = \mathbf{W}(k)\mathbf{W}^T(k)\mathbf{X}(k), \qquad (8)$$

where $\widetilde{\mathbf{s}}_{\mathrm{MWP}}(k)$ represents the demodulated signal component. Because of the orthonormality of the underlying multifilter banks, this can be simplified as

$$\widetilde{\mathbf{s}}_{\mathrm{MWP}}(k) = \mathbf{I}(k)\mathbf{X}(k), \qquad (9)$$

where $\mathbf{I}(k)$ is the identity matrix.

5. MWP-MC-MA System for CR

To exploit the unique features of multiwavelet filter banks within multi-user CR context, a new multicarrier and multiple access scheme called MWP-MC-MA is proposed in this work. It is the multiwavelet extension of WP-MC-MA proposed in [13]. The uplink and downlink system models are described in the subsequent subsections with necessary equations.

5.1. Uplink System Model. The basic uplink scheme of the proposed system is shown in Figure 3. The CR node scans its band of interest (BOI) and generates multiwavelet packet coefficient PSD vector (as described in the previous section) $C_v(n,i)$ where n represents the subband index and i is the corresponding multiwavelet base. Spectrum sensing requires vector input, and hence the signal stream under consideration is repeated based on multiplicity. Data preprocessing does signal repetition and serial-to-parallel conversion. It is evident that based on the number of wavelet functions (multiplicity) the scanned spectrum can be subdivided into a large number of uniform subbands. Based on the value of $C_v(n,i)$ and comparing it with predefined threshold, preliminary decision on vacant spectrum is taken. The information from the preliminary spectrum sensing circuit is input to spectrum decision block. The spectrum decision block is a cross layer approach which involves fine spectrum sensing at physical and MAC layers. Fine sensing at the physical layer incorporates feature extraction techniques to verify the presence of primary user (PU). Finally MAC layer takes the decision after considering certain link layer characteristics of the scanned frequency band and generates a binary information vector regarding spectrum occupancy. Spectrum allocation is made by modified-carrier assignment scheme (CAS) similar to that in [13]. The purpose of the CAS algorithm is to obtain the spectrum index vector I_m and proper allocation of the subbands among CR users. The user's data are baseband encoded, preprocessed to obtain $r \times 1$ vector points instead of scalars, and channeled through P parallel streams where P is the number of subcarriers (subbands) allotted for each user. The data stream is fed into

1: The binary spectrum information vector is obtained.
2: CAS tries to determine CSI of each free subband available within the BOI.
3: CSI of the CR node under consideration along with the neighboring nodes are obtained.
4: Based on the information obtained, CAS assigns subbands for the considered CR node. Two consecutive subbands will be allocated for the same user. The subbands with maximum SNR is the primary choice.
5: If the specified CR as well as a competing neighbor has maximum SNR at the kth consecutive subbands, other CSI factors such as channel delay, phase offset will be taken into consideration to make the final decision.
6: Once the user and band is fixed, final decision is made and that subband index is included in the spectrum index vector I_m and the nth vector data stream of the user is mapped onto those subbands.
7: The process is repeated until all the P data streams of the user are mapped accordingly. The remaining subcarriers carry no data and are padded with zeros.

ALGORITHM 2

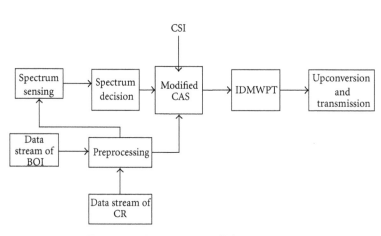

FIGURE 3: MWP-MC-MA uplink transmitter.

CAS, which will allocate subbands to the selected user based on the spectrum measurement vector $C_v(n, i)$ and CSI of the users within the given cell. The symbol stream is allocated to P subbands within available R subbands and by inserting $(R\text{-}P)$ zero arrays an R-dimensional vector is obtained as in OFDMA [38]. Mathematically it can be expressed as

$$d_{n,i}^{(m)} = \begin{cases} c_{n,i}^{(m)} & \text{if } n, i \in I_m; \\ 0 & \text{otherwise,} \end{cases} \quad (10)$$

where $c_{n,i}^m$ represents the constellation of encoded data stream of the user and I_m is the set of the indices of mth subchannel assigned to mth user. The two-variable suffix of the data stream is due to multiwavelet bases and the additional subbands obtained due to them. The vector d^m generated is input to the inverse discrete multiwavelet packet transform (IDMWPT) block for waveform modulation, and the serial data stream s^m is obtained. Due to the time domain overlapping of multiwavelet bases, cyclic prefix (CP) is excluded.

5.1.1. Modified CAS of MWP-MC-MA System. The carrier allocation among different users is a difficult task in multi-filter-based system compared to scalar wavelet-based system. This is due to the vector nature of data processing. When the multiplicity is two, each data vector should be a 2×1 matrix and each filtering in IDMWPT operates on two subbands of the available bandwidth. Hence for a transform size N, the

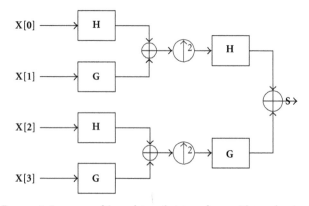

FIGURE 4: Inverse multiwavelet packet transform with two levels of iteration.

total available subbands will be $r \cdot 2^N$. However, dynamic allocation of subcarriers is possible only among 2^N bands. Modified CAS of multiwavelet-based system functions is described by Algorithm 2.

5.1.2. Data Preprocessing and IDWMPT. As mentioned in the spectrum sensing section, multiwavelet signal processing requires vectors instead of scalars. This is because convolution operation involved in wavelet synthesis (analysis) is to be performed with matrix filters. Hence the data stream of the

CR node should also be converted into a vector format. Pre-processing of data performs scalar-to-vector transformation and serial-to-parallel conversion. To keep the block length of each MWPM symbol to be equivalent to that of WPM and OFDM, repeated row preprocessing methodology is not adopted and the available data stream is transformed to $r \times N/r$ vector datum where N is the MWPM block length. IDMWPT is performed on the parallel data stream using vector extension of Mallat's algorithm by using transpose of the low-pass and high-pass matrices H and G. The process involved in IDMWPT block is shown in Figure 4 and the process is similar to that explained in the single-user system model.

5.2. The Uplink Signal Model. The signal transmitted from the mth CR node is

$$s_{\text{MWPm}}(k) = \frac{1}{\sqrt{r2^D}} \sum_{i=1}^{r} \sum_{n=0}^{2^D-1} d_{n,i}^m \Phi_{n,i}(k), \qquad (11)$$

where D is the decomposition level and $\Phi_{n,i}(k)$ corresponds to the multiwavelet synthesis waveform. The signal received at the base station is written as

$$r(k) = \sum_{m=1}^{M} s'_{\text{MWPm}}(k) h_m(k) + n(k), \qquad (12)$$

where $n(k)$ is the noise and $s'_{\text{MWPm}}(k)$ is the multiwavelet packet modulated component of the mth user and $h_m(k)$ the corresponding fading channel. The signal component can be written as

$$s'_{\text{MWPm}}(k) = e^{j\phi_m(k)} \sum_{n=0}^{R-1} \sum_{i=0}^{r} d_{n,i}^m \Phi_{n,i}^{\text{syn}_m}(k - nR - \tau_m), \qquad (13)$$

where $d_{n,i}^m$ is the symbol stream mapped onto the subchannel of the mth user as in (10) and $\Phi_{n,i}^{\text{syn}_m}$ are multiwavelet packet synthesis waveforms for the mth user subchannels. R is the number subcarriers. The term $e^{j\phi_m}$ corresponds to the frequency and phase offset of the mth user and is defined as

$$\phi_m(k) = \frac{2\pi\varepsilon_m k}{rR} + \theta_m(k), \qquad (14)$$

where θ_m is the phase noise component and ε_m is the relative frequency offset of the mth user. The product rR gives the total number of subbands. The frequency offset is normalized to the inter carrier spacing. The integer timing offset τ_m is expressed in sampling periods. It evident that to maintain orthogonality among subcarriers during detection process, proper timing and frequency error estimation are required at the base station.

5.3. The Downlink System. The downlink transmitter and receiver are shown in Figures 5 and 6, respectively. After symbol mapping, the data stream of each user is divided into blocks. Similar to uplink, CAS unit maps the P data symbols of each block onto subcarriers assigned to the corresponding user. The resultant vector will have data stream of all M

users summed up and fed to IDMWPT modulator and the data stream obtained serially is input to digital-to-analog Converter (D/A) and upconversion. At the receiver, the A/D output is the combination of data blocks of all users. Similar to the signal received at BS, frequency and timing errors are likely to be present. Hence the coarse frequency and timing estimation units are required to compute estimates of frequency and timing error. The frequency error estimate can be used to counter rotate the received sequence, and the timing error estimate is used for positioning of DMWPT window correctly. The channel equalization block corrects the channel impairments, if any, as well as the fractional timing errors. After the correction process, the data stream is input to DMWPT block where the serial stream is divided into subbands. For data detection, P subbands of the particular user are considered from the available subbands.

5.4. Downlink Signal Model. The signal transmitted from the BS is

$$\mathbf{s}_{\text{MWP}}(k) = \frac{1}{\sqrt{r2^D}} \sum_{i=1}^{r} \sum_{n=0}^{2^D-1} \mathbf{d}_{n,i} \Phi_{n,i}(k), \qquad (15)$$

where $\mathbf{d}$ denotes the vector representation of the summed data stream. The expression is similar to that of single-user case, but $\mathbf{d}$ includes data of all M users. By adopting matrix representation for data stream and multiwavelet modulation/demodulation, the signal transmitted from the BS can be written as

$$\mathbf{s}_{\text{MWP}}(k) = \mathbf{W}^T(k)\mathbf{X}(k), \qquad (16)$$

where $\mathbf{W}^T(k)$ is the transpose of the toeplitz matrix. Assuming AWGN channel at the receiver, the demodulated signal is

$$\tilde{\mathbf{s}}_{\text{MWP}}(k) = \mathbf{W}(k)\left(\mathbf{W}^T(k)\mathbf{X}(k) + \mathbf{N}(k)\right), \qquad (17)$$

where $\tilde{\mathbf{s}}_{\text{MWP}}(k)$ represents the demodulated signal component. This can be elaborated as

$$\tilde{\mathbf{s}}_{\text{MWP}}(k) = \left(\mathbf{W}(k)\mathbf{W}^T(k)\mathbf{X}(k) + \mathbf{W}(k)\mathbf{N}(k)\right). \qquad (18)$$

Because of the orthonormality of the underlying multifilter banks, this can be simplified as

$$\tilde{\mathbf{s}}_{\text{MWP}}(k) = \mathbf{I}(k)\mathbf{X}(k) + \mathbf{W}(k)\mathbf{N}(k), \qquad (19)$$

where $\mathbf{I}(k)$ is the identity matrix. From the demodulated signal, the corresponding user's subbands can be extracted using the spectrum index vector and then data bits are obtained using symbol demapper.

6. Performance Evaluation

In this section the performance of the proposed system is analyzed in terms of spectrum measurement capability, error rate under different channel conditions, bandwidth efficiency, and computational complexity.

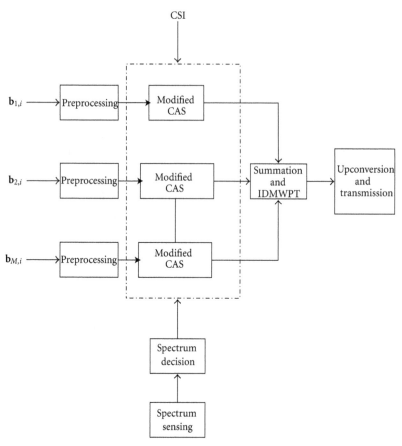

FIGURE 5: MWP-MC-MA downlink transmitter.

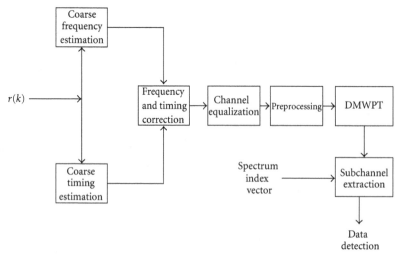

FIGURE 6: MWP-MC-MA downlink receiver.

6.1. Spectrum Measurements. A partial band BPSK signal with 100 symbols embedded in additive white Gaussian noise is considered as the signal to be detected. The carrier frequency is 300 MHz and SNR is kept at 10 dB. For simulation purpose, threshold is determined based on the principle of scalar wavelet-based detection technique explained in [12, 26]. In [12] the threshold for detecting vacant band is kept

as −7 dB as it gives probability of detection equal to 1 for a minimum probability of false alarm. The same threshold is adopted for multiwavelet-based system also due to the inherent similarity of both systems and for making a fair comparison. Figure 7 shows the useful signal detection using both symmetric multiwavelet and Symlet scalar wavelet. The given signal is decomposed into eight subbands with two

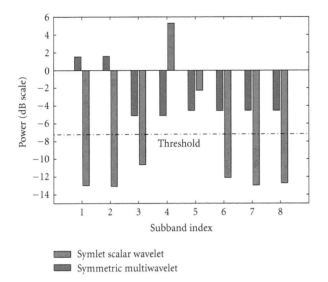

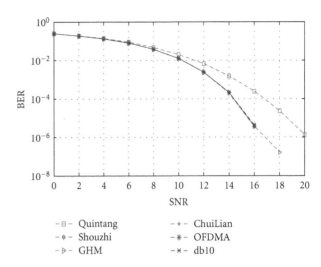

FIGURE 9: Error performance in flat fading channel.

FIGURE 7: Spectrum sensing result of a partial band BPSK signal.

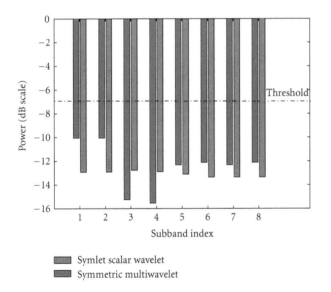

FIGURE 8: Spectrum sensing result of noise signal.

levels of iteration using multiwavelets where scalar wavelet requires three levels of iteration. The subband index is given on x axis and power in dB is plotted on y axis. It is evident that in the proposed system all subband power measurements are well above the threshold giving the presence of the signal. In the case of scalar wavelet, power measurements in only two subbands are above the threshold value. Hence it is proved that multiwavelet system is more powerful in detecting the presence of a primary user. Figure 8 shows the spectrum measurements corresponding to the noise signal detection. Both systems give accurate information about the free spectrum as subband power measurements are well below the threshold.

6.2. Error Performance under Different Channel Impairments.

To evaluate the performance of the proposed system, a multiuser CR environment with 4 users is considered. It is assumed that the BOI is scanned with multiwavelet packet transform and a total frequency band of 64 subbands found vacant. Equal number of subcarriers for all users is considered. Hence there are 4 subchannels with 16 subcarriers for each user in the simulated system. Actually this implies that each MWPM block corresponds to $64/r$ multifilter subcarriers which handle $r \times 1$ vector data. The data of each user is converted into $r \times 1$ vector points and are given to IDMWPT block. It is assumed that there is perfect synchronization between users and base station (BS). The channel index set I_m generated is known at the user end to separate the required data streams. The plots simulated in this work correspond to downlink channel of MWP-MC-MA. It is assumed that QPSK modulation is the baseband symbol mapping scheme adopted by all users. Four different sets of multifilters discussed in [18–21] are used in the simulation and are named after the authors. The filter bank mentioned in [18] is termed as "GHM" (Gerenimo, Hardin, Massopust) and that in [19] as "ChuiLian" (Chui and Lian). The orthogonal multiwavelet with optimum time frequency resolution described in [20] is termed "Quintang" (Quintang Jiang) and the orthogonal filter bank described in [21] is denoted as "Shouzhi" (Yang Shouzhi). All multiwavelet families have multiplicity 2 and hence each filter coefficient is a 2×2 matrix. The number of filter coefficients and support length of each set are different and the details are given in [18–21]. The results obtained are compared with OFDMA and scalar WPM using Daubechies filter of length 20 (db10) with same number of users and subcarriers.

6.2.1. Error Performance in Single-Path Fading Channels.

To incorporate the effects of flat fading, the channel gain is modeled as complex normal distribution $CN(0, 1)$, with variance 1. Figure 9 shows the BER in flat fading channel of different multicarrier schemes. It is assumed that the channel information is known at the receiver and is compensated. The different multiwavelets simulated in the work show similar performance except Quintang multiwavelet with

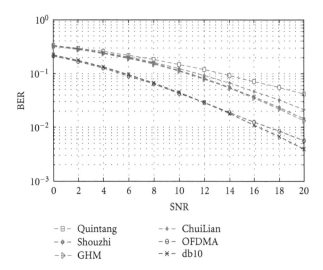

FIGURE 10: Error performance in single-path Rayleigh fading channel.

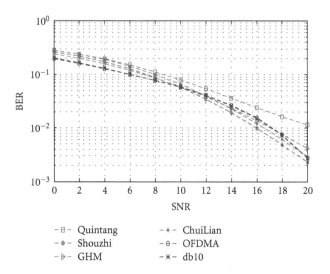

FIGURE 11: Error performance in multi-path channel with fixed fading coefficients.

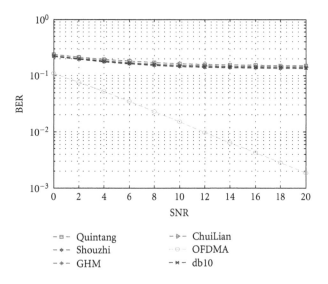

FIGURE 12: Error performance in multi-path channel with the Rayleigh fading coefficients.

optimum time frequency resolution. It is evident that the BER of other multiwavelets are comparable with those of scalar wavelet-based system and OFDMA. In Figure 10 the effect of a single-path Rayleigh fading channel with a maximum Doppler shift of 55 rad/sec is plotted. The channel model is generated based on the Jakes model, and zero forcing equalization algorithm is used at the receiver. The proposed system is highly sensitive to the Doppler shifts compared to OFDMA and scalar WP-MC-MA.

6.2.2. Error Performance in Multipath Fading Channels. To evaluate the capability of the system to mitigate multipath fading channel impairments, three path fading channel with fixed and Rayleigh fading coefficients are considered. The cyclic prefix (CP) of the simulated OFDMA system is higher than the channel delay. At the receiver, the wavelet-based scheme uses a time domain zero forcing equalizer with three taps per sample and OFDMA uses a frequency domain zero forcing equalizer with one tap per subcarrier since the demodulated OFDM signal is in the frequency domain. The fixed channel impulse response used for simulation is $h = [0.407\ 1\ 0.407]$. Figure 11 shows the error performance under fixed fading multi-path and Figure 12 shows that under Rayleigh fading multi-path channel. When the channel coefficients are fixed the proposed multiwavelet based system using symmetric pair multiwavelets termed "Shouzhi" performs better than that of OFDMA and scalar wavelet system. Under multi-path Rayleigh fading channel condition zero-forcing equalizer fail to combat random changes in amplitude and phase, and hence the proposed system gives poor performance similar to scalar wavelet-based system.

6.2.3. Effect of Phase Offset. As in any multicarrier modulation, it is important to consider the effect of frequency, phase and timing offset on error performance of the proposed system. Firstly the effect of phase noise on MWPM is considered. It is known that the presence of phase noise will affect the multicarrier modulation in two ways—(1) it will rotate all the constellation symbols by the same angle which is approximately equal to the average phase noise, (2) it will introduce inter-carrier interference (ICI) due to the spread of subcarriers with a larger bandwidth around the carrier frequency. To simulate the effects of phase noise in a multiuser environment, the phase noise is expressed as a zero mean Gaussian noise and the BER is calculated for different values of noise variance. The channel is assumed to be an AWGN channel and relative frequency error ϵ_m and timing offset to be zero. The signal received at the user terminal can be written as

$$\mathbf{s}_{\text{MWP}}(k) = \mathbf{W}^T(k)\mathbf{X}(k)e^{j\Theta(k)} + \mathbf{N}(k), \qquad (20)$$

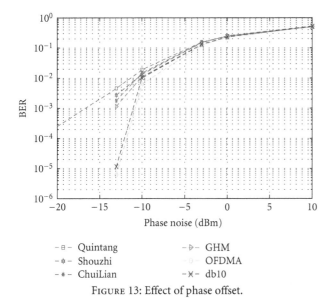

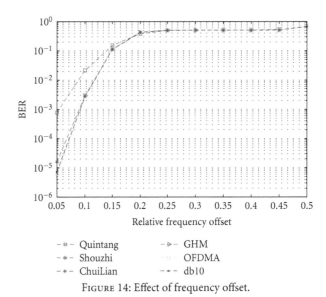

FIGURE 13: Effect of phase offset.

FIGURE 14: Effect of frequency offset.

where Θ denotes the phase-offest vector and $\mathbf{N}(k)$ the noise vector. The demodulated signal would be

$$\tilde{\mathbf{s}}_{\text{MWP}}(k) = \mathbf{W}(k)\mathbf{W}^T(k)\mathbf{X}(k)e^{j\Theta(k)} + \mathbf{W}(k)\mathbf{N}(k)$$

$$= \mathbf{I}(k)\mathbf{X}(k)e^{j\Theta(k)} + \mathbf{W}(k)\mathbf{N}(k)$$

$$= \mathbf{X}(k)e^{j\Theta(k)} + \mathbf{W}(k)\mathbf{N}(k) \qquad (21)$$

$$= \frac{1}{\sqrt{r2^D}}\sum_{i=1}^{r}\sum_{n=0}^{2^D-1}\mathbf{d}_{n,i}e^{j\Theta(k)} + \mathbf{W}(k)\mathbf{N}(k).$$

It is evident that the signal constellations are rotated by the corresponding phase angle and the noise component is altered by the respective multifilter coefficients. Figure 13 shows the effect of phase offset on error performance when the signal-to-noise ratio is kept constant at 15 dB. The phase noise variance is expressed in dB_m and is given on x axis. The bit error rate is depicted on y axis. Figure shows that error increases considerably as the phase noise approaches zero and the type of multifilter does not improve the performance. OFDMA and scalar WPM perform comparatively better than multifilter-bank-based system.

6.2.4. Effect of Frequency Offset.

Frequency offset can occur due to the Doppler shift or by misalignment between the transmitted carrier frequency and the locally generated carrier frequency at the receiver. It destroys orthogonality among subcarriers and hence causes severe ICI. To simulate the effect of frequency offset, AWGN channel is considered and the phase and timing offsets are assumed to be zero. Figure 14 shows the effect of frequency error on performance. BER is plotted as a function of relative frequency offset when the SNR is kept constant as 15 dB. No error compensation is done at the receiver. Other than "Quintang" multifilter, all other systems have comparable error performance. The error degradation of Quintang-based systems is due to optimization of its time frequency resolution.

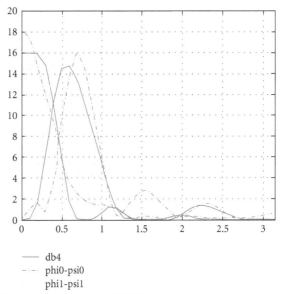

FIGURE 15: Spectrum of "GHM" and the Daubechies wavelets.

6.3. Bandwidth Efficiency and Sidelobe Suppression.

Due to matrix-structured filter bank, multiwavelet-based systems possess higher bandwidth efficiency compared to those of scalar wavelet and OFDMA system. In the proposed system multifilters of multiplicity two are considered. Hence there can be twice the number of subbands compared to those of OFDM and WPM for a given iteration. The spectrum of multiwavelet of multiplicity two and Daubechies scalar wavelet are illustrated in Figure 15 [22]. It is evident that there are only two subcarriers for scalar wavelet (red curves) but four subcarriers for multiwavelet system (blue dotted curves) for a given bandwidth. Thus bandwidth efficiency will be twice that of scalar WPM and OFDM. Moreover similar to scalar WPM, multiwavelet system does not include CP along with the signal, and hence the spectral efficiency will be always higher than that of OFDM. Lastly the spectral

TABLE 1: Complexity analysis.

Name	Filter length	Number of subbands	Number of multiplications
Quintang	7	128	1792
Shouzhi	3	128	768
GHM	4	128	1024
ChuiLian	4	128	1024
Daubechies	20	64	2560
OFDM	—	64	1024

leakage is also minimum in multiwavelet-based system due to nonrectangular waveforms in time domain.

6.4. Complexity Analysis. Conceptually, multiwavelet packet transform suffers from higher complexity involved in each level of its computation. When the filter coefficients are 2×2 matrices, the computations required in one level of iteration will be approximately twice to that of scalar wavelet transform. But as multiwavelet transform can provide twice the number of subbands in a given iteration compared to scalar WPM, it is expected that for a fixed number of subbands, the computational complexity would be almost similar. Theoretically, for an N stage WPT, the number of real multiplications required to calculate the scalar wavelet coefficients is always less than $2LT$ where $T = 2^N$ and L is the filter length [39]. In the case of multiwavelets, this expression can be approximated as $r \cdot 2LT$ since the additional computations in each level of the transform depends on multiplicity. The total number of real multiplications required for different orthonormal multiwavelet systems, Daubechies wavelet (db10), and OFDM for transform stage $N = 6$ is given in Table 1. It is shown that due to lower number of filter taps, "Shouzhi," "GHM," and "ChuiLian" multiwavelet based systems have computational complexity comparable or lower than that of OFDM for a given N.

7. Conclusion and Future Work

In this work, a novel multicarrier multiple-access scheme for CR using multiwavelet packet modulation has been proposed. The MWP-MC-MA system provides spectrum efficiency, flexibility, orthogonality, and multi-user support. A new spectrum sensing method using multifilter bank is proposed. Modified CAS unit has been exploited for adaptive subcarrier allocation. The simulation results show that proposed system insures good flexibility, spectrum efficiency, and comparable error performance. Preliminary spectrum measurement is also possible using DMWPT, and computational complexity is moderate due to lower number of multifilter coefficients. Future work will involve the performance analysis of the multifilter-based spectrum sensing and flexibility enhancement of the proposed system by enabling noncontiguous band operation.

References

[1] S. Haykin, "Cognitive radio: brain-empowered wireless communications," *IEEE Journal on Selected Areas in Communications*, vol. 23, no. 2, pp. 201–220, 2005.

[2] T. A. Weiss and F. K. Jondral, "Spectrum pooling: an innovative strategy for the enhancement of spectrum efficiency," *IEEE Communications Magazine*, vol. 42, no. 3, pp. S8–S14, 2004.

[3] I. F. Akyildiz, W. Y. Lee, M. C. Vuran, and S. Mohanty, "NeXt generation/dynamic spectrum access/cognitive radio wireless networks: a survey," *Computer Networks*, vol. 50, no. 13, pp. 2127–2159, 2006.

[4] C. Carlos, K. Challapali, D. Birru, and S. Shankar, "IEEE 802.22: an introduction to the first wireless standard based on cognitive radios," *Journal on Communications*, vol. 1, no. 1, 2006.

[5] J. Y. Won, S. B. Shim, Y. H. Kim, S. H. Hwang, M. S. Song, and C. J. Kim, "An adaptive OFDMA platform for IEEE 802.22 based on cognitive radio," in *Proceedings of the Asia-Pacific Conference on Communications (APCC '06)*, August 2006.

[6] A. M. Wygliski, M. Nekovee, and Y. T. Hou, *Cognitive Radio Communications and Networks: Principle and Practice*, Academic Press, 2010.

[7] A. Jamin and P. Mähönen, "Wavelet packet modulation for wireless communications," *Wireless Communications and Mobile Computing*, vol. 5, no. 2, pp. 123–137, 2005.

[8] M. K. Lakshmanan, I. Budiarjo, and H. Nikookar, "Maximally frequency selective wavelet packets based multi-carrier modulation scheme for cognitive radio systems," in *Proceedings of the 50th Annual IEEE Global Telecommunications Conference (GLOBECOM '07)*, pp. 4185–4189, November 2007.

[9] D. Karamehmedović, M. K. Lakshmanan, and H. Nikookar, "Performance evaluation of WPMCM with carrier frequency offset and phase noise," *Journal of Communications*, vol. 4, no. 7, pp. 496–508, 2009.

[10] M. Baro and J. Ilow, "Multi-band wavelet-based spectrum agile communications for cognitive radio secondary user communication," in *Proceedings of the IEEE International Symposium on Broadband Multimedia Systems and Broadcasting, Broadband Multimedia Symposium (BMSB '08)*, March 2008.

[11] H. Nikookar and M. K. Lakshmanan, "Comparison of sensitivity of OFDM and wavelet packet modulation to time synchronization error," in *Proceedings of the IEEE 19th International Symposium on Personal, Indoor and Mobile Radio Communications (PIMRC '08)*, September 2008.

[12] M. K. Lakshmanan, D. D. Ariananda, and H. Nikookar, "Cognitive radio transmission and spectrum sensing using a wavelet packet transceiver," in *Proceedings of the IEEE 20th Personal, Indoor and Mobile Radio Communications Symposium, (PIMRC '09)*, September 2009.

[13] M. Mathew, A. B. Premkumar, and C. T. Lau, "Multiple access scheme for multi user Cognitive Radio based on wavelet transforms," in *Proceedings of the IEEE 71st Vehicular Technology Conference (VTC '10)*, May 2010.

[14] V. Strela, *Multiwavelets: theory and applications [Ph.D. thesis]*, Massachusetts Institute of Technology, 1996.

[15] V. Strela, P. N. Heller, G. Strang, P. Topiwala, and C. Heil, "The application of multiwavelet filterbanks to image processing," *IEEE Transactions on Image Processing*, vol. 8, no. 4, pp. 548–563, 1999.

[16] B. Behera, "Multiwavelet packets and frame packets of L2 (ℝd)," *Proceedings of the Indian Academy of Sciences*, vol. 111, no. 4, pp. 439–463, 2001.

[17] G. Strang and V. Strela, "Short wavelets and matrix dilation equations," *IEEE Transactions on Signal Processing*, vol. 43, no. 1, pp. 108–115, 1995.

[18] J. S. Geronimo, D. P. Hardin, and P. R. Massopust, "Fractal functions and wavelet expansions based on several scaling functions," *Journal of Approximation Theory*, vol. 78, no. 3, pp. 373–401, 1994.

[19] C. Chui and J. Lian, *A Study of Orthonormal Multiwavelets*, Centre for Approximation Theory, 1995.

[20] Q. T. Jiang, "On the design of multifilter banks and orthonormal multiwavelet bases," *IEEE Transactions on Signal Processing*, vol. 46, no. 12, pp. 3292–3303, 1998.

[21] Y. Shouzhi, "A fast algorithm for constructing orthogonal multiwavelets," *ANZIAM Journal*, vol. 46, no. 2, pp. 185–201, 2004.

[22] M. L. You and J. Ilow, "An application of multi-wavelet packets in digital communications," in *Proceedings of the 2nd Annual Conference on Communication Networks and Services Research*, pp. 10–18, May 2004.

[23] M. You and J. Ilow, "Adaptive multi-wavelet packet modulation for channels with time-frequency localized interference," in *Proceedings of the IEEE 6th Circuits and Systems Symposium on Emerging Technologies: Frontiers of Mobile and Wireless Communication*, pp. 441–444, June 2004.

[24] X. H. Yan and G. Z. Liu, "Multiwavelet packet based ofdm system," in *Proceedings of the IEEE Asia-Pacific Conference on Circuits and Systems, SoC Design for Ubiquitous Information Technology (APCCAS '04)*, pp. 681–684.

[25] A. H. Kattoush, W. A. Mahmoud, and S. Nihad, "The performance of multiwavelets based OFDM system under different channel conditions," *Digital Signal Processing*, vol. 20, no. 2, pp. 472–482, 2010.

[26] D. D. Ariananda, M. K. Lakshmanan, and H. Nikookar, "A study on application of wavelets and filter banks for cognitive radio spectrum estimation," in *Proceedings of the 2nd European Wireless Technology Conference (EuWIT '09)*, pp. 218–221, September 2009.

[27] D. Cabric, S. M. Mishra, and R. W. Brodersen, "Implementation issues in spectrum sensing for cognitive radios," in *Conference Record of the 38th Asilomar Conference on Signals, Systems and Computers*, pp. 772–776, November 2004.

[28] T. Yücek and H. Arslan, "A survey of spectrum sensing algorithms for cognitive radio applications," *IEEE Communications Surveys and Tutorials*, vol. 11, no. 1, pp. 116–130, 2009.

[29] B. Farhang-Boroujeny, "Filter bank spectrum sensing for cognitive radios," *IEEE Transactions on Signal Processing*, vol. 56, no. 5, pp. 1801–1811, 2008.

[30] Y. Youngwoo, J. Hyoungsuk, J. Hoiyoon, and L. Hyuckjae, "Discrete wavelet packet transform based energy detector for cognitive radios," in *Proceedings of the IEEE 65th Vehicular Technology Conference (VTC '07)*, pp. 2641–2645, April 2007.

[31] Y. Hur, J. Park, W. Woo et al., "A wideband analog Multi-Resolution Spectrum Sensing (MRSS) technique for cognitive radio (CR) systems," in *Proceedings of the IEEE International Symposium on Circuits and Systems (ISCAS '06)*, pp. 4090–4093, May 2006.

[32] L. C. Wang, C. W. Wang, Y. C. Lu, and C. M. Liu, "A concurrent transmission MAC protocol for enhancing throughout and avoiding spectrum sensing in cognitive radio," in *Proceedings of the IEEE Wireless Communications and Networking Conference (WCNC '07)*, pp. 121–126, Hong Kong, China, March 2007.

[33] Y. Zeng and Y. C. Liang, "Maximum-minimum eigenvalue detection for cognitive radio," in *Proceedings of the 18th Annual IEEE International Symposium on Personal, Indoor and Mobile Radio Communications (PIMRC '07)*, September 2007.

[34] Z. Lei and F. Chin, "A reliable and power efficient beacon structure for cognitive radio systems," in *Proceedings of the IEEE International Conference on Communications (ICC '08)*, pp. 2038–2042, May 2008.

[35] H. Arslan and T. Yucek, "Spectrum sensing for cognitive radio applications," in *Cognitive Radio, Software Defined Radio, and Adaptive Wireless Systems*, H. Arslan, Ed., Springer, New York, NY, USA, 2007.

[36] Y. Zeng and Y. C. Liang, "Eigenvalue-based spectrum sensing algorithms for cognitive radio," *IEEE Transactions on Communications*, vol. 57, no. 6, pp. 1784–1793, 2009.

[37] Z. Quan, S. J. Shellhammer, W. Zhang, and A. H. Sayed, "Spectrum sensing by cognitive radios at very low SNR," in *Proceedings of the IEEE Global Telecommunications Conference (GLOBECOM '09)*, pp. 1–6, November 2009.

[38] M. Morelli, C. C. J. Kuo, and M. O. Pun, "Synchronization techniques for orthogonal frequency division multiple access (OFDMA): a tutorial review," *Proceedings of the IEEE*, vol. 95, no. 7, pp. 1394–1427, 2007.

[39] G. Strang and T. Nguyen, *Wavelets and Filter Banks*, Wellesley Cambridge Press, 1996.

2

Improved Handset Antenna Performance via an Electrically Extended Ground Plane

Shirook M. Ali, Huanhuan Gu, Kelce Wilson, and James Warden

Advanced Technology, Research In Motion Limited, 560 Westmount Rd. N., Waterloo, ON, Canada N2L 0A9

Correspondence should be addressed to Huanhuan Gu, hgu@rim.com

Academic Editors: M. Y. W. Chia and J. Park

A novel and practical approach is presented providing improved antenna performance without enlarging the antenna or the ground plane. The approach electrically extends the ground plane using wire(s) that behave as surface metal extensions of the ground plane. The wire extensions can be accommodated within typical handset housing or as part of the stylish metal used on the handset's exterior perimeter; hence don't require enlargement of the device. Consequently, this approach avoids the costs and limitations traditionally associated with physically lengthening of a ground plane. Eight variations are presented and compared with baseline antenna performance. Both far-field patterns and near-field electromagnetic scans demonstrate that the proposed approach controls the electrical length of the ground plane and hence its chassis wavemodes, without negatively impacting the characteristics of the antenna. Improvements in performance of up to 56% in bandwidth at 900 MHz and up to 12% in efficiency with a reduction of up to 12% in the specific absorption rate (SAR) are achieved. An 8% increase in efficiency with a 1.3% improvement in bandwidth and a 20% reduction in SAR is achieved at 1880 MHz. Thus, improvements in bandwidth are achieved without compromising efficiency. Further, improvements at lower frequencies do not compromise performance at higher frequencies.

1. Introduction

Handset users increasingly demand smaller and lighter devices, coupled with long battery life. Unfortunately, compactness, which results in slim and shortened device form factors, is often achieved at the cost of degraded antenna performance. This undesirable tradeoff has inspired numerous research efforts to find a more attractive balance between providing conveniently small and stylish handset dimensions while preserving acceptable antenna performance. In this effort, the influence of the mobile-phone-environment-related parameters, such as chassis (ground plane) size and the antenna position on the ground plane, have been thoroughly investigated, see for example [1–8].

It is known that the total radiation bandwidth of the mobile device is defined by both antenna properties and the chassis physical dimensions [1]. In [5], the authors show that if the chassis is resonant at the antenna-operating frequency, the bandwidth will increase significantly. A more detailed analysis in [1] demonstrated the chassis effects on both specific absorption rate (SAR) and radiation efficiency. It was

demonstrated that the resonance of the chassis leads to an increase in SAR and a decrease in radiation efficiency. These chassis-based analysis efforts have revealed a general trend of exploiting chassis properties for antenna design.

Previous efforts [5, 9, 10] have consistently demonstrated that the optimal dimensions of the ground plane, for achieving the best antenna performance, are those that enable resonance. This has significant consequences for low frequencies, including the 800 MHz and 900 MHZ GSM bands and the proposed 700 MHz band for LTE in the USA. However, a handset that is sized large enough to contain a ground plane that resonates at these low frequencies is often undesirable to consumers.

Some techniques have been proposed to address this issue, for example by controlling the chassis wavemodes [5, 11, 12]. These showed that the incorporation of slots in the chassis plane could lead to significant bandwidth broadening without changing the chassis dimensions. However, the introduction of the quarter wavelength slot effectively acts as an introduction of another antenna, that is, a slot antenna, which resonates around the desired frequency. Therefore, it is the resonance of both the main antenna and this slot antenna that produces the broader bandwidth. References [5, 11] proposed the slot design and optimization process for a single-band broadening, centered at the lower frequency of 900 MHz, whereas [12] demonstrated that the same concept can also be applied to higher frequency bands. However, as indicated in [5], introducing these relatively large quarter wavelength slots is not realizable from a practical stand point, in addition to problematic electromagnetic (EM) interference that results from the slot's proximity to the RF and signal processing modules. Although the approach indicated in [11] overcomes the electromagnetic interference issues in [5] and [12], the layout of PCB design becomes complex. Thus, there have not been any techniques in the literature that control the chassis such that to electrically increase it without altering the antenna ground plane itself.

In this paper, we propose a novel approach of using a wire to electrically extend portions of the chassis ground plane without altering the chassis itself. Forming a closed loop with this wire approximates, at RF, an equivalent solid surface, have the dimensions of the closed wire loop. The dimensions of the wire loop depend on the frequency in which an improvement in the antenna performance is most needed. The wire can be used in a straight form or bent as notches in the interest of shortening its physical length or height.

The remainder of the paper is organized as follows: the proposed approach is implemented using a hex-band antenna, where the antenna is introduced in Section 2. The wired approach is introduced in Section 3. There, eight variations of the proposed approach are introduced. The results and the related discussion are presented in Section 4. The paper is concluded in Section 5.

2. Antenna under Test

The simulation model and prototype of the antenna under test (AUT) are illustrated in Figure 1. The antenna is a 3D monopole-based hex-band antenna, which it supports GSM 800/900/1800/1900 MHz, UMTS 2100 MHz, and Bluetooth 2400 MHz bands [13]. It is designed on a chassis of 100 mm × 60 mm × 1.5 mm, which corresponds to the PCB size of a typical handset device. It is worth mentioning here that the physical dimensions of the ground plane and the antenna structures are kept unchanged throughout this investigation.

A finite difference time domain (FDTD-) based software SEMCAD [14] is used in the simulations. The simulated and measured return losses are compared in Figure 2. As shown, the correspondence between both the simulation and measurement results is quite good.

The antenna and the ground plane characteristics are discussed later in the paper through the near-field properties with the surface current distributions and the EM field scans on the hearing aid compatibility (HAC-) defined plane [15]. The characteristics are also discussed in relation to the far-field performance through the radiation pattern of the antenna. Both the near-field and the far-field discussions are carried out for the proposed models presented and are

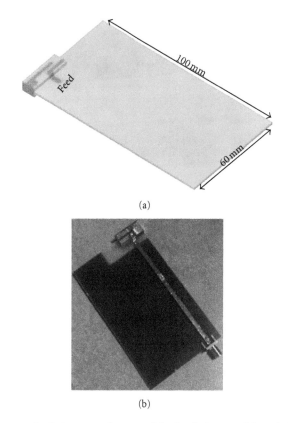

(a)

(b)

FIGURE 1: Antenna under test: (a) simulation model and (b) prototype.

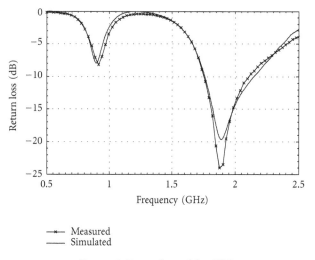

FIGURE 2: Return loss of the AUT.

compared to the initial AUT. We present in this section the near-field and the far-field characteristics of the initial AUT for comparison later in the paper.

Figure 3 illustrates the surface current distributions on the antenna and the ground plane at the frequencies of interest, 900 MHz and 1880 MHz. As expected, the currents are concentrated on the longitudinal edges of the ground plane. Figure 4 shows the HAC scan planes for both the electrical and the magnetic field intensities at the two

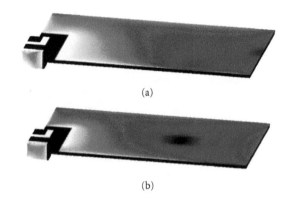

FIGURE 3: Current distribution of AUT: (a) at 900 MHz and (b) at 1880 MHz.

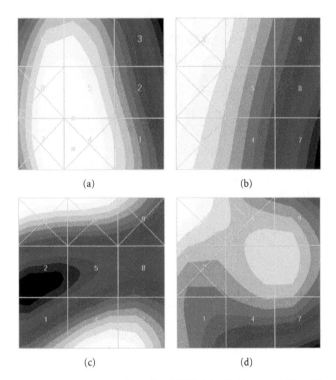

FIGURE 4: HAC-scanned result of AUT: (a) E field at 900 MHz, (b) H field at 900 MHz, (c) E field at 1880 MHz, and (d) H field at 1880 MHz.

frequencies of interest. It is worth noting here that these HAC simulations were validated, with a very good match, using extensive measurements in a HAC certified lab. For brevity, these results are not shown.

3. Electrically Extended Chassis

The genesis of cellular antennas lies in the field of wire antennas such as the monopole and modified monopole antennas. To improve radiation performance, these evolved into the inverted F antenna and the planar inverted F antenna that are widely used in today handsets, [16–18]. In fact, in [19], the authors proposed using the thin wire model to represent the backbone of an antenna to be designed. The

antenna's conductive portions are replaced with a thin wire model, which is physically possible due to the skin effect. Indeed, if we take a closer look at the current distribution on the ground plane of the AUT in Figure 3, we notice that the current is concentrated on the ground plane edges. From this observation, we can replace the ground plane with a closed wire loop with the diameter on the surface ground plane. Or, equivalently, we can have parts of the ground plane represented as a solid metal surface, using the wires to extend it in a desired dimension.

Looking at the HAC plane field scans shown in Figure 5 for the case when the chassis physical length is increased to 120 mm instead of 100 mm, we notice that the field distribution is the same. According to [10], the chassis length of 120 mm is the resonance length of the chassis at 900 MHz, thus optimum chassis-antenna working combination is achieved. However, increasing the chassis physical length is not a desirable option. From this perspective, we propose to control the ground plane length electrically using wires such that it resonates simultaneously with the antenna at the desired frequencies, thereby improving the overall antenna performance. The word "electrically" here means that the increase in the ground plane is done such that the handset device physical dimensions remain the same, while the RF performance is equivalent to that of a larger device.

We show next examples of different ways to achieve the goal of electrically extending the ground plane. The surface dimensions of the original ground plane, prior to applying our approach, are 100 mm × 60 mm. These dimensions are maintained in all examples. The closed wire/wires is/are electrically extended in the vertical direction, making use of the separation height between the ground plane and handset housing. This height is chosen to be within the height of a typical handset, 5 mm. With this, the overall ground plane is now electrically larger than the original plane, even while keeping the handset exterior dimensions unchanged. The proposed models are presented in the following section, together with the antenna performances.

4. Results and Discussion

The proposed wire approach achieves two main objectives. The first is that the introduction and the careful design of these wires significantly improve the overall antenna performance. This is shown through the antenna bandwidth, the antenna efficiency, and SAR values. We also show that the wire extensions compare with a performance improvement when the ground plane is physically extended and this is shown through the near-field EM field intensity scans in the HAC plane. The second achieved objective is that the wire extensions do not affect the antenna characteristics itself but rather control the ground plane characteristics and hence its resonance. Therefore, the proposed approach does not introduce any interference and reradiation issues. This is shown through the far-field radiation patterns.

The proposed approach is shown in eight models. Model I is given in Figure 6(a) and models II–VIII are given in Figure 7. The performance improvements of these

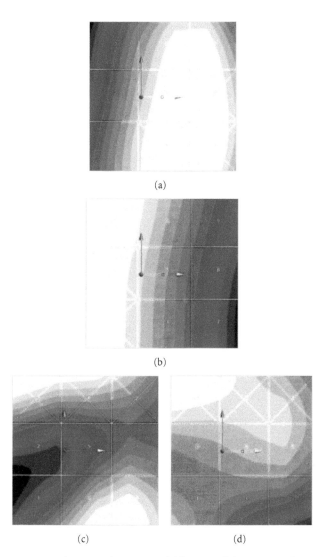

FIGURE 5: Electric and magnetic field scans of the AUT at chassis physical length of 120 mm: (a) HAC scan of E field at 900 MHz, (b) HAC scan of H field at 900 MHz, (c) HAC scan of E field at 1880 MHz, and (d) HAC scan of H field at 1880 MHz.

are listed in Tables 1 and 2 at frequencies 900 MHz and 1880 MHz, respectively. A 6 dB bandwidth definition is used to measure the bandwidth improvement, and the SAR is computed based on the North American standard [20] through simulations [14].

Model I is the first model tested, and it presents an extension of the ground plane length. The presence of the wire loop at the end of the ground plane causes imbalance in the surface current, which then causes the current to extend further on the longitudinal edge, see Figures 6(b) and 6(c) compared to Figure 3. For this model we also compute the HAC scans based on [15] to examine the near-field properties as it become difficult to have a corresponding comparison using the surface currents only. These are compared to the HAC scan plane of the antenna with a physically extended ground plane of 120 mm instead of the original 100 mm length plane, see Figure 5. Notice that Figure 5 of the physically extended ground plane scans

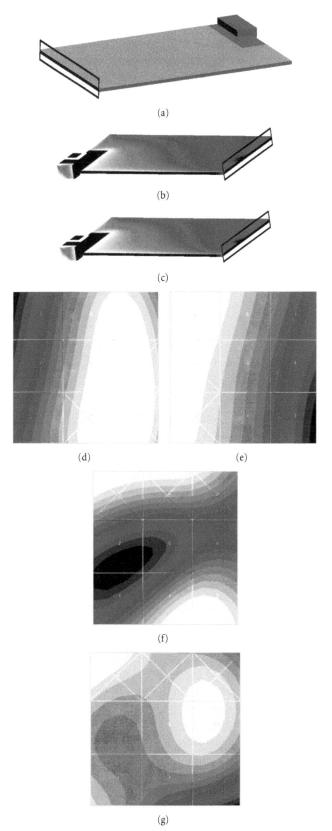

FIGURE 6: First configuration of the proposed approach: (a) model I, (b) current distribution at 900 MHz, (c) current distribution at 1880 MHz, (d) HAC scan of E field at 900 MHz, (e) HAC scan of H field at 900 MHz, (f) HAC scan of E field at 1880 MHz, and (g) HAC scan of H field at 1880 MHz.

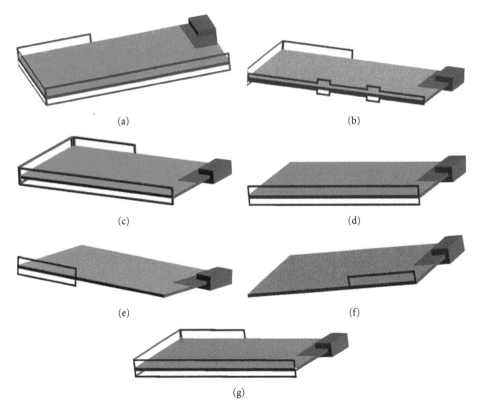

FIGURE 7: Configurations of the proposed approach: (a) model II, (b) model III, (c) model IV, (d) model V, (e) model VI, (f) model VII, and (g) model VIII.

TABLE 1: Percentage performance improvement at 900 MHz.

Model	Increase in efficiency	Increase in bandwidth	Reduction in SAR
I	4.25	28.10	3.12
II	5.06	22.16	10.45
III	2.68	28.13	8.78
IV	2.63	14.81	11.99
V	7.70	56.44	8.11
VI	5.60	34.17	0.33
VII	4.15	44.77	5.50
VIII	6.15	35.23	9.87

TABLE 2: Percentage performance improvement at 1880 MHz.

Model	Increase in efficiency	Increase in bandwidth	Reduction in SAR
I	0	−1.30	12.5
II	−0.35	9.90	0
III	1.19	−3.89	0.39
IV	0.96	5.24	−1
V	1.25	11.66	1.47
VI	0.60	6.06	19.63
VII	0.67	5.10	18.73
VIII	0.77	8.10	−0.3

corresponds better with those of the electrically extended scans in Figures 6(d)–6(g) than to those of Figure 4 of the original antenna. Hence, we have achieved, with the wires, an effective extension comparable to that achieved with the addition of 20 mm to the ground plane length.

Different variations of the proposed wire approach are successfully tried and these are shown in Figure 7. In Figure 7(b), Model III, a bending of the wire, is used to form one of the sides of the loop. With this a reduction of the loop height is achieved for implementation in a slimmer handset. Figure 7(g), Model VIII, is similar to Model II shown in Figure 7(a) but the difference is in the thickness of the wire used to form the closed loop. It is thicker in Model VIII. In both cases a good performance is achieved. Different sizes

and locations of the loop are tried in Figure 7(e), Model VI, and Figure 7(f), Model VII. These different implementations show the flexibility and ease of design of the proposed wire approach.

Comparisons of 2D radiation patterns for the AUT and all the proposed models are illustrated in Figure 8. These results show very similar 2D pattern, which suggests that the introduced wires do not cause interference and hence no reradiation occurs. Therefore, the far field radiation properties of the antenna are unaffected by the presence of the wires, and negative effects are avoided. The wires appear to predominantly affect only the ground plane chassis wavemodes.

Looking at the performance, Tables 1 and 2, the proposed approach offered an increase of up to 56% in bandwidth at

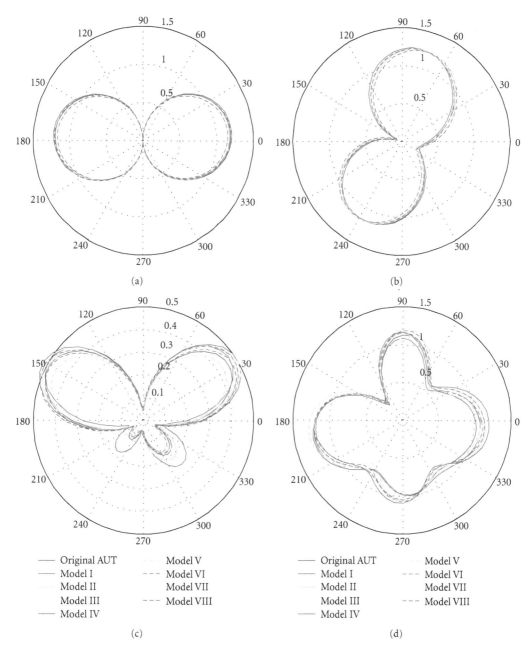

FIGURE 8: 2D radiation pattern comparison result: (a) 2D pattern in φ plane at 900 MHz, (b) 2D pattern in θ plane at 900 MHz, (c) 2D pattern in φ plane at 1880 MHz, (d) 2D pattern in θ plane at 1880 MHz, and (e) legend.

the 900 MHz and a 12% increase at the higher 1880 MHz frequency band. Currently, the proposed approach offers an improvement in the antenna efficiency without the need to enlarge the antenna structure; 8% efficiency was achieved at 900 MHz and 1.3% was achieved at 1880. This is significant, because the improvement in the lower frequency band was not achieved at the expense of performance at the higher frequency band or by degrading the bandwidth.

The implementation of our approach on a handset is easy and cost effective to manufacture. The wires constructing the virtual ground plane extension can be built into the inner surface of the handset device housing or can be designed as part of the device outer metal parts, for example, using part/all of the metal ring surrounding the perimeter of the device and connecting it through the device housing to the ground plane. Additionally, the improvements in the performance are achieved independent of the antenna structure, that is, no change is required in the design or in the location of the antenna. This permits the implementation of our approach without complicating the antenna design cycle.

5. Conclusions

We sidestep the traditional cost and limitations that are imposed when seeking a commonly desired benefit. The traditional cost for improving the antenna performance is an enlarged device, which may be undesirably large, thus limiting the implementation in practice. We accomplish the more desirable solution by electrically extending the length of the ground plane using wires that are placed outside the surface of the ground plane. This exploits a physical phenomenon that the proximity of the wires appears to create a single electrical surface with the ground plane, thereby achieving the enhanced radiation characteristics through controlling the ground plane chassis wavemodes to resonate with the antenna resonance. However, because the wires are outside the surface of the ground plane, they can be placed within the vertical volume normally enclosed by the device housing, without requiring the device housing to be lengthened. This avoids the traditional tradeoff. Performance improvements achieved are simultaneously seen on the antenna bandwidth, efficiency, and the lower specific absorption rates. The proposed wire approach is successfully illustrated in eight models and at a low- and a high-frequency bands.

Acknowledgment

The authors would like to thank Dr. Houssam Kanj from Advanced Technology, Research In Motion Limited, for his comments and fruitful discussions.

References

[1] O. Kivekäs, J. Ollikainen, T. Lehtiniemi, and P. Vainikainen, "Bandwidth, SAR, and efficiency of internal mobile phone antennas," *IEEE Transactions on Electromagnetic Compatibility*, vol. 46, no. 1, pp. 71–86, 2004.

[2] T. Taga and K. Tsunekawa, "Performance analysis of a built-in planar inverted F antenna for 800 MHz band portable radio units," *IEEE Journal on Selected Areas in Communications*, vol. 5, no. 5, pp. 921–929, 1987.

[3] K. Sato, K. Matsumoto, K. Fujimoto, and K. Hirasawa, "Characteristics of a planar inverted-F antenna on a rectangular conducting body," *Electronics and Communications in Japan, Part I*, vol. 72, no. 10, pp. 43–51, 1989.

[4] T. Taga, "Analysis of planar inverted-F antennas and antenna design for portable radio equipment," in *Analysis Design, and Measurement of Small and Low Profile Antennas*, K. Hirasava and M. Heneishi, Eds., Artech House, 1992.

[5] P. Vainikainen, J. Ollikainen, O. Kivekäs, and I. Kelander, "Resonator-based analysis of the combination of mobile handset antenna and chassis," *IEEE Transactions on Antennas and Propagation*, vol. 50, no. 10, pp. 1433–1444, 2002.

[6] D. Manteuffel, A. Bahr, and I. Wolff, "Investigation on integrated antennas for GSM mobile phones," in *Proceedings of the Millennium Conference on Antennas Propagation*, 2000.

[7] D. Manteuffel, A. Bahr, D. Heberling, and I. Wolff, "Design considerations for integrated mobile phone antennas," in *Proceedings of the International Conference on Antennas Propagation*, pp. 252–256, 2001.

[8] A. T. Arkko and E. A. Lehtola, "Simulated impedance bandwidths, gains, radiation patterns and SAR values of a helical and a PIFA antenna on top of different ground planes," in *Proceedings of the International Conference on Antennas Propagation*, pp. 651–654, 2001.

[9] S. M. Ali and H. Gu, "Chassis wavemode effects on hearing aid compatibility at 900 MHz," in *Proceedings of the International Conference on Antennas Propagation*, pp. 651–654, July 2010.

[10] S. M. Ali and H. Gu, "Chassis wavemode effects on hearing aid compatibility (HAC) in the handset".

[11] R. Hossa, A. Byndas, and M. E. Bialkowski, "Improvement of compact terminal antenna performance by incorporating open-end slots in ground plane," *IEEE Microwave and Wireless Components Letters*, vol. 14, no. 6, pp. 283–285, 2004.

[12] T. W. Chiou and K. L. Wong, "Designs of compact microstrip antennas with a slotted ground plane," in *IEEE Antennas and Propagation Symposium*, pp. 732–735, July 2001.

[13] S. M. Ali and H. Kanj, "Hex-band antenna for slim handheld device applications," *Microwave and Optical Technology Letters*, vol. 51, no. 11, pp. 2527–2530, 2009.

[14] *SEMCAD-X Reference Manual*, Zeughausstrasse 43, Schmid & Partner Engineering AG (SPEAG), Zurich, Switzerland, 2007.

[15] ANSI C63.19-2007 (Revision of ANSI C63.19-2006), *American national standard methods of measurement of compatibility between wireless communications devices and hearing aids*, June 2007.

[16] T. Taga and K. Tsunekawa, "Performance analysis of a built-in inverted-F antenna for 800 MHz band portable radio units," *IEEE Journal on Selected Areas in Communications*, vol. 5, no. 5, pp. 921–929, 1987.

[17] H. Nakano, N. Ikeda, Y. Y. Wu, R. Suzuki, H. Mimaki, and J. Yamauchi, "Realization of dual-frequency and wide-band VSWR performances using normal-mode helical and inverted-F antennas," *IEEE Transactions on Antennas and Propagation*, vol. 46, no. 6, pp. 788–793, 1998.

[18] T. Tag, *Analysis, Design, and Measurement of Small and Low-Profile Antennas*, Artech-House, Boston, Mass, USA, 1992.

[19] W. Geyi, Q. Rao, S. Ali, and D. Wang, "Handset antenna design: practice and theory," *Progress in Electromagnetics Research*, vol. 80, pp. 123–160, 2008.

[20] IEEE Std. 1528-2003, *Recommended Practice for Determining the Peak Spatial-Average Specific Absorption Rate (SAR) in the Human Head from Wireless Communications Devices—Measurement Techniques*, Institute of Electrical and Electronics Engineers, New York, NY, USA, 2003.

3

A Three-Tier Architecture for User-Centric Ubiquitous Networked Sensing

Jin Nakazawa and Hideyuki Tokuda

Faculty of Environment and Information Studies, Keio University, 5322 Endo, Fujisawa-shi, Kanagawa 252-0882, Japan

Correspondence should be addressed to Hideyuki Tokuda, hxt@ht.sfc.keio.ac.jp

Academic Editors: D. Cassioli, A. Maaref, and Y. M. Tseng

In a sensor network, sensor data are usually forwarded from sensor nodes to a database. This tight coupling between the nodes and the database has been complicating user-centric applications that traverse multiple different sensor networks. To break this coupling, thus enabling user-centric applications, we propose a three-tier architecture for ubiquitous networked sensing. Its major feature is that it contains the "core" device, which is assumed to be a terminal held by users between sensor nodes and sensor databases. This architecture supports the sensor data directly transmitted to and consumed by the core device, in addition to the classic ones that are transmitted to the sensor database first, and downloaded to the core. The major contribution of this paper are the following three-fold. First, we clarify the architecture itself. Researchers can leverage the architecture as the baseline of their development. Second, we show two types of prototype implementations of the core device. Industry is allowed to develop a new product for practical use of ambient sensing. Finally, we show a range of applications that are enabled by the architecture and indicate issues that need to be addressed for further investigation.

1. Introduction

The recent research and productization of wireless sensor nodes have been enabling ubiquitous networked sensing environment where sensor nodes are densely embedded around users in homes, offices, parks, roads, and so forth. For example, home owners would manage their own sensor networks [1]. A university campus can install its own campus sensing network [2]. Opposing to the node-side, technologies towards sophisticated sensor database have been deeply investigated. Usually, sensor data are directly forwarded from sensor nodes to a database. In the above examples, there would be a sensor database at the home and the campus to store the data captured there. These two sides, sensor nodes and sensor databases, thus form a tightly coupled networked sensing architecture.

This tight coupling has been complicating user-centric applications that traverse multiple different sensor networks. For example, suppose an application that records aerial pollution in the places where its user visits. Since aerial sensors are not small, it is not practical to assume that the user carries

the sensors. This application thus needs to acquire data from the aerial sensors around the user. With the classic tightly coupled architecture, the application is required to identify the databases where the aerial pollution data are stored and query for the particular pieces of data based on the time and the user's location. Observing that the user and the sensor nodes are close to each other, the above indirect data acquisition is inefficient. Therefore, we need a new architecture that support users leveraging in situ sensor applications more efficiently.

To break the tight coupling in the existing architecture, thus enabling user-centric in situ applications, we propose a three-tier architecture for ubiquitous networked sensing. The major feature of the architecture is that it contains the "core" device, which is assumed to be a terminal held by users, between sensor nodes and sensor databases. This architecture support the sensor data directly transmitted to and consumed by the core device, in addition to the classic ones that are transmitted to the sensor database first, and downloaded to the core. This paper contributes to the field of ubiquitous networked sensing by the following three-fold.

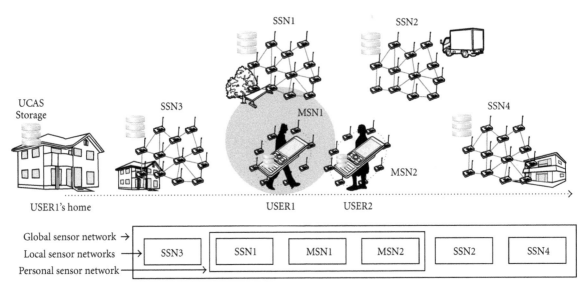

FIGURE 1: UNETS environment: federated sensor networks. Sensor networks are installed everywhere, and users go through them with their own body-worn sensor network and the core device. Each sensor network has its own sensor database to which the data are accumulated. This picture contains four networks of static sensor nodes (SSNs) and two of mobile sensor nodes (MSNs). The user *USER1* walks through this environment collecting the sensor data from surrounding nodes in his handheld device. After a series of activities, he goes back home where his permanent storage is located. The data are transferred from the core to the storage and accumulated there.

First, we clarify the architecture itself. Researchers can leverage the architecture as the baseline of their development. Second, we show two types of prototype implementations of the core device. Industry is allowed to develop a new product for practical use of ubiquitous networked sensing. Finally, we show a range of applications that are enabled by the architecture and indicate issues that needs to be addressed for further investigation.

The rest of this paper is organized as follows. The next section shows the architecture. Section 3 describes the prototyping studies of the core devices and their applications, and Section 4 discusses lessons learnt from the prototyping studies indicating open issues for further investigation. Section 5 surveys related work, and finally Section 6 concludes the paper.

2. Ubiquitous Networked Sensing Architecture

The purpose of defining the architecture is to make a common view of ubiquitous networked sensing, to which one can ground his/her technology. The architecture thus should be common enough to accommodate different aspects of ubiquitous networked sensing. In this section, we first observe the activities of users and the environment we assume, depict the architecture overarching those aspects, then describe components included in the architecture.

2.1. Federated Sensor Networks. We assume in this paper federated sensor networks, depicted in Figure 1, where users are surrounded by static sensor networks installed in many places and the mobile sensor network they carry. The total network view is a three-tier one. First, static and mobile sensor networks form their own local network where a sensor database resides to store the data. Second, the nodes

around a user form a personal sensor network from the user's perspective, whose sink node is the handheld device carried by the user. This network is created in an ad hoc manner. Third, the global sensor network is the collection of sensor databases in the world. They are accessed from applications (not depicted) via the Internet.

Advancement of the research on sensor networks has been enabling such an environment. Urban sensing [3, 4] has been investigated aiming at fine-grained environment monitoring in cities. Sensor networks for generic environment monitoring is also widely researched. AiryNotes [5] is our past project, where we installed more than 200 sensor nodes in Shinjuku Gyoen Park. SenseWeb [6] is aiming at sharing sensor data captured by the sensor nodes embedded in cities to monitor aerial pollution, car traffic, and so forth. Habitat monitoring [7] is used to monitor animals invading farms. Complementing these outdoor sensor networks are indoor sensor networks. SensorAndrew [2] aims at creating a sensed university campus. It monitors buildings, social infrastructures, and students to provide context-aware ubiquitous computing services. AwareHome [8] and PlaceLab [1] are the two major examples of building context-aware homes [9] using sensor networks. Their prototype homes are filled with various types of sensors that are used to capture user activity there. Structural health monitoring [10, 11] protects buildings from being left unwarned when they are damaged due to, for example, an earthquake. Many other places are also targeted such as mountain [12], under water [13], and in a volcano [14]. Observing those places enhanced with a rich sensing capability, users will be surrounded by sensor networks in the future in almost all the places they visit.

Users themselves are also enhanced with sensing capability. Mobile phone sensing [15] leverages the phone carried by users to provide context-aware services on the phone. For

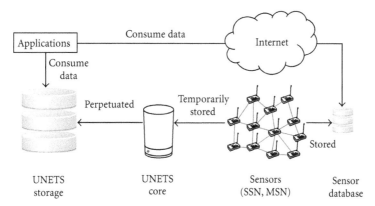

FIGURE 2: UNETS architecture components and data flow.

example, the phone can recognize whether its user is walking, running, sitting, and so forth using an embedded accelerometer. The phone can provide a pedometer capability using this context. Body-area sensor networks [16] is used typically to monitor users' personal health. Thermometer, heart rate meter, and/or tonometer would be able to be networked to the user's cellular phone to record their data, while the user is in an activity. These mobile sensors are also the constituents of the federated sensor networks.

2.2. UNETS Architecture Components. Based on this observation, we describe the user-centric ubiquitous networked sensing (UNETS) architecture from the perspectives of components, interactions, and applications. Figure 2 overviews the components in the architecture and the data flow among them. The users in the UNETS architecture are involved with mobile sensor nodes that are carried by the users, and static ones around them. The data generated by these nodes are first received by the mobile device (UNETS core) carried by the users for temporal storage, and then perpetuated into the user's sensor database (UNETS storage). This sensors—temporal storage—permanent storage configuration constitutes the three-tier architecture.

2.2.1. UNETS Core. A UNETS core is the device that provides sensing (optional), processing, and actuation (optional) capabilities. Readers can suppose, as a virtual example of UNETS core, a cellular phone with an additional network interface (e.g., ZigBee) to communicate with sensor nodes as depicted in Figure 1. It receives the sensor data from the mobile and static nodes and processes them. Processing includes calculating statistics of data and storing the raw and/or calculated data to its internal storage. As the sensing capability, UNETS core can contain its own sensor device like an accelerometer and a GPS receiver on which an application depends to recognize user behavior. It can also contain an LCD, a speaker, and so forth as the actuation capability. Applications on the UNETS core with the actuation capability can provide context-aware digital services using this capability.

2.2.2. Mobile Sensor Nodes (MSNs). MSNs are carried by the user, forming a body-area sensor network with the UNETS

core. Biometric sensors like body temperature sensors and heart rate sensors are their typical examples. Sensors like an accelerometer and a GPS receiver are classified into this class when a user carries them individually instead of having them in his/her UNETS core. A user's mobile sensor nodes can be public or private. Public ones are the sensor nodes that are allowed by the user to serve the data for other users, while private ones are those not. This means a user's UNETS core (e.g., USER1's UNETS core in Figure 1) would be able to receive the data from the public mobile sensor nodes (e.g., MSN2) owned by other users within the UNETS core's radio vicinity (depicted as a gray circle in the figure).

2.2.3. Static Sensor Nodes (SSNs). Immobile sensor nodes, such as those included in sensor networks for campus sensing, environment monitoring at a park, and urban sensing, are classified into this class. Usually, sensor networks are installed and managed by different parties other than the users themselves. This means that the data captured in a sensor network are stored in an individual sensor database in the corresponding facility (campus, park, and city). The immediate SSNs are within a user's vicinity in that the user's UNETS core can receive data via single- or multi-hop communications assuming that they are public. The remote SSNs are outside it; the user's UNETS core would receive the data by referring to the sensor database where the data captured by the remote SSN are stored. Therefore, a sensor node is an immediate for a user close to it, and at the same time a remote one for users far from them. In Figure 1, SSN3 are immediate for USER1 when he is at location 2 and remote for USER2.

2.2.4. UNETS Storage. A UNETS storage serves as a user's personal sensor database where the data collected by his/her UNETS core are transferred and kept. We assume that the storage in a UNETS core is relatively smaller than that in a UNETS storage, since the former is a mobile device with limited computational resource while the latter is static and resource-rich.

2.3. Interactions in UNETS Architecture. The above components interact with one another to exchange sensor data. We analyze the interaction focusing on data flow from the UNETS core's perspective.

2.3.1. Core—MSN. A UNETS core is the sink node for its user's MSN. It receives the current sensor data from his/her own MSN via single- or multi-hop communications. It may also receive the current sensor data from the public ones among the MSN owned by other users when applications running on the UNETS core require to. For example, suppose a toy application that calculates average heart rate of the people around the user. To do this, the UNETS core needs to find the MSN to receive the data from. This can be achieved by either or both of the following two schemes. In both cases, the MSN must be publicized by their owner. First is search basis. This proactive scheme requires the UNETS core to inquire within the network for the MSN that can serve the sensor data of the UNETS core's interest (current heart rate). If there are such MSN, they respond to the inquiry with the data. Second is broadcast basis. Publicized MSN may transmit sensor data periodically via a broadcast channel. The UNETS core receives these broadcast data reactively, filter them, and consume the data of its interest. Typically, the sensor data from publicized MSN are not secured by, for example, encryption, thus can be used by any UNETS core.

2.3.2. Core—SSN. Similar to the above case is the interaction between a UNETS core and immediate SSN. Based on the interest to particular type of sensor data (e.g., temperature and humidity of surrounding environment), a UNETS core locates the nodes that satisfy it. Proactive and reactive schemes can again be used to fulfill this requirement. The architecture assumes that a sensor data dissemination path from SSN to a UNETS core are established by a routing protocol that supports mobile sink nodes, such as [17, 18].

On the other hand, there is no single- or multi-hop communication path between a UNETS core and remote SSN. Therefore, the UNETS core needs to acquire the current sensor data generated by remote SSN indirectly via the Internet. The data are first stored in the sensor database associated to the remote SSN network (e.g., a campus sensing database). The UNETS core then queries for the data to the database via the Internet by using mechanisms for large-scale or global sensor network, such as [19], can be used.

2.3.3. Core—Storage. A user's UNETS core should hold a reasonable amount of sensor data after the user's activities in the UNETS environment. Since the computational resource of the UNETS core is limited, the data should be externalized for permanent storage. Therefore, the UNETS core transfers the data to the user's UNETS storage, and the data are accumulated there to enable applications to refer to the history of sensor data.

While the core—MSN and core—SSN interactions are for collecting the current sensor data, the past data are also important for applications. UNETS core, similarly to the indirect interaction with remote SSN, receives past data of any sensor node from the database where those data are stored. If the UNETS core needs to consume the data generated by the MSN of another user, it queries for the data to the UNETS storage owned by the user. If it needs data generated by SSN, it retrieves them from their sensor database. The

architecture assumes that there exists a mechanism to share sensor data via the Internet such as [6, 20].

2.4. UNETS Applications. We classify the user applications in the architecture from the orthogonal perspectives of location (*here or there: HoT*) and time (*current or past: CoP*). The HoT basis means where the data consumed by the users come from. *Here* indicates that the users acquire the data from the sensor nodes where they reside(d), and *there* indicates that they do from those from remote nodes. For example, sensors here (SH) would be the source for the users to know the degree of aerial pollution around them, while sensors there (ST) would serve as the source for the road traffic information. The CoP basis on the other hand means when the data consumed by the users are captured. *Current* represents that the users acquire the latest data from sensor nodes, and *past* indicates that they use the data captured at some point(s) in the past. This means that all the *here—past* data are stored UNETS Core temporarily, and finally accumulated in the user's UNETS storage. Applications that consumes the past data in a UNETS storage or a UNETS Core are thus classified to *here—past*, and those consuming the data in a sensor database via the Internet are classified to *there—current* or *there—past*. The other class of applications, *here—current*, consumes the current data running in a UNETS Core. To clarify more practically how users behave in the environment, let us discuss how sensor network applications seen in 2.1 can be extended by UNETS architecture in each quadrant of *HoT* and *CoP* space.

Here—Current. Personal health monitoring can be extended by using the data captured by environment monitoring sensors. Users, for example, can correlate their heart rate data with environmental information such as temperature and humidity to calculate the risk of heat stroke at the place where they reside.

Here—Past. Users can know the risk of the building in terms of its structural health by referring to the series of the past data captured by structure monitoring sensors. For example, they can use accelerometer data to calculate the accumulated damage of the building, since the vibration pattern of a building changes when it is damaged.

There—Current. Sensors for Urban monitoring and environment monitoring can be used for users deciding which way to go to when the risk of the heat stroke is high at their place. Instead of immediate sensors, the users consume data from the remote sensors beyond the immediate ones.

There—Past. Users can know the risk of the buildings in the city where they reside in terms of their structural health by referring to the series of the past data captured by structure monitoring sensors. They can decide, using this information, the safest building to go for a certain purpose (e.g., lunch).

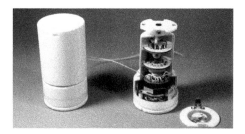

FIGURE 3: uCore Recorder.

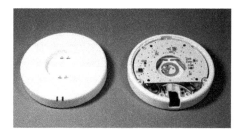

FIGURE 4: uCore Dock.

3. Prototyping Studies

The master piece in the UNETS architecture is the UNETS core, which collects the data from the surrounding sensor nodes, store the data temporarily, and perpetuate them into UNETS storage. However, no such device is available currently, which makes it difficult to experiment on the effectiveness of the architecture. We thus prototyped two types of UNETS core: *uCore Reader* and *Sense Phone*. uCore Recorder is a unique device with our own design, and Sense Phone is a ZigBee interface for Japanese cellular phone. This section first overviews these prototypes and their applications, then the next section discusses lessons learnt.

3.1. Prototyping Study 1: uCore Recorder. The first prototyping study is with uCore Recorder (Figure 3), and its cradle uCore Dock (Figure 4).

3.1.1. Device Configuration. uCore Recorder is a device with great portability embedding a range of sensors capable of communicating with external wireless sensor nodes via a ZigBee network. Figure 5 and Table 1 show its hardware specifications. A user can record three different digital information into the 512KB Flash ROM storage in the uCore Recorder. First, the user can record the interest to a real-world object by reading the RFID tag on the object. We suppose that digital information about the object such as its name and its description can be retrieved by an RFID tag pasted on the object, so the uCore Recorder records the information when it reads the RFID tag. Second, the user can record sensor data from the sensors embedded in the uCore Recorder. For example, the uCore Recorder embeds an accelerometer, whose data can be used to extract the user's status of movement such as walking, running, or sitting. Third, the user can record sensor data transmitted from MSN and SSN through a wireless network. Users of uCore Recorder can perpetuate the stored data to UNETS storage for further analysis, visualization or sharing simply by putting the device on a cradle, called uCore Dock.

The uCore Dock (Figure 4) plays two roles in the system. First, it is the battery charger of the uCore Recorder. It fully recharges the uCore Recorder approximately in four hours. Second, which is more important, it is the entrance to the UNETS storage. When a user finishes a series of activities in a day, he can move the data recorded during the day to the database by putting his uCore Recorder on the uCore Dock. To simplify this data perpetuation, the uCore Dock contains

TABLE 1: Specification of uCore Recorder.

Wireless sensor node	MICA2DOT
Processor	Atmel ATmega128
Wireless	315 MHz ISM Band
Flash ROM	512 K bytes
Rotary encoder	ALPS EC12E24244A3
Resolution	24 pulse
Switch	Yes (Act.Force 6N)
2-axis accelerometer	Analog Devices ADXL311
Range	$\pm 2\,g$
RFID reader	SkyeTek SkyeRead M1-Mini
LED	Full-color LED $\times$ 2
Battery	Korea PowerCell PD2450 (Li-Ion)
Size (mm)	42(W) $\times$ 42(H) $\times$ 77(D)
Weight	63 g

an RFID tag, which is registered to the uCore Recorder as a special tag representing the entrance to the database. The uCore Recorder, when reading this registered tag, flushes the recorded data out to the database through the wireless network interface of the containing MICA2DOT sensor node. The data, then, is received by the storage host, to which another MICA2 node is connected, via the same wireless network. To this extent, uCore Recorder itself does not require users to manipulate computers using classic interface devices like keyboards and mice. Users can record their activities and put the recorded data to the storage through simple interactions with the uCore Recorder, namely, putting it on an RFID tag, and putting it on a uCore Dock.

3.1.2. Applications. uCore Recorder enables various applications that utilizes data accumulated in UNETS storage. The followings are a few examples of the applications that we have implemented.

Click Catalog. Click Catalog [21] is a *here—past* application for mobile memory aid tool using uCore Recorder. In our daily lives, we find many interesting items during shopping, in exposition to events or in conferences. We often try to remember them for later recall by writing memos, taking pictures, and so forth. Those hints (notes and pictures) are, however, easy to be lost. Click Catalog, instead of requiring

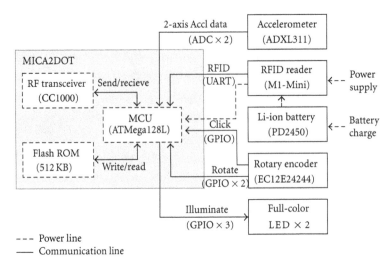

FIGURE 5: Block diagram of uCore Recorder.

the users to do these proactive memory, automatically records the situations of surrounding environment by receiving sensor data from the user's MSN and/or SSN. The user can also record the items, in which he/she was interested, using the uCore Recorder's RFID reading capability.

The recorded data are perpetuated to the user's UNETS storage using the uCore Dock's perpetuation mechanism. The unique feature of Click Catalog is that it enables users to recall the recorded data using the following two types of paper interfaces. One is an interface using a paper calendar (shown in Figure 6(a)), and the other is an interface using a paper atlas (shown in Figure 6(b)). Those paper-based interfaces are pasted RFID tags. A user can easily refer to the past data recorded on a date by putting his/her uCore Recorder on the calendar interface to read the RFID tag pasted on the calendar at the particular date. They can also refer to the past data recorded at a location similarly by putting it on the atlas interface to read the tag pasted on the atlas at the particular location.

ActiBlog and ActiMap. ActiBlog is a *here—past* application that allows users to publish their activities on their weblogs. Figure 7(a) shows its screen image. It visualizes the digital information of the real-world object, and accompanying sensor data. It is implemented as a plug-in module to a weblog system, called Nucleus (http://nucleuscms.org/), thereby enabling users to comment, link, and track back to others' activities with the same manner as ordinary weblogs. Similar, but visually different, application is ActiMap, which visualizes the user activities on GoogleMaps. Figure 7(b) shows its screen image. User activities are marked on the map with icons. The points, on which the activities are placed, are achieved from GPS receivers either public or private. A GPS receiver can be carried with the uCore Recorder as an MSN, or it can be an SSN. The uCore Recorder does not constrain any of these, since it can receive data from those sensors through the same wireless network interface. When a user clicks on an icon, its digital information and the sensor data are shown similarly to the ActiBlog. If multiple users'

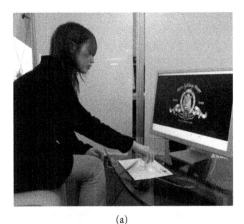

(a)

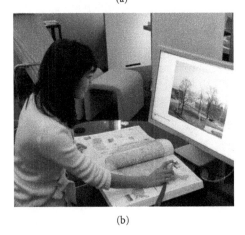

(b)

FIGURE 6: Browsing by a Paper Calendar and by a Paper Map.

activities are published on a same digital map, they can know the geographical relation of their activities on the map.

3.2. Prototyping Study 2: Sense Phone. The second prototyping study is with Sense Phone (Figure 8). The major difference from uCore Recorder is that Sense Phone perpetuates

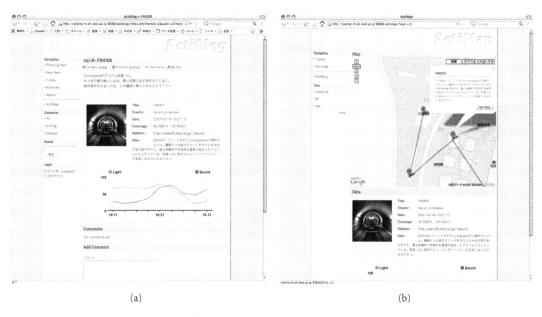

(a)   (b)

FIGURE 7: Screen shots of ActiBlog and ActiMap.

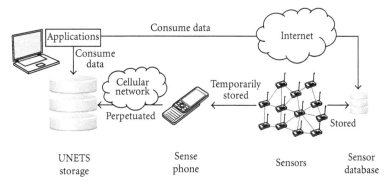

FIGURE 8: Architectural placement of sense phone.

the data via the cellular network. Also, since it contains actuation capability, it can run in situ *here—current* and other classes of applications consuming sensor data captured by MSN and surrounding SSN.

3.2.1. Device Configuration. Sense Phone [22] consists of a sensor data transceiver and the software running on the phone. The transceiver operates as a transport-level bridge between the cellular network and the Internet, and the software as a device-level bridge [23].

This transceiver contains Crossbow MPR2600CA, an OEM module of MICAz Mote, and can operate approximately 8 hours when it receives 3 sensor data packets per second. It connects to a cellular phones via UART as shown in Figure 9. The current prototype can communicate with the series of MICAz Mote sensor nodes and other ZigBee-based nodes if they share the same transport and routing protocols. To achieve this condition, the prototype provides static extensibility; the transceiver embeds one protocol stack that is capable of communicating with one of the different types of nodes.

The software in our technique consists of two layers: middleware and applications. They are implemented with C language on BREW [24]. The middleware operates the transceiver directly and receives the sensor data. The received raw data is stored in the database in the cellular phone and also exported to the applications via APIs. We provide the applications with the following two kinds of APIs. One is the event-driven interface that allows the applications to hook particular range of values, values from particular sensor nodes, and both of them. This enables applications to consume the current data effectively. A special application on the phone uses this interface to perpetuate the received data to the user's UNETS storage over the cellular network. The other is query interface, with which the applications can collect the past data of their interest from the database. Using these APIs, the applications process the sensor data for their purposes, such as abstracting them into contexts, transmitting them to a web service or exporting them to devices on other communication platforms such as nearby Bluetooth devices. Applications can be downloaded to the cellular phone from their carrier' networks (in our case, KDDI),

WSN module	Crossbow MPR2600CA
Wireless	ZigBee (IEEE802.15.4)
External IO	UART, JTAG
Power	DC 3 V
Battery	Li-ion PD3048 (300 mAh)
Operating time	8 hours (for 3 packets/s)
Dimension	$42 \times 80 \times 10$ mm

FIGURE 9: Specifications of Sense Phone transceiver.

sharing the same middleware instance. This feature enables dynamic extensibility in terms of device-level bridge. For example, if a user wants to export the data to another communication platform, he/she can do so just by downloading the application for this purpose. Users can do so from the carrier' application catalogue, such as that for Apple's iPhone, with several clicks or taps of buttons.

3.2.2. Applications. Leveraging the actuation capability of Sense Phone, we have created a here—current application called Infaucet that enables users to acquire digital information being aware of their current context. The application continuously receives sensor data from surrounding SSN and calculates its user's context such that it is raining in the place where the user resides. Meanwhile, the party that installed the SSN can register to the Infaucet server the information that the party wants to disseminate to users of particular context around their SSN. The Infaucet application on the user's cellular phone retrieves the information that comformts to his/her current context.

For example, suppose an urban sensing facility in a city where SSN with weather sensors are installed along the streets. The facility is installed and managed by the city's local government, and the government wants users not to use a slippy street when it is raining. In this case, the government registers to the Infaucet server the recommended road usage information associated with the SSN installed at the intersections to the street. Infaucet users can record the sensor data received from the SSN in the urban sensing facility and simultaneously receive the road usage information.

The application can notify users with this information using the cellular phone's LCD, its speaker set, and so forth.

Readers are reminded that the recorded sensor data would be accumulated in the users' UNETS storage and can be used in *here—past* applications like ActiBlog, ActiMap, and Click Catalog.

4. Lessons Learnt

The aforementioned prototyping studies have pointed out the effectiveness of the architecture and challenges inherent in it. We discuss lessons learnt in the following.

Effectiveness of the Architecture. Researchers are eager to collect sensor data to a centralized computer and export them to the Internet [20, 25]. With such mechanisms, users can consume sensor data on their hand-held device like a cellular phone. However, even if the users want to get the temperature data from the sensor node in front of them, they need to query the data to the computer via the Internet. The two prototypes of UNETS core shown above achieve more efficient utilization of sensor data by enabling users to communicate with sensor nodes directly using uCore Recorder and Sense Phone. Each user having this mechanisms with him/her establishes a distributed, robust, and scalable infrastructure to federate ubiquitous applications to our daily lives. Some existing work shares the same goal [26, 27]. However, their work requires embedding Bluetooth interface to sensor nodes, which is not efficient in energy, and not flexible in network topology.

The applications shown above are enabled by the three-tiered UNETS architecture in that here—past or there—past applications like ActiBlog, ActiMap, and Click Catalog do not need to access multiple sensor databases located with SSN. The past data related to a user are accumulated in his/her UNETS storage (TIER 3), after temporarily stored in a UNETS core (TIER 2) that receives the raw sensor data from MSN and SSN (TIER 1). Therefore, the applications can acquire all the data related to the series of the user activities from his/her UNETS storage. Without having UNETS core in the architecture, the data are spread over the distributed sensor databases associated with SSN, and the applications need to collect the data from all of them. This scheme is inefficient; many transactions required to collect the data would consume network bandwidth and time.

Open Sensor Networks. UNETS core is assumed to communicate with SSN included in sensor networks established for certain purposes by different parties. Usual sensor networks are closed in that the data are collected to a central database, and alien devices like UNETS core are not assumed. The sensor networks, however, need to be open in our architecture; SSN in the networks are required to transmit sensor data to alien UNETS cores. We found the following two issues to achieve this.

First, the communication protocol used between UNETS cores and SSN needs to be standardized. UNETS cores traverse different sensor networks collecting sensor data. If the sensor networks utilize different protocols for sensor data transmission, the UNETS cores required a priori knowledge about all of those protocols. Assuming existence of numerous sensor networks, thus protocols, such UNETS cores having such knowledge is impractical. In addition, the computational resources embedded in UNETS cores are limited based on our prototyping studies of uCore Recorder and Sense Phone. This resource limitation makes it difficult for UNETS cores to have a number of protocol stacks in them. Therefore, we need a standardized communication protocol for sensor data transmissions. Standardization in physical and MAC layers have been addressed by IEEE, resulting in promotion of IEEE802.15.4 (ZigBee). That in network and above layers needs to be addressed.

Second, security would be of a great concern for the parties that open their sensor network to the UNETS architecture. Unlike the current practice of sensor networks where the parties can close their network by using their own protocols and security mechanisms, use of a standard protocol would disclose SSN to malicious users. They might intrude to SSN and disable them. Therefore, a new security mechanisms with assumption of open sensor networks need to be investigated.

Synchronization. We have learnt that synchronization is important between UNETS core and SSN in the following two reasons. Both are for achieving the architecture's requirement that UNETS core is mobile and assumed to communicate with SSN in an ad hoc manner.

First, the amount of energy is limited in SSN and UNETS core, since they usually operate with battery power. Outdoor sensor nodes including Field Server [28] and eKo Mote (http://www.memsic.com/products/wireless-sensor-networks/environmental-systems.html) are operated with solar reactor. This infers that such nodes are operated with an intermittent mode such that a node wakes up to sense and transmit the data once 10 minutes. On the other hand, the mobility pattern of a UNETS core is random. Since the UNETS core's energy is also limited, it is also operated with an intermittent mode. These conclude that without any synchronization mechanism the UNETS core cannot collect sensor data.

Second, if a UNETS core is migrating with a very high speed (e.g., in a running car or a running train with 100 km/h), it may overpass a radio coverage of SSN instantly. Multihop sensor data transmission would take reasonable amount of time to reach the destination. Therefore, the data needs to be routed synchronously to the mobility of the destined UNETS core. This issue is investigated by researchers of mobile sink mechanisms such as [17].

Multiuser Extension. The UNETS architecture described above is focused on a single user's perspective; however, it needs to be extended to support mutual exchange and fusion of sensor data. The data accumulated in UNETS storage would contain personal behavioral information, such as distance of activity of the users and environmental context (e.g., temperature and humidity) where they visited. Such information is valuable for many purposes including dynamic demography and urban strategy. Therefore, the data

in UNETS storage should be able to be reused by third parties.

Privacy is, however, a major issue to achieve this. Since UNETS storage contains the users' private information, the data should not be disseminated without the users' permission. This infers that the users need to (1) grant particular permissions to the third parties, (2) mosaic the data to export if needed, and (3) confirm that the data are deleted by the third parties after they finished using them. Security is also a major issue, since the third parties need to avoid spoofing. When the sensor data are exported from their owner to a third party, the data need to be guaranteed that they actually contain the owner's information.

5. Related Work

There are several classes of research towards effective use of user-side terminals for sensing. One common approach to this direction is the use of cellular phone as a sensor or as a sink node. Use of the phones as a sensor is known as the mobile phone sensing research [15]. Recent cellular phones contain a range of sensors including ubiquitous networked light, proximity, cameras, GPS, accelerometer, compass, and so forth. Due to their richer computational capability, phones can be used to capture context of users in the ubiquitous/pervasive computing perspective. Based on the captured context, they can provide user-aware digital services with them. This approach is limited compared to our architecture. As shown in Figure 10 as a dotted rectangle A, mobile phone sensing can be observed as the model that solely rely on the UNETS core. Applications are limited only to *here—current* and *here—past* that use sensors in the phone. All other applications that consume data from SSN are disabled.

Sensor network deployment projects, such as campus sensing [2], home sensing [1], structure monitoring [10], and environment monitoring [7], focus on the use of SSN. They are seen in the UNETS architecture as the dotted rectangle C in Figure 10. Each deployed sensor network collects data into its associated sensor database. The collected data can then be used by applications that run locally in the network, or remotely via the Internet. This classic model is data-centric instead of user-centric in that it is optimized for efficient data collection into the centralized database, and users are always required to query in the database even when they are directly facing a sensor node.

The model of participatory sensing partly shares user-centric view with us. Some urban sensing projects [3, 4, 29] utilize user-side terminals that correspond to UNETS core in our architecture. Aquiba [3] is a system for achieving human probe capability in urban sensing. They leverage our Sense Phone for their purpose. MetroSense [4] defines a similar architecture that includes the notions of mobile sensors and static sensors. However, their goal is to share the data among users who participate in a sensing project. Their focus is thus closed in the interaction between the user-side terminals and sensors, which is depicted as the dotted circle B in Figure 10.

Besides the sensing models, the following two issues are investigated recently aiming at enhancing interaction between the architectural components. First issue is global

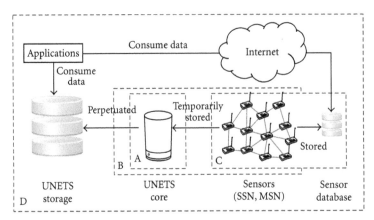

FIGURE 10: Relation of sensing models.

sensor networks as the means to enable for applications to acquire sensor data via the Internet. IrisNet [20] provides a middleware system to share sensors among multiple computers within a city-scale. SenseWeb [6] aims at sharing sensor nodes worldwide. It proposes a software architecture for global sensor sharing assuming sensor, data, and application heterogeneity. GSN [30] also aims at the worldwide sensor sharing. Our architecture does not specify how applications acquire sensor data via the Internet, since sensors may be exported to the Internet through different mechanisms described above. Applications can use the mechanism that exports the sensors needed by the applications. Second, technologies for mobile sink nodes have been investigated. Those technologies can be used to achieve more efficient interaction between UNETS core and SSN in the architecture. Several researchers propose a routing protocol to use mobile nodes as a sink node of a sensor network effectively [17, 18].

6. Conclusions

Human-centric ubiquitous networked sensing is still in its infancy. There is little or no consensus on the sensing, processing, and actuation architecture for the involved devices. Our work contributes to this field in that it gives a generic and total view of such an architecture with component, data flow, and application models. The major feature of our three-tier architecture is that it contains the "core" device, called UNETS Core, which is assumed to be a terminal held by users. The sensor data are directly transmitted to UNETS Core from surrounding sensor nodes including static and mobile nodes. The data are then perpetuated into UNETS Storage. This three-tier sensor—UNETS Core—UNETS Storage enables effective use of sensor data by applications. We classified UNETS applications with location (here or there) and time (current or past) basis. This classification and its associated examples gives insights to researchers of practical sensing about the users' expectation to sensor networks. Our prototype implementations of UNETS Core device can be leveraged by industry to develop a new product for practical use of ubiquitous networked sensing. Finally, we have clarified lessons learnt in which several open issues are indicated for further study.

Acknowledgments

The authors would like to express our gratitude to Dr. Junichi Yura at Fujitsu Laboratories and all members of our laboratory.

References

[1] S. S. Intille, K. Larson, J. S. Beaudin, J. Nawyn, E. M. Tapia, and P. Kaushik, "A living laboratory for the design and evaluation of ubiquitous computing technologies," in *Proceedings of the Conference on extended Abstracts on Human Factors in Computing Systems (CHI '05)*, pp. 1941–1944, ACM Press, New York, NY, USA, 2005.

[2] A. Rowe, M. E. Berges, G. Bhatia et al., "Sensor andrew: large-scale campus-wide sensing and actuation," *IBM Journal of Research and Development*, vol. 55, no. 1, article 6, 2011.

[3] N. Thepvilojanapong, S. Konomi, and Y. Tobe, "A study of cooperative human probes in urban sensing environments," *IEICE Transactions on Communications*, vol. 93, no. 11, pp. 2868–2878, 2010.

[4] A. T. Campbell, S. B. Eisenman, N. D. Lane, E. Miluzzo, and R. A. Peterson, "People-centric urban sensing," in *Proceedings of the 2nd Annual International Workshop on Wireless Internet (WICON '06)*, ACM Press, New York, NY, USA, 2006.

[5] M. Ito, Y. Katagiri, M. Ishikawa, and H. Tokuda, "Airy notes: an experiment of microclimate monitoring in shinjuku gyoen garden," in *Proceedings of the 4th International Conference on Networked Sensing Systems (INSS '07)*, pp. 260–266, June 2007.

[6] A. Kansal, S. Nath, J. Liu, and F. Zhao, "SenseWeb: an infrastructure for shared sensing," *IEEE Multimedia*, vol. 14, no. 4, pp. 8–13, 2007.

[7] R. Szewczyk, E. Osterweil, J. Polastre, M. Hamilton, A. Mainwaring, and D. Estrin, "Habitat monitoring with sensor networks," *Communications of the ACM*, vol. 47, no. 6, pp. 34–40, 2004.

[8] G. D. Abowd, C. G. Atkeson, A. F. Bobick et al., "Living laboratories: the future computing environments group at the georgia institute of technology," in *Proceedings of the Conference on Extended Abstracts on Human Factors in Computing Systems (CHI '00)*, ACM Press, New York, NY, USA, 2000.

[9] S. Meyer and A. Rakotonirainy, "A survey of research on context-aware homes," in *Proceedings of the Australasian Information Security Workshop (AISW '03)*, vol. 21, pp. 159–168, Australian Computer Society, Darlinghurst, Australia, 2003.

[10] N. Kurata, B. F. Spencer, and M. Ruiz-Sandoval, "Risk monitoring of buildings with wireless sensor networks," *Structural Control and Health Monitoring*, vol. 12, no. 3-4, pp. 315–327, 2005.

[11] S. Kim, S. Pakzad, D. Culler et al., "Health monitoring of civil infrastructures using wireless sensor networks," in *Proceedings of the 6th International Symposium on Information Processing in Sensor Networks (IPSN '07)*, pp. 254–263, ACM Press, New York, NY, USA, April 2007.

[12] I. Talzi, A. Hasler, S. Gruber, and C. Tschudin, "PermaSense: investigating permafrost with a WSN in the Swiss Alps," in *Proceedings of the 4th Workshop on Embedded Networked Sensors (EmNets '07)*, pp. 8–12, ACM Press, New York, NY, USA, June 2007.

[13] I. Vasilescu, K. Kotay, D. Rus, M. Dunbabin, and P. Corke, "Data collection, storage, and retrieval with an underwater sensor network," in *Proceedings of the 3rd International Conference on Embedded Networked Sensor Systems (SenSys '05)*, pp. 154–165, ACM Press, New York, NY, USA, 2005.

[14] G. Werner-Allen, K. Lorincz, M. Welsh et al., "Deploying a wireless sensor network on an active volcano," *IEEE Internet Computing*, vol. 10, no. 2, pp. 18–25, 2006.

[15] N. D. Lane, E. Miluzzo, H. Lu, D. Peebles, T. Choudhury, and A. T. Campbell, "A survey of mobile phone sensing," *IEEE Communications Magazine*, vol. 48, no. 9, pp. 140–150, 2010.

[16] A. Natarajan, M. Motani, B. De Silva, K. K. Yap, and K. C. Chua, "Investigating network architectures for body sensor networks," in *Proceedings of the 5th International Conference on Mobile Systems, Applications and Services*, pp. 19–24, ACM Press, New York, NY, USA, June 2007.

[17] J. Luo, J. Panchard, M. Piórkowski, M. Grossglauser, and J.-P. Hubaux, "Mobiroute: routing towards a mobile sink for improving lifetime in sensor networks," in *Distributed Computing in Sensor Systems*, P. Gibbons, T. Abdelzaher, J. Aspnes, and R. Rao, Eds., vol. 4026 of *Lecture Notes in Computer Science*, pp. 480–497, Springer, Berlin, Germany, 2006.

[18] K. Fodor and A. Vidács, "Efficient routing to mobile sinks in wireless sensor networks," in *Proceedings of the 3rd International Conference on Wireless Internet (WICON '07)*, pp. 1–7, ICST, Brussels, Belgium, 2007.

[19] F. Ye, H. Luo, J. Cheng, S. Lu, and L. Zhang, "A two-tier data dissemination model for large-scale wireless sensor networks," in *Proceedings of The 8th Annual International Conference on Mobile Computing and Networking*, pp. 148–159, ACM Press, New York, NY, USA, September 2002.

[20] P. B. Gibbons, B. Karp, Y. Ke, S. Nath, and S. Seshan, "IrisNet: an architecture for a worldwide sensor web," *IEEE Pervasive Computing*, vol. 2, no. 4, pp. 22–33, 2003.

[21] A. Komaki, J. Yura, M. Iwai, J. Nakazawa, K. Takashio, and H. Tokuda, "Clickcatalog: retracing precious memory using paper-based media controller," in *Proceedings of the International Conference on Machine Learning and Cybernetics*, vol. 4, pp. 2077–2082, August 2007.

[22] J. Nakazawa, J. Yura, T. Iwamoto, H. Yokoyama, and H. Tokuda, "Bridging sensor networks and the internet on cellular phones: towards richer and easier-to-use sensor network applications for end-users," in *Proceedings of the 6th International Conference on Networked Sensing Systems (INSS '09)*, pp. 94–97, June 2009.

[23] J. Nakazawa, H. Tokuda, W. K. Edwards, and U. Ramachandran, "A bridging framework for universal interoperability in pervasive systems," in *Proceedings of the 26th IEEE International Conference on Distributed Computing Systems (ICDCS '06)*, July 2006.

[24] Qualcomm Inc. Qualcomm brew.

[25] M. Balazinska, A. Deshpande, M. J. Franklin et al., "Data management in the worldwide sensor web," *IEEE Pervasive Computing*, vol. 6, no. 2, pp. 30–40, 2007.

[26] M. Leopold, M. B. Dydensborg, and P. Bonnet, "Bluetooth and sensor networks: a reality check," in *Proceedings of the 1st International Conference on Embedded Networked Sensor Systems (SenSys '03)*, pp. 103–113, November 2003.

[27] L. Zhong, M. Sinclair, and R. Bittner, "A phone-centered body sensor network platform: cost, energy efficiency & user interface," in *Proceedings of the International Workshop on Wearable and Implantable Body Sensor Networks (BSn '06)*, pp. 179–182, April 2006.

[28] M. Hirafuji, H. Yoichi, and M. Wada, "Field server: multifunctional wireless sensor network node for earth observation," in *Proceedings of the 3rd International Conference on Embedded Networked Sensor Systems (SenSys '05)*, p. 304, ACM Press, New York, NY, USA, 2005.

[29] B. Hull, V. Bychkovsky, Y. Zhang et al., "CarTel: a distributed mobile sensor computing system," in *Proceedings of the 4th International Conference on Embedded Networked Sensor Systems (SenSys '06)*, pp. 125–138, Boulder, Colo, USA, November 2006.

[30] K. Aberer, M Hauswirth, and A. Salehi, "Infrastructure for data processing in large-scale interconnected sensor networks," in *Proceedings of the International Conference on Mobile Data Management*, pp. 198–205, Washington, DC, USA, 2007.

4

Joint MMSE Transceiver Designs and Performance Benchmark for CoMP Transmission and Reception

Jialing Li, Enoch Lu, and I-Tai Lu

Department of ECE, Polytechnic Institute of NYU, 6 Metrotech Center, Brooklyn, NY 11201, USA

Correspondence should be addressed to Jialing Li, jialing.li.phd2@gmail.com

Academic Editors: J. M. Bahi, R. Dinis, M. I. Hayee, and M. Potkonjak

Coordinated Multipoint (CoMP) transmission and reception has been suggested as a key enabling technology of future cellular systems. To understand different CoMP configurations and to facilitate the configuration selection (and thus determine channel state information (CSI) feedback and data sharing requirements), performance benchmarks are needed to show what performance gains are possible. A unified approach is also needed to enable the cluster of cooperating cells to systematically take care of the transceiver design. To address these needs, the generalized iterative approach (GIA) is proposed as a unified approach for the minimum mean square error (MMSE) transceiver design of general multiple-transmitter multiple-receiver multiple-input-multiple-output (MIMO) systems subject to general linear power constraints. Moreover, the optimum decoder covariance optimization approach is proposed for downlink systems. Their optimality and relationships are established and shown numerically. Five CoMP configurations (Joint Processing-Equivalent Uplink, Joint Processing-Equivalent Downlink, Joint Processing-Equivalent Single User, Noncoordinated Multipoint, and Coordinated Beamforming) are studied and compared numerically. Physical insights, performance benchmarks, and some guidelines for CoMP configuration selection are presented.

1. Introduction

Though cellular has many challenges such as multipath fading, cell edge interference, and scarce spectrum, there is a demand for even better cellular performance than what is achieved today. In order to meet this demand, revolutionary ideas are needed. Coordinated Multipoint (CoMP) transmission and reception, a type of Network MIMO (multiple-input and multiple-output) in Long-Term Evolution-Advanced (LTE-A) [1], is one of those ideas and is a key enabling technology of future cellular systems. It, being a MIMO technique, actually exploits the multipath fading. Furthermore, it lowers the cell edge interference by having potential interfering cells cooperate. And lastly, its lowering of the interference allows for better spectrum reuse and, therefore, better use of the scarce spectrum. Since there are various levels of cell cooperation, there are various CoMP configurations [1–4]. As such, the following three categories of configurations are generally considered.

The first category is Noncoordinated Multipoint (Non-CoMP) and does not use CoMP at all. In it, each base station (BS) communicates with its own user(s) and does so without cooperating with the other cells in data sharing or channel state information (CSI) exchange. Each BS either ignores or tries to estimate the intercell interference. It has the lowest level of cooperation.

The second category is Coordinated Beamforming (CBF). (In LTE-A, it is also referred to as Coordinated Scheduling and Coordinated Beamforming (CS/CB).) Here, each BS again only communicates with its own user(s) and there is no data sharing between BSs and no data sharing between users. This time though, the cells do cooperate to minimize the interference they cause to each other through coordination and joint transmitter and/or receiver design. It has the second lowest level of cooperation. Much work has been done for CBF configurations where each cell has one transmitter and receiver pair [5–12] and where each cell has one transmitter and multiple receivers [13–16]. There also are different CSI considerations (e.g., CSI only available at receivers [5–8, 16], full CSI available at a central processing unit [9–14], CSI available only on a per-cell basis [15]) and different design strategies (e.g., centralized [9–14] or distributed [15] designs).

The third category is Joint Processing (JP). Here, the cells fully cooperate; the BSs act as a single equivalent transmitter in downlink (the data is processed and transmitted jointly from the BSs) to form the Joint Processing-Equivalent Downlink (JP-DL) [17–19] and act as a single equivalent receiver in uplink (all received signals are shared and jointly processed) to form the Joint Processing-Equivalent Uplink (JP-UL) [20]. It is shown that JP-UL [20] and JP-DL [17] bring significant gains to both the cell average throughput and the cell edge user throughput. Note that JP-UL and JP-DL have higher level of cooperation than the previous two categories (Non-CoMP and CBF). When the users act as a single equivalent receiver (resp., transmitter) in downlink (resp., uplink), it forms the Joint Processing-Equivalent Single User (JP-SU), which is essentially a point-to-point MIMO system. JP-SU has the highest level of cooperation and is only of theoretical interest.

In addition, a few attempts have also been made to jointly consider different categories/configurations. For example, joint precoder and decoder designs (e.g., SINR balancing, user rate balancing and maximum sum rate) are proposed for Non-CoMP, JP-DL and CBF and numerical comparison of their ergodic sum rates is made in [21–23]. But to the best of our knowledge, there are no comparison and configuration selection guidelines for various CoMP configurations in the literature.

As seen from these previous works, the precoder and decoder designs and performance evaluation for CoMP systems can be very complex and diverse. This is due to the fact that there exist various CoMP configurations, design criteria, and constraints (e.g., the per-antenna power constraint, per-transmitter power constraint). There also exists a vast number of design approaches associated with each of the design criteria, each of the constraints, and each of the CoMP configurations. Moreover, CoMP was not considered mature and was not adopted by 3GPP in LTE release 10 [24]. Thus, performance benchmarks (which show what performance gains are possible) for CoMP configurations are needed to help determine rules for configuration selection. Since different CoMP configurations require different levels of CSI feedback and data sharing, these rules also help to determine CSI feedback and data sharing requirements. There is also a need for a unified approach to enable the cluster of cooperating cells to systematically take care of the transceiver design of whatever configuration they choose to implement. Both of these two needs will be addressed in this paper.

To address the need for performance benchmarks, we consider joint MMSE precoder and decoder designs for JP-UL, JP-DL, JP-SU, Non-CoMP, and CBF. Firstly, this is because joint MMSE designs can be considered as performance benchmarks for other practical design criteria; an MMSE solution is near optimum in some other senses (e.g., maximum sum rate [25, 26], minimum BER [27]) as well. It has been shown that maximizing the sum rate is equivalent to minimizing the *geometric mean* of the MSEs of all data streams [25]. Moreover, minimizing the sum MSE is equivalent to minimizing the upper bound of the

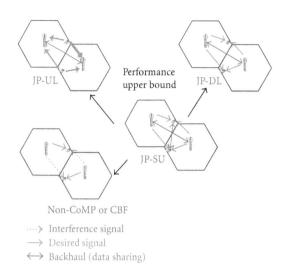

FIGURE 1: Relationship of the five CoMP configurations: an example of two transmitters and two receivers.

MSEs geometric mean. Thus, the MMSE results are nearly optimum in the maximum sum rate sense. Regarding BER, it has been shown that the MMSE design minimizes the lower bound of BER [27]. In addition, the BER results of the MMSE and minimum BER designs in [26] are very comparable. So, the MMSE results are nearly optimum in the minimum BER sense as well. Though studies in [25–27] are for single-user systems, these remarks are also true for CoMP systems. Secondly, note that with full CSI, JP-SU provides a performance upper bound for all CoMP configurations with same total number of transmit antennas and same total number of receive antennas, as shown in Figure 1. Similarly, Non-CoMP and CBF, where each cell has one transmitter and receiver pair, provide performance upper bounds for their respective categories, given same total number of transmit antennas and same total number of receive antennas. Thus, the performance benchmarks can be set forth numerically for various simulation setups; these numerical performance benchmarks can then be used to compare the different configurations and/or categories.

Although not much MMSE work has been published for the CoMP configurations, joint MMSE transceiver designs for the single-user, multiuser downlink, multiuser uplink, and CBF MIMO systems have been studied. For example, for single-user MIMO systems, closed-form expressions of the MMSE design have been derived for the total power constraint [25, 26] and for the shaping constraints [28]. For uplink MIMO systems subject to the per-user power constraint, numerical solutions are provided mainly by the optimal *transmit covariance optimization approach* (*TCOA*) [29, 30] and suboptimal iterative approaches such as in [29]. For downlink systems, numerical solutions are provided mainly by iterative approaches such as in [31] for the total power constraint and in [18] for the per-antenna and per-cell power constraints. Dual uplink approaches [32–34] have also been employed for the total power constraint. Recently, for K-user MIMO interference channels (a case of CBF), a joint MMSE design subject to per-transmitter power constraint, using a linear search for each Lagrange multiplier, is proposed [35].

Note that various CoMP configurations can be considered as special cases of general multiple-transmitter multiple-receiver (MTMR) systems. In this paper, the novel *generalized iterative approach (GIA)* is proposed as the unified approach to take care of the MMSE design of general MTMR MIMO systems subject to general linear power constraints, including the per-transmitter power constraint and the more practical per-antenna power constraint. The *GIA* can provide tradeoff between multiplexing and diversity gains. In addition, the optimum *decoder covariance optimization approach (DCOA)* for the MMSE design of downlink systems (i.e., JP-SU, JP-DL, and Non-CoMP) subject to general linear power constraints is also proposed so that the optimality of the *GIA* can be studied. For this purpose, the equivalence between the *GIA* and the optimum *TCOA* [29, 30] for the uplink or *DCOA* for the downlink is established in the respective configurations.

In the numerical simulations, firstly, aspects pertaining to the proposed *approaches* are investigated. The convergence properties of the proposed approaches are investigated; the optimality and diversity/multiplexing tradeoff of the *GIA* are verified numerically; numerical comparison between the *GIA* and the approach in [35] is investigated. Secondly, aspects pertaining to performance benchmark are investigated. To set forth a benchmark among different CoMP configurations, MSE and BER performances for the five CoMP configurations (JP-SU, JP-DL, JP-UL, CBF, and Non-CoMP) are compared. Since this paper is concerned with performance benchmarks (achievable theoretical upper bounds), fairness-type criteria, and practical issues such as synchronization required by different CoMP configurations are not considered here. Various important factors (level of cooperation, system load, system size, and path loss) are studied though. The performance benchmarks and the resulting physical insights (into the mechanisms and performances of CoMP configurations) are very useful. In particular, much needed guidelines for the configuration selection process are obtained.

Notations are as follows. All boldface letters indicate vectors (lower case) or matrices (upper case). $\mathbf{A}'$, $\mathbf{A}^*$, $\mathbf{A}^{-1}$, $\mathrm{tr}(\mathbf{A})$, $E(\mathbf{A})$, $\mathrm{rank}(\mathbf{A})$, and $\|\mathbf{A}\|_F$ stand for the transpose, conjugate transpose, inverse, trace, expectation, rank, and Frobenius norm of $\mathbf{A}$, respectively. $\mathrm{abs}(\mathbf{A})$ denotes taking the absolute value element-wise of $\mathbf{A}$. $\mathrm{span}(\mathbf{A})$ represents the subspace spanned by the columns of $\mathbf{A}$. Matrix $\mathbf{I}_a$ signifies an identity matrix with rank a. Matrix $\mathbf{0}$ signifies a zero matrix with proper dimension. $\mathrm{diag}[\cdots]$ denotes the diagonal matrix with elements $[\cdots]$ on the main diagonal. $\mathbf{A} > \mathbf{B}\ (\mathbf{A} \geq \mathbf{B})$ means that $\mathbf{A} - \mathbf{B}$ is positive definite (semidefinite). $\mathbf{A} \circ \mathbf{B}$ denotes the Schur product of $\mathbf{A}$ and $\mathbf{B}$ (element-wise product of $\mathbf{A}$ and $\mathbf{B}$). $\mathrm{CN}(\mu, q)$ denotes a complex normal random variable with mean μ and variance q. Finally, i.i.d. stands for independent and identically distributed.

2. Formulation

2.1. A Single Formulation for General MTMR MIMO Systems. In this subsection, we derive a single formulation to describe a general MTMR MIMO system including the five CoMP configurations (JP-UL, JP-DL, JP-SU, Non-CoMP, and CBF) investigated in this paper. Consider an MTMR MIMO system with T transmitters and R receivers. Let τ_n and γ_l denote the numbers of antennas at the nth transmitter and the lth receiver, respectively. Accounting for the path loss (spatial correlation can be easily incorporated as well but has been omitted for simplicity), the channel from the nth transmitter to the lth receiver is modeled as

$$\overline{\mathbf{H}}_{ln} = d_{ln}^{-\beta}\mathbf{H}_{W,ln}. \tag{1}$$

Here, d_{ln} denotes the distance between the lth receiver and the nth transmitter, and 2β is the path loss exponent. The entries of $\mathbf{H}_{w,ln}$ are i.i.d. $\mathrm{CN}(0,1)$. Here, the subscript W represents spatially white noise.

Some of the transmitters (resp., receivers) in the CoMP system may be sharing and jointly processing their data (resp., received signals). Such a collection of transmitters (resp., receivers), which are connected via backhaul, share CSI and data, and act like a single transmitter (resp., receiver) in transmission and data processing, is a *composite* transmitter (resp., receiver) and thus an *equivalent* transmitter (resp., receiver). For the sake of having a single formulation, a transmitter (resp., receiver) which does not collaborate with other transmitters (resp., receivers) in the above way is also considered to be an *equivalent* transmitter (resp., receiver). Thus, this MTMR MIMO system can also be (and will be) considered as having C *equivalent* transmitters (*eq*-transmitters for short) and K *equivalent* receivers (*eq*-receivers for short). Obviously, $C \leq T$ and $K \leq R$.

Let t_c and r_i denote the numbers of antennas at the cth *eq*-transmitter and the ith *eq*-receiver, respectively. Then, $t = \sum_{n=1}^{T}\tau_n = \sum_{c=1}^{C}t_c$ and $r = \sum_{l=1}^{R}\gamma_l = \sum_{i=1}^{K}r_i$ are the total numbers of transmit and receive antennas, respectively. Also let $\mathbf{H}_{ic}$ denote the composite channel matrix from the cth *eq*-transmitter to the ith *eq*-receiver. At the cth *eq*-transmitter, let $\mathbf{s}_{ic}$, m_{ic}, and $\mathbf{F}_{ic}$ denote the data, number of data streams, and precoder for the ith *eq*-receiver, respectively. Furthermore, let $\mathbf{\Phi}_{\mathbf{s}ic} = E(\mathbf{s}_{ic}\mathbf{s}_{ic}^*)$ and $\mathbf{G}_{ic}$ be, respectively, the source covariance matrix for $\mathbf{s}_{ic}$ and the decoder for $\mathbf{s}_{ic}$. Which transmitter transmits to which receiver is configurable. When the cth *eq*-transmitter has no data to transmit to the ith *eq*-receiver, $\mathbf{s}_{ic} = \mathbf{0}$, $m_{ic} = 0$, $\mathbf{\Phi}_{\mathbf{s}ic} = \mathbf{0}$, $\mathbf{F}_{ic} = \mathbf{0}$, and $\mathbf{G}_{ic} = \mathbf{0}$. When it does, $\mathbf{\Phi}_{\mathbf{s}ic}$ is positive definite and $\mathbf{F}_{ic}$ and $\mathbf{G}_{ic}$ must be designed.

In this system, there may be multiple clusters where each cluster jointly designs the MIMO processors for its own *eq*-transmitters and *eq*-receivers but does so independently of the other clusters. There is no CSI sharing between clusters and the intercluster interference is formulated as noise. Let D and S define one such cluster; D being the set of *eq*-transmitter indices in the cluster and S being the set of *eq*-receiver indices in the cluster. D and S are introduced to allow a single formulation to take care of the MMSE transceiver design for different CoMP configurations. At the ith eq-receiver, $i \in S$, the received signal is thus

$$\mathbf{y}_i = \sum_{c \in D} \mathbf{H}_{ic} \sum_{j \in S} \mathbf{F}_{jc} \mathbf{s}_{jc} + \mathbf{n}_i, \tag{2}$$

$$\mathbf{n}_i = \mathbf{a}_i + \mathbf{i}_i, \qquad \mathbf{i}_i = \sum_{l \notin D} \mathbf{H}_{il} \sum_{j \notin S} \mathbf{F}_{jl} \mathbf{s}_{jl}. \tag{3}$$

Here, $\mathbf{n}_i$, $\mathbf{a}_i$ and $\mathbf{i}_i$ are the noise plus intercluster interference vector, the noise vector, and the intercluster interference vector, respectively, at the ith eq-receiver. The interference is from all of the eq-transmitters which do not belong to D. Thus, when there is only one cluster in the system, there is no interference and $\mathbf{n}_i = \mathbf{a}_i$, $\mathbf{i}_i = \mathbf{0}$ for every $i \in S$. Note that, except in Non-CoMP, the possible intercell interference is implicitly included in the first term in (2), and is considered to be manageable.

2.2. Five CoMP Configurations. The needed CSI feedback and data sharing in each CoMP configuration are assumed done through ideal link and of zero delay. The above single formulation is able to describe any general MTMR MIMO system including JP-UL, JP-DL, JP-SU, Non-CoMP, and CBF. There is only one cluster in JP-UL, JP-DL, JP-SU, and CBF. But, there are C clusters in Non-CoMP. Without loss of generality and for convenience, Non-CoMP and CBF considered in this paper have only one transmitter-receiver pair per cluster.

2.2.1. Configuration I: JP-UL. In JP-UL, the system has only one cluster and is just an equivalent uplink MIMO system, that is, there are multiple transmitters (each being an eq-transmitter) but only one eq-receiver (full cooperation among all receivers). Thus,

$$D = \{1, 2, \ldots, C\}, \qquad S = \{1\}, \qquad C = T, \qquad K = 1,$$
$$\mathbf{H}_{ic} = \begin{bmatrix} \overline{\mathbf{H}}'_{1c} & \cdots & \overline{\mathbf{H}}'_{Rc} \end{bmatrix}', \qquad \mathbf{n}_i = \mathbf{a}_i,$$
$$\mathbf{i}_i = \mathbf{0}, \quad c \in D, \ i \in S. \tag{4}$$

For both FDD and TDD systems, each BS estimates all uplink CSI and sends the CSI to a central processing unit via the backhaul (if the BSs are colocated, the backhaul is not needed). The central processing unit performs the system-wide transceiver design and sends each user its optimized precoder through the serving BS. Each user uses the received precoder for transmitting data. Lastly, the BSs share their received signals with the central processing unit for joint decoding.

2.2.2. Configuration II: JP-DL. In JP-DL, the system has only one cluster and is just an equivalent downlink MIMO system, that is, there are multiple receivers (each being an

eq-receiver) but only one eq-transmitter (full cooperation among all transmitters). Thus,

$$D = \{1\}, \qquad S = \{1, 2, \ldots, K\}, \qquad C = 1, \qquad K = R,$$
$$\mathbf{H}_{ic} = \begin{bmatrix} \overline{\mathbf{H}}_{i1} & \cdots & \overline{\mathbf{H}}_{iT} \end{bmatrix}, \qquad \mathbf{n}_i = \mathbf{a}_i,$$
$$\mathbf{i}_i = \mathbf{0}, \quad c \in D, \ i \in S. \tag{5}$$

In TDD systems, the BSs estimate downlink CSI through reciprocity. In FDD systems, each user estimates all intracluster downlink CSI and feeds back the CSI to its serving BS. After obtaining the CSI, each BS sends the CSI to a central processing unit via the backhaul (if the BSs are co-located, the backhaul is not needed). The central processing unit performs the system-wide transceiver design and sends the optimized precoders and decoders to the BSs. Each BS uses the optimized precoder for transmitting data. Each BS also sends the decoder to its users for processing the received data.

2.2.3. Configuration III: JP-SU. In JP-SU, essentially a point-to-point MIMO system, there is only one eq-transmitter (full cooperation among all transmitters) and only one eq-receiver (full cooperation among all receivers). It is only of theoretical interest (showing performance upper bound for all CoMP systems) and the signaling issues are irrelevant and omitted. It is assumed that a central processing unit knows all the channels and performs the system-wide transceiver design. Thus,

$$D = \{1\}, \qquad S = \{1\}, \qquad C = 1, \qquad K = 1,$$
$$\mathbf{H}_{ic} = \begin{bmatrix} \overline{\mathbf{H}}_{11} & \cdots & \overline{\mathbf{H}}_{1T} \\ \vdots & \ddots & \vdots \\ \overline{\mathbf{H}}_{R1} & \cdots & \overline{\mathbf{H}}_{RT} \end{bmatrix}, \qquad \mathbf{n}_i = \mathbf{a}_i, \tag{6}$$
$$\mathbf{i}_i = \mathbf{0}, \quad c \in D, \ i \in S.$$

2.2.4. Configuration IV: Non-CoMP. In Non-CoMP, each transmitter (being an eq-transmitter) is paired with a unique receiver (being an eq-receiver). Each pair is a cluster of the system, so the intercell interference is the inter-cluster interference. Thus, pairwise transceiver design is performed and the system with C eq-transmitter eq-receiver pairs ($C = K = T = R$) is decoupled into C single user clusters with the ith one being

$$D = \{i\}, \qquad S = \{i\}, \qquad \mathbf{H}_{ii} = \overline{\mathbf{H}}_{ii}, \qquad \mathbf{n}_i = \mathbf{a}_i + \mathbf{i}_i,$$
$$\mathbf{i}_i = \sum_{l=1, l \neq i}^{C} \overline{\mathbf{H}}_{il} \mathbf{F}_{ll} \mathbf{s}_{ll}, \quad i \in S. \tag{7}$$

In TDD systems, each transmitter estimates the forward link CSI through reciprocity. The transmitter performs the joint transceiver design and sends the decoder to the receiver. In FDD systems, each receiver estimates the forward link CSI and sends the estimated information to the transmitter. Both transmitter and receiver can independently perform the joint transceiver design. The transmitter will use the resulting precoder to transmit data and the receiver will use the decoder to process the received data.

2.2.5. Configuration V: CBF. Like Non-CoMP, there are multiple pairs of transmitters and receivers in CBF. However, unlike Non-CoMP, there is only one cluster here. Note that in CBF, $\mathbf{F}_{ic} = \mathbf{0}$ for $i \neq c$ and the BSs do not share data. The CSI acquisition and signaling requirement in uplink (resp., downlink) for a central processing unit are the same as in JP-UL (resp., JP-DL). The central processing unit performs the system-wide transceiver design. Thus,

$$D = \{1, 2, \ldots, C\}, \qquad S = \{1, 2, \ldots, C\}, \qquad \mathbf{H}_{ic} = \overline{\mathbf{H}}_{ic},$$
$$\mathbf{n}_i = \mathbf{a}_i, \quad \mathbf{i}_i = \mathbf{0}, \quad c \in D, i \in S. \tag{8}$$

Note that, for the composite channel matrix $\mathbf{H}_{ic}$ in (4)–(8), the subscript i is the *eq-receiver* index and the subscript c is the *eq-transmitter* index. However, for the channel matrix $\overline{\mathbf{H}}_{ln}$, the subscript l is the receiver index and the subscript n is the transmitter index.

2.3. MMSE Design Subject to General Linear Power Constraints.

For a given cluster, define the MSE with respect to the ith *eq-receiver* and the cth *eq-transmitter*, $i \in S, c \in D$, as

$$\eta_{ic} = \mathrm{tr}\left\{ E\left[\left(\mathbf{G}_{ic}\mathbf{y}_i - \mathbf{s}_{ic} \right) \left(\mathbf{G}_{ic}\mathbf{y}_i - \mathbf{s}_{ic} \right)^* \right] \right\}. \tag{9}$$

Note that when the cth *eq-transmitter* has no data for the ith *eq-receiver*, $\eta_{ic} = 0$. The sum MSE η is

$$\eta = \sum_{c \in D} \sum_{i \in S} \eta_{ic}. \tag{10}$$

2.3.1. MMSE Problem. We will jointly choose $\{\mathbf{F}_{ic}, \mathbf{G}_{ic}\}_{i \in S, c \in D}$ to minimize the sum MSE η:

$$\{\mathbf{F}_{ic}, \mathbf{G}_{ic}\}_{\mathrm{MMSE}} = \underset{\{\mathbf{F}_{ic}, \mathbf{G}_{ic} | i \in S, c \in D\}}{\arg\min} \{\eta\}, \tag{11}$$

subject to general linear power constraints, for example, the per-antenna power constraint at the cth *eq-transmitter*

$$\mathbf{I}_{t_c} \circ \left(\sum_{i \in S} \mathbf{F}_{ic}\mathbf{\Phi}_{sic}\mathbf{F}_{ic}^* \right) = \mathrm{diag}[P_{c1}, \ldots, P_{ct_c}], \tag{12}$$
$$P_{c1}, \ldots, P_{ct_c} > 0, \quad c \in D,$$

or the per-transmitter power constraint at the nth transmitter of the cth *eq-transmitter*,

$$\mathrm{tr}\left(\mathbf{Q}_n \circ \left[\sum_{i \in S} \mathbf{F}_{ic}\mathbf{\Phi}_{sic}\mathbf{F}_{ic}^* \right] \right) = P_{bnc} > 0, \quad \forall n \in J_c, \forall c \in D. \tag{13}$$

Here, J_c denotes the set of all cooperating transmitters that form the cth *eq-transmitter*. When there is only one element in J_c, that is, $J_c = \{n\}$, $\mathbf{Q}_n = \mathbf{I}_{t_c}$ in (13). When there are more than one element in J_c, $\mathbf{Q}_n$ is a $t_c \times t_c$ matrix whose entries are all equal to zero except for the diagonal elements corresponding to the antennas of the nth transmitter. The values of these nonzero diagonal elements are equal to one.

2.3.2. Augmented Cost Function. To solve (11) subject to (12) or (13), one can use the method of Lagrange multipliers to set up the augmented cost function for general linear power constraints

$$\xi = \eta + \sum_{c \in D} \mathrm{tr}\left(\mathbf{\Lambda}_c \left(\sum_{i \in S} \mathbf{F}_{ic}\mathbf{\Phi}_{sic}\mathbf{F}_{ic}^* - \mathbf{P}_c \right) \right), \tag{14}$$

where $\mathbf{\Lambda}_c$ represents the Lagrange multipliers. Only the widely considered per-transmitter power constraint and the practical per-antenna power constraint are given as examples. For the per-antenna power constraint in (12),

$$\mathbf{\Lambda}_c = \mathrm{diag}[\lambda_{c1}, \ldots, \lambda_{ct_c}], \quad \mathbf{P}_c = \mathrm{diag}[P_{c1}, \ldots, P_{ct_c}], \quad c \in D. \tag{15}$$

For the per-transmitter power constraint in (13), let $\mathbf{\Delta}_n = \mathbf{I}_{\tau_n}\lambda_{nc}$, $\mathbf{\Gamma}_{nc} = \mathbf{I}_{\tau_n} P_{bnc}/\tau_n$, $c \in D$. Thus

$$\mathbf{\Lambda}_c = \mathrm{diag}\left[\mathbf{\Delta}_n\right]_{n \in J_c}, \quad \mathbf{P}_c = \mathrm{diag}\left[\mathbf{\Gamma}_{nc}\right]_{n \in J_c}, \quad c \in D. \tag{16}$$

2.4. MMSE Decoders and Precoders.

Define the noise covariance matrix and the noise plus interference covariance matrix at the ith *eq-receiver* as $\mathbf{\Phi}_{ai} = E(\mathbf{a}_i\mathbf{a}_i^*)$ and $\mathbf{\Phi}_{ni} = E(\mathbf{n}_i\mathbf{n}_i^*)$, respectively. Assume $\mathbf{\Phi}_{ai}$ is known. Therefore, $\mathbf{\Phi}_{ni}$ is also known in JP-SU, JP-UL, JP-DL and CBF because $\mathbf{\Phi}_{ni} = \mathbf{\Phi}_{ai}$. In Non-CoMP, $\mathbf{\Phi}_{ni}$ can be estimated explicitly as $\mathbf{\Phi}_{ni} = \sum_{l=1,l \neq i}^{C} d_{il}^{-2\beta} P_{bll}\mathbf{I}_{r_i} + \mathbf{\Phi}_{ai}$, and $P_{bll} = \sum_{k=1}^{t_l} P_{lk}$ (see Appendix A).

After some math manipulations, (9) becomes

$$\eta_{ic} = \mathrm{tr}\left(-\mathbf{G}_{ic}\mathbf{H}_{ic}\mathbf{F}_{ic}\mathbf{\Phi}_{sic} - \mathbf{\Phi}_{sic}\mathbf{F}_{ic}^*\mathbf{H}_{ic}^*\mathbf{G}_{ic}^* + \mathbf{\Phi}_{sic} \right.$$
$$\left. + \mathbf{G}_{ic}\left[\sum_{k \in D}\mathbf{H}_{ik}\left(\sum_{j \in S}\mathbf{F}_{jk}\mathbf{\Phi}_{sjk}\mathbf{F}_{jk}^* \right)\mathbf{H}_{ik}^* + \mathbf{\Phi}_{ni} \right]\mathbf{G}_{ic}^* \right). \tag{17}$$

There are two possible directions to solve the MMSE problem.

2.4.1. MMSE Decoder. On one hand, for a given set of precoders $\{\mathbf{F}_{ic}\}_{i \in S, c \in D}$, setting the gradient of η in (10) with respect to $\mathbf{G}_{ic}$ equal to zero yields the MMSE decoder for $\mathbf{s}_{ic}$, $c \in D, i \in S$:

$$\mathbf{G}_{ic} = \mathbf{\Phi}_{sic}\mathbf{F}_{ic}^*\mathbf{H}_{ic}^*\mathbf{M}_i,$$
$$\mathbf{M}_i = \left[\sum_{k \in D}\mathbf{H}_{ik}\left(\sum_{j \in S}\mathbf{F}_{jk}\mathbf{\Phi}_{sjk}\mathbf{F}_{jk}^* \right)\mathbf{H}_{ik}^* + \mathbf{\Phi}_{ni} \right]^{-1}. \tag{18}$$

Substituting (18) into (17), η in (10) is reduced to

$$\eta_1 = \sum_{c \in D}\sum_{i \in S}\mathrm{tr}(-\mathbf{\Phi}_{sic}\mathbf{F}_{ic}^*\mathbf{H}_{ic}^*\mathbf{M}_i\mathbf{H}_{ic}\mathbf{F}_{ic}\mathbf{\Phi}_{sic} + \mathbf{\Phi}_{sic}). \tag{19}$$

The augmented cost function ξ in (14) is also reduced to

$$\xi_1 = \eta_1 + \sum_{c \in D}\mathrm{tr}\left(\mathbf{\Lambda}_c\left(\sum_{i \in S}\mathbf{F}_{ic}\mathbf{\Phi}_{sic}\mathbf{F}_{ic}^* - \mathbf{P}_c \right) \right). \tag{20}$$

Note that η_1 in (19) and ξ_1 in (20) are merely functions of precoders $\{\mathbf{F}_{ic}\}_{i \in S, c \in D}$ (and Lagrange multipliers $\{\mathbf{\Lambda}_c\}_{c \in D}$).

2.4.2. MMSE Precoder. On the other hand, for a given set of decoders $\{\mathbf{G}_{ic}\}_{i\in S, c\in D}$ and Lagrange multipliers $\{\mathbf{\Lambda}_c\}_{c\in D}$, setting the gradient of ξ in (14) with respect to $\mathbf{F}_{ic}$ equal to zero yields the MMSE precoder for $\mathbf{s}_{ic}$, $c \in D$, $i \in S$:

$$\mathbf{F}_{ic} = \mathbf{N}_c \mathbf{H}_{ic}^* \mathbf{G}_{ic}^*,$$

$$\mathbf{N}_c = \left[\sum_{k\in D} \sum_{j\in S} \mathbf{H}_{jc}^* \mathbf{G}_{jk}^* \mathbf{G}_{jk} \mathbf{H}_{jc} + \mathbf{\Lambda}_c \right]^{-1}. \tag{21}$$

Substituting (21) into (14), the augmented cost function ξ in (14) is reduced to

$$\begin{aligned} \xi_2 = &\sum_{c\in D}\sum_{i\in S} \mathrm{tr}(-\mathbf{G}_{ic}\mathbf{H}_{ic}\mathbf{N}_c\mathbf{H}_{ic}^*\mathbf{G}_{ic}^*\mathbf{\Phi}_{sic} + \mathbf{\Phi}_{sic}) \\ &+ \sum_{c\in D}\sum_{i\in S} \mathrm{tr}(\mathbf{G}_{ic}\mathbf{\Phi}_{ni}\mathbf{G}_{ic}^*) - \sum_{c\in D} \mathrm{tr}(\mathbf{\Lambda}_c\mathbf{P}_c). \end{aligned} \tag{22}$$

Note that ξ_2 in (22) is merely a function of precoders $\{\mathbf{G}_{ic}\}_{i\in S, c\in D}$ and Lagrange multipliers $\{\mathbf{\Lambda}_c\}_{c\in D}$.

2.4.3. Transmit and Decoder Covariance Matrices. When the nonzero source covariance matrices are diagonal matrices with the same diagonal elements (i.e., $\mathbf{\Phi}_{sic} = \sigma^2\mathbf{I}_{m_{ic}}$, $i \in S$, $c \in D$, $\mathbf{s}_{ic} \neq 0$), replacing $\mathbf{F}_{ic}$ by $\mathbf{F}_{ic}\mathbf{A}_{ic}$ ($\mathbf{A}_{ic}$ is an arbitrary unitary matrix with proper dimension) does not change the power constraint (12) or (13). Furthermore, $\eta(\mathbf{F}_{ic}, \mathbf{G}_{ic}) = \eta(\mathbf{F}_{ic}\mathbf{A}_{ic}, \mathbf{A}_{ic}^*\mathbf{G}_{ic})$. Define the transmit covariance matrices as

$$\mathbf{U}_{ic} = \mathbf{F}_{ic}\mathbf{F}_{ic}^*, \tag{23}$$

and the decoder covariance matrices as

$$\mathbf{V}_{ic} = \mathbf{G}_{ic}^*\mathbf{G}_{ic}. \tag{24}$$

Essentially, $\eta(\mathbf{U}_{ic}, \mathbf{V}_{ic}) = \eta(\mathbf{F}_{ic}\mathbf{A}_{ic}, \mathbf{A}_{ic}^*\mathbf{G}_{ic})$ for arbitrary unitary matrices $\{\mathbf{A}_{ic}\}_{i\in S, c\in D}$. Therefore, the transmit and decoder covariance matrices $\{\mathbf{U}_{ic}, \mathbf{V}_{ic}\}_{i\in S, c\in D}$ can be used to determine the MSE (in fact, the transmit and decoder covariance matrices $\{\mathbf{U}_{ic}, \mathbf{V}_{ic}\}_{i\in S, c\in D}$ also determine the achievable sum rate) and consequently determine the precoders and decoders. Thus, if the transmit covariance matrices $\{\mathbf{U}_{ic}\}_{i\in S, c\in D}$ which minimize the MSE are found, the precoders $\{\mathbf{F}_{ic}\}_{i\in S, c\in D}$ can be obtained using (23) and the decoders $\{\mathbf{G}_{ic}\}_{i\in S, c\in D}$ can be obtained from (18). Similarly, if the decoder covariance matrices $\{\mathbf{V}_{ic}\}_{i\in S, c\in D}$ which minimize the MSE are found, the decoders $\{\mathbf{G}_{ic}\}_{i\in S, c\in D}$ can be obtained using (24) and the precoders $\{\mathbf{F}_{ic}\}_{i\in S, c\in D}$ can be obtained from (21).

3. Unified Approach for General MTMR MIMO Systems

The *GIA* is proposed as a unified approach for the MMSE design for general MTMR MIMO systems. It is motivated by the fact that, if the Lagrange multipliers $\mathbf{\Lambda}_c$ in (21) are known, we can solve the coupled equations (18) and (21) iteratively for the decoders $\{\mathbf{G}_{ic}\}_{i\in S, c\in D}$ and precoders $\{\mathbf{F}_{ic}\}_{i\in S, c\in D}$. Note that, in most literatures (e.g., [35]), the Lagrange

multipliers are obtained through linear search, in which the search space increases significantly as the system size increases. We herein propose a much more efficient approach using an explicit expression for the Lagrange multipliers.

To obtain an explicit expression for the Lagrange multipliers $\mathbf{\Lambda}_c$, $c \in D$, set the gradient of ξ_1 in (20) with respect to $\mathbf{F}_{ic}$ equal to zero and then left-multiply the resulting equation with $\mathbf{F}_{ic}$. Once this is done for each $i \in S$, sum them all up to obtain the following equation:

$$\left(\sum_{i\in S} \mathbf{F}_{ic}\mathbf{\Phi}_{sic}\mathbf{F}_{ic}^* \right) \mathbf{\Lambda}_c = \mathbf{B}_c, \tag{25}$$

$$\begin{aligned} \mathbf{B}_c = &\sum_{i\in S} \mathbf{F}_{ic}\mathbf{\Phi}_{sic}^2\mathbf{F}_{ic}^*\mathbf{H}_{ic}^*\mathbf{M}_i\mathbf{H}_{ic} - \left(\sum_{i\in S} \mathbf{F}_{ic}\mathbf{\Phi}_{sic}\mathbf{F}_{ic}^* \right) \\ &\times \left(\sum_{k\in D}\sum_{j\in S} \mathbf{H}_{jc}^*\mathbf{M}_j\mathbf{H}_{jk}\mathbf{F}_{jk}\mathbf{\Phi}_{sjk}^2\mathbf{F}_{jk}^*\mathbf{H}_{jk}^*\mathbf{M}_j\mathbf{H}_{jc} \right). \end{aligned} \tag{26}$$

Utilizing (12), for the per-antenna power constraint,

$$\mathbf{\Lambda}_c = \mathbf{P}_c^{-1}(\mathbf{I}_{t_c} \circ \mathbf{B}_c). \tag{27}$$

Utilizing (13), for the per-transmitter power constraint,

$$\lambda_{nc} = P_{bnc}^{-1} \mathrm{tr}(\mathbf{Q}_n \circ \mathbf{B}_c), \quad \forall n \in J_c. \tag{28}$$

Note that the usage of (27) or (28) enforces the corresponding complementary slackness conditions

$$\mathbf{\Lambda}_c \left[\mathbf{I}_{t_c} \circ \left(\sum_{i\in S} \mathbf{F}_{ic}\mathbf{\Phi}_{sic}\mathbf{F}_{ic}^* \right) - \mathbf{P}_c \right] = 0, \tag{29}$$

$$\lambda_{nc} \left[\mathrm{tr}\left(\mathbf{Q}_n \circ \left(\sum_{i\in S} \mathbf{F}_{ic}\mathbf{\Phi}_{sic}\mathbf{F}_{ic}^* \right) \right) - P_{bnc} \right] = 0, \quad \forall n \in J_c. \tag{30}$$

With the explicit expression for the Lagrange multipliers in (27) or (28) in hand, a *GIA* can be developed. There are three steps in each iteration of the *GIA*.

Step 1. Given $\{\mathbf{F}_{ic}\}_{i\in S, c\in D}$, obtain $\{\mathbf{G}_{ic}\}_{i\in S, c\in D}$ using (18).

Step 2. Given $\{\mathbf{F}_{ic}\}_{i\in S, c\in D}$, obtain $\{\mathbf{\Lambda}_c\}_{c\in D}$ using (27) or (28).

Step 3. Given $\{\mathbf{G}_{ic}\}_{i\in S, c\in D}$ and $\{\mathbf{\Lambda}_c\}_{c\in D}$, obtain $\{\mathbf{F}_{ic}\}_{i\in S, c\in D}$ using (21).

The iterative procedure of the *GIA* stops when the Karesh-Kuhn-Tucker (KKT) conditions are all satisfied, that is, when the following three requirements are fulfilled: one, the MSE no longer decreases; two, each precoder (decoder) converges; three, the transmission powers at the transmitter(s) meet the desired power constraints. Since the MSE has a lower bound at zero and each of the *GIA* steps actually enforces one of the KKT conditions of the MMSE problem, the *GIA* can converge quickly to a local minimum at low powers. At high transmit powers, a scaling initialization (scaling the MMSE MIMO precoders and decoders given by the *GIA* at lower powers) is very effective and efficient. Note that the *GIA* can deal with arbitrary source covariance matrices $\{\mathbf{\Phi}_{sic}\}_{i \in S, c \in D}$, thus allowing m_{ic}, the number of data streams intended from the *c*th *eq*-transmitter to the *i*th *eq*-receiver to be prespecified for all $i \in S$, for all $c \in D$, $\mathbf{s}_{ic} \neq \mathbf{0}$. Since the numbers of data streams can be pre-specified, the *GIA* allows for tradeoff between diversity and multiplexing gains.

4. Optimum Approaches for Special MTMR Systems

When the source covariance matrices are diagonal matrices with the same diagonal elements, that is, $\mathbf{\Phi}_{sic} = \sigma^2 \mathbf{I}_{m_{ic}}, i \in S$, $c \in D$, optimum approaches for the MMSE design subject to the general linear power constraints may be developed for special MTMR systems: uplink systems (e.g., JP-UL, JP-SU, and Non-CoMP where S has only one element) in Section 4.1 and downlink systems (e.g., JP-DL, JP-SU, and Non-CoMP where D has only one element) in Section 4.2. For convenience and without loss of generality, in the section, we assume $\sigma^2 = 1$.

4.1. TCOA [29, 30] for Systems with One Eq-Receiver. The *TCOA* [29, 30] can be used for JP-UL, JP-SU, and Non-CoMP where S has only one element (but not for JP-DL and CBF) under general linear power constraint. (Note that in [30, 31], the *TCOA* is only for the per-user power constraint. We use it here to deal with the per-antenna power constraint.) It is motivated by the fact that the MMSE problem may be solved by searching for the transmit covariance matrices $\{\mathbf{U}_{ic}\}_{i \in S, c \in D}$ to jointly minimize η_1 in (19). The optimum numbers of data streams $\{m_{ic}\}_{i \in S, c \in D}$ are determined by the rank of optimum $\{\mathbf{U}_{ic}\}_{i \in S, c \in D}$. The *TCOA* [30] can be reformulated in terms of an SDP formulation which can be solved numerically by SDP solvers (such as SeDuMi [36] and Yalmip [37]) in polynomial time.

4.2. DCOA for Systems with One Eq-Transmitter. The *DCOA* can be developed for JP-DL, JP-SU, and Non-CoMP where D has only one element (but not for JP-UL and CBF). It is motivated by the fact that the MMSE problem may be solved by searching for the decoder covariance matrices $\{\mathbf{V}_{ic}\}_{i \in S, c \in D}$ to jointly minimize ξ_2 in (22). Using (24), ξ_2 in (22) becomes

$$\xi_2 = \mathrm{tr}(\mathbf{\Lambda}_c(\mathbf{N}_c - \mathbf{P}_c)) + \sum_{i \in S} \mathrm{tr}(\mathbf{V}_{ic}\mathbf{\Phi}_{ni}) + \sum_{i \in S} m_{ic} - t_c, \quad (31)$$

where

$$\mathbf{N}_c = \left[\sum_{k \in D} \sum_{j \in S} \mathbf{H}_{jc}^* \mathbf{V}_{jk} \mathbf{H}_{jc} + \mathbf{\Lambda}_c \right]^{-1}. \quad (32)$$

The MMSE transceiver design problem becomes

$$\min_{\{\mathbf{V}_{ic}\}_{i \in S}} \max_{\mathbf{\Lambda}_c} \quad \xi_2,$$

$$\text{subject to} \quad \mathbf{V}_{ic} \geq 0,$$
$$\text{rank}(\mathbf{V}_{ic}) = m_{ic}, \quad (33)$$
$$\mathbf{\Lambda}_c \geq 0,$$
$$i \in S, \quad c \in D.$$

The problem in (33) is not cing with the numbers of data streams, that is, $\text{rank}(\mathbf{V}_{ic}) = m_{ic}$, $i \in S$, $c \in D$. Allowing $\{m_{ic}\}_{i \in S, c \in D}$ to be unspecified, we obtain the rank-relaxed decoder covariance optimization problem:

$$\min_{\mathbf{V}_{ic} \geq 0, i \in S} \max_{\mathbf{\Lambda}_c \geq 0} \xi_{2,\text{rel}}, \quad c \in D,$$

$$\xi_{2,\text{rel}} = \mathrm{tr}(\mathbf{\Lambda}_c \mathbf{N}_c - \mathbf{\Lambda}_c \mathbf{P}_c) + \sum_{i \in S} \mathrm{tr}(\mathbf{V}_{ic}\mathbf{\Phi}_{ni}). \quad (34)$$

The cost function $\xi_{2,\text{rel}}$ in (34) is convex with respect to $\{\mathbf{V}_{ic}\}_{i \in S, c \in D}$ and concave with respect to $\mathbf{\Lambda}_c$. Define $\min_{\mathbf{V}_{ic} \geq 0, i \in S} \max_{\mathbf{\Lambda}_c \geq 0} \xi_{2,\text{rel}}$ as the primal problem and $\max_{\mathbf{\Lambda}_c \geq 0} \min_{\mathbf{V}_{ic} \geq 0, i \in S} \xi_{2,\text{rel}}$ as the dual problem. Since both the primal problem and the dual problem are convex and strictly feasible, strong duality holds, that is, the optimum values of $\{\mathbf{V}_{ic}\}_{i \in S, c \in D}$, $\mathbf{\Lambda}_c$, and $\xi_{2,\text{rel}}$ obtained from the primal problem are the same as those obtained from the dual problem.

4.2.1. Primal-Dual Algorithm. We propose a novel *primal-dual algorithm* to solve the rank-relaxed decoder covariance optimization problem in (34). Denote the feasible set of values for $\{\mathbf{V}_{ic}\}_{i \in S, c \in D}$ as the primal domain and the feasible set of values for $\mathbf{\Lambda}_c$ as the dual domain. In short, the approach consists of iterating between a primal domain step and a dual domain step. (Both subproblems, defined in (30) and (31), are convex because their cost functions are convex and concave, respectively, and their constraints are all linear matrix inequalities. The solution of each sub-problem is optimum for that sub-problem.) For the $(j + 1)$th iteration:

Primal Domain Substep. Given $\mathbf{\Lambda}_c = \mathbf{\Lambda}_c^{(j)}$, find the $\{\mathbf{V}_{ic}^{(j+1)}\}_{i \in S, c \in D}$ which solves

$$\min_{\{\mathbf{V}_{ic}\}} \quad \mathrm{tr}\left(\left[\sum_{j \in S} \mathbf{H}_{jc}^* \mathbf{V}_{jc} \mathbf{H}_{jc} + \mathbf{\Lambda}_c \right]^{-1} \mathbf{\Lambda}_c \right) + \sum_{i \in S} \mathrm{tr}(\mathbf{V}_{ic}\mathbf{\Phi}_{ni}),$$

$$\text{subject to} \quad \mathbf{V}_{ic} \geq 0, \quad i \in S, c \in D.$$
$$(35)$$

Dual Domain Substep. Given $\{\mathbf{V}_{ic}\}_{i \in S, c \in D} = \{\mathbf{V}_{ic}^{(j+1)}\}_{i \in S, c \in D}$, find the $\mathbf{\Lambda}_c^{(j+1)}$ which solves

$$\max_{\mathbf{\Lambda}_c} \quad \mathrm{tr}\left(\left[\sum_{j \in S} \mathbf{H}_{jc}^* \mathbf{V}_{jc} \mathbf{H}_{jc} + \mathbf{\Lambda}_c \right]^{-1} \mathbf{\Lambda}_c - \mathbf{\Lambda}_c \mathbf{P}_c \right), \quad (36)$$

$$\text{subject to} \quad \mathbf{\Lambda}_c \geq 0, \quad c \in D.$$

The convexity of the rank-relaxed decoder covariance optimization problem guarantees the solution provided by the *primal-dual algorithm* is a global optimum. The iterative procedure stops when the $\xi_{2,\text{rel}}$'s corresponding to the primal domain step and the dual domain step converge to the same value and when $\{\mathbf{V}_{ic}\}_{i \in S, c \in D}$ converge and $\mathbf{\Lambda}_c$ converge. In practice, the *DCOA* given by solving (35) and (36) is considered to have converged at the $(j + 1)$th iteration when

$\{\|\mathbf{V}_{ic}^{(j+1)} - \mathbf{V}_{ic}^{(j)}\|_F\}_{i \in S, c \in D}$, $\|\mathbf{\Lambda}_c^{(j+1)} - \mathbf{\Lambda}_c^{(j)}\|_F$, and the duality gap of the values of $\xi_{2,\text{rel}}$ derived from the two steps

$$\text{gap}^{(j+1)} = \xi_{2,\text{rel}}\left(\left\{\mathbf{V}_{ic}^{(j+1)}\right\}, \mathbf{\Lambda}_c^{(j+1)}\right) - \xi_{2,\text{rel}}\left(\left\{\mathbf{V}_{ic}^{(j+1)}\right\}, \mathbf{\Lambda}_c^{(j)}\right) \tag{37}$$

are less than some pre-specified thresholds. Note that, in all this, the power constraints have been accounted for by the Lagrange multipliers. The optimum numbers of data streams $\{m_{ic}\}_{i \in S, c \in D}$ are determined by the rank of optimum $\{\mathbf{V}_{ic}\}_{i \in S, c \in D}$.

4.2.2. Two-Semidefinite Programming (Two-SDP) Procedure.
Similar to the *TCOA* [30] in uplink, (35) and (36) can be reformulated in terms of the SDP formulation:

$$\min_{\mathbf{W}_p, \{\mathbf{V}_{ic}\}_{i \in S}} \quad \text{tr}\left[\mathbf{W}_p \mathbf{\Lambda}_c\right] + \sum_{i \in S} \text{tr}(\mathbf{V}_{ic} \mathbf{\Phi}_{\mathbf{n}i}),$$

$$\text{subject to} \quad \mathbf{V}_{ic} \geq 0, \quad i \in S, c \in D, \tag{38}$$

$$\begin{bmatrix} \mathbf{W}_p & \mathbf{I}_{t_c} \\ \mathbf{I}_{t_c} & \sum\limits_{j \in S} \mathbf{H}_{jc}^* \mathbf{V}_{jc} \mathbf{H}_{jc} + \mathbf{\Lambda}_c \end{bmatrix} \geq 0.$$

$$\min_{\mathbf{W}_d, \mathbf{\Lambda}_c} \quad \text{tr}\left[\mathbf{W}_d\left(\sum\limits_{j \in S} \mathbf{H}_{jc}^* \mathbf{V}_{jc} \mathbf{H}_{jc}\right)\right] + \text{tr}(\mathbf{\Lambda}_c \mathbf{P}_c),$$

$$\text{subject to} \quad \mathbf{\Lambda}_c \geq 0, \quad c \in D, \tag{39}$$

$$\begin{bmatrix} \mathbf{W}_d & \mathbf{I}_{t_c} \\ \mathbf{I}_{t_c} & \sum\limits_{j \in S} \mathbf{H}_{jc}^* \mathbf{V}_{jc} \mathbf{H}_{jc} + \mathbf{\Lambda}_c \end{bmatrix} \geq 0.$$

Both (38) and (39) can be solved numerically by SDP solvers (such as SeDuMi [36] and Yalmip [37]) in polynomial time. However, the *primal-dual algorithm* of the *DCOA* needs both the primal and dual sub-problems to be solved in each iteration. This leads to high computational complexity. Furthermore, the *Two-SDP Procedure* is sensitive to the numerical precisions of the SDP solvers. It works well at low transmit powers, but the duality gap cannot be made arbitrarily small at high transmit powers due to insufficient numerical precisions of the SDP solvers available in public. Nevertheless, a very important contribution here is that the MMSE transceiver design under general linear power constraints provided by the *Two-SDP Procedure* is optimal for downlink.

4.2.3. Numerically Efficient Procedure.
To reduce the computational complexity and improve the convergence properties of the *Two-SDP Procedure*, the SDP formulation in (38) is still employed to solve for the primal domain step in (35). And we employ the explicit expressions of $\mathbf{\Lambda}_c$ derived as follows for the dual domain step in (36).

Substituting (18) into (24) and using (23), we obtain

$$\mathbf{V}_{ic} = \mathbf{M}_i \mathbf{H}_{ic} \mathbf{U}_{ic} \mathbf{H}_{ic}^* \mathbf{M}_i,$$

$$\mathbf{M}_i = \left[\sum_{k \in D} \mathbf{H}_{ik}\left(\sum_{j \in S} \mathbf{U}_{jk}\right)\mathbf{H}_{ik}^* + \mathbf{\Phi}_{\mathbf{n}i}\right]^{-1}. \tag{40}$$

Similarly, substituting (21) into (23) and using (24), we obtain

$$\mathbf{U}_{ic} = \mathbf{N}_c \mathbf{H}_{ic}^* \mathbf{V}_{ic} \mathbf{H}_{ic} \mathbf{N}_c,$$

$$\mathbf{N}_c = \left[\sum_{k \in D} \sum_{j \in S} \mathbf{H}_{jc}^* \mathbf{V}_{jk} \mathbf{H}_{jc} + \mathbf{\Lambda}_c\right]^{-1}. \tag{41}$$

To remove the dependence of $\{\mathbf{V}_{ic}\}_{i \in S, c \in D}$ on $\{\mathbf{U}_{ic}\}_{i \in S, c \in D}$, substitute (41) into (40) to yield

$$\mathbf{V}_{ic} = \mathbf{M}_i \mathbf{H}_{ic} \mathbf{N}_c \mathbf{H}_{ic}^* \mathbf{V}_{ic} \mathbf{H}_{ic} \mathbf{N}_c \mathbf{H}_{ic}^* \mathbf{M}_i,$$

$$\mathbf{M}_i = \left[\sum_{k \in D} \mathbf{H}_{ik}\left(\sum_{j \in S} \mathbf{N}_k \mathbf{H}_{jk}^* \mathbf{V}_{jk} \mathbf{H}_{jk} \mathbf{N}_k\right)\mathbf{H}_{ik}^* + \mathbf{\Phi}_{\mathbf{n}i}\right]^{-1}. \tag{42}$$

Similarly, substituting (23) into $\mathbf{B}_c$ in (26) and using (41), we can express the Lagrange multipliers $\{\mathbf{\Lambda}_c\}_{c \in D}$ in (27) or (28) in terms of $\{\mathbf{V}_{ic}\}_{i \in S, c \in D}$.

5. Equivalence among the Proposed Approaches and Optimality of *GIA*

In this section, we focus the discussions on the optimality of and the relationships between the *GIA*, *TCOA*, and *DCOA*. Then, the optimality of the *GIA* can be established.

5.1. Equivalence of the TCOA and GIA for Systems with One Eq-Receiver.
When the *TCOA* is applicable and the transmit covariance matrices $\{\mathbf{U}_{ic}\}_{i \in S, c \in D}$ obtained from the MMSE designs are of full rank, the *TCOA* and *GIA* are equivalent. Consequently, the solution of the *GIA* is actually optimum because the solution of the *TCOA* is optimum.

To prove the equivalence between the *TCOA* and *GIA*, it suffices to show that the KKT conditions of the two approaches are equivalent. This is because the *TCOA* is a convex approach. The KKT conditions common to both approaches are (18), the power constraint (12) or (13), the complementary slackness condition (29) or (30), and the nonnegativeness of the Lagrange multipliers. To obtain the unique KKT condition of the *TCOA*, we set up the following augmented cost function to include the nonnegative definite constraint on $\{\mathbf{U}_{ic}\}_{i \in S, c \in D}$:

$$\zeta_1 = \text{tr}(\mathbf{\Phi}_{\mathbf{n}i} \mathbf{M}_i) + \sum_{c \in D} \text{tr}(\mathbf{\Lambda}_c(\mathbf{U}_{ic} - \mathbf{P}_c) - \mathbf{\Psi}_{uic} \mathbf{U}_{ic}), \tag{43}$$

where $\{\mathbf{\Psi}_{uic}\}_{i \in S, c \in D}$ are the Lagrange multipliers satisfying $\text{tr}(\mathbf{\Psi}_{uic} \mathbf{U}_{ic}) = 0$, $\mathbf{\Psi}_{uic} \geq 0$, $i \in S$, $c \in D$. When $\{\mathbf{U}_{ic}\}_{i \in S, c \in D}$ are of full rank, the Lagragian variables $\{\mathbf{\Psi}_{uic}\}_{i \in S, c \in D}$ are zero matrices. Making the gradients of (43) with respect to $\{\mathbf{U}_{ic}\}_{i \in S, c \in D}$ to be zeros, we have

$$\mathbf{\Lambda}_c = \mathbf{H}_{ic}^* \mathbf{M}_i \mathbf{\Phi}_{\mathbf{n}i} \mathbf{M}_i \mathbf{H}_{ic}, \quad i \in S, c \in D. \tag{44}$$

The task of showing the equivalence of the KKT conditions of the two approaches boils down to showing that the above KKT condition of the *TCOA*, (44), can be derived from (and can be used to derive) the KKT conditions unique to the *GIA*, (21). Substitute (18) and (23) into (21) to obtain

$$\mathbf{F}_{ic} = \left[\mathbf{H}_{ic}^*\mathbf{M}_i\left(\sum_{k \in D}\mathbf{H}_{ik}\mathbf{U}_{ik}\mathbf{H}_{ik}^*\right)\mathbf{M}_i\mathbf{H}_{ic} + \mathbf{\Lambda}_c\right]^{-1}\mathbf{H}_{ic}^*\mathbf{M}_i\mathbf{H}_{ic}\mathbf{F}_{ic}.$$

(45)

Then right multiply (45) by $\mathbf{F}_{ic}^*\mathbf{U}_{ic}^{-1}$ to get

$$\mathbf{I}_{t_c} = \left[\mathbf{H}_{ic}^*\mathbf{M}_i\left(\sum_{k \in D}\mathbf{H}_{ik}\mathbf{U}_{ik}\mathbf{H}_{ik}^*\right)\mathbf{M}_i\mathbf{H}_{ic} + \mathbf{\Lambda}_c\right]^{-1}\mathbf{H}_{ic}^*\mathbf{M}_i\mathbf{H}_{ic}.$$

(46)

With some matrix manipulations, we can show that (46) and (44) are equivalent. Since (21) and (44) can be derived from each other, this proof is complete. The above proof is done assuming $\mathbf{\Phi}_{sic} = \sigma^2\mathbf{I}_{m_{ic}}$ with $\sigma^2 = 1$, $i \in S$, $c \in D$. It is also applicable when $\sigma^2 \neq 1$.

5.2. Equivalence of the DCOA and GIA for Systems with One Eq-Transmitter. When the *DCOA* is applicable and the decoder covariance matrices $\{\mathbf{V}_{ic}\}_{i \in S, c \in D}$ obtained from the MMSE designs are of full rank, the *DCOA* and *GIA* are equivalent. Consequently, the solution of the *GIA* is actually optimum because the solution given by the *DCOA* is optimal.

To prove the equivalence between the *DCOA* and *GIA*, it suffices to show that the KKT conditions of the two approaches are equivalent. This is because the *DCOA* is a convex approach, so that its KKT conditions are sufficient conditions for optimality. The KKT conditions common to both approaches are (21), the power constraint (12) or (13), the complementary slackness condition (29) or (30), and the non-negativeness of the Lagrange Multipliers. To obtain the unique KKT condition of the *DCOA*, we set up the following augmented cost function from (34) to include the non-negative definite constraint on $\{\mathbf{V}_{ic}\}_{i \in S, c \in D}$

$$\zeta_2 = \mathrm{tr}\left(\left[\sum_{j \in S}\mathbf{H}_{jc}^*\mathbf{V}_{jc}\mathbf{H}_{jc} + \mathbf{\Lambda}_c\right]^{-1}\mathbf{\Lambda}_c - \mathbf{\Lambda}_c\mathbf{P}_c\right)$$
$$+ \sum_{i \in S}\mathrm{tr}(\mathbf{V}_{ic}\mathbf{\Phi}_{ni} - \mathbf{\Psi}_{vic}\mathbf{V}_{ic}),$$

(47)

where $\{\mathbf{\Psi}_{vic}\}_{i \in S, c \in D}$ are the Lagrange multipliers satisfying $\mathrm{tr}(\mathbf{\Psi}_{vic}\mathbf{V}_{ic}) = 0$, $\mathbf{\Psi}_{vic} \geq 0$, $i \in S$, $c \in D$. When $\{\mathbf{V}_{ic}\}_{i \in S, c \in D}$ are of full rank, the Lagrange variables $\{\mathbf{\Psi}_{vic}\}_{i \in S, c \in D}$ are zero matrices. Making the gradients of (47) with respect to $\{\mathbf{V}_{ic}\}_{i \in S, c \in D}$ to be zeros, we have

$$\mathbf{H}_{ic}\mathbf{N}_c\mathbf{\Lambda}_c\mathbf{N}_c\mathbf{H}_{ic}^* = \mathbf{\Phi}_{ni}, \quad i \in S, c \in D.$$

(48)

The task of showing the equivalence of the KKT conditions of the two approaches boils down to showing that the above KKT condition of the *DCOA*, (48), can be derived from (and can be used to derive) the KKT conditions unique to the *GIA*, (18). Substitute (21) and (24) into (18) to obtain

$$\mathbf{G}_{ic} = \mathbf{G}_{ic}\mathbf{H}_{ic}\mathbf{N}_c\mathbf{H}_{ic}^*\left[\mathbf{H}_{ic}\mathbf{N}_c\left(\sum_{j \in S}\mathbf{H}_{jc}^*\mathbf{V}_{jc}\mathbf{H}_{jc}\right)\mathbf{N}_c\mathbf{H}_{ic}^* + \mathbf{\Phi}_{ni}\right]^{-1}.$$

(49)

Then left-multiply (49) by $\mathbf{V}_{ic}^{-1}\mathbf{G}_{ic}^*$ to get

$$\mathbf{I}_{r_i} = \mathbf{H}_{ic}\mathbf{N}_c\mathbf{H}_{ic}^*\left[\mathbf{H}_{ic}\mathbf{N}_c\left(\sum_{j \in S}\mathbf{H}_{jc}^*\mathbf{V}_{jc}\mathbf{H}_{jc}\right)\mathbf{N}_c\mathbf{H}_{ic}^* + \mathbf{\Phi}_{ni}\right]^{-1}.$$

(50)

With some matrix manipulations, we can show that (50) and (48) are equivalent. Since (18) and (48) can be derived from each other, this proof is complete. The above proof is done assuming $\mathbf{\Phi}_{sic} = \sigma^2\mathbf{I}_{m_{ic}}$ with $\sigma^2 = 1$, $i \in S$, $c \in D$. It is also applicable when $\sigma^2 \neq 1$.

6. Simulation Setup

In all of the simulations, the noise and nonzero source covariance matrices, $\mathbf{\Phi}_{ai}$ and $\mathbf{\Phi}_{sic}$, are all identity matrices of dimension r_i and m_{ic}, respectively. The nonzero source (data) vectors consist entirely of uncoded binary phase shift keying (BPSK) modulated bits. For the per-antenna power constraint, $P_{cd} = P$, $d = 1, 2, \ldots, t_c$, $c = 1, 2, \ldots, C$ (see (12)), and for the per-transmitter power constraint $P_{bnc} = \tau_n P$, for all $n \in J_c$, $c = 1, 2, \ldots, C$ (see (13)). Thus, the maximum transmission power from the nth transmitter is always the same (i.e., $\tau_n P$) for both power constraints in (12) and (13).

Without loss of generality, in all of the simulations, the numbers of transmitters and receivers are the same and each cell has only one transmitter and receiver. Since the transmitter in the lth cell always (no matter which configuration) has data for the receiver in the lth cell, they are labeled the lth transmitter and receiver, respectively. Furthermore, for simplicity, d_{ll} (see (1)) is normalized to be equal to 1 for all l. Since all other links are possibly (depending on the configuration) interfering links, they are normalized such that $d_{ln} \geq 1$, $l \neq n$. Again, for the sake of simplicity, all d_{ln}'s, $l \neq n$, are set equal thus giving rise to the parameter

$$\delta = \frac{d_{ll}^{-2\beta}}{d_{ln}^{-2\beta}} = d_{ln}^{2\beta}.$$

(51)

Note that, in a cellular context, the users (base stations) are the receivers (transmitters) in downlink and the transmitters (receivers) in uplink. Thus, $d_{ln} = 1$ ($\delta = 1$) means that all of the users are cell edge users (system is in a cell edge scenario). Furthermore, as d_{ln} increases, δ increases and each user moves away from the cell edge toward its own base station. In all of the simulations, $2\beta = 4$ in the path loss model of (1).

All of the setups (1a, 1b, ..., 5b) used in these simulations for the five CoMP configurations are defined in Table 1. (Note though that the distances are not specified in these baseline setups because they are example dependent.) For each CoMP configuration, there are various setups. The differences between the different setups for a particular CoMP configuration are marked in bold. For example, for JP-UL, setups 1a and 1b are exactly the same except for the values of $\{m_{ic}\}$ and m. Unlike setups 1a–3b where each setup corresponds to only one configuration, setups 4a, 4b, 5a, and 5b can correspond to either Non-CoMP or CBF. Thus, to

TABLE 1: The different setups for numerical simulations.

Setup	JP-UL		JP-DL		JP-SU				Non-CoMP & CBF			
	1a	1b	2a	2b	3a	3b	3c	3d	4a	4b	5a	5b
T	2	2	2	2	2	2	2	2	2	2	3	4
τ_n	2	2	2	2	2	2	1	2	2	2	2	2
C	2	2	1	1	1	1	1	1	2	2	3	4
t_c	2	2	4	4	4	4	2	4	2	2	2	2
t	4	4	4	4	4	4	2	4	4	4	6	8
R	2	2	2	2	2	2	2	2	2	2	3	4
γ_l	2	2	2	2	2	2	2	1	2	2	2	2
K	1	1	2	2	1	1	1	1	2	2	3	4
r_i	4	4	2	2	4	4	4	2	2	2	2	2
r	4	4	4	4	4	4	4	2	4	4	6	8
m_{ic}	2	1	2	1	4	2	2	2	2	1	1	1
m	4	2	4	2	4	2	2	2	4	2	3	4

T: number of transmitters; τ_n: number of antennas of the nth transmitter; C: number of eq-transmitters; t_c: number of antennas of the cth eq-transmitter; t: total number of transmit antennas; $1 \le n \le T$, $1 \le c \le C$; R: number of receivers; γ_l: number of antennas of the lth receiver; K: number of eq-receivers; r_i: number of antennas of the ith eq-receiver; r: total number of receive antennas; $1 \le l \le R$, $1 \le i \le K$; m_{ic}: number of data streams from the cth eq-transmitter to the ith eq-receiver if $\mathbf{s}_{ic} \ne \mathbf{0}$; m: total number of data streams; $1 \le c \le C$, $1 \le i \le K$.

TABLE 2: The applicability of the proposed approaches in different setups.

Setup	JP-UL		JP-DL		JP-SU				Non-CoMP				CBF			
	1a	1b	2a	2b	3a	3b	3c	3d	4a	4b	5a	5b	4a	4b	5a	5b
GIA	Y	Y	Y	Y	Y	Y	Y	Y	Y	Y	Y	Y	Y	Y	Y	Y
TCOA	Y	N	N	N	Y	N	Y	Y	Y	N	N	N	N	N	N	N
DCOA	N	N	Y	N	Y	N	Y	Y	Y	N	N	N	N	N	N	N

"Y" means an approach is applicable in a setup, while "N" means it is not.

help distinguish whether a setup belongs to Non-CoMP or CBF, the name of the configuration is placed next to the setup number, for example, 5a (Non-CoMP) denotes setup 5a for Non-CoMP.

Note that not every approach can be used for every configuration and every setup in Table 1. Also note that the channel matrices generated numerically usually have full column and/or row rank. This in general results in maximum feasible rank transmit covariance matrices and/or decoder covariance matrices in the MMSE designs if the numbers of data streams are not pre-specified. Therefore, in such cases, the TCOA and DCOA are applicable in corresponding setups. The applicability of the proposed approaches in the setups is summarized in Table 2, where "Y" means an approach is applicable in a setup while "N" means it is not.

One last note, the results for setup 4b (Non-CoMP) under the per-antenna power constraint are obtained using the optimum closed-form solution (see Appendix B). The results for setups 5a (Non-CoMP) and 5b (Non-CoMP) can also be obtained by the optimum closed-form solution. But, they are omitted for the clarity of the figures.

7. Investigation into the Proposed Approaches

In this section, the convergence properties, optimality, and diversity/multiplexing tradeoff of the GIA, and numerical comparison of the GIA with the approach in [35] for CBF are investigated. All results except for the ones in Section 7.1 are obtained by averaging over 20 channel realizations. These results are consistent with those obtained by averaging over more channel realizations.

7.1. Convergence Properties of the Approaches. Consider setup 3a (JP-SU). All approaches are applicable. The convergence property (expressed as MSE, dG, and dP) of the GIA for the per-antenna power constraint for one set of channel realizations is shown in Figure 2. The difference in decoders dG and the difference in the per-antenna power constraint dP between the jth and $(j + 1)$th iteration are defined as

$$dG^{(j)} = \left\| \mathbf{G}_{11}^{(j+1)} - \mathbf{G}_{11}^{(j)} \right\|_F,$$

$$dP^{(j)} = \frac{\mathrm{tr}\left[\mathrm{abs}\left(\mathbf{F}_{11}^{(j)} \left(\mathbf{F}_{11}^{(j)} \right)^* - \mathbf{P}_1 \right) \right]}{P}. \tag{52}$$

The convergence property for the per-transmitter power constraint is similar and is omitted due to page limit. As shown in Figure 2, both the MSE and dG converge quickly. It is remarkable that the dPs converge much slower in higher power. This is due to the fact that, when P increases, the Lagrange multipliers decrease quickly (see (27) or (28)). Note that the usage of (27) or (28) enforces the corresponding

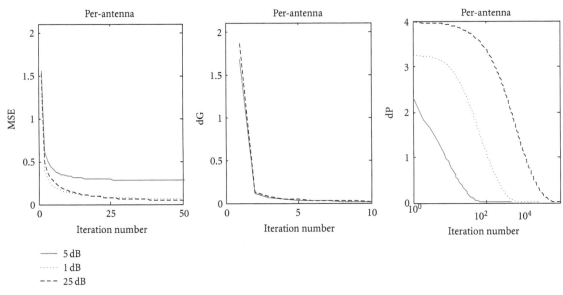

FIGURE 2: Convergence of the *GIA* for setup 3a (JP-SU) under the per-antenna power constraint. The MSEs and differences, dG and dP defined in (52), as functions of the iteration number. Solid, dotted, and dashed lines are results with $10\log_{10} P = 5, 15$, and 25 dB, respectively.

complementary slackness conditions (29) or (30). For large P's, the Lagrange multipliers are very small. For example, when $10\log_{10} P = 30$ dB, they can be as small as 10^{-10}. Thus, the number of iteration increases drastically as P increases if equality in the power constraints in (12) or (13) is insisted. The slow convergence behavior of the dP's is also observed in other configurations.

In Non-CoMP and CBF, the power constraints may not be met with equality for the MMSE results (where the corresponding Lagrange multipliers are essentially zeros). Although the Lagrange multipliers are formulated in this paper using equality power constraints to derive explicit expressions of the Lagrange multipliers, the *GIA* can be in fact used to solve inequality power constraints. When the equality of a particular power constraint is not met, the corresponding Lagrange multiplier becomes zero (which shows the complementary slackness condition).

For the *DCOA*, the convergence properties of the *Two-SDP Procedure* and *Numerically Efficient Procedure*, using SDP solvers SeDuMi [36] and Yalmip [37], are shown in Figure 3 for setup 3a (JP-SU) for the per-antenna power constraint for one set of channel realizations. It is found (from observing the convergence rates of the duality gap in (37) and the antenna powers in Figure 3) that the *Numerically Efficient Procedure* converges faster than the *Two-SDP Procedure*.

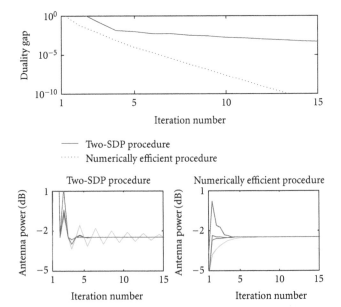

FIGURE 3: Convergence of the *DCOA* for setup 3a (JP-SU) under the per-antenna power constraint with $10\log_{10} P = -2.5$ dB. Duality gap and four antenna powers, as functions of the iteration number. The 4 different colors in the two lower sub-plots correspond to 4 transmit antennas.

7.2. Optimality of the GIA . This sub-section investigates numerically the equivalence relationships stated in Section 5 and verifies the optimality of the *GIA*. Only examples for the per-antenna power constraints are shown for simplicity. In setup 1a (JP-UL), the MSE curves of the *GIA* and *TCOA* merge in the left sub-plot of Figure 4. The *GIA* is equivalent to the *TCOA* and yields the globally optimum solution. On the other hand, in setup 2a (JP-DL), the MSE curves of the *GIA* and *DCOA* merge in the right subplot of Figure 4.

The *GIA* is equivalent to the *DCOA* and yields the globally optimum solution. Similarly, in setups 3a, 3c, and 3d (JP-SU) (see Figure 5), the MSE curves of all approaches merge. The *GIA* is equivalent to both the *TCOA* and *DCOA* and yields globally optimum solution.

7.3. Diversity/Multiplexing Tradeoff by the GIA . In setups 1a (JP-UL), 2a (JP-DL), and 3a (JP-SU), the *GIA* is able

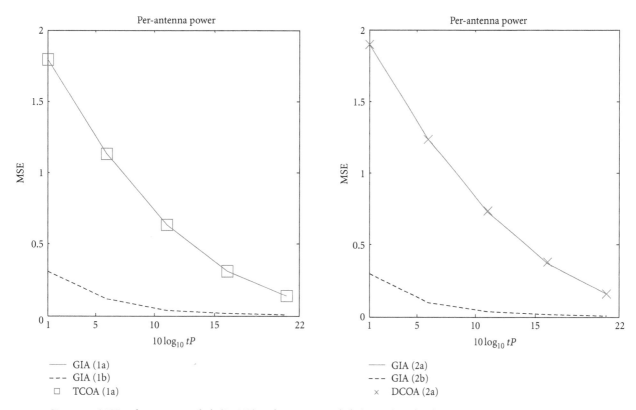

FIGURE 4: MSEs of setups 1a and 1b (JP-UL) and setups 2a and 2b (JP-DL) under the per-antenna power constraints.

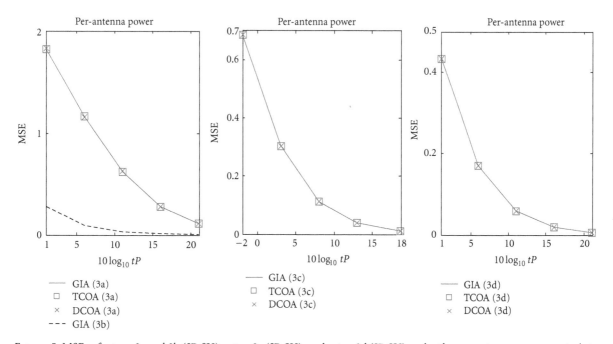

FIGURE 5: MSEs of setups 3a and 3b (JP-SU), setup 3c (JP-SU), and setup 3d (JP-SU) under the per-antenna power constraints.

to transmit the maximum number of data streams as other proposed approaches. On the other hand, in setups 1b (JP-UL), 2b (JP-DL), and 3b (JP-SU), the *GIA* is also able to transmit a fewer number of data streams resulting in a lower MSE and BER performance (see the dashed curves in Figures 4 and 5), while the other proposed approaches are not applicable. In other words, the *GIA* is able to, unlike the other approaches, provide a tradeoff between multiplexing gain and diversity gain.

7.4. Comparison between the GIA and the Approach in [35]. As in Section 7.1, our proposed *GIA* in fact can solve the

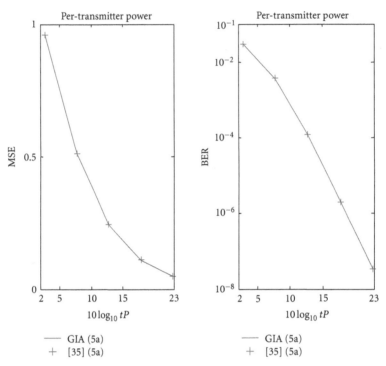

FIGURE 6: MSEs and BERs of setup 5a (CBF) under the per-transmitter power constraint. The proposed *GIA* and the approach in [35] have the same MSE and BER performances.

inequality power constraint. So, both our proposed *GIA* and the approach in [35] are 3-step iteratively approaches applicable in CBF with the per-transmitter power constraint. The only difference is the way of finding the Lagrange multipliers. Reference [35] uses a linear search method to find the Lagrange multipliers when the equality power constraint is enforced, while the *GIA* uses a more efficient explicit expression (28). In setup 5a (CBF), the MSE (BER) curves of the *GIA* and the approach in [35] merge, as in Figure 6. It shows that the *GIA* performs as good as the approach in [35] numerically, but is more efficient. Furthermore, the approach in [35] is only applicable with the per-transmitter power constraint while the *GIA* can deal with the more practical per-antenna power constraint.

8. Performance Benchmark

As in the previous section, the proposed unified approach, the *GIA*, is applicable to all setups. It is optimal when the number of data streams is equal to the rank of the channel, and it provides diversity gain when the number of data streams is less than the rank of the channel (e.g., in setups 1b, 2b, and 3b). In this section, all results are generated using the *GIA* for simplicity. The performances of the five different CoMP configurations will be studied. In particular, the impacts of the level of cooperation (Section 8.1), system load (Sections 8.1 and 8.3), system size (Sections 8.2 and 8.3), and severity of the path loss (Section 8.3) on the performance are analyzed and used to come up with some guidelines for configuration selection (Section 8.4). All of the MSE and BER results are obtained by averaging over 20 channel

realizations. These results are consistent with those obtained by averaging over more channel realizations.

8.1. Impact of the Level of Cooperation and System Load. To understand the impact of different levels of cooperation on the performance of MTMR MIMO systems, we compare the performance of the five configurations. Case A consists of setups 1a (JP-UL), 2a (JP-DL), 3a (JP-SU), 4a (Non-CoMP), and 4a (CBF), and Case B consists of setups 1b (JP-UL), 2b (JP-DL), 3b (JP-SU), 4b (Non-CoMP), and 4b (CBF). For all of the setups in Cases A and B, the total number of transmit (receive) antennas are the same, the power constraints are the same, and the distances are the same ($d_{ln} = 1$ for $l, n = 1, 2$). (Note that this choice of d_{ln} makes $\delta = 1$. It also makes all of the users be at the cell edge). The difference between the two cases lies in the number of data streams transmitted; all setups in Case A have four data streams transmitted in total (i.e., fully loaded systems) while all setups in Case B have two data streams transmitted in total (i.e., partially loaded systems). Figures 7(a) and 7(b) show the MSE and BER results, respectively.

Before comparing the results of Case A and Case B, let us compare the individual setups within each case first. Firstly, observe that, in both cases, the performance order of the configurations is exactly the same as the level of cooperation order. The performance improves as the level of cooperation increases. Note that, the MSE and BER performance order agrees with that of the ergodic sum rate in [22, 23]. Secondly, note that in both cases, the per-transmitter power constraint in CBF does not usually meet with equality for every pair. However, it always does for the Non-CoMP one. The reason

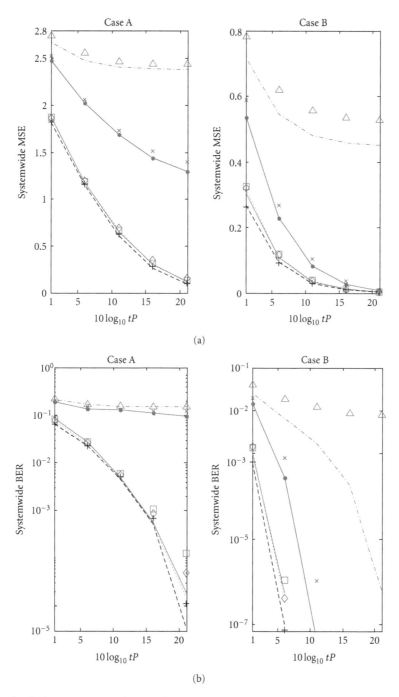

FIGURE 7: (a) Impact of the level of cooperation and system load: system-wide MSEs for Case A (setups 1a, 2a, 3a, 4a (Non-CoMP), and 4a (CBF)) and Case B (setups 1b, 2b, 3b, 4b (Non-CoMP), and 4b (CBF)) under the per-antenna and per-transmitter power constraints. The blue solid lines, red dotted lines, black dashed lines, magenta dash-dot lines, and olive solid lines with dots represent, respectively, the results of setups 1x, 2x, 3x, 4x (Non-CoMP) and 4x (CBF) under the per-transmitter power constraint. And the blue □'s, red ◊'s, black +'s, magenta △'s, and olive ×'s represent the corresponding results under the per-antenna power constraint, (b) Impact of the level of cooperation and system load: System-wide BER's for Case A (setups 1a, 2a, 3a, 4a (Non-CoMP), and 4a (CBF)) and Case B (setups 1b, 2b, 3b, 4b (Non-CoMP), and 4b (CBF)) under the per-antenna and per-transmitter power constraints. (Legends: same as those of Figure 7(a).)

is quite interesting. In Non-CoMP, each pair designs its precoder and decoder to minimize its own MSE. Thus, there is no reason for any of the pairs to limit their transmit power. However, in CBF, all the pairs jointly design their precoders and decoders to minimize the system-wide MSE. Thus, it

may not be always beneficial for all transmitters to transmit on full power since the mutual interference may be large. Thirdly, note that both the per-transmitter and per-antenna power constraints usually meet with equality for the three JP configurations.

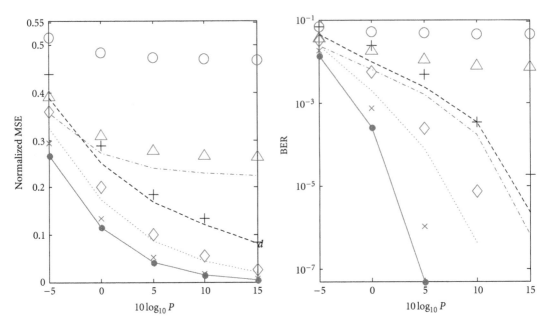

FIGURE 8: Impact of the size of the system (number of transmitter receiver pairs): normalized MSEs and system-wide BERs of various Non-CoMP and CBF setups under the per-antenna and per-transmitter power constraints. The olive solid lines with dots, red dotted lines, black dashed lines correspond to, respectively, setups 4b (CBF), 5a (CBF) and 5b (CBF) under the per-transmitter power constraint. The olive ×'s, red ◇'s, black +'s correspond to, respectively, setups 4b (CBF), 5a (CBF) and 5b (CBF) under the per-antenna power constraint. The magenta dash-dot lines and the green ◯'s correspond to, respectively, setups 4b (Non-CoMP) and 5a (Non-CoMP) under the per-transmitter power constraint. The magenta △'s correspond to setup 4b (Non-CoMP) under the per-antenna power constraint.

With that done, let us now compare the results of Cases A and B. The first observation is that limiting the numbers of data streams is crucial for the performance. The second observation is that, in Case B, the MSE performances of CBF and the *higher* level of cooperation configurations (JP-UL, JP-DL, and JP-SU) are actually similar at high transmit power. The last observation, somewhat related to the first, is that the performances of Non-CoMP and CBF are much more dependent on the number of data streams than JP-UL, JP-DL, and JP-SU. Comments similar to this last observation are made in [22, 23] for the ergodic sum rate results of JP-DL and CBF with multiple receivers per cell.

The difference in the BERs of Non-CoMP and CBF between the two cases is remarkable and can be explained as follows. Using (2) and (3d), we have

$$\hat{\mathbf{s}}_{cc} = \mathbf{G}_{cc}\mathbf{H}_{cc}\mathbf{F}_{cc}\mathbf{s}_{cc} + \mathbf{G}_{cc}\mathbf{H}_{ck}\mathbf{F}_{kk}\mathbf{s}_{kk} \\ + \mathbf{G}_{cc}\mathbf{a}_c, \quad c,k \in \{1,2\}, \ c \neq k, \quad (53)$$

where $\hat{\mathbf{s}}_{cc}$ is the soft output data at the cth *eq*-receiver. As can be easily seen, $\mathbf{G}_{cc}\mathbf{H}_{cc}\mathbf{F}_{cc}\mathbf{s}_{cc}$ is the desired term, $\mathbf{G}_{cc}\mathbf{H}_{ck}\mathbf{F}_{kk}\mathbf{s}_{kk}$ is the interference term, and $\mathbf{G}_{cc}\mathbf{a}_c$ is the noise term. Since each of the channels is 2×2 and will be of full rank with probability 1, their nonsingularity will be assumed throughout this explanation.

In Case A, the cth receiver, $c = 1, 2$, needs $\mathbf{G}_{cc}\mathbf{H}_{cc}\mathbf{F}_{cc}$ (the effective channel from input data to output data) to be of full rank in order to successfully receive its two data streams. But, if $\mathbf{G}_{cc}\mathbf{H}_{cc}\mathbf{F}_{cc}$ is of full rank for both receivers (i.e., for $c = 1, 2$), $\mathbf{G}_{cc}\mathbf{H}_{ck}\mathbf{F}_{kk}$, $c, k = 1, 2$, $k \neq c$, are of full rank as well. Thus, the interference and desired signals *cannot* be separated. If

the interference is significant, as is likely at the cell edge, the performance will suffer greatly. On the other hand, it is possible in Case B for both pairs to successfully receive each of their data streams and null out the interference. This is because $\text{rank}(\mathbf{H}_{cc}\mathbf{F}_{cc}) = \text{rank}(\mathbf{H}_{ck}\mathbf{F}_{kk}) = 1$ and therefore $\text{span}(\mathbf{H}_{cc}\mathbf{F}_{cc})$ is not necessarily equal to $\text{span}(\mathbf{H}_{ck}\mathbf{F}_{kk})$, $c, k = 1, 2$, $k \neq c$. In CBF, the precoders can be chosen to steer $\mathbf{H}_{ck}\mathbf{F}_{kk}$, $k \neq c$, away from $\mathbf{H}_{cc}\mathbf{F}_{cc}$ and the decoders can be chosen to sufficiently null out $\mathbf{H}_{ck}\mathbf{F}_{kk}$, $k \neq c$. In Non-CoMP, the cth pair does not know $\mathbf{H}_{ck}\mathbf{F}_{kk}$, $k \neq c$, but it knows the estimated noise plus interference covariance matrix $\mathbf{\Phi}_{nc}$ (see Appendix A). It can therefore design $\mathbf{F}_{cc}$ and $\mathbf{G}_{cc}$ based on its knowledge of $\mathbf{\Phi}_{nc}$. As can be seen, the performance of Non-CoMP is quite good under the per-transmitter power constraint; it is poor under the more stringent per-antenna power constraint though.

8.2. Impact of System Size (the Number of Transmitter Receiver Pairs). To gain some understanding on what happens when the number of transmitter receiver pairs increases, we consider five different setups: 4b (Non-CoMP), 5a (Non-CoMP), 4b (CBF), 5a (CBF), and 5b (CBF) in Table 1. For convenience, we choose $d_{ln} = 1$ for $l, n = 1, 2$ (cell edge scenario). Figure 8 shows the resulting MSEs and BERs. Note that the maximum antenna power is P in all of the setups. The normalized MSE shown in Figure 8 is defined to be the average MSE per data stream.

Firstly, we compare the results of CBFs setups 4b, 5a, and 5b to see the performance degradation when more transmitter receiver pairs join the wireless environment.

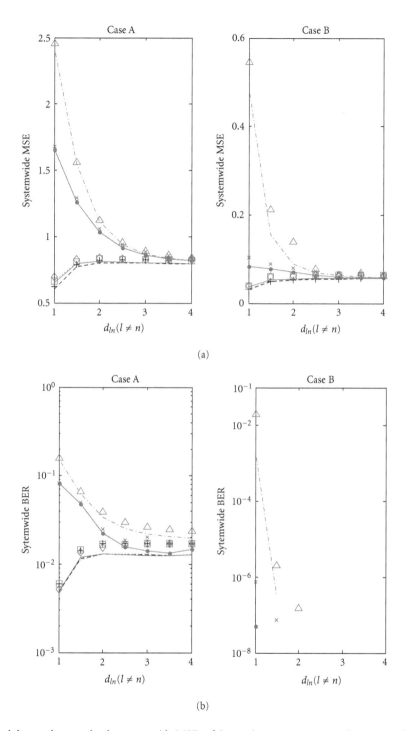

FIGURE 9: (a) Impact of path loss and system load: system-wide MSEs of Case A (setups 1a, 2a, 3a, 4a (Non-CoMP), and 4a (CBF)) and Case B (setups 1b, 2b, 3b, 4b (Non-CoMP), and 4b (CBF)) under the per-antenna and per-transmitter power constraints with $10 \log_{10} P = 5$ dB. (Legends: same as those of Figure 7(a).) (b) Impact of path loss and system load: System-wide BER's of Case A (setups 1a, 2a, 3a, 4a (Non-CoMP), and 4a (CBF)) and Case B (setups 1b, 2b, 3b, 4b (Non-CoMP), and 4b (CBF)) under the per-antenna and per-transmitter power constraints with $10 \log_{10} P = 5$ dB. (Legends: same as those of Figure 7(a).)

Consider setup 4b (CBF) as a baseline system. We observe that setups 5a (CBF) and 5b (CBF), respectively, have 2–5 dB and 7–14 dB loss in the normalized MSE results. In addition, the BER results of setups 5a (CBF) and 5b (CBF) have smaller diversity gains (absolute values of the slopes) than setup 4b

(CBF). However, more data streams are transmitted in setups 5a and 5b.

How does CBF handle the $C = K = 3$ (setup 5a) and $C = K = 4$ (setup 5b) systems when each node has only 2 antennas? Does it perform IA, that is, does its precoders and

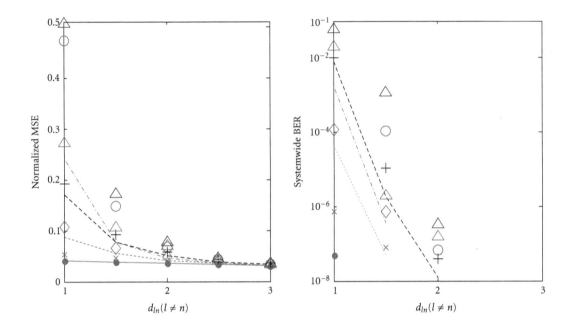

FIGURE 10: Impact of path loss and system size: Normalized MSEs and system-wide BER's of various Non-CoMP and CBF configuration setups under the per-antenna and per-transmitter power constraints with $10\log_{10}P = 5$ dB. The brown $\triangle$'s correspond to setup 5b (Non-CoMP) under the per-transmitter power constraint. The legends for the other curves are the same as those of Figure 8.

decoders satisfy $\text{rank}(\mathbf{G}_{cc}\mathbf{H}_{cc}\mathbf{F}_{cc}) = m_{cc}$ and $\mathbf{G}_{cc}\mathbf{H}_{ck}\mathbf{F}_{kk} = \mathbf{0}$, $c, k = 1, 2, \ldots, C, k \neq c$ [9–12, 38]? Well, MMSE designs are more general than IA because IA is not always feasible and does not take into account arbitrary $\mathbf{\Phi_{nc}}$. But, even so, the MMSE design is seen, at times, to exhibit IA-like features, that is, the interference projections, $\mathbf{H}_{ck}\mathbf{F}_{kk}$, for all $k \neq c$, are steered by the MMSE design such that they lie *predominantly* in a subspace not containing the signal projection, $\mathbf{H}_{cc}\mathbf{F}_{cc}$. As to be expected, the MMSE decoders take into account both the noise and interference—not merely always nulling out the interference as the IA conditions would dictate. In addition, better IA is generally achieved at higher transmit SNR's due to the reduction in the significance of the noise. Furthermore, it is seen that our MMSE design supports more transmitter receiver pairs than [38]'s upper bound for IA designs.

Secondly, we compare Non-CoMP and CBF to see how important joint system-wide transceiver design is to systems with more than 2 transmitter-receiver pairs. BER-wise, it can be seen that, under the per-transmitter power constraint, the best curve for Non-CoMP (the setup 4b (Non-CoMP) one) only has a 1 dB gain over the worst of CBF curves. Actually, only 2 transmitter receiver pairs are communicating in setup 4b (Non-CoMP) as opposed to the 4 transmitter receiver pairs in setup 5b (CBF). When under the per-antenna constraint, *all* of the CBF BER curves are better than the *best* Non-CoMP one. Furthermore, the performance for setup 5a (Non-CoMP) is terrible. Thus, it is clear that joint system-wide transceiver design can greatly help systems with multiple transmitter receiver pairs by mitigating multiple intercell interferences.

8.3. Impact of the Path Loss. Firstly, using Cases A and B (as defined in Section 8.1), the system performance of all five CoMP configurations under different path losses and system loads is studied. As such, d_{ln}, $l \neq n$, varies between 1 and 4 ($d_{ll} = 1$, $l = 1, 2$ as always). Figures 9(a) and 9(b) show, respectively, the MSE and BER results against d_{ln}, $l \neq n$, for $10\log_{10}P = 5$ dB.

In both Cases A and B, as $d_{ln}, l \neq n$, (and thus δ) gets larger, the performances of both Non-CoMP and CBF improve while the performances of JP-UL, JP-DL, and JP-SU worsen. This is because d_{ln}, $l \neq n$, corresponds to interference channels (channels which do not carry desired data) in Non-CoMP and CBF and to desired channels (channels which can carry desired data) in JP-UL, JP-DL, and JP-SU. As d_{ln}, $l \neq n$, (and thus δ) increases, the path losses of the interference channels increase for Non-CoMP and CBF and the path losses of some of the desired channels increase for JP-UL, JP-DL and JP-SU. Actually, the MSE performances of the five configurations eventually merge when d_{ln}, $l \neq n$, (and thus δ) is large. This is because the system essentially ends up consisting of two independent and interference-free transmitter-receiver pairs when d_{ln}, $l \neq n$, (and thus δ) is large enough. It is remarkable that this merging of performances can already be seen when $d_{ln} = 3$, $l \neq n$, in Case A and when $d_{ln} = 2$, $l \neq n$, in Case B. It is also remarkable (but to be expected) that this merging phenomenon of JP-DL and CBF is also seen with ergodic sum rates in [22, 23].

Secondly, using the five setups (4b (Non-CoMP), 5a (Non-CoMP), 4b (CBF), 5a (CBF), and 5b (CBF)) employed in Section 8.2, further path loss studies are conducted for

Non-CoMP and CBF with respect to different system sizes. With $d_{ll} = 1$, for all l, and $10\log_{10} P = 5\,\text{dB}$, Figure 10 shows the MSE and BER results against d_{ln}, $l \neq n$. As d_{ln}, $l \neq n$, (and thus δ) gets larger, it is clearly seen that the performances of the setups improve and merge together. This behavior is because d_{ln}, $l \neq n$, corresponds to the interference channels for both Non-CoMP and CBF. As d_{ln}, $l \neq n$, increases, both the inter-pair interference and the importance of joint design across the pairs decrease.

8.4. Guidelines for Configuration Selection. The purpose of this sub-section is to gain some understanding about when should each configuration be used. The understanding also helps to determine CSI feedback and data sharing requirements, since different CoMP configurations require different levels of CSI feedback and data sharing. For example, if based on the BER performance, only Non-CoMP is needed, a downlink user only needs to feed back the desired channel and inter-cluster interference covariance matrix but not intercell channels,

To this end, consider the following example: there are two transmitters and two receivers (i.e., $T = R = 2$). The MMSE design of their precoders and decoders is subject to the per-transmitter power constraint with $10\log_{10} P = 5\,\text{dB}$. If the desired BER threshold is 3×10^{-2}, when should JP-UL, JP-DL, JP-SU, Non-CoMP, and CBF be used?

Well, looking at Figures 9(a) and 9(b), it is surprising but clear that, for Case B (partially loaded systems), Non-CoMP should always be used—even at the cell edge. (Note though that, for the per-antenna power constraint, the performance of Non-CoMP is marginally acceptable at the cell edge.) Non-CoMP is good enough; the other configurations with their greater network overheads (e.g., information exchange and synchronization) are not needed. For Case A (fully loaded systems), on the other hand, which configuration should be used depends on d_{ln} (and thus δ). For small enough d_{ln}, $l \neq n$ (and thus small enough δ), that is, for a cell edge type scenario, either JP-UL or JP-DL should be used. The interference is too much for Non-CoMP and CBF. However, for larger d_{ln}, $l \neq n$, Non-CoMP should be used. With respect to JP-SU, it is remarkable that, in both Cases A and B, it has no significant performance advantage over JP-UL and JP-DL and is not needed here.

Looking at Figure 10, it is clear that CBF should be used when there are a few transmitter receiver pairs, all at the cell edge, who want to have 1 data stream each. In that case, CBF's interference management capabilities aid it in being able to satisfy the BER threshold when Non-CoMP cannot. It is also clear that for any number of transmitter receiver pairs, there will be a d such that, when $d_{ln} > d$, $l \neq n$, Non-CoMP is good enough and should be employed.

9. Conclusion

For developing a practical CoMP technology in future cellular systems, there are two crucial needs: a performance benchmark and a unified approach for different CoMP configurations. For the need of a performance benchmark,

joint MMSE transceiver designs of various CoMP configurations are considered. The joint MMSE design is nearly optimum in maximizing sum rate. The MSE and BER performances of five CoMP systems (JP-SU, JP-DL, JP-UL, CBF, Non-CoMP) under various levels of cooperation, system loads, system sizes, and path losses are investigated thoroughly. Guidelines for CoMP configuration selection are then established. For the need of a unified approach, the *GIA* is proposed for performing joint MMSE transceiver designs for general MTMR MIMO systems subject to general linear power constraint. In addition, the optimum *DCOA* for downlink is developed to validate the optimality of the *GIA* results when applicable. Remarkably, the *GIA* is shown equivalent to the *TCOA* when each of them converges and the transmit covariance matrices obtained from them are of full rank. They are also shown equivalent to the *DCOA* when each of them converges and the decoder covariance matrices obtained from them are of full rank. This means that the *GIA* gives globally optimum results under the abovementioned special conditions. Convergence properties of the proposed approaches, optimality, and diversity/multiplexing tradeoff of the *GIA* are verified numerically.

The performance analysis of the five CoMP configurations is conducted using the *GIA* to provide physical insights and performance benchmark. Firstly, in the cell edge scenario, it is found that the higher the level of cooperation, the better the performance. Actually, JP-UL and JP-DL achieve essentially the same performance as JP-SU. Note that CBF and Non-CoMP considered in this paper give the achievable performance upper bound for the respective category, given same number of total transmit antennas and same number of total receive antennas.

Secondly, in the cell edge scenario, it is found that the performances of Non-CoMP and CBF are much more dependent on the number of data streams than JP-UL, JP-DL, and JP-SU. When the system is fully loaded, both Non-CoMP and CBF suffer severe interference and thus have poor performances. However, for a partially loaded, two transmitter receiver pairs, system, CBF is able to give good performances under both the per-transmitter and per-antenna power constraints. Non-CoMP also gives good performances, but only for the per-transmitter power constraint (the per-antenna power constraint turns out to be too stringent for it). Thirdly, CBF is able to take care of even more than two transmitter receiver pairs because of its superior interference management capabilities (such as its ability to perform IA-like maneuvers). Not only that, it can actually support more pairs than the upper bound for IA designs in [38]. Fourthly, it is found that the per-transmitter power constraint in the CBF configuration does not usually meet with equality for every pair. However, it always does for the Non-CoMP configuration. This phenomenon is due to the following: (a) in Non-CoMP, each pair cares only about its own MSE while, in CBF, each pair cares for the system-wide MSE and (b) increasing the power at a pair will always be good for the MSE of that pair but not necessarily good for the MSE of the entire system. Fifthly, for a given system, as the path loss of the channels corresponding to the interfering links of Non-CoMP and CBF increases, interesting trends are observed; the performances of CBF and Non-CoMP improve greatly whereas the performances of JP-UL, JP-DL, and JP-SU worsen. Actually, the MSE performances of the five configurations eventually merge together.

In addition to producing these findings, these simulations numerically put forth performance benchmarks for the JP, CBF, and Non-CoMP categories—actually, due to JP-SU, performance benchmarks are given for all CoMP configurations. Moreover, due to the use of the MMSE criterion, benchmarks are put forth for the transceiver designs under other criteria as well (such as maximum capacity and minimum BER). These simulations also provide some guidelines for configuration selection.

These performance benchmarks and guidelines are produced under ideal conditions; for example, the synchronization requirements, and so forth of the configurations are not taken into account. The modulation coding scheme (MCS) selection and CSI error are not accounted for either. Even so, they can be used to greatly simplify the complex configuration selection problem under practical conditions; they can help to show which schemes need or do not need to be considered in a particular scenario. Take, for example, the typical two BS-user pair downlink system with the users at the cell edge. In the partially loaded case, it is clear from this paper that Non-CoMP and CBF should be considered first. In the fully loaded case, it is even simpler: it is clear that JP-DL should be considered first. After such large reductions in scope as these, accounting for the various parameters (MCS, limited feedback, etc.) will thus be much more manageable to perform. Furthermore, one can use the guidelines to choose the CSI feedback and data sharing schemes, since different CoMP configurations require different levels of CSI feedback and data sharing. For example, in one of our papers, we demonstrate a practical scheme for decentralized CBF in TDD systems [39].

Appendices

A. Noise Plus Interference Covariance Matrix in Non-CoMP

Since $E(\mathbf{H}_{W,ic}\mathbf{M}\mathbf{H}_{W,ic}^*) = \text{tr}(\mathbf{M})\mathbf{I}_{\gamma_i}$ for any deterministic matrix $\mathbf{M}$, the noise plus interference covariance matrix for the ith eq-receiver in Non-CoMP can be expressed as

$$\mathbf{\Phi}_{\mathbf{n}i} = \sum_{l=1,l\neq i}^{C} E\left(\overline{\mathbf{H}}_{il}\mathbf{F}_{ll}\mathbf{\Phi}_{\mathbf{s}ll}\mathbf{F}_{ll}^*\overline{\mathbf{H}}_{il}^*\right) + \mathbf{\Phi}_{\mathbf{a}i}$$

$$= \sum_{l=1,l\neq i}^{C} d_{il}^{-2\beta}\,\text{tr}\left(\mathbf{F}_{ll}\mathbf{\Phi}_{\mathbf{s}ll}\mathbf{F}_{ll}^*\right)\mathbf{I}_{r_i} + \mathbf{\Phi}_{\mathbf{a}i}. \tag{A.1}$$

If each transmitter transmits with full power, the trace in (A.1) can be replaced by P_{bll} and the following expression is exact:

$$\mathbf{\Phi}_{\mathbf{n}i} = \sum_{l=1,l\neq i}^{C} d_{il}^{-2\beta}P_{bll}\mathbf{I}_{r_i} + \mathbf{\Phi}_{\mathbf{a}i}. \tag{A.2}$$

Note that even when there is receive spatial correlation (not considered in (1)), (A.2) still holds. When some transmitters

do not transmit with full power, (A.2) is a "worst case" approximation and is still used for the design in this paper.

B. Alternative Approach to the MMSE Transceiver Design of Non-CoMP under the Per-Antenna Power Constraint

For Non-CoMP with one data stream, this appendix shows a different approach to the MMSE transceiver design problem subject to the per-antenna power constraint. Without loss of generality, consider the ith eq-transmitter eq-receiver pair and let $\mathbf{\Phi}_{\mathbf{s}ii} = \sigma_{ii}^2\mathbf{I}_{t_i}$ for all i. Given the MMSE decoder (18), the reduced MMSE problem can be written as

$$\min_{\mathbf{F}_{ii}}\left[\left(\sigma_{ii}^2\mathbf{F}_{ii}^*\mathbf{H}_{ii}^*\mathbf{\Phi}_{\mathbf{n}i}^{-1}\mathbf{H}_{ii}\mathbf{F}_{ii} + 1\right)^{-1}\sigma_{ii}^2\right], \tag{B.1}$$

or equivalently,

$$\max_{\mathbf{F}_{ii}}\mathbf{F}_{ii}^*\mathbf{B}\mathbf{F}_{ii}, \quad \mathbf{B} = [b_{mn}] \equiv \mathbf{H}_{ii}^*\mathbf{\Phi}_{\mathbf{n}i}^{-1}\mathbf{H}_{ii}, \tag{B.2}$$

subject to (12). Here, b_{mn} is the mnth element of the nonnegative definite Hermitian matrix $\mathbf{B}$. Expressing $\mathbf{F}_{ii}^*$ in polar form,

$$\mathbf{F}_{ii}^* = \left[a_1\sqrt{\frac{P_{i1}}{\sigma_{ii}^2}}e^{-j\theta_1} \quad \cdots \quad a_{t_i}\sqrt{\frac{P_{it_i}}{\sigma_{ii}^2}}e^{-j\theta_{t_i}}\right], \tag{B.3}$$

the original problem is further reduced to

$$\max_{\substack{0\leq\theta_1,\ldots,\theta_{t_i}\leq2\pi \\ 0\leq a_1,\ldots,a_{t_i}\leq1}}\gamma, \quad \gamma = \left\{\sum_{n=1}^{t_i}\sum_{m=1}^{t_i}a_na_m\sqrt{P_{in}P_{im}}b_{mn}e^{j(\theta_n-\theta_m)}\right\}. \tag{B.4}$$

A closed-form solution can be easily obtained for solving (B.4) when $t_i = 2$. For $t_i > 2$, however, one generally needs to use some solvers for nonlinear equations.

Let $t_i = 2$ and express $b_{12} = |b_{12}|e^{j\angle(b_{12})}$. Then,

$$\gamma = a_1^2P_{i1}b_{11} + a_2^2P_{i2}b_{22} + 2a_1a_2\sqrt{P_{i1}P_{i2}}|b_{12}|$$
$$\times \cos[\theta_1 - \theta_2 - \angle(b_{12})], \quad b_{11}, b_{22} \geq 0. \tag{B.5}$$

If $b_{12} \neq 0$, γ is maximized if and only if

$$a_1 = a_2 = 1, \quad \theta_1 - \theta_2 - \angle(b_{12}) = 2k\pi, \tag{B.6}$$

for some integer k. If $b_{12} = 0$, γ is maximized if and only if $a_1 = a_2 = 1$. It is remarkable that, in this case, optimality happens *only* when the equality in the per-antenna power constraint in (12) is met.

Acknowledgment

Note that different parts of the work have been published in our conference papers [40–47].

References

[1] "Further advancements for E-UTRA," 3GPP TR36.814, 2009.

[2] F. Zheng, M. Wu, and H. Lu, "Coordinated multi-point transmission and reception for LTE-advanced," in *Proceedings of the 5th International Conference on Wireless Communications, Networking and Mobile Computing (WiCOM '09)*, September 2009.

[3] S. Parkvall, E. Dahlman, A. Furuskär et al., "LTE-Advanced - Evolving LTE towards IMT-Advanced," in *Proceedings of the 68th Semi-Annual IEEE Vehicular Technology Conference (VTC '08)*, September 2008.

[4] R. Irmer, H. Droste, P. Marsch et al., "Coordinated multipoint: concepts, performance, and field trial results," *IEEE Communications Magazine*, vol. 49, no. 2, pp. 102–111, 2011.

[5] S. Catreux, P. F. Driessen, and L. J. Greenstein, "Simulation results for an interference-limited multiple-input multiple-output cellular system," *IEEE Communications Letters*, vol. 4, no. 11, pp. 334–336, 2000.

[6] R. S. Blum, J. H. Winters, and N. R. Sollenberger, "On the capacity of cellular systems with MIMO," *IEEE Communications Letters*, vol. 6, no. 6, pp. 242–244, 2002.

[7] H. Dai and H. V. Poor, "Asymptotic spectral efficiency of multicell MIMO systems with frequency-flat fading," *IEEE Transactions on Signal Processing*, vol. 51, no. 11, pp. 2976–2988, 2003.

[8] M. Chiani, M. Z. Win, and H. Shin, "MIMO networks: the effects of interference," *IEEE Transactions on Information Theory*, vol. 56, no. 1, pp. 336–349, 2010.

[9] V. R. Cadambe and S. A. Jafar, "Interference alignment and degrees of freedom of the K-user interference channel," *IEEE Transactions on Information Theory*, vol. 54, no. 8, pp. 3425–3441, 2008.

[10] K. Gomadam, V. R. Cadambe, and S. A. Jafar, "Approaching the capacity of wireless networks Through distributed interference alignment," in *Proceedings of the IEEE Global Telecommunications Conference (GLOBECOM '08)*, pp. 4260–4265, December 2008.

[11] A. Ö. Zgür and D. Tse, "Achieving linear scaling with interference alignment," in *Proceedings of the IEEE International Symposium on Information Theory (ISIT '09)*, pp. 1754–1758, July 2009.

[12] R. Tresch, M. Guillaud, and E. Riegler, "On the achievability of interference alignment in the K-user constant MIMO interference channel," in *Proceedings of the IEEE/SP 15th Workshop on Statistical Signal Processing (SSP '09)*, pp. 277–280, September 2009.

[13] C. B. Chae, S. H. Kim, and R. W. Heath, "Linear network coordinated beamforming for cell-boundary users," in *Proceedings of the IEEE 10th Workshop on Signal Processing Advances in Wireless Communications (SPAWC '09)*, pp. 534–538, June 2009.

[14] H. Dahrouj and W. Yu, "Coordinated beamforming for the multi-cell multi-antenna wireless system," in *Proceedings of the 42nd Annual Conference on Information Sciences and Systems (CISS '08)*, pp. 429–434, March 2008.

[15] R. Zakhour, Z. K. M. Ho, and D. Gesbert, "Distributed beamforming coordination in multicell MIMO channels," in *Proceedings of the IEEE 69th Vehicular Technology Conference (VTC '09)*, April 2009.

[16] H. Dai, A. F. Molisch, and H. V. Poor, "Downlink capacity of interference-limited MIMO systems with joint detection," *IEEE Transactions on Wireless Communications*, vol. 3, no. 2, pp. 442–453, 2004.

[17] W. Qixing, J. Dajie, L. Guangyi, and Y. Zhigang, "Coordinated multiple points transmission for LTE-advanced systems," in *Proceedings of the 5th International Conference on Wireless Communications, Networking and Mobile Computing (WiCOM '09)*, September 2009.

[18] S. Shi, M. Schubert, N. Vucic, and H. Boche, "MMSE optimization with per-base-station power constraints for network MIMO systems," in *Proceedings of the IEEE International Conference on Communications (ICC '08)*, pp. 4106–4110, May 2008.

[19] J. Zhang, R. Chen, J. G. Andrews, and R. W. Heath, "Coordinated multi-cell MIMO systems with cellular block diagonalization," in *Proceedings of the 41st Asilomar Conference on Signals, Systems and Computers (ACSSC '07)*, pp. 1669–1673, November 2007.

[20] J. Dajie, W. Qixing, L. Jianjun, L. Guangyi, and C. Chunfeng, "Uplink coordinated multi-point reception for LTE-advanced systems," in *Proceedings of the 5th International Conference on Wireless Communications, Networking and Mobile Computing (WiCOM '09)*, September 2009.

[21] A. Tölli, M. Codreanu, and M. Juntti, "Linear multiuser MIMO transceiver optimization in cooperative networks," in *Proceedings of the 2nd International Conference on Communications and Networking in China (ChinaCom '07)*, pp. 513–517, August 2007.

[22] A. Tölli, H. Pennanen, and P. Komulainen, "On the value of coherent and coordinated multi-cell transmission," in *Proceedings of the IEEE International Conference on Communications Workshops (ICC '09)*, June 2009.

[23] A. Tölli, H. Pennanen, and P. Komulainen, "SINR balancing with coordinated multi-cell transmission," in *Proceedings of the IEEE Wireless Communications and Networking Conference (WCNC '09)*, April 2009.

[24] M. Boldi, A. Tölli, M. Olsson et al., "Coordinated MultiPoint (CoMP) Systems," in *Mobile and Wireless Communications for IMT-Advanced and Beyond*, A. Osseiran, J. F. Monserrat, and W. Mohr, Eds., pp. 121–155, John Wiley & Sons, Chichester, UK, 2011.

[25] D. P. Palomar, J. M. Cioffi, and M. A. Lagunas, "Joint Tx-Rx beamforming design for multicarrier MIMO channels: a unified framework for convex optimization," *IEEE Transactions on Signal Processing*, vol. 51, no. 9, pp. 2381–2401, 2003.

[26] A. Scaglione, P. Stoica, S. Barbarossa, G. B. Giannakis, and H. Sampath, "Optimal designs for space-time linear precoders and decoders," *IEEE Transactions on Signal Processing*, vol. 50, no. 5, pp. 1051–1064, 2002.

[27] C.-C. Weng and P. P. Vaidyanathan, "MIMO transceiver optimization with linear constraints on transmitted signal covariance components," *IEEE Transactions on Signal Processing*, vol. 58, no. 1, pp. 458–462, 2010.

[28] D. P. Palomar, "Unified framework for linear MIMO transceivers with shaping constraints," *IEEE Communications Letters*, vol. 8, no. 12, pp. 697–699, 2004.

[29] S. Serbetli and A. Yener, "Transceiver optimization for multiuser MIMO systems," *IEEE Transactions on Signal Processing*, vol. 52, no. 1, pp. 214–226, 2004.

[30] Z. Q. Luo, T. N. Davidson, G. B. Giannakis, and K. M. Wong, "Transceiver optimization for block-based multiple access through ISI channels," *IEEE Transactions on Signal Processing*, vol. 52, no. 4, pp. 1037–1052, 2004.

[31] J. Zhang, Y. Wu, S. Zhou, and J. Wang, "Joint linear transmitter and receiver design for the downlink of multiuser MIMO systems," *IEEE Communications Letters*, vol. 9, no. 11, pp. 991–993, 2005.

[32] M. Schubert, S. Shi, E. A. Jorswieck, and H. Boche, "Downlink sum-MSB transceiver optimization for linear multi-user MIMO systems," in *Proceedings of the 39th Asilomar Conference on Signals, Systems and Computers*, pp. 1424–1428, November 2005.

[33] G. Zheng, T.-S. Ng, and K. K. Wong, "Optimal beamforming for sum-MSE minimization in MIMO downlink channels," in *Proceedings of the IEEE 63rd Vehicular Technology Conference (VTC '06)*, pp. 1830–1834, July 2006.

[34] A. J. Tenenbaum and R. S. Adve, "Minimizing sum-MSE implies identical downlink and dual uplink power allocations," *IEEE Transactions on Communications*, vol. 59, no. 3, pp. 686–688, 2011.

[35] S. W. Peters and R. W. Heath, "Cooperative algorithms for MIMO interference channels," *IEEE Transactions on Vehicular Technology*, vol. 60, no. 1, pp. 206–218, 2011.

[36] J. F. Sturm, "Using SeDuMi 1.02, a MATLAB toolbox for optimization over symmetric cones," *Optimization Methods and Software*, vol. 11, no. 1, pp. 625–653, 1999.

[37] J. Lofberg, "YALMIP: a toolbox for modeling and optimization in MATLAB," in *Proceedings of the IEEE International Symposium on Computer-Aided Control System Design (CACSD '04)*, Taipei, Taiwan, 2004.

[38] C. M. Yetis, S. A. Jafar, and A. H. Kayran, "Feasibility conditions for interference alignment," *IEEE Transactions on Signal Processing*, vol. 58, no. 9, pp. 4771–4782, 2010.

[39] E. Lu and I-T. Lu, "Practical decentralized high-performance coordinated beamforming," in *Proceedings of the 34th IEEE Sarnoff Symposium, (SARNOFF '11)*, May 2011.

[40] I-T. Lu, "Joint MMSE precoder and decoder design for downlink multiuser MIMO systems with arbitrary transmit power constraints," in *Proceedings of the IEEE Sarnoff Symposium (SARNOFF '09)*, April 2009.

[41] I-T. Lu, "Joint MMSE precoder and decoder design subject to arbitrary power constraints for uplink multiuser MIMO systems," in *Proceedings of the IEEE 70th Vehicular Technology Conference Fall (VTC '09)*, September 2009.

[42] I-T. Lu, J. Li, and E. Lu, "Novel MMSE precoder and decoder designs subject to per-antenna power constraint for uplink multiuser MIMO systems," in *Proceedings of the 3rd International Conference on Signal Processing and Communication Systems (ICSPCS'09)*, September 2009.

[43] J. Li, I-T. Lu, and E. Lu, "Optimum mmse transceiver designs for the downlink of multicell mimo systems," in *Proceedings of the IEEE Military Communications Conference (MILCOM '09)*, October 2009.

[44] J. Li, I-T. Lu, and E. Lu, "Unified framework and MMSE transceiver designs for multiple-transmitter- multiple-receiver MIMO systems," in *Proceedings of the 33rd IEEE Sarnoff Symposium*, April 2010.

[45] E. Lu, J. Li, and I-T. Lu, "Comparison of coordinated beamforming and non-coordinated multipoint using MMSE transceiver designs," in *Proceedings of the 33rd IEEE Sarnoff Symposium*, April 2010.

[46] J. Li, I-T. Lu, and E. Lu, "Novel MMSE precoder and decoder designs for single-user MIMO systems under general power constraints," in *Proceedings of the IEEE 71st Vehicular Technology Conference (VTC '10)*, May 2010.

[47] J. Li, E. Lu, and I-T. Lu, "Performance benchmark for network MIMO systems: a unified approach for mmse transceiver design and performance analysis," in *Proceedings of the 53rd IEEE Global Communications Conference (GLOBECOM '10)*, December 2010.

5

Evolution of Signaling Information Transmission

Jasmina Baraković Husić,[1] Himzo Bajrić,[2] and Sabina Baraković[3]

[1] BH Telecom, Joint Stock Company, Sarajevo, Directorate BH Mobile, Obala Kulina bana 8, 71000 Sarajevo, Bosnia and Herzegovina
[2] BH Telecom, Joint Stock Company, Sarajevo, Executive Directorate for Technology and Service Development, Obala Kulina bana 8, 71000 Sarajevo, Trg BiH 1, 71000 Sarajevo, Bosnia and Herzegovina
[3] Department for Informatics and Telecommunication Systems, Ministry of Security of Bosnia and Herzegovina, Trg BiH 1, 71000 Sarajevo, Bosnia and Herzegovina

Correspondence should be addressed to Jasmina Baraković Husić, jasmina.barakovic@bhtelecom.ba

Academic Editors: R.-I. Chang and J. Song

Next Generation Network (NGN) faces the challenge of the rapidly increasing amount of signaling. The growing amount of signaling is a consequence of several reasons arising from the fact that signaling is the main source of network intelligence, analysis, and user behavior monitoring. With the increase in signaling load and complexity, the network management becomes a challenging issue that can impact overall Quality of Service (QoS). To confront this issue, there is a need for reliable and forehand signaling transmission in NGN. As there is much confusion about the interpretation of this concept, this paper aims to provide an overview of the evolution of signaling transmission. Migration towards NGN is analyzed from the signaling perspective. The NGN signaling protocols and related transmission requirements are identified. Through the discussion of standard approaches, the paper considers our previously published approach to signaling transmission along with the current issues and emerging opportunities.

1. Introduction

The rapid growth in subscribers, devices, and applications increases the signaling volume that is causing congestion and impacting the Quality of Service (QoS) [1]. In order to deliver the desired levels of service and user's Quality of Experience (QoE), it is necessary to process significant and growing volume of signaling in real time. There is the need to manage signaling updates and to ensure that service performance is maintained. With the migration to Next Generation Networks (NGNs), the need to manage the growth in signaling has become critical to optimize the network and ease congestion in real time [2].

As networks migrate toward all Internet Protocol (IP) based networks, the growing amount of intelligence is sent through the network [3]. Intelligence means more control over network resources. The optimal source of that intelligence is the signaling. Several advantages are offered using the signaling as the main source of network intelligence, for example, signaling contains the valuable and strategic information in the network that is available nowhere except in the NGN control plane. Therefore, with the growing volume of signaling, the network management becomes the challenging issue. To confront this issue, there is a need for reliable and forehand signaling transmission in NGN. As there is much confusion about the interpretation of this concept, this paper aims to provide an overview of the evolution of approaches to signaling transmission.

The NGN is an IP-based packet-switched network, which does not rely on separate signaling network as in the case of circuit-switched networks [4]. Building such a signaling network is either not possible or it makes no sense. In traditional telecommunication networks, signaling is transported by the separate Signaling System Number 7 (SS7) network fulfilling a number of reliability and performance requirements. Although there is no separate signaling network in the NGN, signaling transport must have similar performance to SS7 [5]. As IP-based transport network is inherently unreliable and lacks the QoS guarantees, there is a need to provide differentiated treatment to signaling traffic. In this respect, several standards and recommendations were proposed by the International Telecommunication Union Telecommunication Standardization Sector (ITU-T), the Internet Engineering Task Force (IETF), the Institute of Electrical and Electronics Engineers (IEEE), and 3rd Generation Partnership Project (3GPP) [6]. In addition to summarizing the approaches of these standards bodies, this paper aims to discuss our approach [7] emerged from the need for reliable and forehand signaling transmission.

The paper is organized as follows. Section 2 analyzes migration towards NGN from the signaling perspective. The NGN signaling protocols and related transmission requirements are identified in Section 3. Through the discussion of standard approaches, Section 4 describes our previously proposed approach to signaling transmission along with the current issues and emerging opportunities. Section 5 gives concluding remarks and identifies open issues for future work.

2. Signaling Perspective on NGN Migration

The migration to NGN has shown to be an evolutionary rather than a revolutionary transition, which has generated a significant impact on the signaling [3]. As signaling is a starting point of the network's evolution, this section reviews its origins and purpose along with the transmission requirements. Signaling has posed many challenges as its history has been linked to the history of telecommunication and switching [8]. Signaling, as it is known today, began around 1890, with the invention of the automatic switching exchange. The period from 1890 to 1976 was characterized by the use of Channel Associated Signaling (CAS), where the speech (in-band), or a channel closely associated with a speech channel (out-band), is used for signaling. Alternative form of signaling was introduced in 1976, that is, Common Channel Signaling (CCS), where a dedicated channel, completely separate from speech channel, is used for signaling. CCS has been used to implement SS7.

SS7 constitutes a separate network within a telecommunication network. SS7 network includes a number of different types of Signaling Points (SPs). In fact, there can be three different types of SPs in an SS7 network: Service Switching Point (SSP), Service Control Point (SCP), and Signal Transfer Point (STP). SSPs provide the SS7 functionality of a switch. SCPs interface the SS7 network to query telecommunication databases, allowing service logic and additional routing information to be obtained to execute services. STPs are used to transfer signaling messages. In SS7, control messages are used by the relevant SPs for call management purposes [8].

Besides it is the signaling network, SS7 is a protocol suite that provides the mechanisms for exchanging control messages using the packet-switching facilities. The Message Transfer Part (MTP) and the Signaling Connection Control Part (SCCP) provide the transfer protocols. MTP is used to reliably transport messages between nodes, and SCCP is used for noncircuit-related signaling. MTP provides the means of reliable transport and delivery of User Parts (UPs)/Application Parts (APs) information across the SS7 network [8].

In addition to transfer of control messages, the signaling network has to meet a number of reliability and performance requirements [5]: (1) probability of message delivered with undetected errors less than 10^{-10}; (2) message loss probability less than 10^{-7}; (3) signaling network unavailability less than 10 minutes per year; (4) probability of message delivered out-of-sequence (including message duplication) less than 10^{-10}; (5) message transfer delay in the STPs less than 100 ms. To fulfill these strict requirements, a reliable transfer of messages between any two SPs is offered by the MTP routing functions and network redundancy. The quality of the underlying physical transport and the probability of system internal errors affect the fulfillment of the first requirement. The redundant signaling links and change-over procedure that allows the loss-free switching of traffic from a failed links to other links are deployed by the MTP to fulfill the second requirement. Several procedures supporting redundancy in the signaling network enable the fulfillment of the third requirement. The MTP performs explicitly timer-based sequence control procedures when rerouting traffic via alternative routes or reverting traffic back to the original routes in order to meet the fourth requirement. Several mechanisms to limit outgoing queues and overall signaling transfer delay are provided by MTP to fulfill the fifth requirement.

When SS7 was formalized, direct signaling connections were utilized to transport control messages. In this case, resources were dedicated to the transmission of these messages. In all forms of telecommunications, certain higher layer protocols are required to perform certain tasks. These higher layers had to have a common transport protocol to deliver them efficiently and reliably. In the beginning the Time-Division Multiplexing (TDM) network provided a 64 kb/s signaling link between two elements that could transfer on a link-to-link basis. This is traditionally known as narrowband SS7. Then when the core network model was introduced, Asynchronous Transfer Mode (ATM) was considered to be the common transport mechanism. The use of ATM to transfer SS7 messages is known as broadband SS7. As IP networks become more extensive, the need to utilize the resources becomes more apparent. This is the way the concept of SS7 over IP is introduced, where existing SS7 protocols can be merged into the same common transport mechanisms as speech and data traffic.

In the creation of NGN it is necessary to transfer SS7 information over IP network. This is why Signaling Transport (SIGTRAN) working group of the IETF was created. The SIGTRAN was tasked with defining the architecture for transporting real-time signaling information over an IP network [9]. The working group's effort yielded three key results: (1) new architecture framework centered on a restructuring of the circuit switch into three functional entities that are Media Gateway Controllers (MGCs), Media Gateways (MGs), and Signaling Gateways (SGs); (2) Stream Control Transmission Protocol (SCTP) as a new transport protocol suitable for meeting the requirements of carrying telecommunication protocols, especially SS7, over a packet network; (3) numerous adaptation layers that support the primitives of Switched Circuit Network (SCN) telephony signaling protocols, such as MTP Level 3 User Adaptation (M3UA), SCCP User Adaptation (SUA), MTP Level 2 User

Adaptation (M2UA), MTP Level 2 Peer Adaptation (M2PA), and Integrated Services Digital Network (ISDN) User Adaptation (IUA). Both SCTP and the adaptation layers include mechanisms designed to handle redundant configurations and improve availability required by signaling.

Deploying SIGTRAN brings the IP infrastructure into the signaling network, allowing the interworking between NGN and circuit-switched networks. The SIGTRAN traffic increases the total signaling load in IP network. The estimation of SIGTRAN traffic volume is useful, if it is going to receive preferential treatment in IP network. Both Differentiated Services (DiffServ) and Multiprotocol Label Switching (MPLS) Traffic Engineering (TE) are used for this purpose [10]. These mechanisms provide better QoS to signaling traffic transported over IP network. Additionally, fast rerouting capability of MPLS helps to reduce the number of network failures that have to be recovered by SCTP and M3UA. Since the QoS and reliability are two fundamental requirements for signaling network, DiffServ and MPLS-TE are mechanisms that complement SIGTRAN in order to meet such requirements. Therefore, the necessity of using them should be assessed as part of the overall NGN design.

A challenging issue with the design of NGN architecture is the implementation of a suitable signaling and session control layer that has proven its importance in the SS7 signaling network. The appropriate signaling and session control layer need to be implemented in the NGN to offer highly available signaling with the reliability and scalability of SS7 network. These requirements present an opportunity to introduce IP Multimedia Subsystem (IMS) technology in the NGN requiring the interoperability and integration of different technologies and protocols as the networks evolve [3].

3. Signaling Protocols in NGN

The NGN is being developed using a number of different technologies. The NGN architecture recognizes the differences between the technologies that can be employed in the access part of the network from those used in the core part of the network. The core network consists of four major candidate transport technologies, that is, ATM, Ethernet, IP, and IP/MPLS. The access networks uses various wireless and wireline access technologies, such as Universal Mobile Telecommunications System (UMTS), Long-Term Evolution (LTE), Worldwide Interoperability for Microwave Access (WiMAX), Ultrawideband (UWB), Wireless Local Area Network (WLAN), Wireless Personal Area Network (WPAN), Bluetooth, Ethernet cable, Digital Subscriber Line (DSL), and optical fiber, to provide consistent and ubiquitous services to subscribers [11].

To implement several technologies in a unified infrastructure, there is a need for standards development to optimize the migration to the NGN architecture. Standardization efforts led by the ITU-T and other standards development organizations have generated a consensus on the basic NGN architecture model and services. The NGN architecture is described with a set of Functional Entities (FEs). Each FE is located in the transport or the service stratum of the NGN architecture. Transport stratum provides user functions for data transfer as well as functions that control and manage transport resources to carry such data among communicating entities. Service stratum provides user functions for service-related data transfer and functions that control and manage service resources and network services to enable user's services and applications [12].

Transport stratum includes Transport Functions and Transport Control Functions. Transport Functions include access network functions, edge functions, core transport functions, gateway functions, and media-handling functions. Transport Control Functions include three groups of functions: Network Attachment and Control Functions (NACF), Resource and Admission Control Functions (RACF), and Mobility Management and Control Functions (MMCF). Service stratum includes Service Control and Content Delivery Functions and Application Support Functions and Service Support Functions [13]. Although the NGN functional blocks have been described in detail, their relationship to the actual protocols used to support these functions have not been described so far. This is the result of assumption that NGN will be based on existing transport-, control-, and management-related technologies. Therefore, there is the need to define the relationship of these protocols to the overall NGN architecture.

Although each NGN stratum is composed of three planes, that is, user plane, control plane, and management plane [12], this paper is focused only on the control plane that includes both routing and signaling protocols, and the associated interfaces. As they constitute a separate and distinct category of protocols, there is a need to clarify this separation in NGN architecture in order to facilitate the development of the interoperable protocols and interfaces. A number of control plane protocols are allowed by the NGN architecture. The control plane protocols depend on whether the connectionless or connection-oriented categories of the NGN are to be implemented. This section considers both routing and signaling protocols for connectionless categories of NGN as shown in Figure 1.

3.1. Transport Stratum Control Plane Protocols. The transport stratum control plane is responsible for routing information exchange and label distribution between adjacent devices. Transport Functions use standard routing protocols such as Routing Information Protocol (RIP), Open Shortest Path First (OSPF), Intermediate System to Intermediate System (IS-IS), and Border Gateway Protocol (BGP) to exchange information in order to build IP forwarding table or label forwarding information base in MPLS environment. Labels are distributed by means of Label Distribution Protocol (LDP), as well as Constraint-based Routing Label Distribution Protocol (CR-LDP) that has been deprecated because IETF decided to focus purely on Resource Reservation Protocol-Traffic Engineering (RSVP-TE). Routing protocols are part of control plane regardless of their transport mechanism; for example, RIP runs over User Datagram Protocol (UDP), OSPF runs directly over IP, BGP runs over Transmission

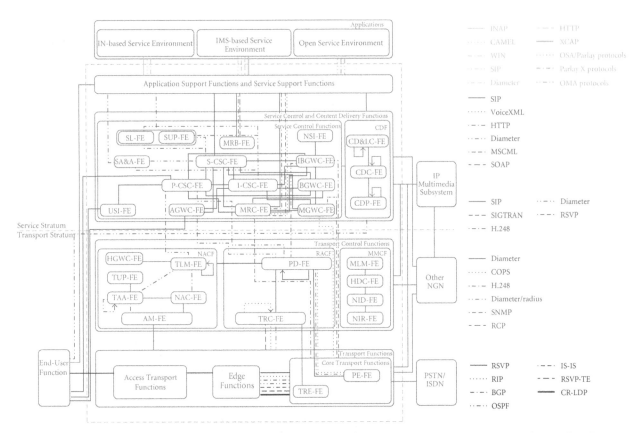

FIGURE 1: NGN control-plane protocols. AGWC-FE (*Access Gateway Control FE*); AM-FE (*Access Management FE*); BGP (*Border Gateway Protocol*); BGWC-FE (*Breakout Gateway Control FE*); CAMEL (*Customized Application for Mobile network Enhanced Logic*); CDC-FE (*Content Delivery Control FE*); CDF (*Content Delivery Function*); CD&LC-FE (*Content Distribution and Location Control FE*); CDP-FE (*Content Delivery Processing FE*); COPS (*Common Open Policy Service*); CR-LDP (*Constraint-based Routing Label Distribution Protocol*); FE (*Functional Entity*); HDC-FE (*Handover Decision and Control FE*); HGWC-FE (*Home Gateway Configuration FE*); HTTP (*Hypertext Transfer Protocol*); IBGWC-FE (*Interrogating Breakout Gateway Control FE*); I-CSC-FE (*Interrogating Call Session Control FE*); INAP (*IN Application Protocol*); IP (*Internet Protocol*); ISDN (*Integrated Services Digital Network*); IS-IS (*Intermediate System to Intermediate System*); MGWC-FE (*Media Gateway Control Function FE*); MLM-FE (*Mobile Location Management FE*); MMCF (*Mobility Management Control Function*); MRB-FE (*Media Resource Broker FE*); MRC-FE (*Media Resource Control FE*); NACF (*Network Attachment and Control Functions*); MSCML (*Media Server Control Markup Language*); NAC-FE (*Network Access Configuration FE*); NGN (*Next Generation Network*); NID-FE (*Network Information Distribution FE*); NIR-FE (*Network Information Repository FE*); NSI-FE (*Network Signaling Interworking FE*); OSPF (*Open Shortest Path First*); P-CSC-FE (*Proxy Call Session Control FE*); PD-FE (*Policy Decision FE*); PE-FE (*Policy Enforcement FE*); PSTN (*Public Switched Telephone Network*); RACF (*Resource and Admission Control Function*); RCP (*Resource Control Protocol*); RIP (*Routing Information Protocol*); RSVP-TE (*Resource Reservation Protocol-Traffic Engineering*); SA&A-FE (*Service Authentication and Authorization FE*); S-CSC-FE (*Serving Call Session Control FE*); SIGTRAN (*Signaling Transport*); SIP (*Session Initiation Protocol*); SL-FE (*Subscription Locator FE*); SNMP (*Simple Network Management Protocol*); SOAP (*Simple Object Access Protocol*); SUP-FE (*Service User Profile FE*); TAA-FE (*Transport Authentication and Authorization FE*); TLM-FE (*Transport Location Management FE*); TRE-FE (*Transport Resource Enforcement FE*); TRC-FE (*Transport Resource Control FE*); TUP-FE (*Terminal User Profile FE*); USI-FE (*User Signaling Interworking FE*); XCAP (*XML Configuration Access Protocol*); XML (*eXtensible Markup Language*); WIN (*Wireless Intelligent Network*).

Control Protocol (TCP), and so forth. Routing traffic is important as it keeps the network operational, and it needs to be forwarded in a timely manner. A minimum bandwidth needs to be guaranteed to ensure that routing traffic always receives timely service and probability of packet drop under peak load is very low [14].

Transport Control Functions are responsible for the admission decision and the resource control of the transport function. The RACF comprises Policy Decision Functional Entity (PD-FE) that takes the final decision over the resource and admission control and delivers it to the corresponding Policy Enforcement Functional Entity (PE-FE)

through Common Open Policy Service Policy Provisioning (COPS-PR), Media Gateway Control (MEGACO)/H.248, or Diameter based interface. Derived from its predecessor Remote Authentication Dial-In User Service (RADIUS), Diameter is used by the RACF to interact with NACF, including network access registration, authentication and authorization, and parameter configuration for checking user profiles and Service Level Agreements (SLAs) held by them. Most of these protocols require reliable transport mechanism, for example, Diameter runs over TCP or SCTP, COPS-PR runs over TCP, MEGACO/H.248 runs over UDP, TCP, or SCTP, and so forth. Applications that use these protocols require a low packet loss, but are relatively not sensitive to delay. Therefore, it is necessary to ensure sufficient bandwidth in the network to provide high assurance of delivery [14].

3.2. Service Stratum Control Plane Protocols. The service stratum control plane provides a variety of functions that control and manage service resources and network services to enable user services and applications. Service Control Functions include resource control, registration, authentication and authorization functions at the service level, and functions for controlling media resources [15]. The actual protocols used to support these functions are Diameter, MEGACO/H.248, and Session Initiation Protocol (SIP). The use of SIP has received substantial attention since it has been selected as the basis of IMS specifications developed by 3GPP and adopted as an integral part of the overall NGN architecture. Many signaling protocols came before SIP, such as ITU-T H.323 umbrella protocol [16]. The Voice over IP (VoIP) signaling protocols evolution is reviewed in [17].

Content Delivery Functions (CDFs) receive content from the Application Support Functions and Service Support Functions and then store, process, and convey this content to the End-User Functions using the means of the Transport Functions. Real-Time Streaming Protocol (RTSP) is intended to control content delivery sessions and provide a means for choosing delivery mechanisms. RTSP can use UDP or TCP as a transport protocol.

Application Support Functions and Service Support Functions include the registration, authentication, and authorization functions at the application level offered to the Applications and the End-User Functions. Cooperation between the Application Support Functions and Service Support Functions and the Service Control Functions offers the requested NGN services to the Applications and the End-User Functions. This cooperation is realized using SIP, Hypertext Transfer Protocol (HTTP), Simple Object Access Protocol (SOAP), Diameter, Voice eXtensible Markup Language (VoiceXML), and Media Server Control Markup Language (MSCML) [15]. SIP is designed to be independent of the underlying transport protocol. Although HTTP definitions presume reliable transport protocol, such as TCP, it has found application even with unreliable protocols, such as UDP. SOAP, as the envelope syntax for sending and receiving XML messages with the Web services can be used over any transport protocol such as HTTP, Simple Mail Transfer Protocol (SMTP), or even TCP. Additionally, HTTP transport is used for VoiceXML, and SIP transport is used for MSCML. This kind of traffic requires sufficient bandwidth in the network to provide high assurance of delivery and low delay. As it does not respond dynamically to packet loss, probability of packet drop or queuing delay under peak load should be very low for this type of traffic [14].

In order to facilitate the implementation of value-added services, NGN capabilities and resources are offered to applications through the use of a standard Application Network Interface (ANI). NGN supports the following three classes of value-added service environments [18]: (1) IN-based service environment (examples of ANI-specific protocols include IN

Application Protocol (INAP), Customized Application for Mobile network Enhanced Logic (CAMEL), and Wireless Intelligent Network (WIN)); (2) IMS-based service environment (examples of ANI-specific protocols include SIP, Diameter, HTTP, and XML Configuration Access Protocol (XCAP)); (3) open service environment (examples of this environment using ANI include Open Service Access (OSA)/Parlay, Parlay X, and Open Mobile Alliance (OMA)). In regard to open interfaces, there are ongoing efforts to provide standardized Application Programming Interfaces (APIs) for RESTful Web services [19], which meets many NGN service provisioning requirements.

4. Signaling Transmission in NGN

The previous section provides an overview of the main signaling protocols in use in current and next generation networks. All of them have the common objective of providing some form of control over and support of user traffic and services, thus contributing to good operation of the network.

Signaling messages can be transmitted using path-coupled or path-decoupled approach. In case of path-coupled approach, signaling nodes must be collocated with routers and signaling messages are routed only through the nodes that are on the data path. In case of path-decoupled approach, signaling nodes should be dedicated and separate from routers and signaling messages are routed through nodes that are not assumed to be on the data path. The RSVP is path coupled and the SIP is path decoupled.

From QoS aspect, signaling can be classified in another two categories: in-band and out-of-band. In-band QoS signaling assumes that signaling traffic is a part of the associated data traffic. It is typically presented in a particular header field of the IP packets, for example, Type of Service (ToS), DiffServ Code Point (DSCP), Traffic Class, and so forth. It neither introduces additional traffic into the network nor incurs setup delay for the data traffic. By definition in-band signaling is path-coupled signaling. Out-of-band QoS signaling assumes that signaling traffic is carried by dedicated packets, separate from the associated data traffic. It entails the use of a signaling protocol and further processing above the network layer. Depending on whether the signaling path is closely tied to the associated data path, it is path-coupled or path-decoupled signaling.

Out-of-band signaling is used in Integrated Services (IntServ), while in-band signaling is used in DiffServ, which are both class-based QoS models proposed by IETF. IntServ is not suitable for signaling transmission due to issues raised by the resource reservation for every flow in intermediate routers across the end-to-end path. This introduces additional delay caused by signaling path establishment process, which is unacceptable due to strict time constraints posed by signaling. DiffServ avoids this processing complexity and signaling overhead in network routers. It concentrates on aggregated flows and Per Hop Behaviors (PHBs) applied to a network-wide set of traffic classes.

The idea of QoS classification appears in a few more standards and recommendations. However, the most important

TABLE 1: ITU-T QoS classes [6].

QoS[f] class	Application (examples)	IPTD[e]	IPDV[b]	IPLR[d]	IPER[c]
Class 0	Real-time, jitter sensitive, high interaction (VoIP[g], VTC[h])	100 ms	50 ms	1×10^{-3}	1×10^{-4}
Class 1	Real-time, jitter sensitive, interactive (VoIP[g], VTC[h])	400 ms	50 ms	1×10^{-3}	1×10^{-4}
Class 2	Transaction data, highly interactive (signaling)	100 ms	U[i]	1×10^{-3}	1×10^{-4}
Class 3	Transaction data, interactive	400 ms	U[i]	1×10^{-3}	1×10^{-4}
Class 4	Low loss only (short transactions, bulk data, video streaming)	1 s	U[i]	1×10^{-3}	1×10^{-4}
Class 6	Traditional applications of default IP[a] networks	U[i]	U[i]	U[i]	U[i]

[a] IP: Internet Protocol; [b] IPDV: IP Packet Delay Variation; [c] IPER: IP Packet Error Ratio; [d] IPLR: IP Packet Loss Ratio; [e] IPTD: IP Packet Transfer Delay; [f] QoS: Quality of Service; [g] VoIP: Voice over IP; [h] VTC: Video Telepresence; [i] U: Unspecified.

QoS classes are defined by ITU-T, IETF, 3GPP, and IEEE [6]. The QoS class is term that is often interchangeably used in the meaning of service class. Services belonging to the same class are described by a specific set of parameters, which can be expressed qualitatively or quantitatively.

ITU-T Recommendation Y.1541 introduced five service classes. There are four QoS parameters to be guaranteed for each service class, that is, IP Packet Transfer Delay (IPTD), IP Packet Delay Variation (IPDV), IP Packet Loss Ratio (IPLR), and IP Packet Error Ratio (IPER). The defined bounds for these QoS parameters are shown in Table 1 and should not be exceeded.

IETF standardized two QoS models, as mentioned above. Within IntServ model, three service classes are defined, that is, Controlled-Load, Guaranteed QoS, and best-effort service classes. DiffServ model introduced a number of PHBs that can be used for realization of various service classes. IETF defined twelve classes in Request for Comments (RFC) 4594, which are listed in Table 2. It recommends how to construct these service classes using DiffServ mechanisms. Although the requirements of each service class are described in terms of a tolerance to packet loss, delay, and jitter, strict values or bounds for QoS parameters are not provided. As defined by RFC 5127, these service classes are aggregated into four QoS classes, that is, Network Control, Real-Time, Assured Elastic, and Elastic Treatment Aggregate.

3GPP specification TS 23.107 defined four QoS classes in Universal Mobile Telecommunications System (UMTS) networks, that is, Conversational, Streaming, Interactive, and Background. Additionally, some features of each QoS class are distinguished in terms of fundamental characteristics, transfer delay, transfer delay variation, low bit error rate, guaranteed bit rate, buffering, and so forth. Fundamental characteristics of each QoS class are shown in Table 3.

IEEE 802.1d standard proposed eight traffic types to be supported in Local Area Network (LAN). The traffic types are mapped to User Priorities (UPs) that are used to differentiate QoS. Requirements for QoS parameter values on traffic types and UPs are not imposed except for voice and video traffic types. For wireless networks, four Access Categories (ACs) are defined to differentiate services in IEEE 802.11e. Mappings between IEEE 802.1d UPs and IEEE 802.11e ACs are shown in Table 4.

Standardization bodies make an effort to define mapping between QoS classes to improve the cooperation between various techniques. It is shown in [6] that, despite some

TABLE 2: IETF QoS classes.

RFC[f] 5127	RFC[f] 4594
Ctrl (CS[b])	Network control (CS[b]6)
Real time (EF[d])	Telephony (EF[d])
	Signaling (CS[b]5)
	Multimedia conferencing (AF[a]4)
	Real-time interactive (CS[b]4)
	Multimedia streaming (AF[a]3)
Assured elastic (AF[a])	Broadcast video (CS[b]3)
	Low latency data (AF[a]2)
	OAM[e] (CS[b]2)
	High priority data (AF[a]1)
Elastic (DF[c])	Low priority data (CS[b]1)
	Standard (DF[c])

[a] AF: Assured Forwarding; [b] CS: Class Selector; [c] DF: Default Forwarding; [d] EF: Expedited Forwarding; [e] OAM: Operations, Administration, and Management; [f] RFC: Request For Comments.

inconsistencies, it is possible to find mappings between ITU-T, IETF, IEEE and 3GPP QoS classes. This paper considers only on signaling-specific QoS classes, as shown in Table 5.

The focus is on the Signaling service class, as defined in the IETF RFC 4594. This service class is included in the Real-Time treatment aggregate, as proposed in IETF RFC 5127. It should be supported by the UMTS Interactive QoS class. Signaling service class is marked with DSCP value CS5. This DSCP value can be mapped to IEEE 802.1d UP 5, and IEEE 802.11e AC AC_VI. This service class is mapped to Class 2 that is specified in ITU-T Recommendation Y.1541. Therefore, it should be configured to assure the target values for IPTD and IPLR: the upper bound on IPTD below 100 ms and the upper bound on IPLR below 1×10^{-3}.

RFC 4594 proposed to configure Signaling service class to provide a minimum bandwidth assurance for CS5 marked packets. This service class should use a rate queuing system, such as Weighted Fair Queuing (WFQ) or Weighted Round Robin (WRR). The single rate with burst size token bucket policer should be used to ensure that the signaling traffic stays within its negotiated or engineered bounds. Traffic in this service class does not respond dynamically to packet loss, so Active Queue Management (AQM) should not be applied to CS5 marked packets [14]. Since RFC 4594 is

TABLE 3: UMTS QoS classes.

QoS[a] class	Fundamental characteristics	Example of application
Conversational	Preserve time relation (variation) between information entities of the stream Conversational pattern (stringent and low delay)	Voice
Streaming	Preserve time relation (variation) between information entities of the stream	Streaming video
Interactive	Request response pattern Preserve payload content	Web browsing
Background	Destination is not expecting the data within a certain time Preserve payload content	Background download of emails

[a] QoS: Quality of Service.

TABLE 4: IEEE QoS classes [6].

Priority	802.1d			802.11e	
	UP[b]	Designation	Traffic type	AC[a]	Designation
Low	1	BK	Background	AC_BK	Background
	2	—	spare	AC_BK	Background
	0	BE	Best effort	AC_BE	Best effort
	3	EE	Excellent effort	AC_BE	Best effort
	4	CL	Controlled load	AC_VI	Video
	5	VI	Video	AC_VI	Video
	6	VO	Voice	AC_VO	Voice
High	7	NC	Network control	AC_VO	Voice

[a] AC: Access Category; [b] UP: User Priority.

TABLE 5: Mapping of signaling-specific QoS classes.

Signaling-specific QoS classes		
Standard body	Document	QoS class
ITU-T[g]	Y.1541	Class 2
IETF[f]	RFC 4594 RFC 5127	Signaling (CS5)[c] Real time (EF)[d]
IEEE[e]	802.1d 802.11e	UP[k] 5 AC_VI[b]
3GPP[a]	TS 23.107 TS 23.203	UMTS[j]/Interactive LTE[h]/QCI[i] 5

[a] 3GPP: 3rd Generation Partnership Project; [b] AC_VI: Access Category_Video; [c] CS: Class Selector; [d] EF: Expedited Forwarding; [e] IEEE: Institute of Electrical and Electronics Engineers; [f] IETF: Internet Engineering Task Force; [g] ITU-T: International Telecommunication Union Telecommunication Standardization Sector; [h] LTE: Long-Term Evolution; [i] QCI: QoS Class Identifiers; [j] UMTS: Universal Mobile Telecommunications System; [k] UP: User Priority.

to be viewed as industry best-practice recommendation, enterprises and service providers are encouraged to adopt this recommendation, with the aim of improving QoS consistency, compatibility, and interoperability. However, since it is a set of formal DiffServ QoS configuration best practices, and not a requisite standard, modifications can be made to these recommendations as required by specific needs and constraints. To meet the QoS requirements as defined in ITU-T Recommendation Y.1541, we proposed

a modification of these configuration guidelines with regard to Signaling service class [20].

The approach proposed in our previous work is based on configuring Signaling service class by using Priority Queuing (PQ) system to give it absolute preferential treatment over all other User service classes. A packet assigned to Signaling service class should be marked with a new DSCP value, which should be requested from the Internet Assigned Numbers Authority (IANA). This DSCP value should be lower than the one used to configure the Network Control service class and higher than the one reserved for all User service classes defined in RFC 4594 and RFC 5865.

Applying the proposed modification to the Signaling service class configuration, it is possible to improve the QoS performances of real-time services. Since this approach is signaling protocol independent, it is considered in one of our previous works with regard to Real-time Transport Control Protocol (RTCP). The standard approach regarding control information prioritization requires RTCP packets to be marked with the same DSCP as the Real-time Transport Protocol (RTP) packets. Our approach is based on marking the RTCP packets with the higher DSCP than the one used by RTP packets. In other words, RTCP packets are classified into the Signaling service class that is assigned the highest priority level in order to transmit user control information reliably and efficiently and thereby increase QoS. In this regard, Figure 2 shows the impact of control information prioritization on the RTP throughput. Both approaches provide the same throughput when the network is unloaded.

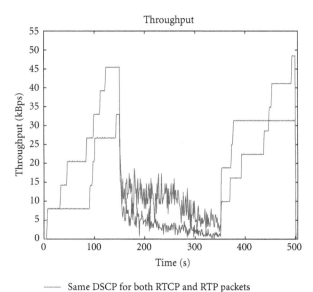

FIGURE 2: Impact of prioritizing of signaling/control information transmission on RTP throughput [21].

Our approach provides higher throughput than the standard approach when the network is heavy loaded. This is because our approach lets RTCP packets adjust the sending rate of RTP packets more dynamically than standard approach and in dependence upon the status of network. Conversely, the standard approach may allow RTCP packets to establish the improper sending rate resulting in higher throughput because QoS statistics determined by delayed RTCP packets may be different than the actual QoS experienced by RTP packets [21].

Signaling service class should be assigned with the highest priority level in order to ensure reliable and forehand signaling transmission. It has been recognized that reliable and forehand signaling transmission is the main condition to guarantee service reachability and enable dynamic end-to-end QoS control depending on the availability of network resources [7].

This concept has also been recognized by 3GPP and incorporated in LTE QoS framework [22]. The Evolved Packet System (EPS) uses QoS Class Identifiers (QCI), which specifies the class to which the bearer belongs. The EPS bearer carrying IMS signaling has a QCI value of 5, which characterizes the highest-priority nonguaranteed bit rate bearer suitable for IMS control messages. Since the bearer is not visible in the transport network, a QCI to DSCP mapping function is implemented. The purpose of this function is to make a translation from bearer-level QoS (QCI) to transport level QoS (DSCP). Using this function, signaling packets on a bearer associated with the highest priority QCI should be marked with the highest priority DSCP for forwarding in the transport network. As mentioned before, the traffic forwarding treatment is determined by queue management schemes and scheduling algorithms for uplink and downlink traffic. For downlink packets, the gateway performs this mapping, while the LTE Radio Access Network (RAN) performs it for uplink packets.

Signaling service class should be used by a number of different applications, such as peer-to-peer IP telephony signaling (e.g., using SIP, H.323), peer-to-peer signaling for multimedia applications, client-server IP telephony signaling (e.g., using H.248, MEGACO, MGCP, etc.), signaling to control IP Television (IPTV) applications (e.g., using Internet Group Management Protocol (IGMP)), and so forth. Different applications have different characteristics and latency requirements. However, in current transport networks, all signaling messages receive uniform treatment regardless of any special application requirements because they are associated with the same DSCP value in their IP packet headers. The transport network uses different DSCP values to apply different forwarding treatment to Signaling service class and all other service classes. The same mechanism could be applied signaling messages having different priorities which are sent over the network. In this case, signaling messages are associated to different DSCP values relating to their priorities. Being linked to various research areas, this idea is hopefully going to become a new starting point for research activities in the future.

5. Conclusion and Future Work

As networks migrate toward NGN, the growing amount of intelligence is sent through network. The main source of that intelligence is the signaling. With the growing amount of signaling, network management becomes the challenging issue that impacts overall QoS. To overcome this issue, there is a need for reliable and forehand signaling transmission. To clarify the interpretation of this concept, this paper provides the overview of evolutionary transition to NGN from signaling perspective.

Since the signaling is a starting point of the network's evolution, its origins and purpose are reviewed along with the transport requirements. Signaling has proven its importance in the SS7, which is separate signaling network fulfilling a number of reliability and performance requirements. Although there is no separate signaling network in the NGN, signaling transport must have similar performance to SS7. Since the NGN transport network is unreliable and lacks the QoS guarantees, there is a need to provide differentiated treatment to signaling traffic. Both routing and signaling protocols in use in current and next generation networks are identified along with their relationship to the overall NGN in order to understand their transmission requirements.

Through the discussion of different standard approaches, this paper finds the mappings between ITU-T, IETF, IEEE, and 3GPP signaling-specific QoS classes. The focus is put on the Signaling service class defined by IETF, which is used as the basis for our approach to signaling transmission. This service class should be assigned with the highest priority level in order to ensure reliable and forehand signaling transmission. This concept has been recognized by 3GPP and incorporated in LTE QoS framework.

Our previously proposed approach could be further improved, if signaling messages having different priorities are marked with different DSCP values to apply different forwarding treatment when transported over the network.

Since the significant growth in Machine-to-Machine (M2M) communications is generating the enormous increases in signaling traffic, this approach could help to meet each M2M's application requirements while protecting the network and making more efficient use of available resources. This idea is hopefully going to become a new starting point for our future research activities.

References

[1] J. M. Batalla, J. Sliwinski, H. Tarasiuk, and W. Burakowski, "Impact of signaling system performance on QoE in next generation network," *Journal of Telecommunications and Information Technology*, pp. 117–130, 2010.

[2] T. Magedanz, M. Corici, and H. Coskun, "Telecom signaling evolution for IMS, OTT and M2M services," in *Proceedings of the 13th Annual NGN Signaling Evolution Forum*, Berlin, Germany, 2012.

[3] E. Mikoczy, I. Kotuliak, and O. van Deventer, "Evolution of the converged NGN service platforms towards future networks," *Future Internet*, vol. 3, no. 1, pp. 67–86.

[4] B. Orimoloye and H. Hanrahan, "Formalizing the next generation "signaling network"," in *Proceedings of the Southern Africa Telecommunication Networks and Application Conference (SATNAC '04)*, Western Cape, South Africa, 2004.

[5] D. K. Grandischnig and M. Tuxen, "Signaling transport over IP-based networks using IETF standards," in *Proceedings of the 3rd International Workshop on the Design of Reliable Communication Network (DRCN '01)*, pp. 168–174, Budapest, Hungary, 2001.

[6] R. Stankiewicz, P. Cholda, and A. Jajszczyk, "QoX: what is it really?" *IEEE Communications Magazine*, vol. 49, no. 4, pp. 148–158, 2011.

[7] J. Baraković, H. Bajrić, M. Kos, S. Baraković, and A. Husić, "Prioritizing signaling information transmission in next generation network," *Journal of Computer Networks and Communications*, vol. 2011, Article ID 470264, 11 pages, 2011.

[8] J. G. Van Bosse and F. U. Devetak, *Signaling in Telecommunication Networks*, John Wiley & Sons, Hoboken, NJ, USA, 2nd edition, 2007.

[9] E. Vazquez, M. Alvarez-Campana, A. Hernandez, and J. Vinyes, "Reliable signalling transport in next generation networks," in *Proceedings of the 6th International Conference on Wired/Wireless Internet Communications (WWIC '08)*, pp. 53–66, Tampere, Finland, 2008.

[10] J. Baraković, H. Bajrić, and A. Husić, "QoS design issues and traffic engineering in next generation IP/MPLS network," in *Proceedings of the 9th International Conference on Telecommunications (ConTEL '07)*, pp. 203–209, June 2007.

[11] J. Zhang and N. Ansari, "On assuring end-to-end QoE in next generation networks: challenges and a possible solution," *IEEE Communications Magazine*, vol. 49, no. 7, pp. 185–191, 2011.

[12] *General principles and general reference model for next generation networks*, ITU-T Recommendation Y.2011, 2004.

[13] *Functional requirements and architecture of next generation networks*, ITU-T Recommendation Y.2012, 2010.

[14] J. Bariarz, K. Chan, and F. Baker, "Configuration guidelines for DiffServ service classes," Tech. Rep. RFC 4594, IETF, 2006.

[15] *Signalling architecture for the NGN service control plane*, ITU-T Recommendation Q.3030, 2008.

[16] H. Liu and P. Mouchtaris, "Voice over IP signaling: H.323 and beyond," *IEEE Communications Magazine*, vol. 38, no. 10, pp. 142–148, 2000.

[17] B. Khasnasish, *Implementing Voice over IP*, vol. 2003, John Wiley & Sons, Hoboken, NJ, USA.

[18] ITU-T NGN FG Proceedings, Part II. Working Group 1 Deliverables—Service Requirements, 2005.

[19] F. Belqasmi, R. Glitho, and C. Fu, "RESTful web services for service provisioning in next-generation networks: a survey," *IEEE Communication Magazine*, vol. 4912, pp. 66–73, 2011.

[20] J. Baraković, H. Bajrić, and S. Baraković, "Priority level configuration for signaling service class," in *Proceedings of the 3rd International Conference on Communication Theory, Reliability, and Quality of Service*, pp. 122–127, Athens, Greece, June 2010.

[21] J. Baraković, S. Baraković, and H. Bajrić, "The impact of control information prioritization on QoS performance metrics," in *Proceedings of the 4th International Conference on Communication Theory, Reliability, and Quality of Service (CTRQ '11)*, pp. 60–65, Budapest, Hungary, 2011.

[22] M. Alasti, B. Neekzad, J. Hui, and R. Vannithamby, "Quality of service in WiMAX and LTE networks," *IEEE Communications Magazine*, vol. 48, no. 5, pp. 104–111, 2010.

6

Game Theoretic Modeling of NGANs: Impact of Retail and Wholesale Services Price Variation

João Paulo R. Pereira[1] and Pedro Ferreira[2]

[1] *School of Technology and Management, Polytechnic Institute of Bragança (IPB), 5301-857 Bragança, Portugal*
[2] *Institute for Systems and Robotics, Technical University of Lisbon (IST), 1049-001 Lisbon, Portugal*

Correspondence should be addressed to João Paulo R. Pereira, jprp@ipb.pt

Academic Editors: L. Pavel and R. Szabo

The increasing demand for broadband access leads operators to upgrade the existing access infrastructures (or building new access network). Broadband access networks require higher investments (especially passive infrastructures such as trenches/ducts and base station towers/masts), and before making any decision it is important to analyze all solutions. The selection of the best solution requires understanding the technical possibilities and limitations of the different access technologies, as well as understanding the costs of building and operating the networks. This study analyzes the effect of asymmetric retail and wholesale prices on operators' NPV, profit, consumer surplus, welfare, retail market, wholesale market, and so on. For that, we propose a techno-economic model complemented by a theoretic-game model. This tool identifies all the essential costs of building (and operating) access networks and performs a detailed analysis and comparison of the different solutions in various scenarios. Communities, operators/service providers, and regulators can use this tool to compare different technological solutions, forecast deployment costs, compare different scenarios, and so on, and help them in making deployment (or regulatory) decisions. The game-theory analyses give a better understanding of the competition and its effect on the business case scenarios' economic results.

1. Introduction

Service providers, network operators, and Internet access providers are faced with the challenge of providing higher-capacity access to the end user and offering wider services [1]. Consequently, new Internet infrastructure and technologies that are capable of providing high-speed and high-quality services are needed to accommodate multimedia applications with diverse quality of service (QoS) requirements. Until a few years ago, Internet access for residential users was almost exclusively provided via public switched telephone networks (PSTN) over the twisted copper pair [2]. The new quadruple play services (i.e., voice, video, data, and mobility), which require high-speed broadband access, created new challenges for the modern broadband wireless/ wired access networks [3]. The new services led to both the development of several different last-mile solutions to make the access network capable of supporting the requirements and a stronger integration of optical and wireless access networks.

The move toward next-generation networks (NGNs) has significant implications for the technical architecture and design of access network infrastructure, as well as the value chains and business models of electronic communications' service provision [4]. This migration has begun to transform the telecommunication sector from distinct single-service markets into converging markets [5]. NGNs allow consumers to choose between different access network technologies to access their service environment. In our work, the NGN architecture will be limited to the developments of network architectures in the access network (local loop), referred to as the next-generation access network (NGAN).

Although the cost of bandwidth in the active layer has reduced significantly (and continually) in recent years, the cost of civil works (such as digging and trenching) represents a major barrier for operators to deploy NGA infrastructure. Studies and deployments [7] show that civil infrastructure is the largest proportion of the costs of fixed access deployment (up to 80%). Duct is a critical part of the next-generation access networks, and its sharing would

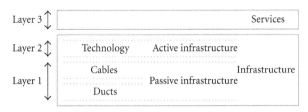

FIGURE 1: Network layers [6].

TABLE 1: Average lengths assumptions.

Segment	Region 1 (urban)	Region 2 (rural)
Feeder	750 m	1500 m
Distribution	300 m	750 m
Drop	15 m	25 m

TABLE 2: Service profile characteristics: retail prices.

Service profiles	One-time activation fees (Connection)	Expected tariff evolution (%)	Monthly subscription fees	Expected tariff evolution (%)
Serv. 1	100€	−10%	20€/month	−5%
Serv. 2	100€	−10%	50€/month	−8%

reduce or eliminate this capital cost and barrier to entry. However, duct access may need to be complemented by extra civil work to increase infrastructure capacity, the use of dark fiber (where available), or the use of conduits of alternative infrastructure providers. This also highlights that different and/or complementary regulatory tools may be required in different parts of the network [8].

2. Effects of NGNs on Market Definition

The entry of new competitors can be based on the resale of services from the incumbent, on building up their own infrastructures, on renting unbundled infrastructure from incumbents, or on the combination of the above elements. The availability of these options to competitors and price definition are generally determined by regulatory policies [9]. So, the introduction of NGNs by telecommunication network operators obligates the national regulators to adapt their access regulation regimes to the new technological conditions. Regulation and/or promotion of competition by regulatory measures need to be analyzed and compared.

The access network is usually the most expensive component in terms of capital investment (specifically passive infrastructure) and OA&M costs. Of the several costs, civil engineering costs are greatest when it is necessary to run a new fiber or copper connection to the cabinet, building, or home. Moreover, access to existing infrastructure, such as the ducts of the incumbent or other market players or sewage pipes, is critically important to avoid digging.

For [6], a local loop network can be divided into three main layers or segments: a service layer and two infrastructure layers (see Figure 1). Layer 1 includes passive infrastructures, such ducts and cables, and requires the greatest investment. Layer 2 consists of active infrastructures, such as the technical installations at the end of the fibers that send, receive, and manage the optical signals. Layer 3 includes several services that consumers buy from telecommunication operators.

3. Business Case Definition

The definition of a business case implies a great number of assumptions, such as the penetration rate, components prices, and the market share rate. However, it is difficult to get an exact forecast of its performance. The utility of a business case is to offer a more approximated estimation that allows the construction of scenarios for the future. A business case should be as realistic as possible in order to be useful and

reflect all the variables of interest of the market, as well as their evolution and expected behavior [10]

3.1. Territory and Demography. The geographical areas considered are an area with high population density and an area with low population density and high coverage. For the rural area, the roll-out strategy does not cover the whole area (1173 km^2)—the target area is limited to 34.04 km^2 with 23,000 inhabitants (see Table 1). In our model, we consider the last 10 years to estimate the average rate of increase: 0.62% for the urban area and value of 0.01% for rural target area. The population density in the urban area is 3,748 inhabitants per square kilometer and 675 in the rural area.

Parameters presented in Table 1 are important to calculate the cost of trenches/ducts, which are the most significant proportion of the costs of fixed-access deployment.

Several studies and models [11–13] assume that, in urban areas, the duct availability rate is about 60% for feeder segments and 40% for the distribution segment. In rural areas, the duct availability rate is 25% for feeder and 0% for the distribution network. The report from [14] assumes that a substantial proportion (80% near to the CO and 30% nearer to the premises) of existing ducts can be reused for fiber deployment [15].

3.2. Service Profile Assumptions. In this business case, we define two different services: slow Internet browsing service with downstream throughput of 2 Mbps and triple play service with 20 Mbps of downstream rate. The expected tariff evolution (the factor by which the tariff is expected to increase or decrease annually) is defined for both tariffs: connection and monthly fee (see Table 2).

The assumptions presented are based on the data from the review of the literature. We observe that several studies and deployments [11, 16–20] use the yearly price erosion of between 5% and 15%. The service price assumptions (prices and annual variation) are presented in Table 2.

3.3. Broadband Market Forecasts. Figure 2 shows the penetration forecast for DSL, HFC, fiber, and WiMAX for urban areas. In 2020, for the urban area, the expected penetration rates for the fixed technologies are 1.5% for WiMAX, 14.25%

Table 3: Willingness assumptions.

Parameters	Region 1 (urban area)		Region 2 (rural area)	
	Serv. 1	Serv. 2	Serv. 1	Serv. 2
Monthly subscription fee (Year 1)	20€	50€	20€	50€
Willingness value	26€	65€	22€	55€
Willingness multiplier	1.3	1.3	1.1	1.1

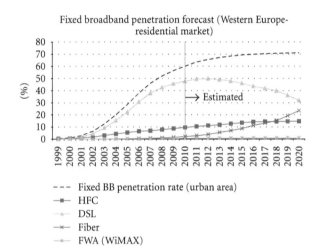

Figure 2: Fixed broadband penetration forecasts (2010–2020).

for HFC, 22.71% for fiber, and 30.97% for DSL. In the rural area, the expected penetration rate in 2020 is 10.95% for HFC, 23.7% for DSL, 16.41% for fiber, and 7.5% for FWA. We also assume that in rural areas the FWA operator has higher market share than in urban areas.

3.4. Competitive Situation and Operators' Market Share. In this section, the market share (relative size) of all the firms (operators) is projected. As competition between operators is different in each area, we estimate the market share for each operator depending on the area, technology, service, and the market (see Figure 3).

4. Game Theory for Competing Modeling

With game theory, we want to understand the effects of the interaction between the different players defined in our business case. In the proposed games, the profit (outcome) of each operator (player) will be dependent not only on their actions, but also on the actions of the other operators in the market.

This section analyzes the impact of the price (retail and wholesale) variations on several output results: players' profit, consumer surplus, welfare, costs, service adoption, and so on. For that, two price-setting games are played (Figure 4). Players' profits and NPV are used as the payoff for the players in the games analyzed.

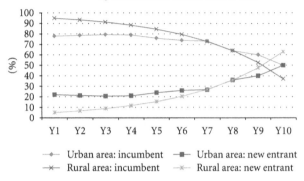

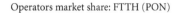

Figure 3: Market share per operator and region (FTTH market).

From the several markets presented previously, in this section we present the results for FTTH (PON) market. We assume that two competing FTTH (PON) networks (incumbent operator and new entrant) are deployed in both areas. For the game-theoretic model, it is necessary to change the adoption model used in the technoeconomic model in a way that reflects the competition between players (see Figure 5). We assume that the variation of the services prices of one player has an influence on the market share of all players (detailed in the next section).

In our model we also use the Nash equilibrium to find equilibrium. Proposed tools include a module to search the Nash equilibrium in the game. One strategy is a Nash equilibrium when both competitors play their best strategy related to the other strategies selected (players know each other's strategy in advance).

4.1. Strategies. To analyze the impact of retail and wholesale services price variations, we propose two games (see Figure 4): (1) analysis of the impact of retail price variation on NPV (wholesale prices are defined by regulator) and (2) analysis of the impact of retail and wholesale price variations on profit, consumer surplus, welfare, and retail/wholesale market (different wholesale prices in each region). For the game-theoretic evaluation, the model calculates the NPV and operator's profit for both operators' pricing strategies. Operators' NPVs are used as payoffs for the players in the first and second games, and operators' profits for the third game.

From the several assumptions, we posit (a) the price that players charge for their services (retail and wholesale) will be varied; (b) the retail price setting will influence the market share of both players (resulting in a higher or lower market share); (c) consumers only buy a retail service if the price is less than their willingness to pay.

As stated above, we assume that when one player increases/decreases the retail price, the market share of all players will be affected. For example, if one player offers cheaper services, it will be able to capture a higher market share. If a price decreases to nearly zero, everyone will use the service, and the market share of this operator will be close to 100% (total market). On the other hand, if an operator charges a higher price for a service, no one will subscribe to

Table 4: Wholesale infrastructure assumptions.

Parameters	Region 1 (urban)		Region 2 (rural)	
	Feeder segment	Distribution segment	Feeder segment	Distribution segment
Provider 1				
Duct availability	100%	100%	90%	90%
Wholesale price charged to access ducts (€/Km)	€110	€110	€90	€90
Proportion of ducts leased	0%	0%	10%	10%
From operator	—	—	2	2
Provider 2				
Duct availability	0%	0%	10%	10%
Wholesale price charged to access ducts (€/Km)	€110	€110	€90	€90
Proportion of ducts leased	75%	75%	100%	100%
From operator	1	1	1	1

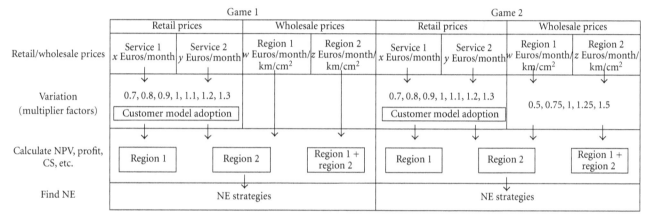

Figure 4: Games proposed.

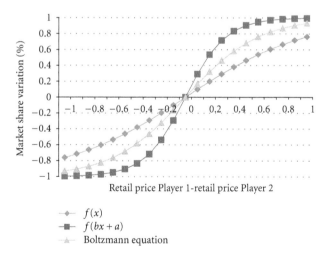

Figure 5: Models to estimate the impact of the price on the service adoption ($a = 0.4$, $b = 3$, $dx = 0.3$).

the service from this player and its market share will decrease to 0%.

4.2. Adoption Model.
The impact of varying retail prices on market shares is estimated using the Boltzmann equation.

4.3. Main Assumptions.
We assume that the willingness to pay for each retail service is different in both regions. In the urban area (region 1), the maximum amount subscribers would be willing to pay for service 1 is 26 Euros and 65 Euros for service 2. In the rural area we assume a willingness value of 22 Euros for service 1 and 55 Euros for service 2 (see Table 3).

For the wholesale infrastructure, we assume a duct availability of player 1 100% in the urban area and 90% in the rural area. We also assume that operator 2 (new entrant) leases 100% of the ducts available in the urban area and 100% of the ducts available (operator 1 has only 90% and the remaining 10% are deployed by operator 2) in the rural area from operator 1 (incumbent operator). In the other hand, player 1 leases the 10% remaining (in region 2) from operator 2. The wholesale prices assumptions are 9.1€ (month/km/cm²) for urban area and 7.5€ (month/km/cm²) for the rural area. The wholesale infrastructure assumptions are described in Table 4.

The next sections present the three game results and analyses. In the first game, retail prices vary between tariff multiplier by 0.7 and 1.3 (in increments of 0.1). For the second game, retail prices vary between 0.8 and 1.2, and wholesale prices between 0.5 and 1.5.

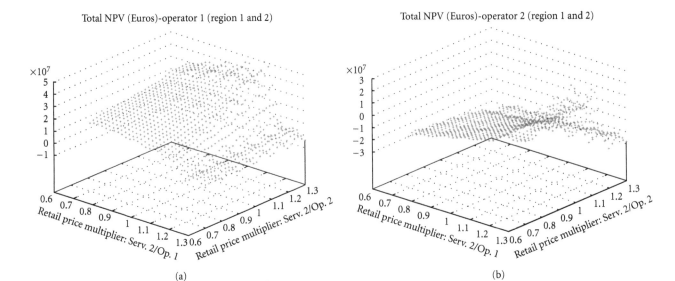

(a)   (b)

FIGURE 6: NPV variation: Operator 1 and 2/retail service 2.

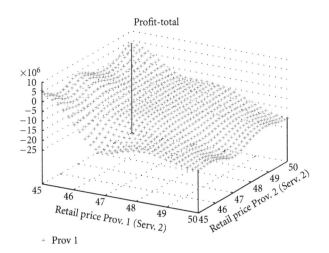

FIGURE 7: Profit variation: retail service 2.

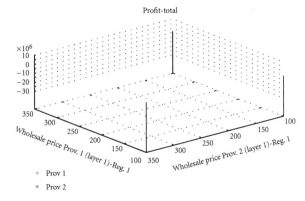

FIGURE 8: Profit variation: wholesale service.

TABLE 5: Retail prices variation values.

Tariff multiplier factor	0.7	0.8	0.9	1	1.1	1.2	1.3
Service 1 price	14	16	18	20	22	24	26
Service 2 price	35	40	45	50	55	60	65

Game 1: Impact of Retail Prices Variation on NPV. In this game we assume that wholesale prices are fixed and that operators choose retail prices to maximize their profit. The impact of varying retail prices on market shares is estimated using the Boltzmann equation (described above). The main goal of this analysis is to determine the optimal retail price strategy for both players. The retail prices vary between −30% and 30%, with increasing steps of 10% (Table 5).

The combination of the two retail prices and seven multiplier factors leads to 49 possible strategies for each player (49 × 49 matrix) in each region (2,401 total strategies).

Table 6 presents the structure of the combinations and calculated NPV.

The results (payoff matrix) of this game are presented in Figure 11 which shows the sum of the payoffs of each player in both regions. This table presents the NPV for both players for each possible combination of strategies (one strategy for each player); Nash equilibrium strategies are also identified. The first two rows represents the prices multiplier factor of Player 2 (for services 1 and 2) and the first two columns show the variation (multiplier factors) of Player 1. Each cell contains two values: The left value corresponds to the NPV of Player 1, and the value on right side corresponds to the NPV of Player 2. For example, the first value calculated (15831024€) corresponds to the NPV of Player 1 when the strategy of Player 1 is to decrease the price of Service 1 and service 2 by about 30% (multiplier factor 0.7) and the strategy of Player 2 is also to decrease the price of service 1 and service 2 by about 30%.

From these results presented in Figure 11, we find three pure NE strategies (black cells) that are described in Table 7. Table 7 shows the NE strategies that maximize the profit of

TABLE 6: Structure of combinations and results for Game 1.

Strategies	Player 1 Retail Price R1 and R2		Player 2 Retail Price R1 and R2		NPV					
					Player 1		Player 2		Tot. P1	Tot. P2
	S1	S2	S1	S2	R1	R2	R1	R2	R1 + R2	R1 + R2
1	0.7	0.7	0.7	0.7	$\cdots$	$\cdots$	$\cdots$	$\cdots$	$\cdots$	$\cdots$
2	0.7	0.7	0.7	0.8	$\cdots$	$\cdots$	$\cdots$	$\cdots$	$\cdots$	$\cdots$
n	$\cdots$	$\cdots$	$\cdots$	$\cdots$	$\cdots$	$\cdots$	$\cdots$	$\cdots$	$\cdots$	$\cdots$

TABLE 7: Pure NE strategies for both regions.

Strategy	Player 1 (incumbent)		Player 2 (new entrant)		NPV K€ Player 1	NPV K€ Player 2
	Retail serv. 1	Retail serv. 2	Retail serv. 1	Retail serv. 2		
1	1.1 (22€)	1.1 (55€)	0.7 (14€)	0.8 (40€)	9.565	555
2	1.2 (24€)	1.2 (60€)	1.3 (26€)	1.1 (55€)	1.435	23.715
3	1.3 (26€)	1 (50€)	1.2 (24€)	0.7 (35€)	5.015	3.295

TABLE 8: Retail and wholesale prices variation values for Game 2.

Service	Tariff multiplier factor				
Retail price	0.8	0.9	1	1.1	1.2
Wholesale price	0.5	0.75	1	1.25	1.5

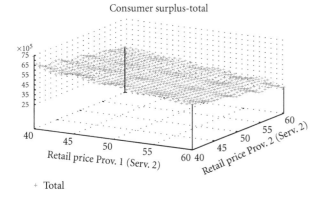

FIGURE 9: Consumer surplus variation.

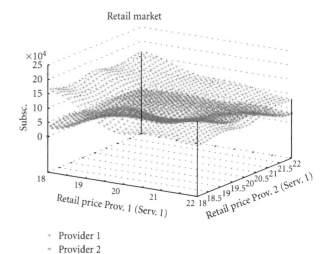

FIGURE 10: Retail market variation.

both players. To maximize profit, in the first equilibrium strategy, Operator 1 increases retail prices by 10%. Operator 2, in face of the imposed wholesale prices, decreases the price of service 1 and service 2 by 30% and 20%, respectively. A new entrant has to pay the wholesale to the incumbent, but if increase the retail prices, their market share will decrease (see model above).

Figure 6 shows the impact of service 2 variation on NPV of both operators. From the analysis of Figure 6, we can conclude that the variation of retail prices of Service 2 has a greater influence in the NPV than the variation of Service 1 price. Service 2 price variation can drop the NPV of Operator 1 to negative. On the other hand, Operator 2 can turn the NPV positive when the tariff of service 2 increases.

Game 2: Impact of Retail and Wholesale Prices Variation on NPV. In this game we assume that wholesale prices are not preimposed, and we investigate what is the reaction of operators when they can also choose different wholesale prices in different regions (see Table 8). In game 2 we assume that has the same variation for both regions. Retail prices vary between 0.8 (−20%) and 1.2 (20%) (in increments of 0.1). For wholesale price we assume a variation between 0.5 and 1.5 (in increments of 0.25).

In this context, the combination of the three prices and variation multipliers (described in Table 8) leads to 625 (5^4) possible strategies for each player (625 × 625 matrix) in each region (390625 strategies in both regions) Table 9 shows the structure used.

As the matrix is too bigger, for this game we decide to present the NE strategies (players profit is used as payoff) and the graphs that show the impact of variation in several results (presented in Figure 12).

The analysis of the results finds five NEs strategies. As Player 2 does not operate in the wholesale market of region 1, the variation of this price is not significant (see Table 10). We

TABLE 9: Structure of combinations and results for Game 2.

Strategies	Player 1				Pl 2	Results-NPV					
	Retail price R1 and R2		Wholesale price		...	Player 1		Player 2		Tot. P1	Tot. P2
			R1	R2	...	R1	R2	R1	R2	R1 + R2	R1 + R2
	S1	S2	Duct Access		...						
1	0.8	0.8	0.8	0.8	...						
2	0.8	0.8	0.8	0.8	...						
n	...	...	...	...	...						

TABLE 10: Pure NE strategies in both regions (Game 2).

Player 1 (incumbent operator)				Player 2 (new entrant)				Profit (K€) Player 1	Profit (K€) Player 2
Retail		Wholesale		Retail		Wholesale			
S1	S2	R1	R2	S1	S2	R1	R2		
0.8	0.8	1.25	1.25	0.8	0.8	0.50 / 0.75 / 1 / 1.25 / 1.5	1.25	22402	101
0.8	0.9	1.25	1	0.8	0.8	0.50 / 0.75 / 1 / 1.25 / 1.5	1.25	19543	6.198

Player 2 (new entrant) strategies

Price S1 (incumbent)	Price S2 (incumbent)	S1=0.7 S2=0.7		S1=0.7 S2=0.8		S1=0.7 S2=1.3		S1=1.2 S2=0.7		S1=1.2 S2=1.3		S1=1.3 S2=0.7		S1=1.3 S2=1.1	
0.7	0.7	15831024	−18582287	18183087	−19363781	28936533	−30770826	17496173	−19795217	30601681	−31983756	18113915	−20768607	26428738	−25938555
	0.8	14472132	−14083788	19556293	−16693988	34299456	−30618352	16137281	−15296719	35964604	−31831283	16755023	−16270109	29303695	−23304216
	0.9	12185918	−9824136	17582209	−11580297	39612688	−30427158	13851067	−11037066	41277837	−31640088	14468808	−12010456	31362952	−20234582
	1	9338223	−5994009	14713466	−6738115	44866176	−30195243	11003372	−7206939	46531325	−31408173	11621113	−8180329	32577289	−16820707
	1.1	6280874	−2707019	11341982	−2384199	50053039	−29925006	7946023	−3911949	51718187	−31137937	8563765	−4893339	33014991	−13215411
	1.2	−7258790	6298197	−6933535	11368737	−4619767	−29519466	−5593641	5085267	−2954619	−30732396	−4975899	4111877	−3280895	23715662
	1.3	−7216198	6452291	−6935595	11588571	−4402383	−29202072	−5551049	5239361	−2737234	−30415002	−4933308	4265971	−3375080	24186698
1.1	0.7	14054700	−15642494	16406763	−16423988	27160208	−27831033	19064485	−17729134	32169993	−29917673	21886956	−20768607	30201779	−25938555
	0.8	12695808	−11143995	17779969	−13754195	32523131	−27678559	17705593	−13230635	37532916	−29765199	20528064	−16270109	33076737	−23304216
	0.9	10409594	−6884343	15805885	−8640503	37836364	−27487364	15419379	−8970983	42846148	−29574004	18241850	−12010456	35135994	−20234582
	1	7561899	−3054215	12937141	−3798322	43089852	−27255449	12571684	−5140855	48099637	−29342089	15394155	−8180329	36350330	−16820707
	1.1	4504550	232775	9565657	555595	48276714	−26985213	9514335	−1853865	53286499	−29071853	12336806	−4893339	36788033	−13215411
	1.2	−9035114	9237091	−8709859	14308530	−6396091	−26579672	−4025329	7151351	−1386307	−28666312	−1202858	4111877	492146	23715662
	1.3	−8992522	9392085	−8711919	14528364	−6178707	−26262279	−3982737	7305445	−1168922	−28348918	−1160266	4265971	397962	24186698
1.2	0.7	13511514	−15140682	15863576	−15922176	26617022	−27329221	19138606	−17069339	32244114	−29257878	22830217	−20768607	31145040	−25938555
	0.8	12152622	−10642183	17236783	−13252383	31979945	−27176747	17779714	−12570840	37607037	−29105404	21471325	−16270109	34019997	−23304216
	0.9	9866407	−6382531	15262698	−8138692	37293177	−26985553	15493499	−8311188	42920269	−28914210	19185110	−12010456	36079254	−20234582
	1	7018712	−2552404	12393955	−3296511	42546666	−26753638	12645805	−4481060	48173758	−28682294	16337416	−8180329	37293591	−16820707
	1.1	3961364	734586	9022471	1057406	47733528	−26483401	9588456	−1194070	53360620	−28412058	13280067	−4893339	37731293	−13215411
	1.2	−9578300	9739802	−9253046	14810342	−6939278	−26077861	−3951208	7811146	−1312186	−28006517	−259597	4111877	1435407	23715662
	1.3	−9535709	9893896	−9255106	15030176	−6721894	−25760467	−3908617	7965240	−1094801	−27689124	−217006	4265971	1341222	24186698
1.3	0.7	11507889	−13885393	13859352	−14666887	24613397	−26073932	11507889	−9292724	24613397	−21481263	11492351	−20732168	19807074	−25902216
	0.8	10148997	−9386894	15233158	−11997094	29976320	−25921458	10148997	−4794225	29976320	−21328789	10133359	−16233669	22682032	−23267776
	0.9	7862782	−5127242	13259073	−6883402	35289552	−25730264	7862782	−534573	35289552	−21137595	7847145	−11974017	24741289	−20198142
	1	5015088	−1297114	10390330	−2041221	40543041	−25498349	5015088	3295555	40543041	−20905679	4999450	−8143889	25955625	−16784268
	1.1	1957739	1989876	7018846	2312695	45729903	−25228112	1957739	6582545	45729903	−20635443	1942101	−4856909	26393328	−13178971
	1.2	−11581925	10995092	−11256671	16065631	−8942903	−24822571	−11581925	15587761	−8942903	−20229902	11597563	4148317	−9902559	23752102
	1.3	−11539334	11149186	−11258730	16285465	−8725518	−24505178	−11539334	15741855	−8725518	−19912509	11554971	4302411	−9996743	24223138

FIGURE 11: Game 1 results—summary.

conclude that, in the business case defined, when operators can charge different retail and wholesale prices, they choose to increase wholesale prices. To maximize profits, operators increase wholesale prices and decrease retail prices. However, the increase in wholesale prices precludes entry of new operators into the market.

The main results of this game are summarized in the next figures. In the graphs we can see the impact of retail prices (Figure 7) and wholesale prices (Figure 8) on players

profit. We can verify that both prices can turn profit positive/negative.

As expected, consumer surplus decreases with the increase of prices (Figure 9). As also predictable and modeled above the impact of retail prices, variation has higher influence in the market share of competitors (see Figure 10).

The comparison of the two games above shows that when the regulator defines wholesale prices, operators increase retail prices to maximize profit. However, when wholesale

Player 1 strategies			W Price R1	W Price R2	Player 2 strategies 0.80 / 0.80										...
					0.50 (W R1)		0.50		0.75		0.50				0.75 ...
					0.50		0.75		1.00		1.25		1.50		0.50
0.8	0.8	0.5	0.5	0.5	20981654	1704052	20954077	1728871	20926500	1753691	20898923	1778510	20871345	1803330	20981654 1704052
				0.75	21232678	1425137	21205100	1449956	21177523	1474776	21149946	1499595	21122369	1524415	21232678 1425137
				1	21483701	1146222	21456124	1171041	21428547	1195861	21400969	1220680	21373392	1245500	21483701 1146222
				1.25	21734724	867307	21707147	892127	21679570	916946	21651993	941766	21624416	966585	21734724 867307
				1.5	21985748	588392	21958171	613212	21930593	638031	21903016	662851	21875439	687670	21985748 588392
			0,75	0.5	21113446	1557616	21085869	1582436	21058292	1607255	21030715	1632075	21003137	1656894	21113446 1557616
				0.75	21364470	1278701	21336892	1303521	21309315	1328340	21281738	1353160	21254161	1377979	21364470 1278701
				1	21615493	999786	21587916	1024606	21560339	1049425	21532761	1074245	21505184	1099064	21615493 999786
				1.25	21866516	720872	21838939	745691	21811362	770511	21783785	795330	21756207	820150	21866516 720872
				1.5	22117540	441957	22089963	466776	22062385	491596	22034808	516415	22007231	541235	22117540 441957
		1	1	0.5	21245238	1411181	21217661	1436000	21190084	1460820	21162506	1485639	21134929	1510459	21245238 1411181
				0.75	21496261	1132266	21468684	1157085	21441107	1181905	21413530	1206724	21385953	1231544	21496261 1132266
				1	21747285	853351	21719708	878171	21692130	902990	21664553	927809	21636976	952629	21747285 853351
				1.25	21998308	574436	21970731	599256	21943154	624075	21915577	648895	21887999	673714	21998308 574436
				1.5	22249332	295521	22221754	320341	22194177	345160	22166600	369980	22139023	394799	22249332 295521
			1,25	0.5	21377030	1264745	21349453	1289565	21321876	1314384	21294298	1339204	21266721	1364023	21377030 1264745
				0.75	21628053	985830	21600476	1010650	21572899	1035469	21545322	1060289	21517745	1085108	21628053 985830
				1	21879077	706916	21851500	731735	21823922	756555	21796345	781374	21768768	806194	21879077 706916
				1.25	22130100	428001	22102523	452820	22074946	477640	22047369	502459	22019791	527279	22130100 428001
				1.5	22381124	149086	22353546	173905	22325969	198725	22298392	223544	22270815	248364	22381124 149086
			1,5	0.5	21508822	1118310	21481245	1143129	21453668	1167949	21426090	1192768	21398513	1217588	21508822 1118310
				0.75	21759845	839395	21732268	864214	21704691	889034	21677114	913853	21649536	938673	21759845 839395
				1	22010869	560480	21983291	585300	21955714	610119	21928137	634939	21900560	659758	22010869 560480
				1.25	22261892	281565	22234315	306385	22206738	331204	22402607	101928	22151583	380843	22261892 281565
				1.5	22512915	2650	22485338	27470	22457761	52289	22430184	77109	22402607	101928	22512915 2650
...	...														
...	...														

FIGURE 12: Game 2 results—summary.

prices are not regulated, operators maximize profit by decreasing retail prices and increasing wholesale prices. However, without regulation, the higher wholesale prices will limit the entrance of new competitors.

5. Conclusions

The European Commission argues that infrastructure-based competition is the best and fastest way for broadband development. The arguments are that infrastructure-based competition provides efficiency incentives to operators, reduces prices, increases penetration, stimulates innovation, and so on. On the other hand, service-based competition implies that the new entrants (alternative operators) are dependent on the incumbent. However, because of the high costs of deploying infrastructures (especially trenching and ducting), service competition has been used as a substitute or complement to infrastructure competition. In regions with lower numbers of existing access infrastructures, new entrants are obligated to build their own infrastructure. In this way, infrastructure sharing can stimulate the construction of new access infrastructures that can be leased to other operators.

The results of this investigation show that the sharing of passive infrastructures (e.g., ducts, trenching, base station sites, and antenna masts) is a viable strategy, particularly in the context of new building (in scenarios with developed access infrastructure). When an operator deploys an access network, the access to existing civil engineering significantly reduces the investment. There are strong arguments to be made for allowing infrastructure sharing.

In this context, regulators must guarantee new entrant operators access to civil engineering; this will stimulate investment in new networks. The reduction of the barriers to new infrastructure investment by opening passive existing infrastructure would be key in the future. This study has shown that in rural areas, characterized by a small number of developed access infrastructure, the access to civil engineering does not make the scenario economically viable for the operator.

References

[1] S. L. Kota, *Satellite Multimedia Networks and Technical Challenges*, Microwave Review, 2006.

[2] O. C. Ibe, *Fixed Broadband Wireless Access Networks and Services*, John Wiley & Sons, 2002.

[3] J. P. R. Pereira and P. Ferreira, "Access networks for mobility: a techno-economic model for broadband access technologies," in *Proceedings of the 5th International Conference on Testbeds and Research Infrastructures for the Development of Networks and Communities and Workshops (TridentCom '09)*, pp. 1–7, April 2009.

[4] J. S. Marcus, D. Elixmann, C. Wernick et al., "Next Generation Networks (NGNs), European Parliament," 2009.

[5] F. Kirsch and C. Von Hirschhausen, "Regulation of NGN: structural separation, access regulation, or no regulation at all?" in *Proceedings of the 1st International Conference on Infrastructure Systems and Services: Building Networks for a Brighter Future (INFRA '08)*, pp. 1–8, November 2008.

[6] C. Jaag and M. Lutzenberger, "Approaches to FTTH-regulation. An International Comparison," in *Proceedings of the 2nd Annual Conference on Competition and Regulation in Network Industries*, p. 23, 2009.

[7] J. P. Pereira, "Telecommunication Policies for Broadband Access Networks," in *Proceedings of the 37th Research Conference on Communication, Information and Internet Policy*, pp. 1–13, 2009.

[8] Analysys-Mason, Telecoms infrastructure access—sample survey of duct access, Ofcom, 2009.

[9] J. P. Pereira and P. Ferreira, "Next Generation Access Networks (NGANs) and the geographical segmentation of markets," in *Proceedings of the 10th International Conference on Networks (ICN '11)*, p. 6, 2011.

[10] J. Rendón, F. Kuhlmann, and J. P. Aranis, "A business case for the deployment of a 4G wireless heterogeneous network in Spain," in *Proceedings of the 18th European Regional International Telecommunications Society*, 2007.

[11] T. Monath, N. K. Elnegaard, P. Cadro, D. Katsianis, and D. Varoutas, "Economics of fixed broadband access network strategies," *IEEE Communications Magazine*, vol. 41, no. 9, pp. 132–139, 2003.

[12] F. Loizillon, J. Harno, I. Welling et al., "Final results on seamless mobile IP service provision economics," IST-Information Society Technologies, 2002.

[13] T. Monath, "Techno-economic results for fixed access network evolution scenarios," in *Book Techno-Economic Results for Fixed Access Network Evolution Scenarios*, Techno-Economic Results for Fixed Access Network Evolution Scenarios, p. 28, 2005.

[14] "Analysys-Mason, The costs of deploying fibre-based next-generation broadband infrastructure," Analysys-Mason, Broadband Stakeholder Group, 2008.

[15] CSMG, "Economics of Shared Infrastructure Access," 2010.

[16] K. Stordahl, "Broadband demand and the role of new technologies," in *Proceedings of the The 13th International Telecommunications Network Strategy and Planning Symposium*, pp. 1–23, 2008.

[17] K. Stordahl, "Market development up to 2015, MARCH—Multilink architecture for multiplay services," 2010.

[18] K. Stordahl, L. A. Ims, and B. T. Olsen, "Risk methodology for evaluating broadband access network architectures," *Telektronikk*, vol. 2, no. 3, pp. 273–285, 1999.

[19] V. Riihimäki, "Managing Uncertainties in Broadband Investments—Case Studies of Real Options for Rural Area Access Networks," Department of Communications and Networking, Aalto University, Aalto, Fnland, 2010.

[20] European-Union, "Europe's Digital Competitiveness Report 2010," European Union, 2010.

7

A Joint Channel-Network Coding Based on Product Codes for the Multiple-Access Relay Channel

Tafzeel ur Rehman Ahsin and Slimane Ben Slimane

Department of Communication Systems (CoS), School of Information and Communication Technology, KTH Royal Institute of Technology, 16440 Stockholm, Sweden

Correspondence should be addressed to Slimane Ben Slimane, slimane@kth.se

Academic Editors: S. S. Pietrobon and Y. T. Su

The multiple access relay channel with network coding has the potential to achieve diversity and improve coverage of wireless networks. Its network coding scheme provides an extra redundancy that can be used at the receiver to improve the performance of the cooperating users. This paper shows that the combination of channel coding and network coding, in the multiple access relay channel, can be seen as a product code with rows formed by the code-words of the individual channel codes of the users and columns formed by the network coding code-words. This new representation allows the use of any decoding algorithm of product codes at the receiver to decode the information data of the cooperating users. This decoding process is a complete joint channel-network decoding algorithm as it sees the combination of the two coding schemes as a single coding scheme. It also gives the possibility to use network coding schemes more powerful than conventional XOR-based network coding. The obtained results show that the proposed product-based network coding structure can improve the performance of the multiple-access relay channel without reducing its efficiency and allow a very flexible cooperation between the involved users.

1. Introduction

Cooperative communication [1–4] via relay nodes in cellular networks is an efficient and inexpensive way to achieve spatial diversity gain. Relay nodes deployed in the network can act as a cooperating node by listening to the transmissions performed by different nodes and forwarding them towards the destination. The throughput of cellular networks can be improved further by allowing relay nodes to forward linear combinations, based on network coding [5], of received packets instead of forwarding each packet separately. A well-known scheme that employs cooperation via a fixed relay node is the multiple-access relay channel (MARC) which could be used for the cooperation of two mobile users to a base station with the help of a relay node. Several research work in the literature has shown that network coding in cellular relaying systems provides the same diversity gain as that of conventional two-hop relay channels while improving the system throughput by a factor of 4/3 [6–13]. However, most of these studies were based on computing the outage probability without considering the interaction between channel and network coding. In fact, a relay cannot only be used to gain diversity, its transmission can be seen as an extra redundancy at the receiver, which gives the possibility to improve the link performance as compared to point-to-point communication.

As network coding combines packets of different users, it creates a redundancy common to all these cooperating users. This redundancy will not be fully utilized if separate network-channel decoding is employed at the receiver where channel decoding is performed for each transmission followed by network decoding [9, 11, 14]. To fully utilize the redundancy of network coding, joint channel-network decoding should be employed at the receiver where all users involved in the cooperation process can benefit.

Distributed channel coding has been used to exploit the redundancy provided by the relay link in a two-hop relay channel as described in [15–18]. The idea was to use the principle of turbo coding where one constituent code is employed at the source and one constituent code is employed at the relay node, which gives the possibility to employ turbo decoding at the receiver. Joint network-channel coding based on turbo codes was considered in [19] where the same convolutional code was employed at the source and the relay node with interleaved user data. Iterative network and channel decoding was used at the receiver. In [11], nested codes were proposed and applied to cooperation diversity with two nodes transmitting to a common destination. These codes assume that individual nodes employ low-rate codes that are a subset of a higher-rate codes, such that the XORed codewords at the relay node can be seen as produced by a higher-rate code. Iterative decoding of the direct transmission and the relayed transmission was employed at the receiver. However, the principle of nested codes requires that nodes employ different codes. In [12], a joint channel-network coding scheme was proposed for MARC where the two transmitting nodes perform channel coding with a low-density parity-check (LDPC) code and their combinations, with the network code described by a Tanner graph on which the decoder performs iterative decoding to jointly decode the network and the channel code. The obtained results in all previous work have shown that joint channel-network coding can exploit the diversity gain and the redundancy provided by the relay node at the receiver in cooperative communication. However, most of these previous contributions apply convolutional codes and LDPC codes with a decoding algorithm based on iterative decoding.

This paper considers joint channel-network coding for the multiple-access relay channel when the transmitting nodes employ linear block codes. It will be shown that the combination of channel coding of the transmitting nodes and the network coding scheme of the relay node can be seen as a product code. The rows of the obtained matrix codewords are the codewords of the cooperating users and the columns are the codewords of the linear network code, employed at the relay node(s). This new representation gives the possibility to use any linear block code as a network code at the relay node(s). It also gives us the possibility to use product decoding algorithms, which represent real joint channel-network decoding algorithms where the combination of network and channel coding schemes are seen as a single channel code. Several algorithms for decoding product codes exist in the literature [20–25] and can be used in our proposed scheme for MARC. These existing decoding algorithms range from simple hard decision decoding to iterative turbo-type soft decoding with performance quite close to maximum likelihood decoding [22, 25]. With this new representation of channel-network coding in MARC and the variety of decoding algorithms that exist in the literature, one can consider using more powerful network coding schemes at the relay node and adapt its rate according to the number of cooperating users and the quality of the different links. Such a flexibility will provide more robust MARC schemes with a better throughput.

This article is organized as follows. Section 2 describes the system model of the scenario under consideration. Section 3 discusses the reference system using XOR-based network coding. Section 4 describes the proposed

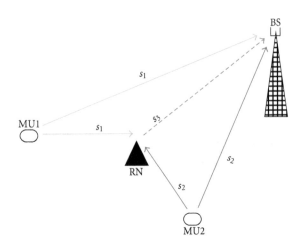

FIGURE 1: A multiple-access relay channel with 2 cooperating users and one relay node.

representation of channel-network coding in the multiple-access relay channel. It also illustrates the benefits of this new representation with the possibility of using better network coding schemes in order to generate more powerful joint channel-network coding schemes for the MARC scheme. Section 5 highlights the diversity gain achieved by the proposed scheme using an analytical approach. Section 6 illustrates the importance of using joint channel-network coding using computer simulations. It also highlights the gain achieved by the proposed network coding scheme as compared to the conventional XOR-based combining scheme. Finally, Section 7 provides concluding remarks and suggestions for future work.

2. System Model

Let us consider the multiple-access relay channel (MARC) shown in Figure 1 which consists of two transmitting mobile users, one relay node, and one receiving base station. Here, we assume that the two mobile users and the relay node are using orthogonal channels with the relay node operating in a half-duplex mode. First, each user transmits its own packet toward the base station. These packets are received at the base station and also at the relay node. The relay node decodes the received packets, reencodes them, linearly combines them into one packet using bit-by-bit XOR (network coding), and forwards the network-coded packet to the base station. Figure 1 illustrates the case of two cooperating users via one relay node but this can be generalized to N users cooperating via r relay nodes as indicated in [26].

The base station receiver then receives a total of three packets, two packets from the cooperating users and one packet from the relay node. Using these three packets, the base station tries to decode the information data of the two different users. It is assumed that each user is using an (n, k, d) linear block code with packet length n, a minimum Hamming distance d, and a code rate $R_c = k/n$. Taking into account the extra packet transmitted by the relay node,

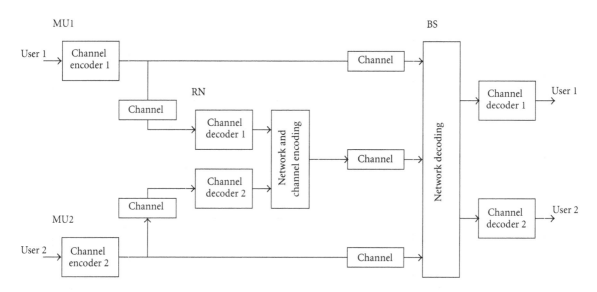

FIGURE 2: Separate channel-network decoding at the base station receiver for a multiple-access relay channel with two users and one relay node.

the overall code rate of the channel-network coding of this multiple-access relay channel is given by

$$R_e = \frac{2k}{3n} = \frac{2R_c}{3}. \tag{1}$$

In the case when users are employing channel codes with different rates, but with the same packet length n, the overall code rate of the channel-network coding of the multiple-access channel can be written as

$$R_e = \frac{k_1 + k_2}{3n} = \frac{R_1 + R_2}{3}, \tag{2}$$

where $R_i = k_i/n$ is the code rate of user i.

It is further assumed that the cooperating users are close to the relay node allowing the relay node to decode the transmitted packets without error. In the case of a decoding error, the relay drops the packet in error and does not use it in the combination process.

2.1. Channel Model. Assuming that the system is employing orthogonal frequency division multiplexing (OFDM) modulation, the radio channel can be assumed to be flat Rayleigh fading on each subcarrier of the OFDM scheme. We denote by $y_l = \{y_{0l}, y_{1l}, \ldots, y_{(n-1)l}\}$ the received packet from link l at the base station with

$$y_{il} = h_{il}s_{il} + z_{il}, \quad l = 1, 2, 3; \quad i = 0, 1, \ldots, n - 1, \tag{3}$$

where n is the packet length, s_{il} is the transmitted symbol i on link l with $E\{|s_{il}|^2\} = E_l$. The coefficient h_{il} denotes the complex multiplicative channel coefficient gain and is assumed constant over at least one symbol interval with $2\sigma^2 = E\{|h_{il}|^2\}$. The sample z_{il} denotes the complex Gaussian noise experienced by link l during the ith symbol interval with double-sided power spectral density $N_0/2$. The received packets from the different users and the relay station

are then used by the base station to make a decision on the transmitted information of the different users. How to use these received packets at the base station receiver will play an important role on the link quality of the different users.

3. Separate Channel and Network Decoding

With separate channel and network decoding, it is assumed that the receiver uses network decoding to separate the two user packets and then feeds each packet to its corresponding decoder as illustrated in Figure 2. In this case, network decoding can be done in two different ways as follows.

(1) We may use joint symbol-by-symbol detection where every three received signal samples $\mathbf{y}_i = \{y_{i1}, y_{i2}, y_{i3}\}$ are used to estimate the symbols $\mathbf{s}_i = \{s_{i1}, s_{i2}, s_{i3}\}$ for all symbols of the packets with $i = 0, 1, \ldots, n-1$. Each estimated packet is then fed to the corresponding individual channel decoder to extract the information data of the user.

(2) We may also use single-packet detection followed by successive cancellation where the strongest packet is decoded first, removed from the network-coded packets, the result is used to decode the next strongest packet, and so on until the last packet is decoded [27].

The first method gives better performance and is the one considered in this paper. Hence, to estimate the symbols $\{s_{i1}, s_{i2}, s_{i3}\}$ the network decoder computes the following metric:

$$\mathcal{C}(\hat{m}) = \sum_{l=1}^{3} |y_{il} - h_{il}\hat{s}_{il}|^2, \quad i = 0, 1, \ldots, n-1 \tag{4}$$

and chooses the set of symbols that minimizes this metric, where $\hat{s}_{il}$ denotes the estimate of s_{il}.

Assuming uncorrelated radio links and perfect interleaving for the link packets, the conditional pairwise error probability can be written as

$$
P_2(\mathbf{s}_i \longrightarrow \hat{\mathbf{s}}_i \mid \mathbf{h}_i) = Q\left(\sqrt{\frac{\sum_{l=1}^{3} |h_{il}|^2 |s_{il} - \hat{s}_{il}|^2}{2N_0}}\right)
$$

$$
\leq \frac{1}{2} \exp\left(-\sum_{l=1}^{3} \frac{|h_{il}|^2 |s_{il} - \hat{s}_{il}|^2}{4N_0}\right),
$$

$$(5)$$

where $\mathbf{h}_i = \{h_{i1}, h_{i2}, h_{i3}\}$ is the channel state information.

The pairwise error probability is then obtained by averaging the expression in (5) over the fading coefficients of the channel. To illustrate the diversity gain obtained from this detection scheme, Chernoff bounds can be used to derive the pairwise error probability [28]. For Rayleigh fading with uncorrelated radio links, an upper bound on the pairwise error probability can be written as follows:

$$
P_2(\mathbf{s}_i \longrightarrow \hat{\mathbf{s}}_i) \leq \frac{1}{2} \prod_{l=1}^{3} \left(\frac{1}{1 + \left(\sigma^2 |s_{il} - \hat{s}_{il}|^2/2N_0\right)}\right). \quad (6)
$$

The average symbol error probability for user 1 is obtained by averaging the pairwise error probability over all possible transmitted symbols and can be written as follows [29]:

$$
P_s \leq \sum_{s_{i1}} \sum_{s_{i2}} P(s_{i1}) P(s_{i2})
$$

$$
\times \sum_{\hat{s}_{i1} \neq s_{i1}} \sum_{\hat{s}_{i2}} \frac{1}{2} \prod_{l=1}^{3} \left(\frac{1}{1 + \left(\sigma^2 |s_{il} - \hat{s}_{il}|^2/2N_0\right)}\right),
$$

$$(7)$$

where $P(s_{il})$ is the probability of transmitting s_{il} for $l = 1, 2$. For equally likely transmitted symbols we have, $P(s_{i1}) = P(s_{i1}) = 1/2^m = 1/M$, where M is the modulation level and m is the number of bits per transmitted symbol. A similar expression can be obtained for user 2 by interchanging s_{i1} with s_{i2} and vice versa in (7).

For linearly multilevel-modulated signals with symbols having equal decision regions, such as $MPSK$ modulation, any symbol can be taken as a reference and the upper bound on the average symbol error probability given in (7) simplifies to

$$
P_s \leq \sum_{s_{i2}} P(s_{i2}) \sum_{\hat{s}_{i1} \neq s_{i1}} \sum_{\hat{s}_{i2}} \frac{1}{2} \prod_{l=1}^{3} \left(\frac{1}{1 + \left(\sigma^2 |s_{il} - \hat{s}_{il}|^2/2N_0\right)}\right). \quad (8)
$$

In general, the average symbol error probability is dominated by the shortest error event path and the minimum-squared Euclidean distance between the modulated symbols. For a given transmitted symbol, we have a total of $2(M - 1)$ error events of length 2 and $(M - 1)(M - 2)$ error event paths of length 3. This is illustrated in Table 1 for the case of $M = 4$ when the transmitted symbol is $s_{i1} = 00$ for user 1. Hence,

TABLE 1: Possible error events when the symbol $s_{i1} = 00$ is transmitted for the case $M = 4$.

s_{i1}	s_{i2}	$s_{i3} = s_{i1} \oplus s_{i2}$	Error event
00	00	00	s_{i1} correct
00	01	01	s_{i1} correct
00	10	10	s_{i1} correct
00	11	11	s_{i1} correct
01	00	01	s_{i1}, s_{i3}
01	01	00	s_{i1}, s_{i2}
01	10	11	s_{i1}, s_{i2}, s_{i3}
01	11	10	s_{i1}, s_{i2}, s_{i3}
10	00	10	s_{i1}, s_{i3}
10	01	11	s_{i1}, s_{i2}, s_{i3}
10	10	00	s_{i1}, s_{i2}
10	11	01	s_{i1}, s_{i2}, s_{i3}
11	00	11	s_{i1}, s_{i3}
11	01	10	s_{i1}, s_{i2}, s_{i3}
11	10	01	s_{i1}, s_{i2}, s_{i3}
11	11	00	s_{i1}, s_{i2}

the average symbol error probability for user 1 can be upper bounded as

$$
P_s \leq \frac{1}{2M} \left(\frac{M - 1}{1 + \delta_{i1}\gamma_1}\right)
$$

$$
\times \left[\frac{1}{1 + \delta_{i2}\gamma_2} + \frac{1}{1 + \delta_{i3}\gamma_3} + \frac{M - 2}{(1 + \delta_{i2}\gamma_2)(1 + \delta_{i3}\gamma_3)}\right],
$$

$$(9)$$

where

$$
\delta_{il} = \min_{s_{il} \neq \hat{s}_{il}} \frac{|s_{il} - \hat{s}_{il}|^2}{4E_l}, \qquad \gamma_l = \frac{2\sigma^2 E_l}{N_0} \quad (10)
$$

with γ_l denoting the average received signal-to-noise (SNR) of packet l and E_l is the average energy per transmitted symbol of packet l and $2\sigma^2 = E\{|h_{il}|^2\}$.

For binary phase shift keying (BPSK), an upper bound on the average symbol error probability can be obtained from (9) by letting $M = 2$ and is written as

$$
P_s \leq \frac{1}{4} \left[\frac{1}{(1 + \delta_{i1}\gamma_1)(1 + \delta_{i2}\gamma_2)} + \frac{1}{(1 + \delta_{i1}\gamma_1)(1 + \delta_{i3}\gamma_3)}\right].
$$

$$(11)$$

Assuming a high received SNR, that is, $|s_{il} - \hat{s}_{il}|^2/4N_0 \gg 1$, for all $s_{il} \neq \hat{s}_{il}$, the average symbol error probability in (9) can be upper bounded as

$$
P_s \leq \frac{M - 1}{2M} \left[\frac{1}{\delta_{i1}\delta_{i2}\gamma_1\gamma_2} + \frac{1}{\delta_{i1}\delta_{i3}\gamma_1\gamma_3} + \frac{M - 2}{\delta_{i1}\delta_{i2}\delta_{i3}\gamma_1\gamma_2\gamma_3}\right].
$$

$$(12)$$

It is observed from (12) that a diversity gain of order 2 is obtained in the MARC scheme. For instance, for the particular case of coherent BPSK modulation, we have

$s_i = \pm\sqrt{E_l}$ giving $\delta_{il} = 1$ and the average symbol error probability of (12) reduces to

$$P_s \leq \frac{1}{4}\left[\frac{1}{\gamma_1\gamma_2} + \frac{1}{\gamma_1\gamma_3}\right]. \quad (13)$$

Once all the symbols of the user packets are separated via network decoding, each packet is fed to the channel decoder of the corresponding user. As each symbol of a packet is wrongly detected with a probability P_s and that all symbols of a packet are assumed uncorrelated (ideal interleaving), the average packet error probability at the output of the channel decoder of the user can be upper bounded as [28, page 456]

$$P_p \leq \left(2^k - 1\right)[4P_s(1 - P_s)]^{d/2}. \quad (14)$$

Using the expression of (12) in (14), assuming BPSK modulation and a high-average-received SNR, an upper bound on the user packet error probability becomes

$$P_p \leq \left(2^k - 1\right)\left[\left(\frac{1}{\delta_{i1}\delta_{i2}}\right)^{d/2}\left(\frac{1}{\gamma_1\gamma_2}\right)^{d/2}\right.$$
$$\left. + \left(\frac{1}{\delta_{i1}\delta_{i3}}\right)^{d/2}\left(\frac{1}{\gamma_1\gamma_3}\right)^{d/2}\right]. \quad (15)$$

For the case of equal-received average SNRs on the three links with $\gamma_1 = \gamma_2 = \gamma_3 = \gamma_0$, the above expression reduces to

$$P_p \leq \left(2^k - 1\right)\left[\left(\frac{1}{\delta_{i1}\delta_{i2}}\right)^{d/2} + \left(\frac{1}{\delta_{i1}\delta_{i3}}\right)^{d/2}\right]\left(\frac{1}{\gamma_0}\right)^d. \quad (16)$$

It is observed from the packet error rate expression in (16) that separate network and channel decoding can achieve a diversity gain of order d which is double of that obtained in a point-to-point direct transmission. This result is similar to that obtained in [26] when considering the outage probability as a performance measure. It is worth mentioning that the total diversity gain order is the product of the diversity gain order obtained from network coding and that obtained from channel coding. Even though the diversity gain order is achieved through separate network-channel decoding, the redundancy provided by the relay node is not properly exploited at the base station receiver.

4. Equivalent Representation of Channel-Network Coding in MARC

Let us consider the case of conventional XOR-based network coding for the multiple-access relay channel and assume cooperation between two users (see Figure 1). Here, every two packets received by the relay node are combined into one packet using bit-by-bit XOR operation and forwarded to the base station. The network-coded packet is then of the same length as the packets of the individual users. Hence, the base station receiver receives three different packets: the packet of user 1, the packet of user 2, and the packet forwarded by the relay node.

TABLE 2: XOR-based network coding and its possible codewords in MARC.

	c_{1i}	c_{2i}	$c_{1i} \oplus c_{2i}$
codeword 0	0	0	0
codeword 1	0	1	1
codeword 2	1	0	1
codeword 3	1	1	0

We denote the transmitted packet of user i by

$$\mathbf{C}_i = \{c_{i1}, c_{i2}, \ldots, c_{in}\}, \quad i = 1, 2, \quad (17)$$

where $c_{ij} = 0$ or 1 with equal probabilities and n is the packet length. With XOR-based network coding, the packet generated by the relay node after reception of the user packets can be written as

$$\mathbf{C}_3 = \{c_{31}, c_{32}, \ldots, c_{3n}\}$$
$$= \{c_{11} \oplus c_{21}, c_{12} \oplus c_{22}, \ldots, c_{1n} \oplus c_{2n}\}, \quad (18)$$

where $\oplus$ is the modulo 2 sum.

Looking at the XOR-based network coding operation at the relay node, we see that for every transmitted *two* bits (one bit for each user) the relay node transmits *one* bit. Hence, the corresponding *three* received bits at the base station consist of two uncoded bits (one bit for each user) and one redundancy bit (relay node bit), that is,

$$\{c_{1i}, c_{2i}, c_{1i} \oplus c_{2i}\}, \quad i = 1, 2, \ldots, n. \quad (19)$$

In fact, it is quite easy to see that the network coding operation at the relay node with the directly received packets forms a $(3, 2, 2)$ linear block code with a minimum Hamming distance $d_{\min} = 2$ and a code rate $R_n = 2/3$. The different codewords of this linear block code are illustrated in Table 2.

Taking the three transmitted packets of MARC and placing them in rows, one over the other, we obtain a $3 \times n$ channel coding matrix. This operation is illustrated in Figure 3. It is observed that the channel coding operation of the individual user codes is done along the rows of this formed channel coding matrix and the linear network coding operation is done along the columns. Looking at the structure of this matrix, one can deduce that this $3 \times n$ matrix formed by the individual packets of the cooperating users and that of the relay node is a codeword matrix of a product code [30]. The obtained product code is an

$$(n, k, d) \times (3, 2, 2) = (3n, 2k, 2d) \quad (20)$$

block code with a code rate $R_e = 2k/3n$.

This coding structure can now be used at the base station receiver to decode the information of the cooperating users. Seen as one single code, the correction capability of the corresponding decoder is now $\lfloor(2d - 1)/2\rfloor = d - 1$ as compared to $\lfloor(d - 1)/2\rfloor$ for the case of separate channel-network decoding [28].

Product codes have been studied extensively in the literature and several algorithms for decoding product codes

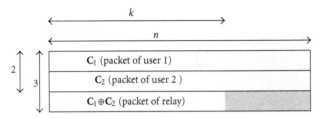

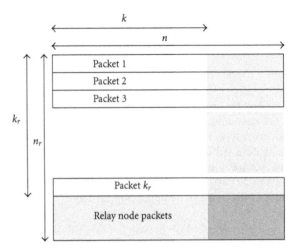

FIGURE 3: Representation of channel and XOR-based network coding in a multiple-access relay channel with two users and one relay node.

FIGURE 4: Joint channel-network coding based on product codes for MARC with k_r user packets and $n_r - k_r$ relay node packets.

also exist in the literature [20–25]. These existing decoding algorithms range from simple hard decision decoding to iterative turbo decoding having performance quite close to maximum likelihood decoding [22, 25]. This new representation of channel-network coding in MARC allows us to use the variety of decoding algorithms that exist in the literature. In addition, more powerful network coding schemes can also be considered at the relay node and their rate can be adapted according to the number of cooperating users and the quality of the different links. This flexibility is capable of making MARC schemes more robust along with providing better throughput.

5. Channel-Network Coding Based on Product Codes

We have just seen in the previous section that the combination of channel coding and linear network coding in the MARC scheme can be seen as a product code with matrix codewords having as rows the codewords of the cooperating users and as columns the codewords of the linear network coding employed at the relay node(s). This new representation gives the possibility to use any linear block code as a network code at the relay node(s). It also gives us the possibility to use product decoding algorithms, which represent real joint channel-network decoding algorithms where the combination of network and channel coding schemes are seen as a single channel code.

Based on the new representation of Figure 3, we can generalize the channel-network coding structure of multiple-access relay channels as shown in Figure 4. Here, we have the first k_r row packets belonging to the cooperating users. They are generated using an (n, k, d) linear block code. These packets can belong to one user, two users, or any number of users up to k_r different users. It is also possible to have packets generated using linear block codes with different code rates or different versions of the same packet. The result of this operation is a very flexible structure that can be adapted to help the user(s), within the cooperating set of users, that need(s) help. The remaining $n_r - k_r$ row packets are the ones forwarded by the relay node. They are obtained by applying a linear block code, denoted by (n_r, k_r, d_r), along the columns of the formed k_r row packets of the cooperating users. Here, the column linear block encoder represents the network coding scheme of the multiple-access relay channel.

This network coding scheme is quite general and can be selected according to our need and the channel quality of the different links. This gives a motivation to use more powerful network coding schemes for MARC.

As the first k_r rows (packets) of this formed matrix are received by the base station receiver via the direct links of the cooperating users, the relay node only forwards the remaining $n_r - k_r$ row packets of this formed channel coding matrix. These forwarded packets by the relay node are in fact the redundancy produced by the network coding scheme. The base station receiver takes the packets received directly from the cooperating users and the packets received from the relay node to form a received version of the complete product code matrix. Hence, a single decoder as shown in Figure 5, for joint channel-network decoding can be used at the base station receiver. A single decoder can take advantage of the channel variations in the different branches of MARC and, as a result, better diversity gain can be obtained due to the involvement of the different radio links at the receiver. As mentioned earlier, several decoding algorithms for product codes exist in the literature and can be used at the base station receiver for a joint channel-network decoding of the proposed coding structure of the multiple-access relay channel. These decoding algorithms range from the simple generalized minimum distance decoding algorithm to the complex iterative turbo decoding of product codes [20–25].

To illustrate the performance of the proposed channel-network coding structure and the possible diversity gain order that can be achieved, we will consider the performance limits of two basic decoding structures: hard decision decoding and soft decision decoding as given in the following subsections. In Section 6, some variations of different decoding algorithms are used to generate bit error rate performance of MARC using computer simulations.

5.1. Hard Decision Decoding. Consider the multiple-access relay channel of Figure 1 and assume that the product code $(n_r n, k_r k, d_r d)$ is used as the channel-network coding structure. The base station receiver collects the received packets

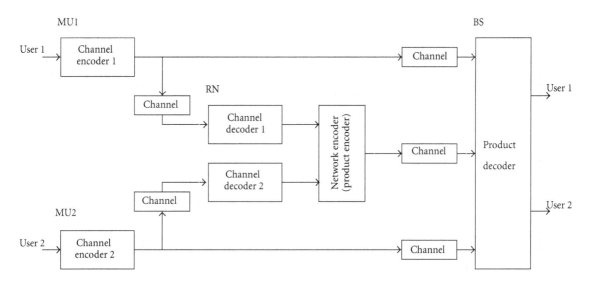

FIGURE 5: Joint channel-network decoding structure for a multiple-access relay channel based on the new proposed representation.

from the cooperating users and the network-coded packets received from the relay node and forms the received product code codeword matrices. These codeword matrices are then demodulated and decoded using a hard decision product decoder to estimate the information data of the cooperating users. To illustrate the diversity gain order for this decoding algorithm, let us consider the case when the different links have the same received SNR.

Let us denote the modulated coded symbols of the codeword matrix m shown in Figure 4 by

$$s_{i,m}, \quad i = 0, 1, \ldots, n \times n_r \quad (21)$$

and the corresponding received sample by y_i with

$$y_{i,m} = h_i s_{i,m} + z_i, \quad i = 0, 1, \ldots, n \times n_r, \quad (22)$$

where h_i is the channel fading coefficient and z_i is a complex additive white Gaussian noise sample.

With hard-decision decoding, demodulation and decoding are accomplished separately. Assuming uncorrelated radio links and full interleaving for the different link packets, the codeword error probability can be upper bounded as [28, page 456]

$$P_p \leq \left(2^{k_r k} - 1\right)\left[4p(1-p)\right]^{d_r d/2}, \quad (23)$$

where p is the bit error probability of the link and depends on the modulation scheme employed. For the particular case of coherent BPSK modulation and a Rayleigh fading channel, p is given by [28, page 891]

$$p = \frac{1}{2}\left(1 - \sqrt{\frac{\gamma_0}{1 + \gamma_0}}\right) \leq \frac{1}{4\gamma_0}, \quad (24)$$

where $\gamma_0 = \gamma_1 = \gamma_2 = \gamma_3$ is the average received SNR of the coded symbol.

Substituting (24) into (23), the upper bound on the codeword error probability can be rewritten as follows:

$$P_p \leq \left(2^{k k_r} - 1\right)\left(\frac{1}{\gamma_0}\right)^{d_r d/2}. \quad (25)$$

Hence, when all the links have the same SNR, a diversity gain of order $d_r d/2$ is obtained with this hard decision decoding. Hence, with a simple hard decision decoder it is possible to achieve a diversity gain of order $d_r d/2$ as compared to $d/2$ for the direct link of the user. Note that this diversity gain is of the same order as that obtained in Section 3 for separate channel-network coding where soft decision decoding is employed for network decoding and hard decision decoding for the individual channel coding of the cooperating users. With more powerful decoders, it will be possible to achieve even higher diversity gain.

5.2. Soft Decision Decoding. With soft decision decoding based on joint detection, the receiver performs demodulation and decoding of the coded matrix simultaneously. Using the expression of the received codeword samples, the receiver computes the following metric:

$$\mathcal{C}(\hat{m}) = \sum_{i=0}^{n_r n - 1} |y_{i,m} - h_i s_{i,\hat{m}}|^2, \quad (26)$$

for all possible codewords of the product code.

The receiver then chooses the codeword matrix that gives the minimum metric in (26) and declares it as the network and channel decoded symbols of links $1, 2, \ldots, k_r$.

Assuming uncorrelated links with Rayleigh fading channels and coherent BPSK modulation, an upper bound on the pairwise error probability of choosing a wrong codeword can be derived in a similar manner as done in Section 3. Assuming that codeword k was transmitted, the pairwise error probability of choosing a codeword m instead of k can be written as follows:

$$P_2(\mathbf{s}_k \longrightarrow \mathbf{s}_m)$$

$$\leq \frac{1}{2} \prod_{i=0}^{N_{k,m}-1} \left(\frac{1}{1 + \left(\sigma^2 \left| s_{p_{i,k,m},k} - s_{p_{i,k,m},m} \right|^2 / 2N_0 \right)} \right), \quad (27)$$

where $N_{k,m}$ is the number of positions within the codeword matrix for which the two codewords differ and $p_{i,k,m}$ is the ith index of the position.

An upper bound on the codeword error probability is then obtained by averaging the pairwise error probability of (27) over all possible codewords and is written as [31, page 460]

$$P_p \leq \frac{1}{2} \sum_{m=1}^{2^{k_r k}-1} \prod_{i=0}^{N_{0,m}-1} \left(\frac{1}{1 + \left(\sigma^2 \left| s_{p_{i,0,m},0} - s_{p_{i,0,m},m} \right|^2 / 2N_0 \right)} \right)$$

$$\leq \frac{1}{2} \sum_{m=1}^{2^{k_r k}-1} \prod_{i=0}^{N_{0,m}-1} \left(\frac{1}{1 + \delta_{i,m} \gamma_{i,m}} \right), \quad (28)$$

where

$$\delta_{i,m} = \frac{\left| s_{p_{i,0,m},0} - s_{p_{i,0,m},m} \right|^2}{4 E_{p_{i,0,m}}}, \quad \text{with } s_{p_{i,0,m},0} \neq s_{p_{i,0,m},m}, \quad (29)$$

$$\gamma_{i,m} = \frac{2\sigma^2 E_{p_{i,0,m}}}{N_0}.$$

Here $E\{|s_{p_{i,0,m},m}|^2\} = E_{p_{i,0,m}}$ and $2\sigma^2 = E\{|h_i|^2\}$.

At high SNR on the links, the codeword error probability in (28) is limited by the minimum Hamming distance $d_r d$ of the product code. Hence, for high SNR values, the codeword error probability can be upper bounded as

$$P_p \leq \frac{2^{k_r k} - 1}{2} \prod_{i=0}^{d_r d-1} \left(\frac{1}{1 + \delta_i \gamma_i} \right), \quad (30)$$

where

$$\delta_i = \min_{m \neq 0} \frac{\left| s_{p_{i,0,m},0} - s_{p_{i,0,m},m} \right|^2}{4 E_{p_{i,0,m}}}. \quad (31)$$

For the case of coherent BPSK modulation and assuming the same average received SNR on the three link of MARC, that is, $\gamma_i = \gamma_0$, for all i, we have ($\delta_i = 1$) and the expression in (30) becomes

$$P_p \leq \frac{2^{k_r k} - 1}{2} \left(\frac{1}{1 + \gamma_0} \right)^{d_r d}, \quad (32)$$

which shows that a diversity gain of order $d d_r$ can be obtained with soft decision decoding, which is double of that obtained with hard decision decoding. However, soft decision decoding has a high complexity that increases exponentially with the number of codewords. One possibility to reduce the complexity of such decoders is to employ soft decision decoding on the column codes of the product channel-network coding scheme and apply hard decision decoding on the row codes. Further improvement can be obtained by using multiple iterations. This is illustrated in the numerical results section for different coding schemes and compared to that of separate channel-network decoding.

Depending on the type of decoding scheme used at the receiver, a diversity gain order ranging from $d_r d/2$ to $d_r d$ can be obtained. This diversity gain depends on the complexity of the decoder used. A practical and efficient decoding structure for product codes is to employ iterative decoding where each iteration consists of a column decoder followed by a row decoder [20, 25]. This type of decoding algorithm is a good compromise between performance and complexity and is well suited for large product codes.

6. Numerical Results

In this section we will focus on two things. First, we will show that joint network and channel coding based on product code representation improves the error performance of users as compared to separate network-channel decoding. Then, we will illustrate that by using a better network coding scheme at the relay node, links can be made more reliable as compared to the conventional XOR-based method. The radio channel is modeled as flat Rayleigh fading channel and uncorrelated for the different links. It is further assumed that the different links have the same average received SNR, unless specified. Moreover, the γ_i for link i in the simulation results represents the average received SNR for the uncoded symbols.

6.1. XOR-Based Network Coding. Consider the MARC scheme with two users and XOR-based network coding at the relay node. The user channel encoder is taken as a $(7, 4, 3)$ Hamming code. Hence, with the new representation presented in Section 3, the equivalent channel-network coding scheme is a $(21, 8, 6)$ block code. For separate channel-network decoding, we assume soft decision decoding for the network coding and hard decision decoding for the user channel coding as discussed in Section 3. For joint network-channel coding, we assume a soft-decision product decoder as discussed in Section 5.2. Figure 6 illustrates the average bit error rate of the MARC scheme for both separate channel-network decoding and joint channel-network decoding based on the product representation. It is observed that joint channel-network decoding based on the new representation outperforms separate channel-network decoding over all ranges of SNRs. For instance, at a bit error rate of 10^{-3}, a coding gain of about 3 dB is obtained as compared to separate channel-network decoding.

Figure 6 also illustrates the average bit error rate of the MARC for both separate and joint channel-network decoding when the relay link is 10 dB better than that of the direct link. It can be observed that both separate and joint decoding algorithms benefit from the good quality of the relay link in

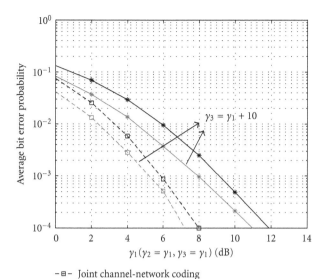

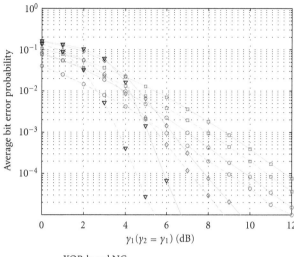

FIGURE 6: Performance of the proposed joint channel-network coding scheme for the XOR-based network coding over Rayleigh fading channels for a $(7, 4, 3)$ user channel code. All the links have the same average received SNR unless specified.

FIGURE 7: Performance of the product-based NC scheme for MARC over Rayleigh fading channels for different network coding schemes and fixed user channel coding. Same average received SNR on the direct links and two SNR cases for the relay node-to-base station link.

the same way. The relative coding gain is about the same, a 3 dB gain is obtained with joint channel-network decoding at a bit error rate of 10^{-3} as compared to separate channel-network decoding.

6.2. Channel-Network Coding Based on Product Codes.

The proposed new representation of channel-network coding for the MARC scheme gives the possibility to employ more powerful network coding schemes. In this subsection, we look at the interaction between channel and network coding for joint channel-network decoding based on the proposed representation. For that, we will fix one coding scheme, vary the other coding scheme, and assess the benefit that they can provide to the MARC scheme.

First, we assume a fixed channel encoder for the individual users. For that we consider the linear block code $(15, 11, 3)$ as the individual channel code of the user and look at different channel coding schemes for the network coding scheme, (n_r, k_r, d_r). To keep the efficiency or rate almost the same as that of XOR-based network coding scheme, network coding schemes with feasible code rates close to 2/3 are considered. Figure 7 illustrates the average bit error rate of MARC as a function of the average received uncoded SNR over Rayleigh fading channels when all the links have the same average received SNR. The product decoder considered at the base station is an iterative hard decision decoder [25] with a total of 4 iterations. It is observed that, without affecting the efficiency of MARC, the average bit error probability of the link has been improved considerably in comparison to that of conventional XOR-based network coding. For instance, using $(7, 4, 3)$ as a network coding scheme, a gain of nearly 2 dB can be observed at a bit error rate of 10^{-3}, as compared to conventional XOR-based

network coding. With the proposed new representation, the cooperating users benefit from the use of more powerful network encoders at the relay node.

More powerful network coding schemes can improve the error performance of MARC further as illustrated in Figure 7. For instance, a gain of nearly 3 dB and 4 dB can be obtained by using $(31, 21, 5)$ and $(63, 39, 9)$, respectively, as compared to the conventional XOR-based network coding, at a bit error rate of 10^{-3}.

Having a good link between the relay node and the base station improves the performance of all schemes as illustrated in Figure 7. It is observed that a better link quality between the relay node and the base station improves the performance of the MARC scheme and this improvement is more pronounced with powerful network coding schemes.

Another type of interaction between channel coding and network coding can be obtained by fixing the network coding scheme and varying the user channel coding schemes. Figure 8 shows the average bit error probability of MARC for different user channel coding schemes and a fixed network coding scheme when all links have the same average received SNR. It is observed that the relative gain of product-based network coding is higher than that of the XOR-based network coding scheme. For instance, the relative gain between the user channel codes $(7, 4, 3)$ and $(15, 5, 7)$ is nearly 2 dB for the XOR-based scheme at a bit error rate equal to 10^{-4}. On the other hand, the relative gain between the two codes is nearly 3 dB for the product-based scheme at the same bit error rate. This improvement is due to the joint decoding

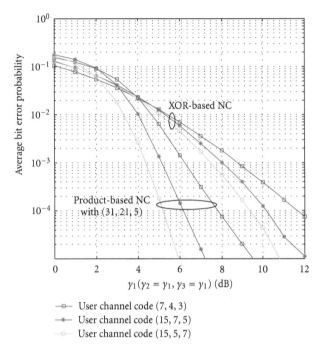

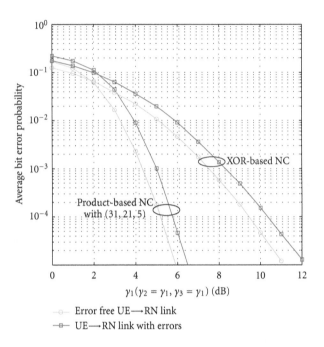

FIGURE 8: Performance of the proposed joint channel-network coding scheme for MARC over Rayleigh fading channels for different user channel coding schemes. All links have the same average received SNR.

FIGURE 9: Performance of the product-based network coding scheme for the case of nonideal links between the mobile users (UE) and the relay (RN). The user channel code is a $(15, 5, 7)$ block code and the UE-RN SNR is assumed 10 dB higher than that of the direct link.

structure, based on the new representation, where channel coding and network coding are seen as one single code at the receiver.

So far, we considered a MARC scheme with perfect links between the cooperating users (UE) and the relay node (RN). Nonideal links will of course have an impact on the link performance of MARC. In general, there are many relay nodes within the cell and users cooperate via the relay node that is closest to them. Here, we assume that the average SNR between the cooperating users and the relay node is 10 dB higher than that of the direct link between the mobile users and the base station. Figure 9 illustrates the obtained bit error probability of the product-based NC and that of the XOR-based NC as a function of the average received SNR of the direct link. It is observed that the nonideal nature of the link between the cooperating users and the relay node affects the performance of both schemes in the same way with an experienced degradation of about 0.5 dB over most ranges of SNRs.

Grouping users with different received average SNRs will have an impact on the link performance of both users. Figure 10 illustrates a study case where the sum of SNRs for the direct links of the users is assumed constant, that is, $\gamma_2 + \gamma_1 = 10$ dB and the average received SNR of the relay node link is assumed constant with $\gamma_3 = 10$ dB. Here, it is assumed that half of the packets are sent by user 1 with an average received SNR equal to γ_1, while the other half is sent by user 2 with an average received SNR equal to γ_2. The channel code used for both methods is $(15, 7, 5)$. However, the code of the product-based NC is $(31, 21, 5)$; that is, user

1 has $N_1 = 10$ packets and user 2 has $N_2 = 11$ packets. The network coding scheme has about the same efficiency as that of the XOR-based NC scheme. It is observed from Figure 10 that the cooperating users benefit most from the cooperation when the average received SNRs of their direct links are almost equal. This is true for both XOR-based and product-based network coding schemes. When one of the cooperating users has a bad direct link, both users will experience bad link performance regardless of the other user's direct link quality. This causes a problem for the XOR-based NC scheme where only two packets are involved in the NC operation at the relay node. The proposed product-based NC scheme involves many packets in the NC operation which gives some flexibility in the allocation process and might help ensuring a good quality of service for both users.

For instance, one simple way to balance the performance of the cooperating users in the product-based NC scheme is by splitting the total number of packets between the users according to their experienced average received SNRs on their direct links. For a product-based NC scheme with a code (n_r, k_r, d_r), we have a total of k_r packets for the cooperating users. Hence, we may define the number of packets allocated to user 1 as

$$N_1 = \text{round}\left(k_r \times \frac{\gamma_1}{\gamma_1 + \gamma_2}\right) \tag{33}$$

and that allocated to user 2 as $N_2 = k_r - N_1$, where round $(\cdot)$ denotes the nearest integer function. Figure 11 illustrates the allocated packets as a function of the average received SNR of user 1 direct link with $\gamma_2 = 10 - \gamma_1$. It is observed

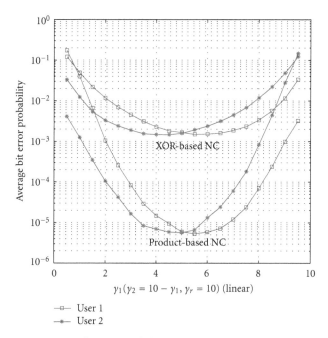

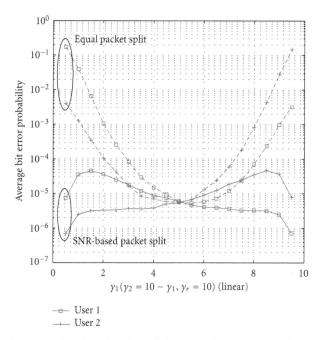

FIGURE 10: Performance of the proposed joint channel-network coding scheme for MARC over Rayleigh fading channels for different average received SNRs with $\gamma_3 = 10\,\text{dB}$ and $\gamma_2 = 10 - \gamma_1$.

FIGURE 12: SNR-based packet split in the product-based NC scheme and its effect on the bit error probability of the cooperating users. Different average received SNRs are considered with $\gamma_3 = 10\,\text{dB}$ and $\gamma_2 = 10 - \gamma_1$.

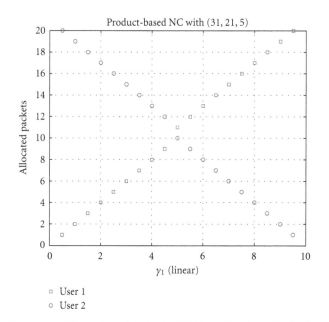

FIGURE 11: Allocated packets in the SNR-based packet split for the product-based NC scheme as a function of the average received SNR of user 1 direct link. Different average received SNRs are considered with $\gamma_3 = 10\,\text{dB}$ and $\gamma_2 = 10 - \gamma_1$.

that this allocation procedure allocates more packets to the user having a better direct link quality. This should allow the strong user to help the weak user and provide a good link quality for both cooperating users. The benefits of the strong user is of course a higher data rate as it gets more packets than the weak user.

It is observed from the obtained results in Figure 12 that, with this simple SNR-based allocation procedure, the gap between the error probabilities of the users is reduced considerably and now both cooperating users can enjoy good link performance even if one of them has a weak direct link.

7. Conclusions

This paper looked at the interaction between channel coding and network coding in a MARC scheme. It was shown that this interaction can be represented by a product code with rows formed by the individual packets of the users and columns formed by the network coding scheme used at the relay node. This new structure allowed performing network and channel decoding jointly by using a single decoder at the base station receiver. This decoder takes advantage of the channel variations of the different links of MARC and allows a better interaction between their coding schemes. With this new representation, more powerful network coding schemes can be used without affecting the overall efficiency of the MARC scheme. The obtained results showed that, even with simple linear network codes, the proposed method outperforms conventional XOR-based network coding schemes over all ranges of SNRs. The relative gain between joint channel-network coding using the proposed method, and the separate network and channel coding is comparable to that obtained in [19], where distributed turbo codes are used as the joint network and channel decoding algorithm. The proposed new representation also provides a good flexibility in the cooperation process where several packets can be combined at the relay node. These packets can be allocated in a way that ensures good link quality for both cooperating users. For that, we have proposed an SNR-based packet allocation scheme that splits the packets between the users according to their experienced average received SNRs on their direct links. This procedure provides a trade-off between data rate and link quality where the strong user can increase its data rate and help improve the link quality of the weak user.

In our work, we have assumed that all cooperating users are employing the same channel encoder and it will be interesting to investigate the case when users have different channel encoders. It will also be interesting to consider convolutional codes instead of block codes and their implication on the proposed representation of the joint channel-network coding structure of MARC schemes.

References

[1] A. Sendonaris, E. Erkip, and B. Aazhang, "Increasing uplink capacity via user cooperation diversity," in *Proceedings of the IEEE International Symposium on Information Theory (ISIT '98)*, Cambridge, Mass, USA, August 1998.

[2] J. N. Laneman and G. W. Wornell, "Energy-efficient antenna sharing and relaying for wireless networks," in *Proceedings of the IEEE Wireless Communications and Networking Conference (WCNC '00)*, pp. 7–12, September 2000.

[3] A. Sendonaris, E. Erkip, and B. Aazhang, "User cooperation diversity—part I: system description," *IEEE Transactions on Communications*, vol. 51, no. 11, pp. 1927–1938, 2003.

[4] J. N. Laneman, D. N. C. Tse, and G. W. Wornell, "Cooperative diversity in wireless networks: efficient protocols and outage behavior," *IEEE Transactions on Information Theory*, vol. 50, no. 12, pp. 3062–3080, 2004.

[5] R. Ahlswede, N. Cai, S.-Y. R. Li, and R. W. Yeung, "Network information flow," *IEEE Transactions on Information Theory*, vol. 46, no. 4, pp. 1204–1216, 2000.

[6] Y. Wu, P. A. Chou, and S. Y. Kung, "Information exchange in wireless networks with network coding and physical layer broadcast," in *Proceedings of the Conference on Information Sciences and Systems*, The Johns Hopkins University, March 2005.

[7] S. Katti, D. Katabi, W. Hu, H. Rahul, and M. M. Medard, "The importance of being opportunistic: practical network coding for wireless environments," in *Proceedings of the 43rd Annual Allerton Conference on Communication, Control, and Computing*, Monticello, Ill, USA, September 2005.

[8] P. Larsson, N. Johansson, and K. E. Sunell, "Coded bi-directional relaying," in *Proceedings of the IEEE 63rd Vehicular Technology Conference (VTC '06)*, pp. 851–855, Melbourne, Australia, May 2006.

[9] X. Bao and J. Li, "Matching code-on-graph with network-on-graph: adaptive network coding for wireless relay networks," in *Proceedings of the 43rd Allerton Conference on Communication, Control, and Computing*, September 2005.

[10] X. Bao and J. Li, "On the outage properties of Adaptive Network Coded Cooperation (ANCC) in large wireless networks," in *Proceedings of the IEEE International Conference on Acoustics, Speech and Signal Processing (ICASSP '06)*, pp. IV57–IV60, May 2006.

[11] L. Xiao, T. E. Fuja, J. Kliewer, and D. J. Costello Jr., "Nested codes with multiple interpretations," in *Proceedings of the 40th Annual Conference on Information Sciences and Systems (CISS '06)*, pp. 851–856, March 2006.

[12] C. Hausl, F. Schreckenbach, I. Oikonomidis, and G. Bauch, "Iterative network and channel decoding on a tanner graph," in *Proceedings of the 43rd Allerton Conference on Communication, Control, and Computing*, September 2005.

[13] L. Chen, R. A. Carrasco, S. LeGoff, and I. J. Wassell, "Cooperative amplify-and-forward with trellis coded modulation," in *Proceedings of the IEEE Wireless Communications and Networking Conference (WCNC '09)*, April 2009.

[14] D. Tuninetti and C. Fragouli, "Processing along the way: forwarding vs. coding," in *Proceedings of the International Symposium on Information Theory and its Applications (IEEE ISITA '04)*, October 2004.

[15] M. Janani, A. Hedayat, T. E. Hunter, and A. Nosratinia, "Coded cooperation in wireless communications: space-time transmission and iterative decoding," *IEEE Transactions on Signal Processing*, vol. 52, no. 2, pp. 362–371, 2004.

[16] B. Zhao and M. C. Valenti, "Distributed turbo coded diversity for relay channel," *Electronics Letters*, vol. 39, no. 10, pp. 786–787, 2003.

[17] Y. Cao and B. Vojcic, "Cooperative coding using serial concatenated convolutional codes," in *Proceedings of the IEEE Wireless Communications and Networking Conference (WCNC '05)*, pp. 1001–1006, March 2005.

[18] A. Chakrabarti, A. de Baynast, A. Sabharwal, and B. Aazhang, "LDPC code design for half-duplex decode and forward relaying," in *Proceedings of the 43rd Allerton Conference on Communication, Control, and Computing*, September 2005.

[19] C. Hausl and P. Dupraz, "Joint network-channel coding for the multiple-access relay channel," in *Proceedings of the 3rd Annual IEEE Communications Society on Sensor and Ad hoc Communications and Networks (Secon '06)*, pp. 817–822, September 2006.

[20] G. D. Forney Jr., "Generalized minimum distance decoding," *IEEE Transactions on Information Theory*, vol. 12, no. 2, pp. 125–131, 1966.

[21] J. Hagenauer, L. Papke, E. Offer, and L. Papke, "Iterative decoding of binary block and convolutional codes," *IEEE Transactions on Information Theory*, vol. 42, no. 2, pp. 429–445, 1996.

[22] R. M. Pyndiah, "Near-optimum decoding of product codes: block turbo codes," *IEEE Transactions on Communications*, vol. 46, no. 8, pp. 1003–1010, 1998.

[23] A. R. Calderbank, "Multilevel codes and multistage decoding," *IEEE Transactions on Communications*, vol. 37, no. 3, pp. 222–229, 1989.

[24] L. R. Bahl, J. Cocke, F. Jelinek, and J. Raviv, "Optimal decoding of linear codes for minimizing symbol error rate," *IEEE Transactions on Information Theory*, vol. 20, no. 2, pp. 284–287, 1974.

[25] O. Al-Askary, *Coding and iterative decoding of concatenated multi-level codes for the rayleigh fading channel [Ph.D. thesis]*, Royal Institute of Technology (KTH), Stockholm Sweden, 2006.

[26] Y. Chen, S. Kishore, and J. Li, "Wireless diversity through network coding," in *Proceedings of the IEEE Wireless Communications and Networking Conference (WCNC '06)*, pp. 1681–1686, April 2006.

[27] T. U. R. Ahsin and S. B. Slimane, "Detection strategies in cooperative relaying with network coding," in *Proceedings of the IEEE 21st International Symposium on Personal Indoor and Mobile Radio Communications (PIMRC '10)*, pp. 12–17, September 2010.

[28] J. G. Proakis, *Digital Communications*, McGraw-Hill International, 4th edition, 2001.

[29] S. Haykin, *Digital Communications*, John Wiley & Sons, 1988.

[30] P. Elias, "Error free coding," *IEEE Transactions on Information Theory*, vol. 4, pp. 29–37, 1954.

[31] L. Ahlin, J. Zander, and S. B. Slimane, *Principles of Wireless Communications*, Narayana Press, Copenhagen, Denmark, 2006.

8

Approximate Core Allocation for Large Cooperative Security Games

Saman Zonouz[1] and Parisa Haghani[2]

[1] *University of Miami, Coral Gables, FL, USA*
[2] *University of Illinois, Champaign, IL, USA*

Correspondence should be addressed to Parisa Haghani, parisa.haghany@gmail.com

Academic Editors: S. Cheng, T. Erseghe, W. Jiang, and V. Tralli

Coalition games have been recently used for modeling a variety of security problems. From securing the wireless transmissions in decentralized networks to employing effective intrusion detection systems in large organizations, cooperation among interested parties has shown to bring significant benefits. Motivating parties to abide to a solution is, however, a key problem in bridging the gap between theoretical models and practical solutions. Benefits should be distributed among players (wireless nodes in a network, different divisions of an organization in security risk management, or organizations cooperating to fight spam), such that no group of players is motivated to break off and form a new coalition. This problem, referred to as *core allocation*, grows computationally very expensive with a large number of agents. In this paper, we present a novel approximate core allocation algorithm, called the bounding boxed core (BBC), for large cooperative security games in characteristic form that rely on superadditivity. The proposed algorithm is an *anytime* (an algorithm is called *anytime* if it can be interrupted at any time point during execution to return an answer whose value, at least in certain classes of stochastic processes, improves in expectation as a function of the computation time) algorithm based on iterative state space search for better solutions. Experimental results on a 25-player game, with roughly 34 million coalitions, show that BBC shrinks the 25-dimensional bounding-box to 10^{-15} times its initial hypervolume.

1. Introduction

In the recent years, there has been a growing interest for modeling defenders in different security problems with coalition games. This is mainly due to results which confirm that many security goals can be better reached through cooperation among the interested parties. Millions of connected computers and networks of them have turned security to a problem characterized by interdependence [4]. In this interconnected world of computers, the security of a particular user is not independent of others and it heavily depends on the efforts of other users. As a prominent example in Internet security, in combating spam and unsolicited communications, the Organization for Economic Co-operation and Development recommends international cooperation and promotes cross-border enforcement cooperation on spam-related problems [18].

With regard to cyber attacks originated from any particular country, a recent study [13] shows that international cooperation in enforcement as measured by the indicator of joining the convention on cybercrimes, can deter cyber attacks by up to 24%. Cooperative attack and defense for a range of distributed network applications, with an emphasis on phishing, has been examined in [23] and the results highlight the need for cooperative information sharing.

Building suitable models based on cooperation for a variety of security problems has been the subject of some recent studies. Coalition game theory has been used for security risk management [22] in divisions of an organization as well as secure wireless transmissions [16] in ad hoc wireless networks, and against network security attacks [5]. In detecting [12, 19] and mitigating [21] DDos attacks, cooperation has been affirmed. While many studies advocate the use of coalition games for modeling large scale security problems, the question of revenue allocation, as an important step in turning these game theoretical models to practical robust solutions, has not been studied and warrants greater attention.

Cooperative game theory studies the problem of revenue allocation for a set of n participants, called players, in a joint project where a value function v is defined for each subset of players, representing the revenue achieved by the players in that subset without assistance of other players. In the context of security, we call these games *cooperative security games*. In cooperative security games players are the defenders (e.g., organizations cooperating for intrusion detection) and revenue is the security benefit they achieve through cooperation. We will present a formal definition in the next Section. In general, each solution concept defines a set $\mathcal{X}$ of allocation vectors. Obtaining $\mathcal{X}$ is usually a nontrivial problem and has always been an important issue in the study of cooperative game theory. A particularly interesting theme to the study of such decision problems is that of the bounded rationality, which argues that decisions made by real-life agents may not spend an unbounded amount of resources to evaluate all the possibilities for optimal outcome [17]. Much effort has been made in the study of the bounded rationality in computational resource for solution concepts of cooperative games.

The definition of a cooperative game involves an exponential number (in the number of players) of values, one for each subset of players. Moreover, the definitions of many solution concepts, for example, the core [1], would involve an exponential number of constraints. Therefore, it becomes infeasible to get the set of fair allocation vectors $\mathcal{X}$ for a large cooperative game using traditional approaches, such as linear programming. Megiddo [25] observed that, for many games, the game value is calculated through succinctly defined structures and for such games, he suggested that finding a solution should be done by a good algorithm (following Edmonds [28]), that is, within time polynomial in the number of players. Deng and Papadimitriou [14] suggested computational complexities be taken into consideration as another measure of fairness for evaluating and comparing different solution concepts.

In this paper, we present bounding-boxed core (BBC), an approximate revenue allocation algorithm for large cooperative security games that are intractable to be solved using traditional algorithms such as linear programming. Previous work in security revenue allocation investigate all coalitions and their corresponding values before computing the core. This is not feasible with large number of players, that is, organizations that attempt to protect security of their assets, because increasing number of players result in exponential growth of the coalition space. Our algorithm, to the best of our knowledge, is the first algorithm to provide an approximate solution to this problem. In addition, we utilize the special characteristics of the core, namely, its convexity, to analyze the approximation error and provide bounds on the worst case errors.

This paper is organized as follows. In Section 2, we describe the security game model and the revenue allocation problem. In Section 3 we present an overview of related background literature. The BBC algorithm is briefly explained in Section 4. Section 5 is devoted to the bounding box shrinking algorithm. Approximate core allocation approach is discussed in Section 6. Finally, experimental results for a case study cooperative game with 25 players is presented in Section 7 and Section 8 concludes the paper.

2. Security Model and Basic Definitions

We start by describing a simplified security problem and subsequently formally define a cooperative security game. Assume a finite set of organizations denoted by $\mathcal{N} = \{1, 2, \ldots, n\}$. Each organization has its own security resources and valuable assets which it protects against security attacks. Any subset $S \subseteq \mathcal{N}$ is called a coalition. The *security profit* function $v : \mathcal{P}(\mathcal{N}) \rightarrow \mathbb{R}$ is a function with $v(\phi) = 0$, where $\mathcal{P}(\mathcal{N})$ denotes the power set of $\mathcal{N}$. For each coalition $S \subseteq \mathcal{N}$, $v(S)$ is the value of S that is interpreted as the security profit achieved by the collective action of organizations in S without any assistance of organizations in $\mathcal{N} - S$. A security cooperative game is given by specifying the security profit function, that is, a value for every coalition. The security profit can be defined based on different measures, such as security resources of a coalition, the type and probability of successful attacks against these security measures, and the expected cost of such attacks. Instead of a security profit function, a *security cost* function can be used. In this paper we only deal with profit games, however, symmetric statement holds for cost games. Security profit functions are assumed to be superadditive, that is, the value of a union of disjoint coalitions is no less than the sum of the coalitions' separate values:

$$v(S) + v(T) \le v(S \cup T) \quad \forall S, T \subseteq \mathcal{N} \ni S \cap T = \phi. \quad (1)$$

Given a pair $(\mathcal{N}, v)$, the focus is how to fairly distribute the collective income. We denote the income distributed to individual organizations by a payoff vector $x = \{x_1, x_2, \ldots, x_n\}$ satisfying $\sum_{i \in \mathcal{N}} x_i = v(\mathcal{N})$, called an allocation. An allocation vector x is called an *imputation* of the game $(\mathcal{N}, v)$ if it also satisfies the individual rationality condition:

$$v(\{i\}) \le x_i \quad \forall i \in \mathcal{N}. \quad (2)$$

As an illustrative example, consider a set of online shopping sites which are willing to cooperate against intrusion detection attacks by sharing worm and virus signatures identified by their antivirus systems. The valuable assets in this scenario consists of a database of credit-card information. We consider a dollar value as the security profit associated with an attack. Let us consider two of these shopping sites $\{1, 2\}$. Let the expected security profit of site 1 be $v(\{1\}) = c_1 - 300$, while this value is $v(\{2\}) = c_2 - 50$ for site 2. If they cooperate by sharing their signatures, the expected security profit of their coalition would be $v(\{1, 2\}) = c_1 + c_2 - 400$. The allocation problem involves assigning x_1 and x_2 in a fair manner, which also motivates the formation of a coalition.

Additional requirements for fairness, stability, and rationality lead to different sets of allocations, which are generally referred to as solution concepts. Here, we shall discuss the most important one that is the core.

Sum of the coalitions' separate values.

The concept of the core was first introduced by Gillies [1] based on the concept of subgroup rationality.

Definition 1. The core of a game $(\mathcal{N}, v)$ is defined by

$$C(v) = \left\{ x \in \mathbb{R}^{|\mathcal{N}|} : \sum_{i \in \mathcal{N}} x_i = v(\mathcal{N}); \right.$$

$$\left. \sum_{i \in S} x_i \geq v(S) \quad \forall S \subseteq \mathcal{N} \right\}. \tag{3}$$

The constraints imposed on $C(v)$ ensure that no coalition would have an incentive to split from the grand coalition $\mathcal{N}$ and do better on its own. The core is a subset of the hyperplanes defined by the equation $\sum_{i \in S} x_i = v(S)$ [16], and since the inequalities $x_i \geq v(\{i\})$ are included in (3), the core is bounded. Thus, $C(v)$ is a compact convex polyhedron, and possibly empty, of dimension at most $n - 1$. The definition of the core, involves an exponential number of constraints, therefore, exact computation of the core is infeasible in large scale games. In this paper, we present an approximate algorithm for core allocation.

3. Related Work

In the security community, there has been considerable effort in introducing models based on cooperation for defenders of a security attack, see for example [12, 19, 21, 23]. Here, we review the ones which explicitly use coalition games as their models. The authors in [22] define a coalition game for modeling risk management. In their model, divisions of an organization are the players of the game. They use an influence graph to specify the positive and negative effects that each division of the organization can have on other divisions. The security benefit of each coalition is then defined as a function involving the influence graph, the security resources of each division, and threats against vulnerabilities. They further enrich their model by introducing a friction graph which denotes the costs associated with cooperation. They analyze the formation of coalitions based on this model. Coalition game theory has also been used in modeling secure transmissions in a wireless network [16]. In this problem a set of wireless transmitters try to transmit a message to a set of destinations in presence of eavesdroppers. The goal is to avoid the overhead of cryptography and self-organize the wireless transmitter such that secure wireless communication can be achieved. Coalition of transmitters can decode-and-forward (DF) or amplify-and-forward (AF) a signal, and in this way, completely null the signal at the eavesdroppers. In another recent study, [5] models defenders of a network security attack with coalition games. They analyze coalition formation in three canonical security games described previously in [26] for non-cooperative games.

The above mentioned papers mostly consider the problem of coalition formation. In this paper, we consider another important problem, namely, revenue allocation. Much of cooperative game theory is built around the question of distributing the collective income in fair and rational manners. Different philosophies result in different solution concepts that constitute the bargaining set family, that is, the various bargaining sets [15, 24], the Kernel [20]

and the Nucleolus [11]; in effect, these notions are defined separately for each coalition structure. By contrast, the Shapley value [3], Core [1], and Von Neumann-Morgenstern solutions [6] are not a priori defined with reference to a coalition structure. In this part, we review related literature on determining the core.

One of the most important problems regarding the core is *testing nonemptiness* that is determining whether a given instance of the game has a nonempty core. Generally, determining core nonemptiness is NP-complete for cooperative games both with and without transferable utility [8]. However, recently there has been increasing interest in investigating this problem in more specific games with a description polynomial in n (number of players). As a case in point, the core nonemptiness testing problem is solvable in polynomial time for weighted graph games [14]; for minimum base game with no all-negative circuits can be solved in oracle-polynomial time [10].

Since the core is usually empty, some related solution concepts arise from the core via relaxing its constraints. Shapley and Shubik [27] recommended the concepts of (strong) ε-core and weak ε-core for a cooperative game. Their main idea is to relax the requirements of subgroup rationality by $x(S) \geq v(S) - \varepsilon$ and $x(S) \geq v(S) - \varepsilon|S|$ for each proper subset S of $\mathcal{N}$, respectively.

Later, Tijs and Driesssen [7] introduced the concept of multiplicative ε-tax core by using $x(S) \geq v(S) - \varepsilon[v(S) - \sum_{i \in S} v(\{i\})]$ instead. Faigle and Kern [9] modified the requirement of Tijs and Driessen as $x(S) \geq (1 - \varepsilon)v(S)$ to define another approximate core, called multiplicative ε-core. One explanation of these concepts is that cooperation may not be as hopeless even when the core is empty. Cooperation may be possible with the subsidies of the central authority.

All of the above mentioned algorithms need to investigate all coalitions and their corresponding values before computing the core; however, this is not feasible in cooperative games with large number of players due to the exponential growth of the coalition space.

4. The Bounding Boxed Core

The bounding-boxed Core (BBC) algorithm is a practical best-effort approach to distribute the collective security profit in an approximately fair manner among the involved organizations (players) in a given large cooperative security game $(\mathcal{N}, v)$.

More specifically, BBC consists of two main stages: tightening bounding box, and approximate core allocation. The former is an iterative global search algorithm to solve an axis-aligned smallest enclosing box problem. It finds the minimum-hypervolume n-dimensional bounding box enclosing the core, that is, closed and convex set, subject to the constraint that the edges of the box are parallel to the (Cartesian) coordinate axes. Starting from some initial large bounding box, BBC iteratively tries to tighten the bounding box, obtained at the previous iteration, by heuristically considering some useful subset of constraints by the core (3).

Consequently, a bounding box $B = [a_1, b_1] \times [a_2, b_2] \times \cdots \times [a_n, b_n]$ is generated once a given deadline is passed or some convergences condition is met. In the approximate core allocation step, BBC computes a unique payoff vector in the generated bounding box B. The allocation values for individual players are determined by calculating the gravity center of the resulting bounding box B.

5. Bounding Box Tightening

In this section, the iterative bounding box tightening algorithm is explained in details. The goal is to find the minimum-hypervolume bounding box enclosing the core $B(C(v))$ using an iterative search algorithm. We use B_t to denote the bounding box, obtained at t-th iteration step. Initially, we know that player i gets a payoff of $x_i \in [v(\{i\}), v(\mathcal{N}) - v(\mathcal{N} - \{i\})]$ in the core $C(v)$. The lower bound denotes individual rationality, that is, no player receives less than what it could get on its own; and the upper bound is obtained using one of the core constraints:

$$\sum_{j \in \mathcal{N} - \{i\}} x_j \geq v(\mathcal{N} - \{i\}), \tag{4}$$

along with the efficiency condition:

$$\sum_{i \in \mathcal{N}} x_i = v(\mathcal{N}). \tag{5}$$

Therefore, we assign as shown in (13) to be the initial, that is, $t = 0$, bounding box enclosing the core. Throughout this paper, we will use notations $B_t^l(i)$ and $B_t^u(i)$ to denote the lower and upper bounds for the ith player in the tth bounding box.

The initial bounding box B_0 is further tightened during several iterations. First, we describe the single iteration t of the tightening procedure given a permutation $\pi \in \Pi$ on the set of players:

$$\pi = (\pi(1), \pi(2), \ldots, \pi(n)), \tag{6}$$

where, π is in fact a one-to-one function from $\mathcal{N}$ onto $\mathcal{N}$. Moreover, as a shorthand notation, we use π_i^j ($i \leq j$) to denote $(\pi(i), \pi(i+1), \ldots, \pi(j))$.

5.1. Recursive Tree Construction. At each iteration t, tightening algorithm starts with constructing a full binary tree on a given permutation of players π, in a top-down manner. The root node, which covers all players π_1^n, has two children nodes denoting two disjoint subsets of $\mathcal{N}$: $\pi_1^{i_0}$ and $\pi_{i_0+1}^n$ ($1 \leq i_0 < n$). Breaking point i_0 is *optimally* determined in a way that the bounding box is tightened the most (discussed later). Recursively, children nodes are further partitioned into two disjoint subsets of their corresponding players: $\pi_1^{i_1}$, $\pi_{i_1+1}^{i_0} \subseteq \pi_1^{i_0}$, and $\pi_{i_0+1}^{i_2}$, $\pi_{i_2+1}^n \subseteq \pi_{i_0+1}^n$. Leaf nodes of the tree represent individual players, for example, $\pi_i^i = (\pi(i))$.

To determine the optimal breaking point, let us consider an arbitrary parent node which covers a subset of players π_i^k. Suppose j ($i \leq j < k$) is the breaking point so that π_i^k is

partitioned into children nodes $\pi_i^j, \pi_{j+1}^k \subseteq \pi_i^k$. Using the core constraints (3), and the bounding box B_{t-1}, obtained at the previous iteration $t - 1$, we know

$$\underline{\sum_{q \in \pi_i^k} x_q} \leq \sum_{q \in \pi_i^k} x_q \leq \overline{\sum_{q \in \pi_i^k} x_q}, \tag{7}$$

where in the root node both bounds are equal to $v(\mathcal{N})$, but in lower level nodes

$$\underline{\sum_{q \in \pi_i^k} x_q} = \max\left(\sum_{q \in \pi_i^k} B_{t-1}^l(q), v(\pi_i^k)\right),$$

$$\overline{\sum_{q \in \pi_i^k} x_q} = \min\left(\sum_{q \in \pi_i^k} B_{t-1}^u(q), v(\mathcal{N}) - v(\mathcal{N} - \pi_i^k)\right). \tag{8}$$

Similar conditions hold for children nodes, that is, π_i^j, π_{j+1}^k. Furthermore, each child node can make use of its sibling's bounds to update, that is, tighten, its own bounds. As a case in point, we update bounds on the left child, that is, π_i^j:

$$\mathcal{L}_{\pi_i^j} \leq \sum_{q \in \pi_i^j} x_q \leq \mathcal{U}_{\pi_i^j}, \tag{9}$$

where,

$$\mathcal{L}_{\pi_i^j} = \max\left(\underline{\sum_{q \in \pi_i^j} x_q}, \underline{\sum_{q \in \pi_i^k} x_q} - \overline{\sum_{q \in \pi_j^k} x_q}\right),$$

$$\mathcal{U}_{\pi_i^j} = \min\left(\overline{\sum_{q \in \pi_i^j} x_q}, \overline{\sum_{q \in \pi_i^k} x_q} - \underline{\sum_{q \in \pi_j^k} x_q}\right). \tag{10}$$

The right child also updates her bounds using the same justification. Consequently, the optimal breaking point j^* is determined using

$$j^* = \arg \max_{x_i \leq j < k, j \in \mathbb{Z}} \left(\mathcal{T}_i^j + \mathcal{T}_{j+1}^k\right), \tag{11}$$

where,

$$\mathcal{T}_i^j = \left[\left(\overline{\sum_{q \in \pi_i^j} x_q} - \underline{\sum_{q \in \pi_i^j} x_q}\right) - \left(\mathcal{U}_{\pi_i^j} - \mathcal{L}_{\pi_i^j}\right)\right], \tag{12}$$

and $\mathcal{T}_{j+1}^k$ is defined similarly. Once the optimal breaking point j^* is determined: (1) players in the parent node π_i^k are partitioned into two children coalitions $\pi_i^{j^*}, \pi_{j^*+1}^k \subseteq \pi_i^k$; (2) upper and lower bounds on children are updated. As a result, recursive tree construction procedure is terminated when it gets to leaf nodes, that is, the players' payoffs, and updates their upper and lower bounds.

Figure 1 shows how the recursive tree construction algorithm updates the initial bounding box for a sample 3-player game, that is, $\mathcal{N} = \{1, 2, 3\}$. Characteristic values for

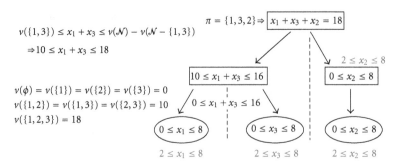

$$v(\{1,3\}) \le x_1 + x_3 \le v(\mathcal{N}) - v(\mathcal{N} - \{1,3\})$$

$$\Rightarrow 10 \le x_1 + x_3 \le 18$$

$$v(\phi) = v(\{1\}) = v(\{2\}) = v(\{3\}) = 0$$
$$v(\{1,2\}) = v(\{1,3\}) = v(\{2,3\}) = 10$$
$$v(\{1,2,3\}) = 18$$

FIGURE 1: A Sample 3-player game: tightening the initial boundingbox.

different coalitions of the game are given in the Figure 1. The initial bounding box enclosing the core

$$B_0 = ([v(\{1\}), v(\mathcal{N}) - v(\mathcal{N} - \{1\})]), \ldots, \tag{13}$$
$$[v(\{n\}), v(\mathcal{N}) - v(\mathcal{N} - \{n\})])$$

is obtained as $0 \le x_i \le 8 \ \forall i \in \mathcal{N}$ that results in $0 \le x_1 + x_3 \le 16$ as shown in Figure 1. The updated values are illustrated in red font.

5.2. Iterative Search. In the previous section, we described how a given permutation of players is used in constructing a binary tree for tightening the bounding box. The permutation used, can be chosen at random, or as we describe in this section, it can be produced by an evolutionary algorithm which tends to generated permutations which result in larger reductions of the bounding box volume. During each iteration t of the algorithm, we have a population P, for example, $P = 100$, of permutations $\Pi_t \subseteq \Pi$, which are used for tightening the bounding box as explained in Section 5.1. Once the bounding box around feasible point in the core is updated, the fitness function is calculated as follows for each permutation in current population $\pi \in \Pi_t$ and measures its quality, that is, how helpful it was in tightness improvement:

$$lcl\psi_t(\pi) = \sum_{i \in \mathcal{N}} \left| \left[B_{t,a_\pi}^u(i) - B_{t,a_\pi}^l(i) \right] - \left[B_{t,b_\pi}^u(i) - B_{t,b_\pi}^l(i) \right] \right|, \tag{14}$$

where B_{t,b_π} (B_{t,a_π}) denote bounds, at iteration t, just before (after) they are updated using recursive tree construction on permutation π. Once we have the population and the fitness function defined, iterative search algorithm proceeds to initialize a population of permutations randomly, then improves tightness of the bounding box through repetitive application of mutation, crossover, inversion and selection operators (discussed later).

Initialization. Initially, P permutations are randomly generated from the search space Π to form an initial population.

Selection. During each iteration t, a proportion 2α ($\alpha \in [0, 0.5]$) of the existing population Π_t is selected to breed a new generation of permutations Π_{t+1}. Individual permutations are selected through a fitness-based process, where top $2\alpha \cdot P$ fittest permutations, as measured by $\psi_t(.)$ (14), are selected.

Reproduction. The next step is to generate the next generation population of permutations Π_{t+1} from those selected. For each new permutation to be produced, a pair of *parent* permutations, that is, π_{p_1} and π_{p_2}, is selected for breeding from the pool selected previously. By producing a *child* permutation π_{child} using function composition, that is, $\pi_{child}(i) = \pi_{p_1} \circ \pi_{p_2}(i)$, a new permutation is created. New parents are selected for each child, that is, $\alpha \cdot P$ children permutations. Furthermore, $(1 - \alpha) \cdot P$ new permutations are randomly generated. These processes ultimately result in the next generation population Π_{t+1} of permutations. Generally, the average fitness will have increased by this procedure for the population, since only the most useful permutation from the previous generation are selected.

Termination. This iterative search process is repeated until a termination condition has been reached. Terminating conditions can be defined regarding various criteria, such as: (1) all possible permutations Π are investigated; (2) a predefined deadline is passed deadline < t; (3) tightness improvement in the last iteration t was less than some nonnegative threshold ϵ, that is, $\sum_{\pi \in \Pi_t} \psi_t(\pi) \le \epsilon$.

6. Approximate Core Allocation

Once the bounding box around feasible points in the core is generated (see Section 5) $B = [a_1, b_1] \times [a_2, b_2] \times \cdots \times [a_n, b_n]$, the candidate approximate core is computed as follows:

$$C_B(v) = \left(\frac{a_1 + b_1}{2}, \frac{a_2 + b_2}{2}, \ldots, \frac{a_n + b_n}{2} \right). \tag{15}$$

However, $C_B(v)$ may not be in the actual core; therefore, here we analyze the worst case error, that is, distance between the core $C(v)$ and the approximate $C_B(v)$. First, we need to define the distance between the point $C_B(v)$ and the core $C(v)$, that is, a convex set of points:

$$d(C_B(v), C(v)) = \min_{x \in C(v)} d(x, C_B(v)). \tag{16}$$

In other words, the distance between a point and a set is the infimum of the distances between the point and those in the set.

Here, we exploit the convexity of the core in analyzing the worst case error of the the approximate core, $C_B(v)$, that is defined as follows

$$\Upsilon(B) = \max_{Q \in \mathcal{C} \text{ s.t. } B(Q)=B} d(C_B(v), Q), \qquad (17)$$

where $\mathcal{C}$ is the convex set space in $\mathbb{R}^{|\mathcal{N}|}$; and $B(Q)$ denotes the minimum-volume axis-aligned bounding box around the set Q.

We first obtain Υ when $|\mathcal{N}| = 3$, and then, generalize the result to higher dimensional spaces. Given $B = [a_1, b_1] \times [a_2, b_2] \times [a_3, b_3]$, w.l.o.g. we transfer B to the origin using the linear transformation $B' = B - ((a_1 + b_1)/2, (a_2 + b_2)/2, (a_3 + b_3)/2)$; therefore, we get the bounding box B' that consists of $2 \times 3 = 6$ planes:

$$B' = \left[-\frac{\Delta_1}{2}, \frac{\Delta_1}{2}\right] \times \left[-\frac{\Delta_2}{2}, \frac{\Delta_2}{2}\right] \times \left[-\frac{\Delta_3}{2}, \frac{\Delta_3}{2}\right], \qquad (18)$$

and $C_{B'}(v) = (0, 0, 0)$, where $\Delta_i = b_i - a_i$. As discussed earlier (Section 2), the core is a convex subset of the hyperplanes. It can be shown that the worst case error $\Upsilon(B')$ (see (17)) is caused by $Q \in \mathcal{C}$ whose closest hyperplane H_Q to the point $C_{B'}(v)$ includes those 3 vertices of B', any pair of which have exactly one of the 6 bounding box planes in common:

$$p_1 = \left(\frac{\Delta_1}{2}, -\frac{\Delta_2}{2}, \frac{\Delta_3}{2}\right),$$

$$p_2 = \left(-\frac{\Delta_1}{2}, \frac{\Delta_2}{2}, \frac{\Delta_3}{2}\right), \qquad (19)$$

$$p_3 = \left(\frac{\Delta_1}{2}, \frac{\Delta_2}{2}, -\frac{\Delta_3}{2}\right);$$

therefore,

$$H_Q : x + \frac{\Delta_1}{\Delta_2}y + \frac{\Delta_1}{\Delta_3}z - \frac{\Delta_1}{2} = 0. \qquad (20)$$

Hence, $\Upsilon(B')$ is obtained as the distance between the point $C_{B'}(v)$ and H_Q:

$$\Upsilon(B') = \frac{1}{2 \times \sqrt{1/\Delta_1^2 + 1/\Delta_2^2 + 1/\Delta_3^2}}. \qquad (21)$$

As a case in point, let $\Delta_i = \Delta \quad \forall i \in \mathcal{N}$. Without considering convexity of the core, we know $\Upsilon(B') = \Delta.\sqrt{3}/2$ that is the distance between any of the vertices of B' and its gravity center $C_{B'}(v)$. But, exploiting the convexity of the core (21) yields a better result $\Upsilon(B') = \Delta.\sqrt{3}/6 < \Delta.\sqrt{3}/2$.

For higher dimensional spaces, that is, games with more than 3 players, discussions remain exactly the same and the worst case error is obtained as:

$$\Upsilon(B')$$

$$= \frac{1}{2 \times \sqrt{1/(b_1 - a_1)^2 + 1/(b_2 - a_2)^2 + \cdots + 1/(b_n - a_n)^2}}. \qquad (22)$$

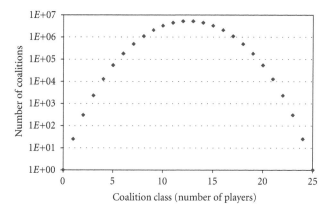

FIGURE 2: Number of coalitions in each coalition class with particular no. of players.

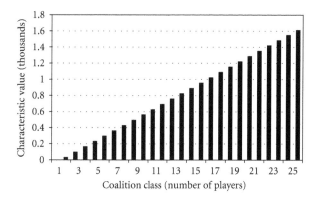

FIGURE 3: Maximum characteristic value distribution on coalition classes.

7. Evaluations

In this section, we present the results from our prototype implementation of BBC on a case study large cooperative game. The system we used for implementation was a 2.20 GHz AMD Athlon 64 processor 3700+ with 2.00 GB of memory and Windows XP SP3 operating system. Because of large number of coalitions the bottleneck is usually the memory that caused our first prototype to crash; hence, we reimplemented the whole algorithm in C++ from scratch using more sophisticated data structures to speed up the iterative search and reduce memory consumption.

Here, we present the evaluation results of the BBC algorithm for a cooperative game with 25 players in which there are about 34 million coalitions of players.

Figure 2 shows the number of coalitions in each coalition class that is defined based on its size, that is, number of players. As discussed earlier, every cooperative game is determined by its characteristic function for each coalition. Figure 3 shows the maximum characteristic value for each coalition class. As shown in the figure, value for grand coalition is 1604. Furthermore, coalition values satisfy superadditivity property.

Given the characteristic values for the cooperative game, we start iterative tightening of the 25-dimensional bounding

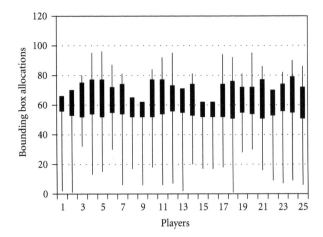

FIGURE 4: Bounding box tightening result for each dimension in $\mathbb{R}^{25}$.

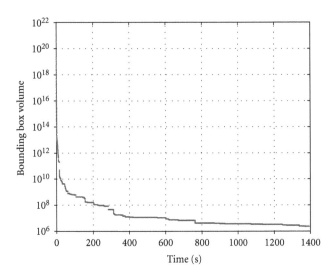

FIGURE 5: Bounding box volume improvement during iterative search.

box. Figure 4 illustrates the initial lower and upper bounds for individual dimensions, that is, players' payoffs, of the initial bounding box, as in (13), and their corresponding updated bounds. In this experiment, we assigned $P = 100$ and $\alpha = 0.3$.

Finally, bounding box volume reduction, during the iterative tightening algorithm, is shown in Figure 5 with 10^{20} scale. As illustrated in the logarithmic-scale graph, although the bounding box volume has shrank more than 10^{12} units during only a few seconds, tightening speed significantly decreases afterwards. Consequently, after about 25 minutes, bounding-box volume is 10^{-15} times its initial value.

8. Conclusion

In this paper, we present an approximate core allocation algorithm, called the bounding-boxed core (BBC), for cooperative security games with large number of organizations (players). Since the definition of core involves an

exponential number of constraints in terms of the number of organizations, it is infeasible to solve this problem for exact solutions. We present an analysis of the maximum approximation error incurred by BBC. We also proposed a heuristic search algorithm based on Genetic algorithms to search the input space. Experimental results show that BBC significantly speeds up core allocation. In modeling cooperation among large number of organizations, this is an important step in achieving a practical solution in limited time.

References

[1] D. B. Gillies, "Solutions to general non-zero-sum games," in *Contributions to the Theory of Games 4*, R. D. Luce and A. W. Tucker, Eds., Annals of Mathematics Studies, pp. 47–85, Princeton, 1959.

[2] L. S. Shapley, "Cores of convex games," *International Journal of Game Theory*, vol. 1, no. 1, pp. 11–26, 1971.

[3] L. S. Shapley, "A value for n-person games," in *Contributions to the Theory of Games 2*, H. W. Kuhn and A. W. Tucker, Eds., Annals of Mathematics Studies, pp. 307–317, Princeton, 1953.

[4] H. Kunreuther and G. Heal, "Interdependent Security," *Journal of Risk and Uncertainty*, vol. 26, no. 2-3, pp. 231–249, 2003.

[5] H. Narasimhan, V. Varadarajan, and U. Rangan, "Towards a cooperative defense model against network security attacks," in *Proceeding of the 9th Workshop on the Economics of Information Security (WEIS '10)*.

[6] J. V. Neumann and O. Morgenstern, *Theory of Games and Economic Behaviour*, Princeton, 1944.

[7] S. H. Tijs and T. S. H. Driessen, "Extensions of solution concepts by means of multiplicative ε-tax games," *Mathematical Social Sciences*, vol. 12, no. 1, pp. 9–20, 1986.

[8] V. Conitzer and T. Sandholm, "Complexity of determining nonemptiness of the core," in *Proceedings of the 4th ACM Conference on Electronic Commerce*, pp. 230–231, June 2003.

[9] U. Faigle and W. Kern, "On some approximately balanced combinatorial cooperative games," *Methods and Models of Operations Research*, vol. 38, no. 2, pp. 141–152, 1993.

[10] H. Nagamochi, D. Z. Zeng, N. Kabutoya, and T. Ibaraki, "Complexity of the minimum base game on matroids," *Mathematics of Operations Research*, vol. 22, no. 1, pp. 146–164, 1997.

[11] D. Schmeidler, "The nucleolus of a characteristic function game," *SIAM Journal of Applied Mathematics*, vol. 17, no. 1163, 1170 pages, 1969.

[12] D. Frincke, D. Tobin, J. Mcconnell, J. Marconi, and D. and Polla, "A framework for cooperative intrusion detection," in *Proceedings of the 21st NIST-NCSC National Information Systems Security Conference*, pp. 361–373, 1998.

[13] Q. Hong Wang and S. Hyun Kim, "Cyber attacks: Cross-country interdependence and enforcement," in *Proceeding of the 8th Work shop on the Economics of Information Security (WEIS 2009)*.

[14] X. Deng and C. Papadimitriou, "On the complexity of cooperative game solution concepts," *Mathematics of Operations Research*, vol. 19, pp. 257–266, 1994.

[15] M. Davis and M. Maschler, "Existence of stable payoff configurations for cooperative games," in *Essays in Mathematical Economics in Honor of Oskar Morgenstern*, M. Shubik, Ed., pp. 39–52, Princeton, 1967.

[16] W. Saad, Z. Han, T. Başar, M. Debbah, and A. Hjørungnes, "Distributed coalition formation games for secure wireless transmission," *Mobile Networks and Applications*, vol. 16, no. 2, pp. 231–245, 2011.

[17] H. A. Simon, "Theories of bounded rationality," in *Decision and Organization*, C. Radner and R. Radner, Eds., pp. 161–176, 1972.

[18] Report of the OECD task force on spam, "Antispam toolkit of recommended policies and measures," Tech. Rep., Directorate for Science, Technology and Industry, Committee on Consumer Policy Committee for Information, Computer and Communications Policy, 2006.

[19] F. Cuppens and A. Miège, "Alert correlation in a cooperative intrusion detection framework," in *Proceedings of the Symposium on Security and Privacy*, pp. 202–215, IEEE Computer Society, Washington, DC, USA, May 2002.

[20] M. Davis and M. Maschler, "The kernel of a cooperative game," *Naval Research Logistics*, vol. 12, pp. 223–259, 1965.

[21] D. Nojiri, J. Rowe, and K. Levitt, "Cooperative response strategies for large scale attack mitigation," in *Proceedings of the 3rd DARPA Information Survivability Conference and Exposition (DISCEX '03)*, pp. 293–302, 2003.

[22] W. Saad, T. Alpcan, T. Başar, and A. Hjørungnes, "Coalitional game theory for security risk management," in *Proceedings of the 5th International Conference on Internet Monitoring and Protection (ICIMP '10)*, pp. 35–40, Washington, DC, USA, May 2010.

[23] T. Moore, "Cooperative attack and defense in distributed networks," Tech. Rep. UCAM-CL-TR-718, Computer Laboratory, University of Cambridge, 2008.

[24] R. J. Aumann and M. Maschler, "The bargaining set for cooperative games," in *Advances in Game Theory*, M. Dresher, L. S. Shapley, and A. W. Tucker, Eds., Annals of Mathematics Studies, pp. 443–476, Princeton, 1964.

[25] N. Megiddo, "Computational complexity and the game theory approach to cost allocation for a tree," *Mathematics of Operations Research*, vol. 3, pp. 189–196, 1978.

[26] J. Grossklags, N. Christin, and J. Chuang, "Secure or insure? a game-theoretic analysis of information security games," in *Proceedings of the 17th International Conference on World Wide Web (WWW '08)*, pp. 209–218, New York, NY, USA, April 2008.

[27] L. Shapley and M. Shubik, "Quasi-cores in a monetary economy with nonconvex preference," *Econometrica*, vol. 34, pp. 805–827, 1966.

[28] J. Edmonds, "Path, tree, and flowers," *Canadian Journal of Mathematics*, vol. 17, pp. 449–469, 1965.

9

Optimizing Virtual Private Network Design Using a New Heuristic Optimization Method

Hongbing Lian and András Faragó

Erik Jonsson School of Engineering and Computer Science, University of Texas at Dallas, Richardson, TX 75083, USA

Correspondence should be addressed to Hongbing Lian, lian0716@yahoo.com

Academic Editors: A. Maaref, C. Pomalaza-Ráez, and A. Zanella

In virtual private network (VPN) design, the goal is to implement a logical overlay network on top of a given physical network. We model the traffic loss caused by blocking not only on isolated links, but also at the network level. A successful model that captures the considered network level phenomenon is the well-known reduced load approximation. We consider here the optimization problem of maximizing the carried traffic in the VPN. This is a hard optimization problem. To deal with it, we introduce a heuristic local search technique called landscape smoothing search (LSS). This study first describes the LSS heuristic. Then we introduce an improved version called fast landscape smoothing search (FLSS) method to overcome the slow search speed when the objective function calculation is very time consuming. We apply FLSS to VPN design optimization and compare with well-known optimization methods such as simulated annealing (SA) and genetic algorithm (GA). The FLSS achieves better results for this VPN design optimization problem than simulated annealing and genetic algorithm.

1. Introduction

In the VPN setting the goal is to implement a logical overlay network on top of a given physical network. We consider here the optimization problem of maximizing the carried traffic in the VPN. In other words, we want to minimize the loss caused by blocking some of the offered traffic, due to insufficient capacity in the logical links.

A key feature in the VPN setting is that the underlying physical network is already given. Thus, our degree of freedom lies only in dimensioning the logical (virtual) links. However, since the given physical link capacities must be obeyed and a physical link may be shared by several logical links, we can reduce the blocking on a logical link possibly only by taking away capacity from other logical links. Therefore, we may be able to improve a logical link only by degrading others. The above described situation leads to a hard optimization problem.

Mitra et al. [1] analyzed a network loss probability caused by blocking with *fixed point equations* (FPEs). They derived the loss probability only based on assumption of link independence. Actual difficulty is posed by the fact that we need to model the traffic loss caused by blocking not only on isolated links, but also at the network level. This means we also need to take into account that the loss suffered on a link reduces the offered traffic of other links and vice versa, so a complex system of mutual influences arise. This situation calls for a more sophisticated machinery than blocking formulas (such as Erlang's formula) that compute the blocking probability only for a single link viewed in isolation. A successful model that captures the considered network level phenomenon is the reduced load approximation. We review it in the next section so that we can then use it in our VPN design model.

In this paper we investigate a virtual private network (VPN) design problem. We adopt a complex model to describe the carried traffic [2–4]. To deal with the arising hard optimization problem, we use a new heuristic local search technique called landscape smoothing search (LSS) proposed by Lian and Faragó, authors of this paper in

[5]. This study first describes the LSS heuristic method and then we modify the original LSS method to a fast landscape smoothing search (FLSS) method to overcome the slow search speed for the case when the objective function calculation is very time consuming. We apply FLSS to VPN design optimization and compare with existing methods such as simulated annealing (SA) [6, 7] and genetic algorithm (GA) [8, 9].

Basically this study consists of two parts. The first part is the proposal and the analysis of carried traffic for virtual private network (VPN). In the second part we propose the landscape smoothing search (LSS) [10] method and the fast LSS (FLSS) heuristic method and apply them to VPN optimization.

The remainder of the paper is organized as follows: Section 2 presents a reduced load approximation to model to capture the VPN carried traffic. Section 3 analyzes a nonlinear network level optimization model. The last part of Section 3 also provides the carried traffic objective function for VPN design optimization. Section 4 presents initial results with the original Landscape Smoothing Search (LSS). Section 5 presents Fast Landscape Smoothing Searching (FLSS). Section 6 presents numerical optimization results for VPN optimization and discussion of the features of three heuristic FLSS, SA and GA. Finally, Section 7 concludes the paper.

2. Reduced Load Approximation

The principle of this approach is "folklore" in traffic engineering and had been presented already in the 1960's by Cooper and Katz [11]. Nevertheless, in-depth exact investigation was done only much later, in the papers by Kelly [2] and Whitt [4]. For a comprehensive exposition of related results see the book of Ross [3].

To present the most fundamental case, let us consider a network of J links. A general link will be denoted by j, that is, we index the edges of the network graph here, rather than the nodes. Link j has capacity C_j. Let us assume that a set R of fixed routes is given in the network. A route $r \in R$, in general, can be an arbitrary subset of the link set. Here we do not need the assumption that it is a path in the graph theoretic sense. Of course, the practically most important case is when it is actually a path. There may be several routes between the same pair of nodes, even on the same sequence of links. The offered traffic V_r (the demand) to a given route $r \in R$ arrives as a Poisson stream and the streams belonging to different routes are assumed to be independent.

The incidence of links and routes is given by a matrix = $[A_{jr}], j = 1, \ldots, J, r \in R$. If link j is on route r, then $A_{jr} = 1$, otherwise $A_{jr} = 0$. The call holding times are independent random variables, and the holding periods of calls on the same route are identically distributed with finite mean. However, this distribution can otherwise be arbitrary. The central approximation assumption of the model is that the blocking of different links are probabilistically independent events. Let us denote the blocking probability of link j by B_j. The reduced load approximation says that the Poisson

stream is thinned by a factor of $(1 - B_j)$ on each traversed link independently. Hence the carried traffic on route r can be expressed as

$$V_r \prod_{j=1}^{J} \left(1 - B_j\right)^{A_{jr}}., \tag{1}$$

Note that the factor $(1 - B_j)^{A_{jr}}$ is 1 if the line is not traversed by the route (because then $A_{jr} = 0$); this is why the product can be taken for all links without taking care of which links are traversed by the route.

The carried traffic on link j is obtained if we sum up the carried traffic of all routes that traverse the link:

$$\sum_{r \in R} A_{jr} V_r \prod_{i} (1 - B_i)^{A_{ir}}. \tag{2}$$

Again, the summation is simply extended for all routes since $A_{jr} = 0$ holds for those that do not contain link j, making their contribution disappear from the sum.

If the total *offered load* to link j is denoted by ρ_j, then (2) should be equal to $\rho_j(1 - B_j)$, since the latter is the carried traffic on link j, obtained by thinning the offered load by the factor $1 - B_j$. Thus, we can write the equation

$$\rho_j\left(1 - B_j\right) = \sum_{r} A_{jr} V_r \prod_{i} (1 - B_i)^{A_{ir}}, \tag{3}$$

or, after canceling the factor $(1 - B_j)$

$$\rho_j = \sum_{r} A_{jr} V_r \prod_{i \neq j} (1 - B_i)^{A_{ir}}. \tag{4}$$

Further equations can be obtained by using that B_j depends on ρ_j and C_j in this model via Erlang's formula:

$$B_j = E\left(\rho_j, C_j\right) = \frac{\rho_j^{C_j}/C_j!}{\sum_{i=0}^{C_j} \rho_j^i/i!}. \tag{5}$$

(Note: in the case C_j is not an integer, we can use an analytic continuation of Erlang's formula, see [12].)

Writing out (4) and (5) for all $j = 1, \ldots, J$, we obtain a system of $2J$ equations for the $2J$ unknown quantities $\rho_j, B_j, j = 1, \ldots, J$. We can observe that B_j can be computed from (5) directly, once the values of the ρ_j variables are known (the link capacities are given). Therefore, the core of the problem is to compute $\rho_j, j = 1, \ldots, J$. Eliminating B_j from (4) by (5), we obtain a system of equations directly for the ρ_j variables:

$$\rho_j = \sum_{r} A_{jr} V_r \prod_{i \neq j} \left(1 - E\left(\rho_j, C_j\right)\right)^{A_{ir}}. \tag{6}$$

This system of equations (or, equivalently, the systems (4) and (5) together) is called *reduced load approximation*.

Alternatively, the equations are also called the *Erlang fixed point equations*.

The concept of *fixed point* comes into the picture in the following way. Let us use a vector notation $\rho = [\rho_1, \ldots, \rho_J]$ and define a function $f\colon R_+^J \to R_+^J$ by

$$f_j(\rho) = [f_1(\rho), \ldots, f_J(\rho)], \tag{7}$$

where $f_j(\rho)$, $j = 1, \ldots, J$ is given as

$$f_j(\rho) = \sum_r A_{jr} V_r \prod_{i \neq j} \left(1 - E(\rho_j, C_j)\right)^{A_{ir}}. \tag{8}$$

Now the system (6) can be compactly formulated as

$$\rho = f(\rho). \tag{9}$$

In other words, we have to find a fixed point of the mapping $f\colon R_+^J \to R_+^J$.

There are some natural questions that arise here immediately. Does a solution (a fixed point) always exist? If one exists, is it unique? How can we find it algorithmically in an efficient way? The fundamental theorem characterizing this model was proven by Kelly [2] (see also [13]). We also outline its proof, since the proof contains some concepts that we are going to use later.

Theorem 1. *The Erlang fixed-point equations always have a unique solution.*

Proof. The existence of the solution follows from the fact that the function f, defined above, is a continuous mapping of the closed J-dimensional unit cube $[0, 1]^J$ into itself, therefore by the well-known Brouwer fixed point theorem it has a fixed point. (Brouwer's fixed-point theorem says that any continuous function that maps a compact convex set into itself always has a fixed point.)

To show the uniqueness of the fixed point, we define an auxiliary function $U(y, C)$ in a tricky way, by the implicit relation

$$U(-\log(1 - E(v, C)), C) = v(1 - E(v, C)), \tag{10}$$

where $E(v, C)$ is Erlang's formula. The interpretation of $U(y, C)$ is that it is the average number of circuits in use (the utilization) on a link of capacity C when the blocking probability is $1 - e^{-y}$. In other words, $U(y, C)$ measures the link utilization as a function of a logarithmically scaled blocking probability $y = -\log(1 - B)$.

Define now an optimization problem, as follows:

$$\text{minimize} \quad \sum_r V_r \exp\left(-\sum_j y_j A_{jr}\right) + \sum_j \int_0^{y_j} U(z, C_j)\, dz,$$

$$\text{subject to} \quad y_j \geq 0, \quad j = 1, \ldots, J. \tag{11}$$

The first sum in objective function is a strictly convex function. Since $U(y, C)$ is strictly increasing, therefore, the integrals in the second sum are also strictly convex. Hence the above optimization problem, being the minimization of a strictly convex function over a convex domain, has a unique

minimum. Consider now the stationary equations obtained by equating the derivative of the objective function with zero:

$$\sum_r V_r \exp\left(-\sum_j y_j A_{jr}\right) = U(y_j, C_j), \quad j = 1, \ldots, J. \tag{12}$$

Using the definition of $U(y, C)$ and applying the transformation $B_j = 1 - e^{-y_j}$, we get back precisely the Erlang fixed-point equations from (12). Since we already know that there is a nonnegative solution to the fixed point equations, this implies that the stationary equations (12) also have a nonnegative solution, which is thus the minimum of the optimization problem (11). Conversely, each solution of (11) corresponds to a fixed point through the transformation $B_j = 1 - e^{-y_j}$. Since by the strict convexity there is a unique minimum, therefore (12) cannot have another solution, which implies the uniqueness of the fixed point, thus completing the proof. □

Having proved the existence and uniqueness of the fixed point, a natural question is how to find it algorithmically. The simplest algorithm is to do iterated substitution using the function defined in (7), (8). We can start with any value, say $\rho^{(0)} = [1, \ldots, 1]$ and then iterate as

$$\rho^{(i+1)} = f(\rho^{(i)}), \tag{13}$$

until $\rho^{(i+1)}$ and $\rho^{(i)}$ are sufficiently close to each other. This method works very well in practice, although convergence is not guaranteed theoretically, since $f(\cdot)$ is not a contraction mapping, that is, $||f(x) - f(y)|| < \alpha||x - y||$ does not necessarily hold for some constant $\alpha < 1$. In fact, there exist examples for nonconvergence, see Whitt [4].

Another algorithmic possibility is solving the convex programming problem (11). Although this is guaranteed to work, nevertheless, it offers a much more complicated algorithm, which is made even worse by the implicit definition of the function $U(y, C)$. Therefore the practical algorithm is the iterated substitution, even though it is not guaranteed to converge in pathological cases.

The presented model is the base case, when routing is fixed and traffic is homogeneous. Various extensions exist for more complicated cases, see for example, [3, 14]. Unfortunately, they lack the nice feature of the unique fixed point. In the next section, extensions to heterogeneous traffic will be used for cases when the reduced load approximation is embedded into optimization models.

3. A Nonlinear Network Level Optimization Model

In this section we build a nonlinear network level optimization model based on the reduced load approximation. Recall that we considered the situation when logical (virtual) sub-networks exist on top of the given physical network. They are realized by logical links. A logical link is, in general, a subset of the physical links. It can be, for example, a route in the physical network. Our objective is to allocate capacity to the logical links such that the physical capacity constraints are obeyed on every physical link and the total carried network traffic is maximized. Note that since the logical links share physical capacities. Therefore if we want to decrease blocking on a logical link by giving more capacity, we can only do this by taking away capacity from others, thus degrading other logical links. It is intuitively clear that an optimization problem arises from this VPN design.

Since the model is built on the reduced load approximation (Section 2), therefore we use the same notation. The network contains J logical links, labeled $1, 2, \ldots, J$. The capacity of logical link j is C_j. Since logical link capacities are not fixed in advance (we want to optimize with respect to them!), therefore the C_j are variables. Let $C = (C_1, C_2, \ldots, C_J)$ be the vector of logical link capacities.

The condition that the sum of logical link capacities on the same physical link cannot exceed the physical capacity can be expressed by a linear system of inequalities. Let C^{phys} be the vector of given physical link capacities. Furthermore, let S be a matrix in which the jth entry in the ith row is 1 if logical link j needs capacity on the ith physical link, otherwise 0. Then the physical constraints can be expressed compactly as $SC \leq C^{\text{phys}}$.

A set R of fixed routes is given in the network. A route is a sequence of logical links. There may be several routes between the same pair of nodes, even on the same sequence of logical links. The offered traffic (the demand) to a given route $r \in R$ is V_r and is assumed to arrive as a Poisson stream. The streams belonging to different routes are assumed independent. Holding times are independent of each other and holding periods of sessions on the same route are identically distributed.

We consider heterogeneous (multirate) traffic. To preserve the nice properties of the Erlang fixed-point equations, we adopt the following homogenization approach: a session (call) that requires b units of bandwidth is approximated by b independent unit bandwidth calls.

The capacity (bandwidth) that a session on route r requires is denoted by b_{jr} on link j (for the sake of generality, we allow that it may be different on different links). If the route does not traverse link j, then $b_{jr} = 0$. Note that b_{jr} plays the same role here as A_{jr} in the description of the reduced load approximation, but b_{jr} can now also take values other than 0 and 1.

According to the applied approximations, the total carried traffic in the network is expressed as

$$\sum_r V_r \prod_j \left(1 - B_j\right)^{b_{jr}}, \tag{14}$$

where B_j is the (yet unknown) blocking probability of logical link j. ($j = 1, 2, \ldots, J$).

Our objective is to find the vector C of logical link capacities, subject to the physical constraints $SC \leq C^{\text{phys}}$ and $C \geq 0$, such that the total carried traffic is maximized:

$$\text{maximize} \quad \sum_r V_r \prod_j \left(1 - B_j\right)^{b_{jr}}, \tag{15}$$

$$\text{subject to} \quad SC \leq C^{\text{phys}}, \quad C \geq 0,$$

where C_j are variables and the dependence of B_j on C_j is defined by the Erlang fixed-point equations:

$$B_j = E\left(\left(1 - B_j\right)^{-1} \sum_{r \in R} b_{jr} V_r \prod_{i \neq j} (1 - B_i)^{b_{ir}}, C_j\right), \tag{16}$$

where $j = 0, 1, \ldots, J$.

4. Heuristic Methods to Solve Network Design Problems

This section presents heuristic methods to solve optimization problems, including network design tasks. Here we only focus on combinatorial optimization algorithms for problems of the following form:

$$\text{minimize} \quad F(x) \text{ for } x \in S, \tag{17}$$

where S is a very large finite set of feasible points (solution space, optimization space). The variable x can take different forms: it can be a binary string, an integer vector, or mixed integer and label combination.

4.1. Well-Known Heuristic Methods. One of the well-known general stochastic methods is *simulated annealing* (SA) [7, 9, 15]. As a local search method, SA also uses the notion of neighborhood, but applies randomness to choosing the next step to avoid getting trapped in local optima. We can refer [5, 7, 9] for SA pseudocode.

Another well-known heuristic method is *genetic algorithm* (GA). The genetic algorithm (GA) is also often applied in combinatorial optimization problems [5, 6, 8, 9]. The procedure first selects parent solutions for generating offspring. Then it performs two basic procedures: crossover (x) with probability P_c and mutation (x) with probability P_m. We can refer [5, 6, 8, 9] for GA pseudocode. Genetic algorithm does not use local search. It may jump away from the best point even when it is very close to it.

4.2. Description of Landscape Smoothing Search (LSS). Our proposed LSS is a general optimization technique suitable for a wide range of combinatorial optimization problems. The authors of this paper proposed the original LSS to solve call admission control optimization problem for cognitive radio network in [5]. To better understand the idea of LSS we give an introduction to its basic form here. LSS can get out of local optima, and effectively conduct local search in the vast search spaces of hard optimization problems. The key idea is that we continuously change the objective/fitness function of the

```
Procedure algorithm LSS (F,λ,X,G)
begin
create initial feasible solution X₀
set dₕ(X) = 0, (h = 1,...,H)
(set all initial smoothing factors to zero)
    for i: = 1 to max-iterations
    begin
        F'(X) = F(X) + Σₕ[λₕ* dₕ(X)]
        Xᵢ = Local search (F', λₕ, Xᵢ₋₁, G)
        for each h: = 1 to H
        begin
            adjust dₕ(X);
            (Xₕ is the local optimum point)
            if F(Xᵢ) < Fᵇᵉˢᵗ then
                Fᵇᵉˢᵗ: = F(Xᵢ);
                Xᵇᵉˢᵗ: = Xᵢ;
            end
            adjust λₕ for adaptive λ;
        end
    end procedure
    LSS returns Xᵇᵉˢᵗ where F(Xᵇᵉˢᵗ) is the minimum of all solutions so far.
```

ALGORITHM 1: Landscape smoothing search (LSS).

problem to be minimized with a set of smoothing functions that are dynamically manipulated during the search process to steer the heuristics to get out of the local optima.

The objective function $F(X)$ is extended with a smoothingfunction $S(X)$ as follows:

$$F'(X) = F(X) + S(X) = F(X) + \sum_h \lambda_h \cdot d_h(X), \qquad (18)$$

where $S(X)$ is the smoothing function:

$$S(X) = \sum_h \lambda_h \cdot d_h(X), \qquad (19)$$

which contains "landscape smoothing functions." We define them as $d_h(X_h) = 0$, if we hit this local optimal point X_h for the first time. $d_h(X_h) = d_h(X_h) + 1$, if we hit this local optimal point X_h for the second or more time. λ_h is the smoothing step constant and it may be adaptively changed.

We also record the best point reached so far, and the local optima during the search. Every time we hit a local optimum, we compare it with the global optimum (best point so far). Then we adjust the landscape smoothing factors to let the local search get away from the local trap.

As we keep changing the objective function, we gradually "smooth out" the landscape to get rid of the local holes that trap the search. We never fill a hole, however, before the second time we reach it. This way the search trace never misses a hole that could be the global optimum. See Figure 1.

We assume F is the objective function; λ is a group of constants that serve as a landscape smoothing step factors, which can be constants or can also be adaptively changed as λ_h. G represents the problem specification (e.g. network topology, demand matrix or some constraints). We give the pseudo code here for landscape smoothing search (LSS) in Algorithm 1.

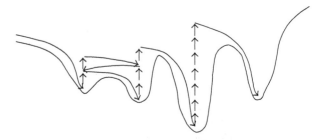

FIGURE 1: Landscape smoothing search (LSS).

5. Initial Results with Original Landscape Smoothing Search (LSS)

In this section we demonstrate a sample non-linear hard VPN design problem and the optimization results achieved with LSS and simulated annealing (SA).

5.1. A Sample VPN. We use a VPN with 40 virtual links and 12 routes shown as in Figure 2 for simulation. For example, $e_2 = c_0 + c_8$ means physical link e_2 consists of two virtual links c_0 and c_8, $e_9 = c_{12} + c_{27} + c_{35}$ means physical link e_9 consists of three virtual links c_{12}, c_{27}, and c_{35}, dashed route $r_2 = c_8 + c_9 + c_{10}$ means route r_2 consists of three virtual links c_8, c_9, and c_{10}, dotted route $r_5 = c_{18} + c_{19} + c_{20} + c_{21}$.

5.2. Initial Results with LSS. We use the sample VPN described in Section 5.1. The diagram in Figure 3 shows initial results with landscape smoothing search (LSS) and simulated annealing (SA).

Our optimization results were obtained through a PC with AMD Sempron 2500+ CPU. The searching time is the

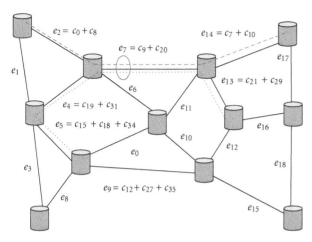

FIGURE 2: A sample VPN structure.

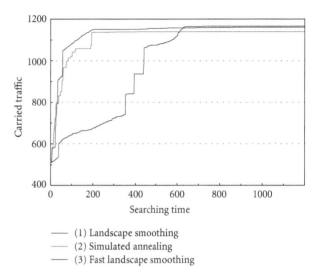

——— (1) Landscape smoothing
——— (2) Simulated annealing
——— (3) Fast landscape smoothing

FIGURE 4: VPN Search trace with fast LSS and SA.

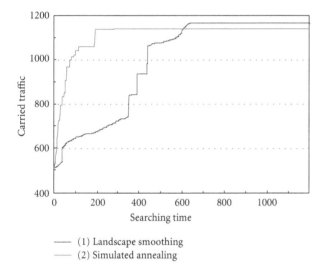

——— (1) Landscape smoothing
——— (2) Simulated annealing

FIGURE 3: VPN design search trace with LSS and SA.

time needed to obtain best solution so far. The searching time unit is 10 seconds. For each heuristic method, these measures were recorded each time there was an improvement in the best carried traffic value. So in each point of the search curve, the X-axis value is the searching time in seconds and the Y-axis value is the best carried traffic value we achieve so far. We find that LSS gives better result in long time, but the search speed is slower than SA. When the objective function takes very long time to calculate we find that the original landscape smoothing searching (LLS) heuristic method is slower than simulated annealing (SA). As we know SA makes a possible move with a random neighbor to find a better objective value. The original LSS makes a possible move by picking the best neighbor of all direct neighbors. If for a case which has N ($N = 40$) direct neighbors it needs to do N ($N = 40$) objective function calculations to make a possible move. The objective function calculation of VPN design itself is a complex iterative process using (16). It may take 50 to 90 iterations to calculate an accurate value. So the objective function calculation of VPN design is a time consuming

process. This explains why the original LSS method is slower than SA here for VPN design case.

6. Fast Landscape Smoothing Search (FLSS)

To improve the search speed of LSS, we modify the original LSS into a fast landscape smoothing search (FLSS). The FLSS has two (or more) phases of search. The first phase we call rough search phase. In the rough search phase we divide the set of N neighbors into several subsets, like $N1$, $N2$, $N3$, and $N4$. We apply the LSS method on subneighborhoods one at a time, and also we apply LSS on subneighbor one by one. This way we make every LSS move with much fewer objective function calculations. The second phase we call fine search phase. In the fine search phase we use the original LSS method on the whole neighborhood, as in the original LSS. This way we will not miss the possible global optima in the process we search all N direct neighbor. The improved result is shown in Figure 4.

7. More Numerical and Optimization Results

This section presents more numerical and optimization results of carried traffic load for the VPN design problem.

7.1. Optimization Results with Simulated Annealing (SA). Figure 5 shows simulated annealing (SA) optimization search traces for function (15) with 3 different T-reduce values (cooling speed factor). We can see SA convergence speed may be affected by setting the temperature reduce cooling value. At the beginning of the SA search procedure, SA converges very fast. Then SA convergence becomes very slow. After a while it takes a long time for SA to find the next better value.

Figure 6 shows simulated annealing (SA) optimization search trace with different initial settings. In all these figures, legend initial settings like [Initial-2 = 4 3 2 1 4 3 2 1] means virtual link capacities

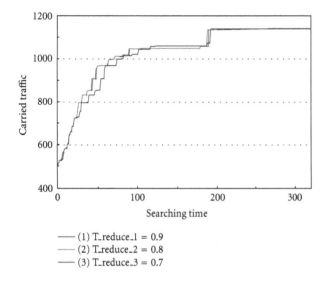

FIGURE 5: Simulated annealing search trace with different T-reduce values.

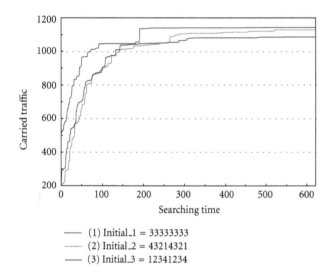

FIGURE 6: Simulated annealing search trace with different initial settings.

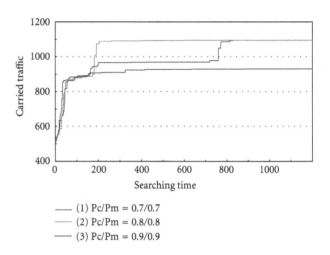

FIGURE 7: Genetic algorithm search trace with different P_c/P_m values.

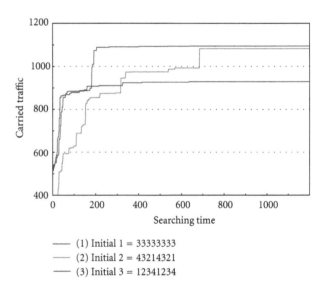

FIGURE 8: Genetic algorithm search trace with different initial settings.

$C_j[0], C_j[1], C_j[2], C_j[3], C_j[4], C_j[5], C_j[6], C_j[7], \ldots = 4\,3\,2\,1\,4\,3\,2\,1,\ldots$. From Figure 6 we can see the SA optima value depends on the initial settings. Different initial settings will lead to a slightly different SA optima value.

7.2. Optimization Results with Genetic Algorithm (GA). Figure 7 shows genetic algorithm (GA) optimization search traces for function (16) with 3 sets of different P_c/P_m values. P_c is the probability for crossover. P_m is the probability for mutation. From Figure 7 we can see GA convergence speed may be affected by settings of crossover/mutation probability values. At the beginning of the GA search procedure, GA converges very fast. Then GA converges very slowly. After a while it takes a long time for GA to find the next better value.

Figure 8 shows Genetic Algorithm (GA) optimization search trace with different initial settings. From Figure 8 we can see the GA near optima value depends on the initial settings. Here the notation like [Initial-2 = 1 2 3 4   1 2 3 4] means virtual link capacities $C_j[0]$, $C_j[1], C_j[2], C_j[3], C_j[4], C_j[5], C_j[6], C_j[7], \ldots = 1\,2\,3\,4\,1\,2\,3\,4,\ldots$. Different initial settings will lead to slightly different GA optima values. This kind of search trend is similar to that which we see in SA.

7.3. Optimization Results with Fast Landscape Smoothing Search (FLSS). Figure 9 shows fast landscape smoothing search (FLSS) optimization search trace with different smoothing step factor λ values. From Figure 9 we can see LSS convergence speed may slightly affected by setting of

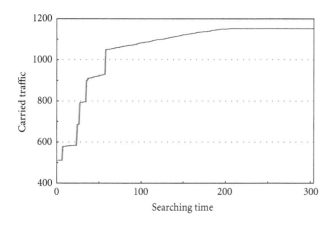

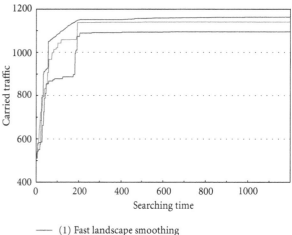

— (1) Fast landscape smoothing
— (2) Simulated annealing
— (3) Genetic algorithm

FIGURE 11: Three optimization methods—search results comparison.

— (1) $\lambda 1 = 2.9$
— (2) $\lambda 2 = 1.9$
— (3) $\lambda 3 = 3.9$

FIGURE 9: Fast landscape smoothing search trace with different λ values.

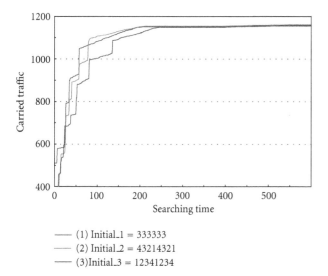

— (1) Initial_1 = 333333
— (2) Initial_2 = 43214321
— (3) Initial_3 = 12341234

FIGURE 10: Fast landscape smoothing search trace with different initials.

smoothing step factor λ value. FLSS converges relatively fast and stabilizes smoothly.

Figure 10 shows Fast Landscape Smoothing Search (FLSS) optimization search trace with different initial settings. Here the notation [Initial-3 = 1 2 3 4 1 2 3 4] means virtual link capacities $C_j[0]$, $C_j[1]$, $C_j[2]$, $C_j[3]$, $C_j[4]$, $C_j[5]$, $C_j[6]$, $C_j[7]$, ... = 1 2 3 4 1 2 3 4,.... From Figure 10 we can see the FLSS optima value depends on the initial settings. Different initial settings will lead to slightly different optima values.

These results show that FLSS is much less sensitive to the adjustable parameters than SA and GA. And FLSS is also much less sensitive to the initial settings of search starting point. With different initial settings, FLSS converges to three

near optima values that are very close. The difference of the three values is almost negligible.

7.4. Three Optimization Methods Comparison. To compare the three optimization methods, we put fast landscape smoothing search (FLSS), simulated annealing (SA), and genetic algorithm (GA) optimization search traces together in Figure 11.

Here the three methods all use the same initial settings of [3 3 3 3 3 3 3 3]. FLSS uses smoothing step factor λ of 2.90. SA uses cooling T-reduce factor of 0.7. GA uses crossover/mutation probabilities P_c/P_m of 0.9/0.9. We can see that FLSS starts slower than SA and GA at the beginning of the search, but FLSS catches up later and achieves a better objective function value.

We can see that SA and GA are not likely to get better results after time unit of 250. FLSS keeps getting better results after time unit of 250 and even 500. In this VPN case, FLSS slightly over performs SA and GA in the long run. So FLSS is a very good candidate for heuristic methods.

The results of these heuristic methods are case dependent. Based on the three network design cases we used, we compare these heuristic method features in Table 1 of the following page.

LSS and FLSS use adaptive smoothing function and they reach the optima by finding the best neighbor. SA jumps randomly with reduced cooling probabilities and reaches the optimum by chance. GA uses crossover and mutation with P_c/P_m probabilities and reaches the optimum by chance. SA and GA might jump away from the global optimum even when they are very close to it.

8. Conclusion

In this paper, we model the VPN traffic loss caused by blocking not only on isolated links, but at the network level.

TABLE 1: Four heuristic method feature comparison.

Method	Neighbor local search used?	Random?	Trap escaping mechanism	Search speed
Simulated annealing (SA)	Yes Use with probability Use random neighbor	Yes	Randomly jump with probability, controlled by cooling schedule. (Reach optima by chance)	Fast
Genetic algorithm (GA)	No	Yes	Use crossover, mutation with probability to jump out. (Reach optima by chance)	Slow
Landscape smoothing search (LSS)	Yes Use best neighbor	No	Use adaptive smoothing function. (Reach optima by best neighbor)	Medium
Fast landscape smoothing search (FLSS)	Yes Use best neighbor	No	Use adaptive smoothing function. (Reach optima by best neighbor)	Fast

We take into account that the loss suffered on a link reduces the offered traffic of other links and vice versa. We formulate the VPN design problem as the optimization problem of maximizing the carried traffic in the VPN. So that the VPN optimization becomes a hard optimization problem. We used a heuristic method called landscape smoothing search (LSS) and applied it to this problem. We find that LSS can get better result than SA but with a slower search speed. The reason is that in this VPN case, the objective function calculation of VPN carried traffic is a very time consuming process. To improve the speed of the original LSS we proposed a new fast landscape smoothing (FLSS) method.

The slow search speed drawback of the original LSS is overcome in the FLSS. Our FLSS method is also compared with popular heuristic methods such as simulated annealing (SA) and genetic algorithm (GA). We find the FLSS technique to be simple to implement. The three techniques were tested in many experiments with different VPN initial settings and different adjustable parameters to compare the optimization performance. The results show that the FLSS is much less sensitive to the adjustable parameters than SA and GA are. The FLSS is also less sensitive to the initial settings of search starting point than SA and GA are. With different initial settings, the FLSS converges to almost the same near optima value each time. The overall results show that FLSS outperforms the SA and the GA techniques both in terms of solution quality and optimization speed. Therefore based on these results, the fast landscape smoothing search (FLSS) technique can be strong candidate in solving hard optimization problems in network design.

Acknowledgment

The authors are grateful for the support of NSF Grant CNS-1018760.

References

[1] D. Mitra, J. A. Morrison, and K. G. Ramakrishnan, "Virtual private networks: joint resource allocation and routing design," in *Proceedings of the 18th Annual Joint Conference of the IEEE Computer and Communications Societie (INFOCOM '99)*, pp. 480–490, March 1999.

[2] F. P. Kelly, "Kelly blocking probabilities in large circuit-switched networks," *Advances in Applied Probability*, vol. 18, no. 2, pp. 473–505, 1986.

[3] K. W. Ross, *Multiservice Loss Models for Broadband Telecommunication Networks*, Springer, New York, NY, USA, 1995.

[4] W. Whitt, "Blocking when service is required from several facilities simultaneously," *AT&T Technical Journal*, vol. 64, no. 8, pp. 1807–1856, 1985.

[5] H. Lian and A. Faragó, "A heuristic optimization method and its application in cognitive radio networks," Computer Science Technical Report UTDCS-39-11, University of Texas at Dallas, Dallas, Tex, USA, 2011.

[6] B. Dengiz, F. Altiparmak, and A. E. Smith, "Local search genetic algorithm for optimal design of reliable networks," *IEEE Transactions on Evolutionary Computation*, vol. 1, no. 3, pp. 179–188, 1997.

[7] O. C. Martin and S. W. Otto, "Combining simulated annealing with local search heuristics," *Annals of Operations Research*, vol. 63, pp. 57–75, 1996.

[8] Y. Leung, G. Li, and Z. B. Xu, "A genetic algorithm for the multiple destination routing problems," *IEEE Transactions on Evolutionary Computation*, vol. 2, no. 4, pp. 150–161, 1998.

[9] M. Pioro and D. Medhi, *Routing, Flow, and Capacity Design in Communication and Computer Networks*, Morgan Kaufmann, San Fransisco, Calif, USA, 2004.

[10] H. Lian and A. Faragó, "Optimizing Call Admission Control for Cognitive Radio Networks Using a New Heuristic Optimization Method," *Science Academy Transactions on Computer and Communication Networks (SATCCN)*, vol. 2, no. 1, pp. 2046–5157, 2012.

[11] R. B. Cooper and S. Katz, "Analysis of alternate routing networks account taken of the nonrandomness of overflow traffic," Tech. Rep., Bell Telephone Laboratories Memorandum, 1964.

[12] A. A. Jagers and E. A. Van Doorn, "On the continued Erlang loss function," *Operations Research Letters*, vol. 5, no. 1, pp. 43–46, 1986.

[13] F. P. Kelly, "Loss networks," *Annals of Applied Probability*, vol. 1, no. 3, pp. 319–378, 1991.

[14] S. P. Chung and K. W. Ross, "Reduced load approximations for multirate loss networks," *IEEE Transactions on Communications*, vol. 41, no. 8, pp. 1222–1231, 1993.

[15] J. Arabas and S. Kozdrowski, "Applying an evolutionary algorithm to telecommunication network design," *IEEE Transactions on Evolutionary Computation*, vol. 5, no. 4, pp. 309–322, 2001.

10

An Overview of Algorithms for Network Survivability

F. A. Kuipers

Faculty of Electrical Engineering, Mathematics and Computer Science, Delft University of Technology, P.O. Box 5031, 2600 GA Delft, The Netherlands

Correspondence should be addressed to F. A. Kuipers, F.A.Kuipers@tudelft.nl

Academic Editors: H. Kubota and M. Listanti

Network survivability—the ability to maintain operation when one or a few network components fail—is indispensable for present-day networks. In this paper, we characterize three main components in establishing network survivability for an existing network, namely, (1) determining network connectivity, (2) augmenting the network, and (3) finding disjoint paths. We present a concise overview of network survivability algorithms, where we focus on presenting a few polynomial-time algorithms that could be implemented by practitioners and give references to more involved algorithms.

1. Introduction

Given the present-day importance of communications systems and infrastructures in general, networks should be designed and operated in such a way that failures can be mitigated. Network nodes and/or links might for instance fail due to malicious attacks, natural disasters, unintentional cable cuts, planned maintenance, equipment malfunctioning, and so forth. Resilient, fault tolerant, survivable, reliable, robust, and dependable, are different terms that have been used by the networking community to capture the ability of a communications system to maintain operation when confronted with network failures. Unfortunately, the terminology has overlapping meanings or contains ambiguities, as pointed out by Al-Kuwaiti et al. [1]. In this paper, we will use the term *survivable networks* to refer to networks that, when a component fails, may "survive" by finding alternative paths that circumvent the failed component. Three ingredients are needed to reach survivability.

(1) *Network connectivity*, that is, the network should be well connected (connectivity properties are discussed in Section 1.1).

(2) *Network augmentation*, that is, new links may need to be added to increase the connectivity of a network.

(3) *Path protection*, that is, a procedure to find alternative paths in case of failures.

These three ingredients will be explained in the following sections.

1.1. Network Connectivity. A network is often represented as a graph $G(\mathcal{N}, \mathcal{L})$, where $\mathcal{N}$ is the set of N nodes (which for instance represent routers) and $\mathcal{L}$ is the set of L links (which for instance represent optical fiber lines or radio channels). Links may be characterized by weights representing for instance their capacity, delay, length, cost, and/or failure probability. A graph is said to be connected if there exists a path between each pair of nodes in the graph, else the graph is said to be disconnected. In the context of survivability, the notion of connectivity may be further specified as k-connectivity, where at least k disjoint paths exist between each pair of nodes. Depending on whether these paths are node or link disjoint, we may discriminate between node and link connectivity. The link connectivity $\lambda(G)$ of a graph G is the smallest number of links whose removal disconnects G. Correspondingly, the node connectivity $\kappa(G)$ of a graph is the smallest number of nodes whose removal disconnects G.

In 1927, Menger provided a theorem [2]—in German—that could be interpreted as follows.

Theorem 1 (Menger's theorem). *The maximum number of link/node-disjoint paths between A and B is equal to the minimum number of links/nodes that would separate A and B.*

Menger's theorem clearly relates to the k link/node connectivity of a graph, in the sense that a k link/node-connected graph has at least k link/node-disjoint paths between any pair of nodes in the graph. The minimum number of links/nodes separating two nodes or sets of nodes is referred to as a minimum cut. In order to assess the link/node connectivity of a network, we therefore need to find its minimum cut.

A somewhat less intuitive notion of connectivity stems from the spectrum of the Laplacian matrix of a graph and is denoted as algebraic connectivity. The algebraic connectivity was introduced by Fiedler in 1973 [3] and is defined as follows.

Definition 2 (algebraic connectivity). The algebraic connectivity equals the value of the second smallest eigenvalue of Q, where Q is the Laplacian matrix $Q = \Delta - A$, with A an $N \times N$ adjacency matrix with elements $a_{ij} = 1$ if there is a link between nodes i and j, else $a_{ij} = 0$, and $\Delta = \text{diag}(d_1, \dots, d_N)$ an $N \times N$ diagonal matrix with d_j the degree of node j.

The algebraic connectivity has many interesting properties that characterize how strongly a graph G is connected (e.g., see [4, 5]). Moreover, the multiplicity of the smallest eigenvalue (of value 0) of the Laplacian Q is equal to the number of components in the graph G. Hence, if the algebraic connectivity $\alpha(G)$ is larger than 0, the network is connected, else the algebraic connectivity is 0, and the network is disconnected. We have that

$$\alpha(G) \le \kappa(G) \le \lambda(G) \le \delta(G), \qquad (1)$$

where $\delta(G)$ is the minimum degree in the network. For ease of notation, when G is not specified, we use α, κ, λ, and δ.

Connectivity properties, may be less obvious when applied to multilayered networks [6, 7], like IP over WDM networks, where a 2-link-connected IP network operated on top of an optical WDM network, with multiple IP links sharing (e.g., groomed on) the same WDM link, could still be disconnected by a single-link failure at the optical layer.

In probabilistic networks, links and/or nodes x are available with a certain probability p_x, which is often computed as $p_x = \text{MTTF}(x)/(\text{MTTF}(x) + \text{MTTR}(x))$, with $\text{MTTF}(x)$ the mean time to failure of x and $\text{MTTR}(x)$ the mean repair time of x. Often the term network availability is used to denote the probability that the network is connected (e.g., see [8]). When the node probabilities are all one and all the link probabilities are independent and of equal value p, then a reliability polynomial (a special case of the Tutte polynomial, e.g., see [9]) is a polynomial function in p that gives the probability that the network remains connected after its links fail with probability p.

1.2. Network Augmentation. The outcome of testing for network connectivity could be that the network is not sufficiently robust (connected). Possibly, rewiring the (overlay) network could improve its robustness properties [10]. However, this is more involved when applied to the physical network, and improving network performance or network robustness is therefore often established by adding new links and possibly also nodes to the network. Adding links or nodes can be costly (which could be reflected by link/node weights), and the new links/nodes should therefore be placed wisely, such that the desired network property is obtained with the fewest amount of links/nodes or such that the addition of a fixed amount of links/nodes maximizes the desired network property. This class of problems is referred to as (network) augmentation problems, and within this class the problems only differ in their objectives. For instance, k-connectivity is an important property in the context of network robustness, and reaching it through link additions might be one such objective. The alternative objective of algebraic connectivity augmentation leads to an NP-hard problem [11]. Similarly, adding a minimum amount of links to make a graph chordal is also NP-hard [12] (a graph is chordal if each of its cycles of four or more nodes has a link connecting two nonadjacent nodes in the cycle).

1.3. Path Protection. Network protocols like OSPF are deployed in the internet to obtain a correct view of the topology and in case of changes (like the failure of a link) to converge the routing towards the new (perturbed) situation. Unfortunately, this process is not fast, and applications may still face unacceptable disruptions in performance. In conjunction with MPLS, an MPLS fast reroute mechanism can be used that, as the name suggests, provides the ability to switch over in subsecond time from a failed primary path to an alternate (backup) path. This fast reroute mechanism is specified in RFC 4090 [13], May 2005, and has already been implemented by several vendors. The concept has also been extended to pure IP networks and is referred to as IP fast reroute [14]. RFC 4090 defines RSVP-TE extensions to establish backup label-switched path (LSP) tunnels for local repair of LSP tunnels. The backup path can either be configured to protect against a link or a node failure. Since the backup paths are precomputed, no time is lost in computing backup paths or performing signalling in the event of a failure. The fast reroute mechanism as described in RFC 4090 assumes that MPLS (primary and backup) paths are computed and explicitly routed by the network operator. Hence, there is a strong need for efficient algorithms to compute disjoint paths.

Depending on whether backup paths are computed before or after a failure of the primary path, survivability techniques can be broadly classified into restoration or protection techniques.

(i) *Protection scheme*: protection is a proactive scheme, where backup paths are precomputed and reserved in advance. In 1:1 protection, traffic is rerouted along the backup path upon the failure of the primary path. In 1+1 protection, the data is duplicated and sent concurrently over the primary and backup paths.

(ii) *Restoration scheme*: restoration is a reactive mechanism that handles a failure after it occurs. Thus, the backup path is not known *a priori*. Instead, a backup path is computed only after the failure in the primary path is sensed.

In general, protection has a shorter recovery time since the backup path is precomputed, but it is less efficient in terms of capacity utilization and less flexible. Restoration, on the other hand, provides increased flexibility and efficient resource utilization, but it may take a longer time for recovery, and there is no guarantee that a backup path will be found. As a compromise between the two schemes, Banner and Orda [15] considered designing a low-capacity backup network (using spare capacity or by installing new resources) that is fully provisioned to reroute traffic on the primary network in case of a failure. The backup network itself is not used to transport "primary" traffic. Backup networks with specific topological features have also been addressed in the literature, for instance protection [16] and preconfigured [17] cycles or redundant trees [18].

Depending on how rerouting is done after a failure in the primary path, there are three categories of survivability techniques.

(i) *Path-based protection/restoration*: in path-based protection, a link- or node-disjoint backup path is precomputed and takes over when the primary path fails. In path-based restoration, a new path is computed between the source and destination nodes of the failed path. If such a backup path cannot be found, the request is blocked.

(ii) *Link-based protection/restoration*: in link-based protection, each link is preassigned a local route that is used when the link fails, and in link-based restoration, the objective is to compute a detour between the two ends of the failed link for all paths that are using the link. Since link-based protection/restoration requires signaling only between the two ends of the failed link, it has a smaller recovery time than path-based protection/restoration, which requires end-to-end signaling between the source and destination nodes.

(iii) *Segment-based protection/restoration*: the segment-based scheme (e.g., see [19]) is a compromise between path-based and link-based schemes. Thus, in segment-based protection, backup routes are precomputed for segments of the primary path. In segment-based restoration, a detour of the segment containing the failed link is computed following a failure.

Depending on whether sharing of resources is allowed among backup paths, protection schemes can be of two types:

(i) *Dedicated protection*: in this scheme, resources (e.g., links, wavelength channels, etc.) are not shared among backup paths and are exclusively reserved for a given path request.

(ii) *Shared protection*: in this scheme, backup paths may share resources as long as their primary paths do not share links. In $M:N$ protection, M backup paths are used to protect N primary paths. The shared scheme

provides a better resource utilization; however, it is more complicated and requires more information, such as the shareability of each link.

In general, path protection requires less capacity than link protection, while shared protection requires less capacity than dedicated protection. However, path protection is more vulnerable to multiple link failures than link protection, and so is shared protection compared to dedicated protection.

1.4. Paper Outline and Objective. The remainder of this paper is structured as follows. In Section 2, we give an overview of several methods for determining the connectivity properties of a network. In case a network is found to be insufficiently connected from a survivability perspective, links may have to be added to increase the connectivity. In Section 3, we list key results in network connectivity augmentation. Once a network is designed to withstand some failures, proper path protection/restoration schemes should be in place that can quickly defer traffic to alternate routes in case of a failure. In Section 4, we survey work on finding disjoint paths in a network. We conclude in Section 5.

Throughout the paper, the objective is not to list and explain all the relevant algorithms. Rather, we aim to briefly explain some fundamental concepts and some polynomial-time algorithms that could easily be deployed by practitioners or which can be (and have been) used as building blocks for more advanced algorithms, and to provide pointers to further reading.

2. Determining Network Connectivity

In Section 1.1, we indicated that Menger's theorem implies that finding a minimum cut corresponds to finding the connectivity of a network. In this section, we will look further at finding cuts in a network.

Definition 3 (link (edge) cut). A link cut refers to a set of links whose removal separates the graph into two disjoint subgraphs, and where all links in the removed cut-set have an end-point in both subgraphs.

The two subgraphs need not be connected themselves.

Definition 4 (node (vertex) cut). A node cut refers to a set of nodes whose removal separates the graph into two disjoint subgraphs, and where all nodes in the removed cut-set have at least one adjacent link to both subgraphs.

Definition 5 (minimum link/node cut). A minimum cut is a cut whose cardinality is not larger than that of any other cut in the network.

Definitions for a cut also have a variant in which a source node s and a terminating node t need to be separated.

Definition 6 (s-t cut). An s-t cut refers to a cut that separates two nodes s and t in the graph such that both belong to different subgraphs.

```
(1) f(u, v) ← 0 ∀(u, v) ∈ 𝓛 and f* ← 0 /*Initialize to zero flow*/
(2) While /*loop until the algorithm terminates in line 9*/
(3)         For all nodes u ∈ 𝒩, compute in G_f the hopcount h(u) to t /*by
              Breadth-First-Search [28] from t*/
(4)         Compute a blocking flow f in G_f thereby skipping links (u, v) for which
              h(v) ≠ h(u) + 1
(5)         If f exists
(6)             f* ← f* + f
(7)             Update G_f
(8)         else
(9)             return f*
```

ALGORITHM 1: Dinitz-Max-Flow (G, c, s, t).

Often, when referring to a cut, a link cut is meant. In the remainder of this paper, we will use the same convention and only specify the type of cut for node cuts.

Definition 7 (maximum cut). A maximum cut is a cut whose cardinality is not exceeded by that of any other cut in the network.

Definition 8 (sparsest cut). The sparsest cut (sometimes also referred to as the (Cheeger) isoperimetric constant) is a cut for which the ratio of the number of links in the cut-set divided by the number of nodes in the smaller subgraph is not larger than that of any other cut in the network.

Finding a maximum or sparsest cut is a hard problem (the maximum-cut problem is APX-hard [20] and the sparsest-cut problem is NP-hard [21, 22]), but fortunately a minimum cut, and consequently the network's connectivity, can be computed in polynomial time as will be indicated below. The algebraic connectivity α could be used to approximate the sparsest cut γ as $\alpha/2 \leq \gamma \leq \sqrt{\alpha(2\delta - \alpha)}$ [4, 21]. Dinh et al. [23] investigated the notion of pairwise connectivity (the number of connected pairs, which bears similarities to the sparsest-cut problem), and proved that finding the smallest set of nodes/links whose removal degrades the pairwise connectivity to certain degree is NP-complete.

2.1. Determining Link Connectivity. In the celebrated paper from Ford and Fulkerson [24] (and independently by Elias et al. [25]) a maximum flow from a source s to a terminal t in a network, where the links have a given capacity, is shown to be equal to the minimum-weight s-t link cut in that network, where the weight of the cut is the sum of the capacities of the links in the cut-set; the so-called *max-flow min-cut theorem*. By using a max-flow algorithm and setting the capacity of all links to 1, one can therefore compute the minimum s-t link cut, or the minimum link cut when repeated over all possible s-t pairs. It is not our goal to overview all maximum-flow algorithms (an excellent discourse of the subject is presented in the book by Ahuja et al. [26]), but we will present Dinitz's algorithm, which can be used to determine the minimum s-t link cut in $O(L \cdot (\min\{N^{2/3}, \sqrt{L}\}))$ time.

We will subsequently present the algorithm of Matula for determining the minimum link cut in $O(NL)$ time.

2.1.1. Dinitz' Algorithm. Dinitz' algorithm, published in 1970 by Yefim Dinitz, was the first maximum-flow algorithm to run in polynomial time (contrary to the pseudopolynomial running time of the Ford-Fulkerson algorithm [24]). The algorithm is sometimes referred to as Dinic's or Dinits' algorithm, and also different variants are known. A historical perspective of the different variants is presented by Dinitz himself in [27]. In order to describe Dinitz' algorithm, as presented in Algorithm 1, some definitions are given.

Definition 9. The residual capacity $c_f(u, v)$ of a link (u, v) is interpreted in two directions as follows:

$$c_f(u, v) = c(u, v) - f(u, v),$$
$$c_f(v, u) = f(u, v), \tag{2}$$

where the flow $f(u, v)$ over a link (u, v) cannot exceed the capacity $c(u, v)$ of that link.

Definition 10. The residual graph G_f of G is the graph in which a directed link (u, v) exists if $c_f(u, v) > 0$.

Definition 11. A blocking flow f_b is an s-t flow such that any other s-t flow f would have to traverse a link already saturated by f_b.

A blocking flow could be obtained by repeatedly finding (via Depth-First-Search [28]) an augmenting flow along an s-t path (or pruning the path from the graph in unit-capacity networks). In unit-capacity networks, the algorithm runs in $O(L \cdot (\min\{N^{2/3}, \sqrt{L}\}))$, which therefore also is the time complexity to determine a minimum s-t link cut with Dinitz' algorithm (for unit node capacities, a complexity of $O(L\sqrt{N})$ can be obtained [29]).

For further reference, in Table 1, we present some key achievements in computing minimum s-t link cuts.

2.1.2. Matula's Algorithm. In this section, we describe the algorithm from Matula [43] for determining the link connectivity of an undirected network. Matula's algorithm is based on the following lemma.

TABLE 1: Related work on computing minimum s-t link cuts.

Year[1]	Reference	Complexity	Description
1951	Dantzig [30]	$O(N^2LU)$	Linear programming, where U is the largest link capacity.
1956	Ford and Fulkerson [31]	$O(NLU)$	Augmenting paths.
1970	Dinitz [27]	$O(N^2L), O\left(L \cdot \left(\min\left\{N^{2/3}, \sqrt{L}\right\}\right)\right)$	Resp. capacitated and unit-capacity graphs. Shortest augmenting paths.
1974	Karzanov [32]	$O(N^3)$	Preflow-push (A simplification of Karzanov's algorithm has been presented by Tarjan [33]).
1980	Galil and Naamad [34]	$O(NL\log^2 N)$	Extension of Dinitz' algorithm.
1982	Shiloach and Vishkin [35]	$O((N^3\log N)/p)$	Parallel algorithm for $p \leq N$ processors.
1983	Sleator and Tarjan [36]	$O(NL\log N)$	Dynamic tree data structure.
1986	Goldberg and Tarjan [37]	$O(NL\log(N^2/L))$	Highest-label preflow-push.
1987	Ahuja et al. [38]	$O\left(NL\log\left((N/L)\sqrt{\log U}+2\right)\right)$	Excess scaling.
1989	Cheriyan and Hagerup [39]	$O(NL + N^2\log^3 N)$	Randomized algorithm.
1990	Alon [40]	$O(NL)$	Deterministic version of Cheriyan and Hagerup's randomized algorithm.
1998	Goldberg and Rao [41]	$O\left(\min\left\{N^{2/3}, \sqrt{L}\right\}L\log(N^2/L)\log U\right)$	Length function.
2011	Christiano et al. [42]	$\tilde{O}(LN^{1/3}\epsilon^{-11/3}), \tilde{O}(L+N^{4/3}\epsilon^{-8/3})$	Resp. $(1-\epsilon)$ and $(1+\epsilon)$ approximation, where $\tilde{O}(f(x))$ denotes $O(f(x)\log^c f(x))$ for some constant c.

[1]Throughout the paper, we take the convention of listing the year of the first (conference) publication, while referring to the extended (journal) version there where applicable.

Lemma 12. *Let G be a graph with a minimum cut of size $\lambda(G) \leq \delta(G)-1$ that partitions the graph G into two subgraphs $G_1(\mathcal{N}_1, \mathcal{L}_1)$ and $G_2(\mathcal{N}_2, \mathcal{L}_2)$, then any dominating set S of G contains nodes of both G_1 and G_2 (a dominating set $S \in \mathcal{N}$ is a subset of the nodes in G, such that every node in $\mathcal{N}$ is either in S or adjacent to a node in S).*

Proof. For subgraph G_i, $i = 1, 2$, holds that the sum of the nodal degrees in G_i is bounded by

$$N_i(N_i - 1) + \lambda(G) \geq \sum_{u \in G_i} d(u) \geq N_i\delta(G). \quad (3)$$

The upper bound occurs if all nodes in G_i are connected to each other and some of the nodes have a link that is part of the cut-set. The lower bound stems from each node having a degree larger or equal than the minimum degree $\delta(G)$. From the bounds in (3), we can derive that

$$(N_i - \delta(G))(N_i - 1) \geq \delta(G) - \lambda(G). \quad (4)$$

Since $\lambda(G) \leq \delta(G) - 1$ is assumed, $(N_i - \delta(G))(N_i - 1) \geq 1$ and consequently both terms on the left-hand side cannot be smaller than 1. Hence, $N_i - \delta(G) \geq 1$, which means that, under the assumption that $\lambda(G) \leq \delta(G) - 1$, there is at least one node in G_1 that does not have a neighbor in G_2 (and vice versa). In other words, any dominating set S of G should contain nodes of both G_1 and G_2. □

The algorithm of Matula (see Algorithm 2) starts with a node of minimum degree (e.g., node s in G_1) and gradually builds a dominating set S by adding nodes not yet part of

or adjacent to the growing set. Since at one point a node, for example u^*, from G_2 needs to be added, keeping track of the minimum cut between newly added dominating nodes, and S will result in finding the overall minimum cut. The algorithm is presented below.

In the algorithm of Matula, an augmenting path is a path in the residual network, where a residual network is the network that remains after pruning the links of a previous augmenting path. There are no 1-hop paths from u^* to S, because then $u^* \in T$. If u^* has n_T neighbors that belong to T, then there exist n_T 2-hop paths from u^* to S, for which either the first hop from u^* to T or the second hop from T to S is part of the minimum cut. These n_T paths form the first augmenting paths, after which $\lambda(G) - n_T$ remains. These remaining augmenting paths can be found in $O(L)$ time each and since there are at most $d(u^*) - n_T$ such paths, the complexity of the algorithm is bounded by $O(NL)$. Finally, if $\lambda(G) = \delta(G)$, then the initialization guarantees that that value would be found.

For directed multigraphs, Shiloach [44] provided a theorem that is stronger than Menger's theorem, namely.

Theorem 13. *Let G be a directed k-link-connected multigraph, then for all $s_1, \ldots, s_k, t_1, \ldots, t_k \in \mathcal{N}$ (not necessarily distinct) there exist link-disjoint paths P_i from s_i to t_i for $i = 1, \ldots, k$.*

We refer to Mansour and Schieber [45] for an $O(NL)$-time algorithm for determining the link connectivity in directed networks.

For further reference, in Table 2 we present some key achievements in computing minimum link cuts.

(1) For a node s of minimum degree set $S \leftarrow \{s\}$, $T \leftarrow \{t \mid t \in \mathrm{adj}(s)\}$, $U \leftarrow \mathcal{N} - S - T$, and $\lambda \leftarrow d(s)$.
(2) While $U \neq \varnothing$
(3)   Choose $u \in U$
(4) $n \leftarrow$ The number of shortest augmenting paths from u to S
(5)   If $n < \lambda$ then $\lambda \leftarrow n$
(6)   Set $S \leftarrow S \cup u$, $T \leftarrow T \cup \{t \mid t \in \mathrm{adj}(u)\}$, followed by $U \leftarrow \mathcal{N} - S - T$

ALGORITHM 2: Matula-Min-Cut (G).

TABLE 2: Related work on computing minimum link cuts.

Year	Reference	Complexity	Description
1971	Podderyugin [70]	$O(NL)$	Undirected graphs. Variation of Ford-Fulkerson max-flow algorithm in how augmenting paths of one and two hops are handled.
1971	Tarjan [67]	$O(N + L)$	Testing for 2-link connectivity in undirected graphs via DFS.
1975	Even and Tarjan [29]	$O(N^{5/3}L)$	Application of Dinitz' algorithm.
1986	Karzanov and Timofeev [59]	$O(\lambda N^2)$	Undirected graphs.
1987	Matula [43]	$O(NL)$, $O(\lambda N^2)$	Undirected graphs. It is also shown that the maximum subgraph link connectivity can be determined in $O(N^2 L)$.
1989	Mansour and Schieber [45]	$O(NL)$, $O(\lambda^2 N^2)$	Directed graphs. Relation between minimum cut and dominating set.
1990	Nagamochi and Ibaraki [71]	$O(L + \lambda N^2)$	Undirected graphs. Algorithm does not use a max-flow algorithm.
1991	Galil and Italiano [72]	$O(N + L)$	Testing for 3-link-connectivity in undirected graphs.
1991	Gabow [73]	$O(\lambda L \log(N^2/L))$, $O(L + \lambda^2 N \log(N/\lambda))$	Directed, resp. undirected graphs. Matroid approach.
1996	Karger [74]	$O\big(L \log^2 N\big)$	Randomized algorithm.

2.2. Determining Node Connectivity. Maximum-flow algorithms can also be used to determine the node connectivity, as demonstrated by Dantzig and Fulkerson [46] (and also discussed in [47]), by transforming the undirected graph $G(\mathcal{N}, \mathcal{L})$ to a directed graph $G'(\mathcal{N}', \mathcal{L}')$ as follows.

For every node $n \in \mathcal{N}$ place two nodes n' and n'' in $\mathcal{N}'$ and connect them via a directed link (n', n''), using the convention that the link starts at n' and ends at n''. For every undirected link $(i, j) \in \mathcal{L}$ place directed links (i'', j') and (j'', i') in G'. All links are assigned unit capacity.

The s-t node connectivity in G can be computed by finding a maximum flow from s'' to t' in G'. This can be seen as follows. Assume that there are κ node-disjoint paths between s and t, then there are also κ corresponding node-disjoint paths from s'' to t' in G'. Since each link has unit capacity, there thus exists a flow of at least κ. Since each link entering a node $n' \in G'$ has to traverse a single unit-capacity link (n', n'') at most one unit of flow can pass through a node, which corresponds to a node-disjoint path. Since there are only κ node-disjoint paths, the maximum flow in G' is equal to κ.

By using Dinitz' algorithm, one may compute the s-t node connectivity in $O(L \cdot (\min\{N^{2/3}, \sqrt{L}\}))$ time, and by using the algorithm of Mansour and Schieber [45], the node connectivity can be determined in $O(NL)$ time. We refer to

Henzinger et al. [48] and Gabow [49] for more advanced algorithms to compute the node connectivity in directed and undirected graphs and to Yoshida and Ito [50] for a κ-node-connectivity property testing algorithm (in property testing the objective is to decide, with high probability, whether the input graph is close to having a certain property. These algorithms typically run in sub-linear time).

3. Network Connectivity Augmentation

In the previous section, we have provided an overview of several algorithms to determine the connectivity of a network. In this section, we will overview several network augmentation algorithms that can be deployed to increase the connectivity (or some other metric) of a network by adding links. Network augmentation problems seem closely related to network deletion problems (e.g., see [51]), where the objective is to remove links in order to reach a certain property. However, there may be significant differences in terms of complexity. For instance, finding a minimum-weight set of links to cut a λ-link-connected graph such that its connectivity is reduced to $\lambda = 0$ is solvable in polynomial time (as discussed in Section 2.1), while adding a minimum-weight set of links to increase a disconnected graph to λ-link-connectivity is NP-complete as shown in Section 3.1. When both link deletions and link additions are permitted, we speak of link modification problems, for example, see [52].

3.1. Link Connectivity Augmentation. In this section, we consider the following link augmentation problem.

Problem 1 (the link connectivity augmentation (LCA) problem). Given a graph $G(\mathcal{N}, \mathcal{L})$ consisting of N nodes and L links, link connectivity λ and an integer β, the link connectivity augmentation problem is to add a minimum-weight set of links, such that the link connectivity of the graph G is increased from λ to $\lambda + \beta$.

We can discriminate several variants based on the graph (directed, simple, planar, etc.) or if link weights are used or not (i.e., in the unweighted case all links have weight 1). Let us start with the weighted link connectivity augmentation problem.

Theorem 14. *The weighted LCA problem is NP-hard.*

We will use the proof due to Frederickson and JáJá [53] to show that the 3-dimensional matching (3DM) problem is reducible to the weighted LCA problem (an earlier proof has been provided by Eswaran and Tarjan [54], but since it aims to augment a network without any links to one that is 2 connected and has N links (a cycle), it has the characteristics of a design rather than an augmentation problem).

Problem 2 (3-dimensional matching (3DM)). Given a set $M \subseteq X \times Y \times Z$ of triplets, where X, Y, and Z are disjoint sets of q elements each, is there a matching subset $M' \subseteq M$ that contains all $3q$ elements, such that $|M'| = q$, and thus no two elements of M' agree in any coordinate?

Proof. For a 3DM instance $M \subseteq X \times Y \times Z$, with $|M| = p$, $X = \{x_i \mid i = 1, \ldots, q\}$, $Y = \{y_i \mid i = 1, \ldots, q\}$, and $Z = \{z_i \mid i = 1, \ldots, q\}$, we create the graph $G(\mathcal{N}, \mathcal{L})$ of the corresponding instance of the weighted LCA problem as follows:

$$\mathcal{N} = \{r\} \cup \{x_i, y_i, z_i \mid i = 1, \ldots, q\}$$

$$\cup \left\{ a_{ijk}, \bar{a}_{ijk} \mid \left(x_i, y_j, z_k \right) \in M \right\},$$

$$\mathcal{L} = \{(r, x_i), (r, y_i), (r, z_i) \mid i = 1, \ldots, q\}$$

$$\cup \left\{ \left(x_i, a_{ijk} \right), \left(x_i, \bar{a}_{ijk} \right) \mid \left(x_i, y_j, z_k \right) \in M \right\}.$$

(5)

The graph G as constructed above forms a tree and therefore is 1 connected. Links from the complement G^c of G can be used to augment the graph to 2-link connectivity. The weights of the links in $G^c(\mathcal{N}, \mathcal{L}^c)$ are $w(a_{ijk}, \bar{a}_{ijk}) = w(y_j, a_{ijk}) = w(z_k, \bar{a}_{ijk}) = 1$ for $(x_i, y_j, z_k) \in M$, and for the remaining links in G^c, the weight is 2.

M contains a matching M' if and only if there is a set $\mathcal{L}' \subseteq \mathcal{L}^c$ of weight $w(\mathcal{L}') = p + q$ such that $G'(\mathcal{N}, \mathcal{L} \cup \mathcal{L}')$ is 2-link connected. Assuming M' exists, then adding links (y_j, a_{ijk}) and $(z_k, \bar{a}_{ijk})$ for each triple $(x_i, y_j, z_k) \in M'$ will establish the (2-connected) cycle $r - y_j - a_{ijk} - x_i - \bar{a}_{ijk} - z_k - r$. Since $|M'| = q$, the weight of these added links is $2q$. The

remaining nodes that are not yet on a cycle are the nodes a_{ijk} and $\bar{a}_{ijk}$ belonging to $(x_i, y_j, z_k) \in \{M - M'\}$. These nodes will be directly connected, thereby creating the cycle $x_i - a_{ijk} - \bar{a}_{ijk} - x_i$. In total, $|M - M'| = p - q$ additional links will be added, leading to a total weight of links that have been added of $p + q$. Since the graph G is a tree with $2(p+q)$ leaves and the minimum link weight is 1, a network augmentation solution of weight $p + q$ is indeed the lowest possible. It remains to demonstrate that an augmentation of weight $p+q$ will lead to a valid matching M'. Since, in a solution of weight $p+q$, each leaf will be connected by precisely one link from $\mathcal{L}^c$, a link (y_j, a_{ijk}) will prevent adding a link $(a_{ijk}, \bar{a}_{ijk})$, and therefore also link $(z_k, \bar{a}_{ijk})$ must be added. The corresponding triple (x_i, y_j, z_k) was not augmented before and is, therefore, part of a valid matching. The remaining $p - q$ links $(a_{ijk}, \bar{a}_{ijk})$ do not contribute to the matching. □

Frederickson and JáJá also used the construction of this proof to prove that the node-connectivity and strong-connectivity variants of the weighted LCA problem are NP-hard (in a directed graph strong connectivity is used, which means that there is a directed path from each node to every other node in the graph). We remark that the unweighted simple graph preserving LCA problem was claimed to be NP-hard by Jordán (reproduced in [55]) by using a reduction to one of the problems treated by Frederickson and JáJá. However, Jordán appears to be using an unweighted problem of which only (in the paper [53] referred to) the weighted version is proved to be NP-hard, and it is therefore not clear whether the unweighted problem is indeed NP-hard. For fixed β, the unweighted simple graph preserving problem can be solved in polynomial time [55].

Eswaran and Tarjan [54] were the first to report on augmentation problems. They considered augmenting a network towards either 2-link connectivity, 2-node connectivity or strong connectivity, and provided for each unweighted problem variant an algorithm of complexity $O(N + L)$ (Raghavan [56] pointed out an error in the strong connectivity algorithm and provided a fix for it). Since most protection schemes only focus on protecting against one single failure at a time (by finding two disjoint paths as discussed in Section 4), we will first present the 2-link-connectivity augmentation algorithm of Eswaran and Tarjan [54].

3.1.1. Eswaran and Tarjan Algorithm. The algorithm of Eswaran and Tarjan as presented in Algorithm 6 makes use of preorder (Algorithm 4) and postorder (Algorithm 3) numbering of nodes in a tree T (the label $l(u)$ of node u denotes its number as a result of the ordering) and a procedure (Algorithm 5) to find 2-link-connected components.

We have assumed that the initial graph was connected. Eswaran and Tarjan's algorithm also allows to start with disconnected graphs, by augmenting the forest of condensed 2-link-connected components to a tree.

3.1.2. Cactus Representation of All Minimum Cuts. The algorithm of Eswaran and Tarjan uses a tree representation of all the 2-link-connected components in G, which is

```
(1) For each v ← adj(u) do PostOrder (v, i)
(2) i ← i + 1
(3) l(u) ← i
```

ALGORITHM 3: PostOrder (T, u, i).

```
(1) i ← i + 1
(2) l(u) ← i
(3) For each v ← adj(u) do PreOrder (v, i)
```

ALGORITHM 4: PreOrder (T, u, i).

subsequently used to find a proper augmentation. By using a so-called cactus representation of all minimum cuts in a network, a similar strategy could be deployed to augment a network to a connectivity >2. A graph G is defined to be a cactus graph if any two distinct simple cycles in G have at most one node in common (or equivalently, any link of G belongs to at most one cycle). In this section, we will present the cactus representation.

We will use the notation (X, Y) to represent a set of links that connect nodes in X to nodes in Y. The link-set $(X, \overline{X})$, with $\overline{X} = \mathcal{N} \setminus X$, refers to a cut-set of links whose removal separates the graph into two subgraphs of nodes X and nodes $\overline{X}$. Dinitz et al. [58] have proposed a cactus structure $\mathcal{H}(G)$ to represent all the minimum cuts of a graph G (possibly with parallel links) and have shown that there can be at most $\binom{N}{2}$ such minimum cuts. The structure $\mathcal{H}(G)$ possesses the following properties.

(1) $\mathcal{H}(G)$ is a cactus graph, that is, any two distinct simple cycles of $\mathcal{H}(G)$ have at most one node in common.

(2) Each proper cut in $\mathcal{H}(G)$ is a minimum cut (a cut is called proper if the removal of the links in that cut partitions the graph in precisely two subgraphs. A minimum cut is always proper).

(3) For any link (u, v) that is part of a cycle in $\mathcal{H}(G)$ the weight $w(u, v) = \lambda/2$, else $w(u, v) = \lambda$.

(4) $w(\lambda(\mathcal{H}(G))) = \lambda(G)$, where $w(\lambda(\mathcal{H}(G)))$ represents the minimum-weight link cut of $\mathcal{H}(G)$.

A cactus graph without cycles is a tree, and if $\lambda(G)$ is odd, then $\mathcal{H}(G)$ is a tree. Cycles in the cactus graph $\mathcal{H}(G)$ reflect so-called crossing cuts in G.

Definition 15. Two cuts $(X, \overline{X})$ and $(Y, \overline{Y})$, with $X, Y \in \mathcal{N}$, are crossing cuts, if all four sets $X \cap Y$, $X \cap \overline{Y}$, $\overline{X} \cap Y$, and $\overline{X} \cap \overline{Y}$ are non-empty.

Karzanov and Timofeev [59] have outlined an algorithm to compute $\mathcal{H}(G)$ that consists of two parts: (1) computing all minimum cuts and (2) constructing the corresponding cactus representation. However, Nagamochi and Kameda [60] reported that their cactus representation may

not be unique. We assume that all minimum cuts are already known (e.g., by computing minimum s-t cuts between all possible source-destination pairs, by the Gomory-Hu tree algorithm [61], or with Matula's algorithm as explained in [62]) and focus on explaining—by following the description of Fleischer [63]—how to build a unique cactus graph $\mathcal{H}(G)$ for the graph G.

Karzanov and Timofeev [59] observe that for a link $(i, j) \in \mathcal{L}$, any two minimum cuts $(X, \overline{X})$ and $(Y, \overline{Y})$ that separate i and j are nested, which means that $X \subset Y$ (or vice versa). If we assign the nodes of G a preorder labelling $\{n_1, \ldots, n_N\}$, such that node n_{i+1} is adjacent to a node in the set $\mathcal{N}_i := \{n_1, \ldots, n_i\}$, and define $\mathcal{M}_i$ to be the set of minimum cuts that contain $\mathcal{N}_{i-1}$ but not n_i, then it follows that all cuts in $\mathcal{M}_i$ are noncrossing for each $i \in \{2, \ldots, N\}$. For instance, consider a 4-node ring $\{(a, b), (b, c), (c, d), (d, a)\}$, where three minimum cuts separate nodes a and d, namely, $(\{a\}, \{b, c, d\})$, $(\{a, b\}, \{c, d\})$, and $(\{a, b, c\}, \{d\})$. Clearly $\{a\} \subset \{a, b\} \subset \{a, b, c\}$, which allows us to represent them as a path graph $a - b - c - d$. The three possibilities to cut this chain correspond to the three minimum cuts that separate a and d in the ring graph. For each $\mathcal{M}_i$ there is a corresponding path graph P_i. These $N - 1$ path graphs are used to create a single cactus graph. We proceed to present the algorithm as described by Fleischer [63] (for an alternative description we refer to [64]), see Algorithm 7. We define η to be the function that maps nodes of G to nodes in $\mathcal{H}(G_{i+1})$, and we define G_i to be the graph G with nodes $\mathcal{N}_i$ contracted to a single node (and any resulting self-loops removed). Let G_r be the smallest graph that has a minimum cut of value λ, where r corresponds to the largest index of such a graph. $\mathcal{H}(G_r)$ is a path graph. The algorithm builds $\mathcal{H}(G_i)$ from $\mathcal{H}(G_{i+1})$ until $\mathcal{H}(G_1) = \mathcal{H}(G)$ is obtained.

Figure 1 gives an example of the execution of the algorithm on a 4-node ring.

3.1.3. Naor-Gusfield-Martel Algorithm. Naor et al. [65] have proposed a polynomial-time algorithm to augment the link connectivity of a graph G from λ to $\lambda + \beta$, by adding the smallest number of (possibly parallel) links. The authors first demonstrate how to augment the link connectivity by one in $O(NL)$ time, after which it is explained how executing this algorithm β times could optimally augment the graph towards $\lambda + \beta$ link connectivity (Cheng and Jordán [66] further discuss link connectivity augmentation by adding one link at a time). In practice, as a result of the costs in network augmentation, a network's connectivity is likely not augmented with $\beta > 1$. We will therefore only present the algorithm to augment the link connectivity by one, see Algorithm 9, and refer to [65] for the extended algorithm. The algorithm uses the cactus structure $\mathcal{H}(G)$ that was presented in the previous section to represent all the minimum cuts of a graph G. The algorithm is similar in approach to the Eswaran-Tarjan algorithm, since a cactus representation of a 1-connected network is the tree representation used by Eswaran and Tarjan, and the algorithm connects "leafs" as Eswaran and Tarjan have done. Naor et al., however, use a different definition of leafs for cactus graphs.

(1) Find a directed spanning tree T in G rooted at a node s
(2) PostOrder $(T, s, 0)$
(3) For $i = 1, \ldots, N$
(4)   For $j \in \mathrm{adj}(i)$ /*Only nodes "downstream"*/
(5)   if $\min(\{i - N_D(i) + 1\} \cup \{N_L(j)\} \cup \{j \mid (i, j) \notin T\}) > j - N_D(j)$ and
            $\max(\{i\} \cup \{N_H(j)\} \cup \{j \mid (i, j) \notin T\}) \le j$ /*$N_D(i)$ is the number of descendants
            in the tree including i*/
(6)   then (i, j) is 1-link-connected. /*Its removal cuts the graph*/

ALGORITHM 5: Tarjan-2-link-components (G), developed by Tarjan [57].

(1) Find the 2-link-connected components of G
(2) Condense G into a tree T for which each node represents one of the 2-link-connected components of G
(3) Number the nodes in T in preorder, starting from an arbitrary non-leaf node s /*PreOrder $(T, s, 0)$*/
(4) For $i = 1, \ldots, \lceil r/2 \rceil$ choose links $(u(i), u(i + \lfloor r/2 \rfloor))$, where $u(i), \ldots, u(r)$ are the r leaves of T ordered in increasing node number
(5) Map the ends of each chosen link to an arbitrary node in the corresponding 2-link-connected component

ALGORITHM 6: Eswaran-Tarjan-2-link-augmentation (G).

Definition 16 (cactus leaf). A node in a cactus representation $\mathcal{H}(G)$ is a cactus leaf if it has degree 1 or is a cycle node of degree 2.

Similarly to a tree, if the cactus $\mathcal{H}(G)$ has k leafs, then $\lceil k/2 \rceil$ links need to be added to increase the connectivity by 1.

The algorithm uses a Depth-First-Search-like procedure, see Algorithm 8, to label the nodes of the cactus graph.

For further reference, in Table 3, we present some key achievements in augmenting link connectivity in unweighted graphs.

Splitting off a pair of links (u, v) and (v, w) refers to deleting those links and adding a new link (u, w). A pair of links is said to be splittable if the s-t min-cut values remain unaffected after splitting off the pair of links and is considered in the context of Mader's theorem.

Theorem 17 (Mader [68, 69]). *Let G be a connected undirected graph where for some node s the degree $d(s) \ne 3$, and the removal of one of the adjacent links of s does not disconnect the graph, then s has a pair of splittable links.*

Mader's theorem has been used by for instance Cai and Sun [75] and Frank [77] in developing network augmentation algorithms. The algorithms (as already outlined in 1976 by Plesník [84]) attach a new node s to the graph with $(\lambda + \beta)$ parallel links between s and all other nodes in the graph and subsequently proceed to split off splittable links.

As indicated by Theorem 14, the weighted LCA problem is NP-complete for both undirected graphs and directed graphs. Frederickson and JáJá [53] provided an $O(N^2)$ algorithm to make a weighted graph 2 connected. The algorithm

is a 2-approximation algorithm if the starting graph is connected, else it is a 3-approximation algorithm. Khuller and Thurimella [85] proposed a 2-approximation algorithm for increasing the connectivity of a weighted undirected graph to $(\lambda + \beta)$ that has a complexity of $O(N(\lambda + \beta) \log N(L + N \log N))$. Taoka et al. [86] compare via simulations several approximation and heuristic algorithms, including their own maximum-weight-matching-based algorithm.

Under specific conditions, the weighted LCA problem may be polynomially solvable, as shown by Frank [77] for the case that link weights are derived from node weights.

3.2. Node Connectivity Augmentation. In this section, we consider the following node augmentation problem.

Problem 3. The Node Connectivity Augmentation (NCA) problem. Given a graph $G(\mathcal{N}, \mathcal{L})$ consisting of N nodes and L links, node connectivity κ and an integer γ, the node connectivity augmentation problem is to add a minimum-weight set of links, such that the node connectivity of the graph G is increased from κ to $\kappa + \gamma$.

Like for the LCA problem.

Theorem 18. *The weighted NCA problem is NP-hard.*

Proof. The proof of Theorem 14 also applies here. □

The unweighted undirected NCA problem has received most attention. The specific case of making a graph 2-node connected was treated by Eswaran and Tarjan [54], Rosenthal and Goldner [87] (a correction to this algorithm has been made by Hsu and Ramachandran [88]). Watanabe

(1) Compute P_i for $i = 2, \ldots, N$

(2) For $i = r - 1, \ldots, 1$

(3)   Replace the node q in $\mathcal{H}(G_{i+1})$ that contains nodes $\{n_1, \ldots, n_{i+1}\}$ with the Path P_{i+1}.
        If $P_{i+1} = X_1, \ldots, X_k$, then remove q and introduce k new nodes $q_1, \ldots, q_k$ with links
        (q_j, q_{j+1}) for $1 \le j < k$.

(4)   Connect path P_{i+1} to $\mathcal{H}(G_{i+1})$. For any tree or cycle link (q, w) in $\mathcal{H}(G_{i+1})$, let $W \ne \varnothing$
        be the set of nodes in w, or if w is an empty node, the nodes in any nonempty
        node w' reachable from w by some path of links disjoint from a cycle containing
        (q, w). Find the subset X_j such that $w \subset X_j$ and connect W to q_j.

(5)   Label the nodes of P_{i+1}. Let Q be the set of nodes mapped to q in $\mathcal{H}(G_{i+1})$.
        Update η by $\eta^{-1}(q_j) := X_j \cap Q$ for all $1 \le j < k$. All other mappings remain
        unchanged.

(6)   Remove all empty nodes of degree ≤ 2 and all empty 2-way cut nodes by contracting
        an adjacent tree link (a node is an x-way cut node if its removal separates the graph into
        x connected parts). Replace all empty 3-way cut nodes with 3 cycles.

ALGORITHM 7: Build-Cactus (G).

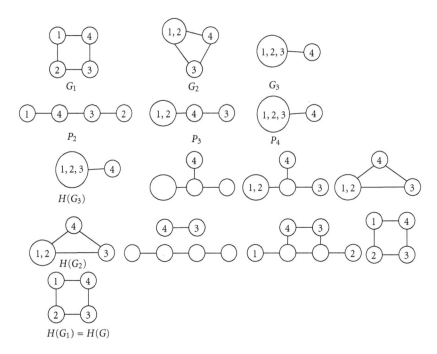

FIGURE 1: Example of a cactus construction for a 4-node ring topology. The top "row" gives the graphs G_i, for $i = 1, \ldots, r$. The second row gives the paths P_i, for $i = 2, \ldots, N$. The third row presents the first iteration of the for loop in algorithm Build-Cactus, while the fourth row presents the last iteration. The last row presents the cactus representation of the ring, which is a ring itself.

(1) Assign different colors to the different simple cycles /*, for example, by finding the articulation
    points [67]*/

(2) DFS traversal that starts at an arbitrary node and obeys the following rule: if a node u is visited
    for the first time via a cycle with some color, then traverse all other differently colored links
    adjacent to u before traversing the adjacent link of the same color. Enumerate the cactus leafs
    $u_1, \ldots, u_k$ in the order in which they are first encountered in the DFS traversal.

ALGORITHM 8: Cactus-DFS $(\mathcal{H}(G))$.

---

(1) $\mathcal{H}(G)$ ←Build-Cactus (G)

(2) Cactus-DFS $(\mathcal{H}(G))$

(3) Form the pairs $\{(U_i, U_{i+\lceil k/2 \rceil}) : 1 \le i \le \lfloor k/2 \rfloor\}$, where U_i is the set of nodes from G that map to the leaf u_i of $\mathcal{H}(G)$.

(4) For each pair $(U_i, U_{i+\lceil k/2 \rceil}) : 1 \le i \le \lfloor k/2 \rfloor$, add a link between a node from G in U_i and a node from G in $U_{i+\lceil k/2 \rceil}$. If k is odd, then connect a node in $U_{\lceil k/2 \rceil}$ to a node in a different leaf U_j.

ALGORITHM 9: Naor-Gusfield-Martel-Aug-1 (G).

and Nakamura [89] and Jordán [90] solved the case for achieving 3-node-connectivity, while Hsu [91] developed an algorithm to upgrade a 3-node connected graph to a 4-node-connected one. Increasing the connectivity of a κ-node-connected graph (where κ can be any integer) by 1 was studied by many researchers [90, 92–97], since it was long unknown whether the problem was polynomially solvable. In 2010, Végh [98] provided a polynomial-time algorithm to increase the connectivity of any κ-node-connected unweighted undirected graph by $\gamma = 1$.

Augmenting the node connectivity of directed graphs has been treated by Frank and Jordán [99]. They found a min-max formula that finds the minimum number of required new links to make an unweighted digraph $(\kappa + \gamma)$-node connected. Frank and Végh [100] developed a polynomial-time algorithm to make a κ-node-connected directed graph $(\kappa + 1)$-node connected.

As the weighted NCA problem is NP-complete, special cases have been considered [88–91, 98, 101]. Most of these articles discuss specific connectivity targets (γ and/or κ have specific values) or specific topologies, like trees. Also heuristic and approximation algorithms have been proposed [85, 102–107].

4. Disjoint Paths

When a network is (made to be) robust, algorithms should be in place that can find link- or node-disjoint paths to protect against a link or node failure. There can be several objectives associated with finding link- or node-disjoint paths.

Problem 4. Given a graph $G(\mathcal{N}, \mathcal{L})$, where $|\mathcal{N}| = N$ and $|\mathcal{L}| = L$, a weight $w(u, v)$ and a capacity $c(u, v)$ associated with each link $(u, v) \in \mathcal{L}$, a source node s and a terminal node t, and two bounds $\Delta_1 \ge 0$ and $\Delta_2 \ge 0$ find a pair of disjoint paths from s to t such as the following.

Min-Sum Disjoint Paths Problem. The total weight of the pair of disjoint paths is minimized.

Min-Max Disjoint Paths Problem. The maximum path weight of the two disjoint paths is minimized.

Min-Min Disjoint Paths Problem. The smallest path weight of the two disjoint paths is minimized.

Bounded Disjoint Paths Problem. The weight of the primary path should be less than or equal to Δ_1, and the weight of the backup path should be less than or equal to Δ_2.

Widest Disjoint Paths Problem. The smallest capacity over all links in the two paths is maximized.

The most common and simpler one is the *min-sum* disjoint paths problem. If the two paths are used simultaneously for load-balancing purposes (or $1 + 1$ protection), then the min-max objective is desirable. Unfortunately, the min-max disjoint paths problem is NP-hard [108]. If failures are expected to occur only sporadically (and in case of $1:1$ protection), then it may be desirable to minimize the weight of the primary (shorter) path (min-min objective), which also leads to an NP-hard problem [109]. The min-max and min-min disjoint paths problems could be considered as extreme cases of the bounded disjoint paths problem, which was shown to be NP-hard [110] and later proven to be APX-hard by Bley [111] (the graph structure referred to as lobe that was used by Itai et al. [110] to prove NP-completeness has since often been used to prove that other disjoint paths problems are NP-complete, e.g., [112–114]). Finding widest disjoint paths can easily be done by pruning "low-capacity" links from the graph and finding disjoint paths. When the capacity requirements for the primary and backup paths are different, disjoint paths problems usually become NP-complete [115].

Beshir and Kuipers [116] investigated the min-sum disjoint paths problem with min-max, min-min, bounded, and widest, as secondary objectives in case multiple min-sum paths exist between s and t. From these variants, only the widest min-sum link-disjoint paths problem is not NP-hard.

Li et al. [112] studied the min-sum disjoint paths problem, where the link-weight functions are different for the primary and backup paths and showed that this problem is hard to approximate. Bhatia [117] demonstrated that the problem remains hard to approximate in the case that the weights for the links of the backup path are a fraction $0 < \rho < 1$ of the normal link weights (for the primary path).

Sherali et al. [118] investigated the time-dependent min-sum disjoint paths problem, where the link weights are time-dependent. They proved that the problem is NP-hard, even if only one link is time-dependent and all other links are static.

4.1. Min-Sum Disjoint Paths. Finding min-sum disjoint paths is equivalent to finding a minimum-cost flow in unit-capacity networks [26]: a minimum-cost flow of k

TABLE 3: Related work on augmenting link connectivity in unweighted graphs.

Year	Reference	Complexity	Description
1976	Eswaran and Tarjan [54]	$O(N + L)$	Augmenting to 2-connectivity.
1986	Cai and Sun [75]	NA	Splitting off links.
1987	Watanabe and Nakamura [76]	$O\big((\lambda + \beta)^2 N^4 ((\lambda + \beta)N + L)\big)$	Based on a derived formula for the minimum number of links to $(\lambda + \beta)$-link-connect G.
1990	Frank [77]	$O(N^6)$	Different s-t connectivities may be specified, instead of one $(\lambda + \beta)$-connectivity for all pairs[1].
1990	Naor et al. [65]	$O(\beta^2 NL + \beta^3 N^2 + NC_{\text{flow}})$	C_{flow} is the complexity of computing a maximum flow. If $\beta = 1$, then the complexity is $O(NL)$.
1991	Gabow [78]	$O\big(L + (\lambda + \beta)^2 N \log N\big)$	Poset representation of cuts applied to the Naor-Gusfield-Martel algorithm.
1994	Benczúr [79]	$\tilde{O}(\min\{N^3, \beta N^2\}), O(N^4)$	Resp. randomized and deterministic algorithms.
1996	Nagamochi and Ibaraki [80]	$O(N(L + N \log N) \log N)$	Splitting off links.
1998	Benczúr and Karger [81]	$O(N^2 \log^8 N)$	Randomized algorithm.
2004	Nagamochi and Ibaraki [82]	$O(NL + N^2 \log N)$	Maximum adjacency ordering[2].

[1] NP-hard variations of this problem and corresponding approximation results are provided by Nutov [83].
[2] Maximum adjacency ordering rule: add a new node n_{i+1} to previously selected nodes $\{n_1, \ldots, n_i\}$ that has the largest number of links to the set $\{n_1, \ldots, n_i\}$. Start with an abitrary node n_1.

will traverse k disjoint paths. In fact, Suurballe's algorithm, which is most often cited as an algorithm to compute two disjoint paths, is an algorithm that uses augmenting paths, like in several max-flow algorithms. The original Suurballe algorithm as presented in [119] allows to compute k node (or link) disjoint paths between a single source-destination pair, by using k shortest path computations. Later, this approach was used by Suurballe and Tarjan [120] to find two link (or node) disjoint paths from a source s to all other nodes in the network (i.e., $N - 1$ source-destination pairs), by using only two shortest-paths computations, that is, in $O(N \log N + L)$ time. Both papers focus on directed networks, but can also be applied to undirected networks.

In directed networks, a link-disjoint paths algorithm can be used to compute node-disjoint paths, if we split each node u into two nodes u_1 and u_2, with a directed link (u_1, u_2), and the incoming links of u connected to u_1 and the outgoing links of u departing from u_2.

In undirected networks, a link-disjoint paths algorithm can be used to compute node-disjoint paths by the transformation described in Section 2.2.

We will present the Suurballe-Tarjan algorithm, see Algorithm 10, for computing two link-disjoint paths between s and every other node in the network.

Instead of finding an augmenting path for each source-destination pair, Suurballe and Tarjan have found a way to combine these augmenting flow computations into two Dijkstra-like shortest-paths computations. First a shortest paths tree T is computed in line 1, and based on the computed shortest path lengths, the link weights are modified in line 2. This link weight modification was also used by Suurballe and is to assure that $w(u, v) \geq 0$ for all links, with equality if (u, v) is in T. In Suurballe's original algorithm the direction of the links on the shortest path from s to d was reversed, after which a shortest (augmenting) path

in the newly modified graph was computed. In Suurballe-Tarjan's algorithm the links maintain their direction, but an additional parameter q is used instead. The algorithm proceeds in a Dijkstra-like fashion. Lines 3–6 correspond to the initialization of the smallest length $l(i)$ from s to i found so far, its corresponding predecessor list $\pi(i)$ and $q(i)$. The algorithm repeatedly extracts a node of minimum length (in line 8) and removes that node from the tree T (in line 9). A slightly different relaxation procedure is used (lines 10–12). Upon termination of the algorithm, the disjoint paths between the source s and a destination t can be retrieved via the lists $\pi()$ and $q()$ with Algorithm 11.

Taft-Plotkin et al. [121] extended the approach of Suurballe and Tarjan in two ways: (1) they return maximally disjoint paths, and (2) they also take bandwidth into account. Their algorithm, called MADSWIP, computes maximum-bandwidth maximally disjoint paths and minimizes the total weight as a secondary objective. Consequently, by assigning all links equal bandwidth, the MADSWIP algorithm returns the min-sum maximally disjoint paths.

For a distributed disjoint paths algorithm, we refer to the work of Ogier et al. [122] and Sidhu et al. [123].

Roskind and Tarjan [124] presented an $O(L \log L + k^2 N^2)$ algorithm for finding k link-disjoint spanning trees of minimum total weight. Xue et al. [125, 126] have considered quality of service and quality of protection issues in computing two disjoint trees (quality of Protection (QoP) as used by Xue et al. refers to the amount of link failures that can be survived. QoP sometimes is used to refer to probabilistic survivability, as discussed in the following section or protection differentiation as overviewed by Cholda et al. [127]). Ramasubramanian et al. [128] proposed a distributed algorithm for computing two disjoint trees. Guo et al. [129] considered finding two link-disjoint paths subject to multiple Quality-of-Service constraints.

```
(1) Compute the shortest paths tree T rooted at s
(2) Modify the weights of each link (u, v) ∈ 𝓛 to w'(u, v) = w(u, v) − l(s, v) + l(s, u)
      /*l(s, i) is the length of the shortest path in G from s to i*/
(3) For i = 1, . . . , N
(4)       l(i) ← ∞, q(i) ← NIL, π(i) ← NIL
(5) l(s) ← 0
(6) Q ← 𝒩
(7) While Q ≠ ∅
(8)       EXTRACT-MIN (Q) → u
(9)       DELETE (T, u) /* T becomes a forest of subtrees*/
(10)      For each non-tree link (i, j) in T  such that i = u or i and j are in different subtrees
(11)          If l(u) + w(i, j) < l(j)
(12)              l(j) ← l(u) + w(i, j), π(j) ← i, q(j) ← u
```

ALGORITHM 10: Suurballe-Tarjan-2-link-disjoint-paths (G, s).

```
(1) x ← t
(2) While x ≠ s
(3)       mark x
(4)       x ← q(x)
(5) For i = 1, 2
(6) x ← t
(7) While x ≠ s
(8)       If x is marked
(9)           unmark x
(10)          P_i ← P_i + (p(x), x)
(11)          x ← p(x)
(10)      Else
(11)          P_i ← P_i + (y, x) /* y is parent of x in T*/
(12)          x ← y
```

ALGORITHM 11: Return-Suurballe-Tarjan-2-link-disjoint-paths (G, s, t).

4.2. Probabilistic Survivability. When two disjoint primary and backup paths are reserved for a connection, any failure on the primary path can be survived by using the backup path. The backup path therefore provides 100% survivability guarantee against a single failure. When no backup paths are available, that is, unprotected paths are used, then the communication along a path will fail if there is a failure on that path. Banner and Orda [130] have introduced the term p-survivable connection to denote a connection for which there is a probability $\geq p$ that all its links are operational (the related notion of Quality of Protection (QoP), as defined by Gerstel and Sasaki [131], was argued to be difficult to apply to general networks). The previous two cases correspond to $p = 1$ and $p = 0$, respectively. Banner and Orda proved that, under the single-link failure model, at most two paths are needed to establish a p-survivable connection, if it exists. Based on this observation, they studied and proposed algorithms for several problem variants, namely establishing p-survivable-B-bandwidth, most survivable, and widest p-survivable connections for $1:1$ and $1 + 1$ protection architectures (the MADSWIP algorithm [121] can also be used to find the most survivable connection). The p-survivable-B-bandwidth problem asks for a connection with survivability $\geq p$ and bandwidth $\geq B$ and solving it provides a foundation for solving the other problems. We will therefore discuss the solution proposed by Banner and Orda for the p-survivable-B-bandwidth problem.

The approach by Banner and Orda to solve the p-survivable-B-bandwidth problem is twofold. First, the graph is transformed, after which a minimum-cost flow is found on the resulting graph. The graph transformation is depicted in Figure 2 and slightly differs for the $1:1$ and $1 + 1$ cases. Clearly, if a link does not have sufficient spare capacity to accommodate the requested bandwidth B, then it does not need to be considered further (Figure 2(a)). If, for $1:1$ protection, $b_e \geq B$, then there is sufficient bandwidth for both disjoint paths, since the backup path is only used after failure of the primary path. To allow for both paths to share that link, it is transformed to two links (Figure 2(b)). If the original link is only used by one path, then that link is protected, and hence the weight 0 is assigned to the top link. If both paths have to use the original link, then the connection's survivability is affected by the failure probability of that link, which is why the weight $-\ln(1 - p_e)$ is assigned to the lower link (the logarithm is used to transform a multiplicative metric to an additive metric).

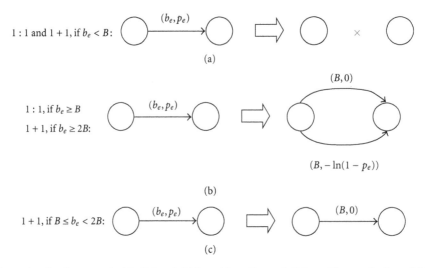

FIGURE 2: Graph transformation for the p-survivable-B-bandwidth problem. For each link e with capacity b_e and failure probability p_e, the new links consist of a bandwidth-weight pair.

The same applies to the $1 + 1$ case, with the exception that the concurrent transmission of data over both paths requires twice the requested bandwidth. For the remaining range $B \leq b_e < 2B$ for $1 + 1$ protection (Figure 2(c)), it holds that only one of the paths can use that link, which is why there is no weight penalty.

In the transformed graph, a minimum-cost flow of $2B$ units corresponds to two maximally disjoint paths of each B bandwidth. The minimum-cost flow could, for instance, be found with the cycle-canceling algorithm of Goldberg and Tarjan [132], while the corresponding maximally disjoint paths could be returned via a flow-decomposition algorithm [26].

Luo et al. [133] studied the min-sum p-survivable connection problem, where each link is characterized by a weight and a failure probability, and the problem is to find a connection of least weight and survivability $\geq p$. Contrary to the min-sum maximally-disjoint paths problem, this problem is NP-hard, since it contains the NP-hard restricted shortest paths problem (e.g., see [134]). Luo et al. proposed an ILP and two approximation algorithms for this problem. Chakrabarti and Manimaran [135] studied the min-sum p-survivable-B-bandwidth problem, for which they considered a segment-based protection strategy.

She et al. [114] have considered the problem of finding two link-disjoint paths, for which the probability that at least one of these paths will not fail is maximized. They refer to this problem as the maximum-reliability (max-rel) link-disjoint paths problem. The rationale behind this problem is to establish two disjoint paths that give 100% protection against a single-link failure, while reducing the failure probability of the connection as much as possible when multiple failures may occur. Assuming that the link-failure probabilities p_i are independent, then the reliability of a connection (consisting of two link-disjoint paths P_1 and P_2) is defined as $\prod_{i \in P_1} q_i + \prod_{j \in P_2} q_j + \prod_{i \in P_1} q_i \cdot \prod_{j \in P_2} q_j$, with $q_i = 1 - p_i$, for $i \in \mathcal{L}$. The max-rel link-disjoint paths problem is proven to be NP-complete. She et al. [114] evaluated two

simple heuristic algorithms that both transform the link probabilities p_i to link weights $\log_q q_i$, with $q_i = 1 - p_i$, for $i \in \mathcal{L}$, and $0 < q < 1$. Based on these weights, one heuristic finds a shortest path, prunes its links from the graphs, and finds a shortest path in the pruned graph. This is often referred to as an active-path-first (APF) approach. The second heuristic uses Suurballe's algorithm to find two link-disjoint paths. Contrary to the first heuristic, the second always returns link-disjoint paths if they exist.

4.3. Multiple Failures.

The single-link failure model has been most often considered in the literature, but multiple failures may occur as follows.

(i) Due to lengthy repair times of network equipment, there is a fairly long time span in which new failures could occur.

(ii) In case of terrorist attacks, several targeted parts of the network could be damaged. With Suurballe's algorithm, k link/node-disjoint paths can be found to establish full protection against $k - 1$ link/node failures.

(iii) In layered networks, for instance IP-over-WDM, one failure on the lowest-layer network, may cause multiple failures on higher-layer networks. Similarly, the links of a (single-layered) network may share the same duct, in which case a damaging of the duct may damage all the links inside. These links are often said to belong to the same shared risk link group (SRLG) (the node variant SRNG also exists. When both nodes and links can belong to a shared risk group, the term Shared Risk Resource Group (SRRG) is used, e.g., see [136]). Finding two SRLG-disjoint paths—paths of which the links in one path may not share a risk link group with links from the other path—is an NP-complete problem [137]. In specific cases, the SRLG-disjoint paths problem is polynomially solvable, as discussed by Bhandari [138], Datta and Somani [139], and Luo and Wang [140]. In those cases, for instance, when the links in a SRLG share the same endpoint, a graph transformation can be made that reflects the shared risk groups, and on which a simple link-disjoint paths algorithm can be run. Lee et al. [141] have generalized the SRLG problem to include failure probabilities. In the deterministic SRLG scenario, when a SRLG r fails (e.g., a cable in the physical network is cut) all higher-layer links that belong to that group fail. In the probabilistic SRLG (PSRLG) scenario, the links (i, j) in that PSRLG r fail with probability $p_{ij}^r > 0$. If $p_{ij}^r \in \{0, 1\}$, for $(i, j) \in \mathcal{L}$, then the problem of finding PSRLG-disjoint paths reduces to the NP-complete problem of finding SRLG-disjoint paths. For SRLG types of problems, often an integer programming formulation is provided (e.g., [137, 142–144]) or an active-path-first (APF) approach is used as a heuristic. Hu [137] provided a basic ILP formulation to return a min-sum pair of SRLG-disjoint paths. Xu et al. [143] gave an ILP and an APF heuristic for the case of shared (backup paths) protection.

(iv) Natural disasters may affect all nodes and links within a certain geographical area. Work on multilink geographic failures has mostly focused on determining the geographic max-flow and min-cut values of a network under geographic failures of circular shape (e.g., Sen et al. [145], Agarwal et al. [146], and Neumayer et al. [147]). Trajanovski et al. [148] proved that, the problem of finding two region-disjoint paths is NP-hard, and they proposed a heuristic for it.

5. Conclusion

We have provided an overview of algorithms for network survivability. We have considered how to verify that a network has certain connectivity properties, how to augment an existing network to reach a given connectivity, and, lastly, how to find alternative paths in case network failures occur. Our focus has been on algorithms for general networks, although much work has also been done for specific networks, such as optical networks, where additional constraints like wavelength continuity and signal impairments induce an increased complexity, for example, see our work [149–151]. We have not discussed how to design a survivable network from scratch. Typically network design problems are hard to solve and involve many constraints, but since they only need to be solved sporadically, longer computation times are permitted. Predominantly, integer programming is used to design a network, as we have done in [152].

Acknowledgment

The author would like to thank Professor Piet Van Mieghem for his constructive comments on an earlier version of this paper.

References

[1] M. Al-Kuwaiti, N. Kyriakopoulos, and S. Hussein, "A comparative analysis of network dependability, fault-tolerance, reliability, security, and survivability," *IEEE Communications Surveys and Tutorials*, vol. 11, no. 2, pp. 106–124, 2009.

[2] K. Menger, "Zur allgemeinen kurventheorie," *Fundamenta Mathematicae*, vol. 10, pp. 96–115, 1927.

[3] M. Fiedler, "Algebraic connectivity of graphs," *Czechoslovak Mathematical Journal*, vol. 23, pp. 298–305, 1973.

[4] P. Van Mieghem, *Graph Spectra for Complex Networks*, Cambridge University Press, 2011.

[5] N. M. M. de Abreu, "Old and new results on algebraic connectivity of graphs," *Linear Algebra and Its Applications*, vol. 423, no. 1, pp. 53–73, 2007.

[6] K. Lee, E. Modiano, and H. W. Lee, "Cross-layer survivability in WDM-based networks," *IEEE/ACM Transactions on Networking*, vol. 19, no. 4, pp. 1000–1013, 2011.

[7] K. Lee, H. W. Lee, and E. Modiano, "Reliability in layered networks with random link failures," *IEEE/ACM Transactions on Networking*, vol. 19, no. 6, pp. 1835–1848, 2011.

[8] W. Zou, M. Janic, R. Kooij, and F. A. Kuipers, "On the availability of networks," in *Proceedings of the BroadBand Europe*, Antwerp, Belgium, December 2007.

[9] C. J. Colbourn, *The Combinatorics of Network Reliability*, Oxford University Press, New York, NY, USA, 1987.

[10] P. Van Mieghem, H. Wang, X. Ge, S. Tang, and F. A. Kuipers, "Influence of assortativity and degree-preserving rewiring on the spectra of networks," *European Physical Journal B*, vol. 76, no. 4, pp. 643–652, 2010.

[11] D. Mosk-Aoyama, "Maximum algebraic connectivity augmentation is NP-hard," *Operations Research Letters*, vol. 36, no. 6, pp. 677–679, 2008.

[12] M. Yanakakis, "Computing the minimum fill-in is NP-complete," *SIAM Journal on Algebraic and Discrete Methods*, vol. 2, no. 1, pp. 77–79, 1981.

[13] P. Pan, G. Swallow, and A. Atlas, "Fast reroute extensions to RSVP-TE for LSP tunnels," IETF Request for Comments RFC 4090, 2005.

[14] M. Shand and S. Bryant, "IP fast reroute framework," IETF Request for Comments RFC 5714, 2010.

[15] R. Banner and A. Orda, "Designing low-capacity backup networks for fast restoration," in *Proceedings of the IEEE INFOCOM*, San Diego, Calif, USA, March 2010.

[16] G. Ellinas, A. G. Hailemariam, and T. E. Stern, "Protection cycles in mesh WDM networks," *IEEE Journal on Selected Areas in Communications*, vol. 18, no. 10, pp. 1924–1937, 2000.

[17] R. Asthana, Y. N. Singh, and W. D. Grover, "p-cycles: an overview," *IEEE Communications Surveys and Tutorials*, vol. 12, no. 1, pp. 97–111, 2010.

[18] M. Médard, S. G. Finn, R. A. Barry, and R. G. Gallager, "Redundant trees for preplanned recovery in arbitrary vertex-redundant or edge-redundant graphs," *IEEE/ACM Transactions on Networking*, vol. 7, no. 5, pp. 641–652, 1999.

[19] K. P. Gummadi, M. J. Pradeep, and C. S. R. Murthy, "An efficient primary-segmented backup scheme for dependable real-time communication in multihop networks," *IEEE/ACM Transactions on Networking*, vol. 11, no. 1, pp. 81–94, 2003.

[20] C. H. Papadimitriou and M. Yannakakis, "Optimization, approximation, and complexity classes," *Journal of Computer and System Sciences*, vol. 43, no. 3, pp. 425–440, 1991.

[21] B. Mohar, "Isoperimetric numbers of graphs," *Journal of Combinatorial Theory, Series B*, vol. 47, no. 3, pp. 274–291, 1989.

[22] D. W. Matula and F. Shahrokhi, "Sparsest cuts and bottlenecks in graphs," *Discrete Applied Mathematics*, vol. 27, no. 1-2, pp. 113–123, 1990.

[23] T. N. Dinh, Y. Xuan, M. T. Thai, E. K. Park, and T. Znati, "On approximation of new optimization methods for assessing network vulnerability," in *Proceedings of the IEEE INFOCOM*, San Diego, Calif, USA, March 2010.

[24] D. R. Fulkerson and G. B. Dantzig, "Computation of maximal flows in networks," *Naval Research Logistics*, vol. 2, no. 4, pp. 277–283, 1955.

[25] P. Elias, A. Feinstein, and C. E. Shannon, "A note on the maximum flow through a network," *IRE Transactions on Information Theory*, vol. 2, pp. 117–119, 1956.

[26] R. K. Ahuja, T. L. Magnanti, and J. B. Orlin, *Network Flows: Theory, Algorithms, and Applications*, Prentice Hall, Upper Saddle River, NJ, USA, 1st edition, 1993.

[27] Y. Dinitz, "Dinitz' algorithm: the original version and Even's version," in *Essays in Memory of Shimon Even*, O. Goldreich, A. L. Rosenberg, and A. L. Selman, Eds., vol. 3895 of *Lecture Notes in Computer Science*, pp. 218–240, Springer, Berlin, Germany, 2006.

[28] T. H. Cormen, C. E. Leiserson, R. L. Rivest, and C. Stein, *Introduction to Algorithms*, MIT Press, Cambridge, Mass, USA, 3rd edition, 2009.

[29] S. Even and R. E. Tarjan, "Network flow and testing graph connectivity," *SIAM Journal on Computing*, vol. 4, pp. 507–518, 1975.

[30] G. B. Dantzig, "Application of the simplex method to a transportation problem," in *Activity Analysis of Production and Allocation*, pp. 359–373, John Wiley & Sons, New York, NY, USA, 1951.

[31] L. R. Ford and D. R. Fulkerson, "Maximal flow through a network," *Canadian Journal of Mathematics*, vol. 8, pp. 399–404, 1956.

[32] A. V. Karzanov, "Determining the maximal flow in a network by the method of preflows," *Soviet Mathematics-Doklady*, no. 15, pp. 434–437, 1974.

[33] R. E. Tarjan, "A simple version of Karzanov's blocking flow algorithm," *Operations Research Letters*, vol. 2, no. 6, pp. 265–268, 1984.

[34] Z. Galil and A. Naamad, "An $O(EV \log^2 V)$ algorithm for the maximal flow problem," *Journal of Computer and System Sciences*, vol. 21, pp. 203–217, 1980.

[35] Y. Shiloach and U. Vishkin, "An $O(n^2 \log n)$ parallel max-flow algorithm," *Journal of Algorithms*, vol. 3, no. 2, pp. 128–146, 1982.

[36] D. D. Sleator and R. E. Tarjan, "A data structure for dynamic trees," *Journal of Computer and System Sciences*, vol. 26, no. 3, 1983.

[37] A. V. Goldberg and R. E. Tarjan, "A new approach to the maximum-flow problem," *Journal of the ACM*, vol. 35, no. 4, pp. 921–940, 1988.

[38] R. K. Ahuja, J. B. Orlin, and R. E. Tarjan, "Improved time bounds for the maximum flow problem," *SIAM Journal on Computing*, vol. 18, no. 5, pp. 939–954, 1989.

[39] J. Cheriyan and T. Hagerup, "Randomized maximum-flow algorithm," *SIAM Journal on Computing*, vol. 24, no. 2, pp. 203–226, 1995.

[40] N. Alon, "Generating pseudo-random permutations and maximum flow algorithms," *Information Processing Letters*, vol. 35, no. 4, pp. 201–204, 1990.

[41] A. V. Goldberg and S. Rao, "Beyond the flow decomposition barrier," *Journal of the ACM*, vol. 45, no. 5, pp. 783–797, 1998.

[42] P. Christiano, J. A. Kelner, A. Madry, D. A. Spielman, and S. H. Teng, "Electrical flows, laplacian systems, and faster approximation of maximum flow in undirected graphs," in *Proceedings of The 43rd ACM Symposium on Theory of Computing, STOC' 11*, pp. 273–281, San Jose, CA, USA, June 2011.

[43] D. W. Matula, "Determining edge connectivity in $O(nm)$," in *Proceedings of the 28th Symposium on Foundations of Computer Science (FOCS '87)*, pp. 249–251, Los Angeles, Calif, USA, October 1987.

[44] Y. Shiloach, "Edge-disjoint branching in directed multigraphs," *Information Processing Letters*, vol. 8, no. 1, pp. 24–27, 1979.

[45] Y. Mansour and B. Schieber, "Finding the edge connectivity of directed graphs," *Journal of Algorithms*, vol. 10, no. 1, pp. 76–85, 1989.

[46] G. B. Dantzig and D. R. Fulkerson, "On the max-flow mincut theorem of networks," in *Linear Inequalities and Related Systems*, Annals of Mathematics Studies, Study 38, pp. 215–221, Princeton University Press, Princeton, NJ, USA, 1956.

[47] S. Even, *Graph Algorithms*, Computer Science Press, 1979.

[48] M. R. Henzinger, S. Rao, and H. N. Gabow, "Computing vertex connectivity: new bounds from old techniques," *Journal of Algorithms*, vol. 34, no. 2, pp. 222–250, 2000.

[49] H. N. Gabow, "Using expander graphs to find vertex connectivity," *Journal of the ACM*, vol. 53, no. 5, pp. 800–844, 2006.

[50] Y. Yoshida and H. Ito, "Property testing on k-vertex-connectivity of graphs," *Algorithmica*, vol. 62, no. 3-4, pp. 701–712, 2012.

[51] P. Van Mieghem, D. Stevanović, F. A. Kuipers et al., "Decreasing the spectral radius of a graph by link removals," *Physical Review E*, vol. 84, no. 1, 2011.

[52] A. Natanzon, R. Shamir, and R. Sharan, "Complexity classification of some edge modification problems," *Discrete Applied Mathematics*, vol. 113, no. 1, pp. 109–128, 2001.

[53] G. Frederickson and J. JáJá, "Approximation algorithms for several graph augmentation problems," *SIAM Journal on Computing*, vol. 10, no. 2, pp. 270–283, 1981.

[54] K. P. Eswaran and R. E. Tarjan, "Augmentation problems," *SIAM Journal on Computing*, vol. 5, no. 4, pp. 653–665, 1976.

[55] J. Jensen and T. Jordán, "Edge-connectivity augmentation preserving simplicity," in *Proceedings of the 9th Annual ACM/SIAM Symposium On Discrete Algorithms (SODA '97)*, pp. 306–315, 1997.

[56] S. Raghavan, "A note on Eswaran and Tarjan's algorithm for the strong connectivity augmentation problem," in *The Next Wave in Computing, Optimization, and Decision Technologies*, vol. 29 of *Operations Research/Computer Science Interfaces Series*, pp. 19–26, Springer, 2005.

[57] R. E. Tarjan, "A note on finding the bridges of a graph," *Information Processing Letters*, vol. 2, no. 6, pp. 160–161, 1974.

[58] E. A. Dinitz, A. V. Karzanov, and M. V. Lomonosov, "On the structure of the system of minimum edge cuts of a graph," in *Issledovaniya po Diskretnoi Optimizatsii*, A. A. Fridman, Ed., pp. 290–306, Nauka, Moscow, Russia, 1976.

[59] A. V. Karzanov and E. A. Timofeev, "Efficient algorithm for finding all minimal edge cuts of a nonoriented graph," *Cybernetics and Systems Analysis*, vol. 22, no. 2, pp. 156–162, 1986.

[60] H. Nagamochi and T. Kameda, "Canonical cactus representation for minimum cuts," *Japan Journal of Industrial and Applied Mathematics*, vol. 11, no. 3, pp. 343–361, 1994.

[61] R. E. Gomory and T. C. Hu, "Multi-terminal network flows," *Journal of the Society for Industrial and Applied Mathematics*, vol. 9, no. 4, pp. 551–570, 1961.

[62] D. Gusfield and D. Naor, "Extracting maximal information about sets of minimum cuts," *Algorithmica*, vol. 10, no. 1, pp. 64–89, 1993.

[63] L. Fleischer, "Building chain and cactus representations of all minimum cuts from Hao-Orlin in the same asymptotic run time," *Journal of Algorithms*, vol. 33, no. 1, pp. 51–72, 1999.

[64] H. Nagamochi, "Graph algorithms for network connectivity problems," *Journal of the Operations Research Society of Japan*, vol. 4, no. 4, pp. 199–223, 2004.

[65] D. Naor, D. Gusfield, and C. Martel, "A fast algorithm for optimally increasing the edge connectivity," *SIAM Journal on Computing*, vol. 26, no. 4, pp. 1139–1165, 1997.

[66] E. Cheng, "Successive edge-connectivity augmentation problems," *Mathematical Programming B*, vol. 84, no. 3, pp. 577–593, 1999.

[67] R. E. Tarjan, "Depth-first search and linear graph algorithms," *SIAM Journal on Computing*, vol. 1, no. 2, pp. 146–160, 1972.

[68] W. Mader, "A reduction method for edge-connectivity in graphs," *Annals of Discrete Mathematics*, vol. 3, pp. 145–164, 1978.

[69] A. Frank, "On a theorem of Mader," *Discrete Mathematics*, vol. 101, no. 1–3, pp. 49–57, 1992.

[70] V. D. Podderyugin, "An algorithm for determining edge-connectivity of a graph," in *Proceedings of the Seminar on Combinatorial Mathematics*, Moscow, Russia, 1971, Doklady Akademii Nauk SSSR, Scientific Council on the Complex Problem "Cybernetics", pp. 136–141, 1973.

[71] H. Nagamochi and T. Ibaraki, "Computing edge-connectivity in multigraphs and capacitated graphs," *SIAM Journal on Discrete Mathematics*, vol. 5, no. 1, pp. 54–66, 1992.

[72] Z. Galil and G.F. Italiano, "Reducing edge connectivity to vertex connectivity," *ACM SIGACT News*, vol. 22, no. 1, pp. 57–61, 1991.

[73] H. N. Gabow, "A matroid approach to finding edge-connectivity and packing arborescences," *Journal of Computer and System Sciences*, vol. 50, no. 2, pp. 259–273, 1995.

[74] D. R. Karger, "Minimum cuts in near-linear time," *Journal of the ACM*, vol. 47, no. 1, pp. 46–76, 2000.

[75] G. Cai and Y. Sun, "The minimum augmentation of any graph to a K-edge-connected graph," *Networks*, vol. 19, no. 1, pp. 151–172, 1989.

[76] T. Watanabe and A. Nakamura, "Edge-connectivity augmentation problems," *Journal of Computer and System Sciences*, vol. 35, no. 1, pp. 96–144, 1987.

[77] A. Frank, "Augmenting graphs to meet edge-connectivity requirements," *SIAM Journal on Discrete Mathematics*, vol. 5, no. 1, pp. 25–53, 1992.

[78] H. N. Gabow, "Applications of a poset representation to edge connectivity and graph rigidity," in *Proceedings of the 32nd Annual Symposium on Foundations of Computer Science (FOCS '91)*, pp. 812–821, October 1991.

[79] A. A. Benczúr, "Augmenting undirected connectivity in RNC and in randomized $\tilde{O}(n^3)$ time," in *Proceedings of the 26th Annual ACM Symposium on Theory of Computing (STOC '94)*, pp. 658–667, New York, NY, USA, May 1994.

[80] H. Nagamochi and T. Ibaraki, "Deterministic $\tilde{O}(nm)$ time edge-splitting in undirected graphs," *Journal of Combinatorial Optimization*, vol. 1, no. 1, pp. 5–46, 1997.

[81] A. A. Benczúr and D. R. Karger, "Augmenting undirected edge connectivity in $\tilde{O}(n^2)$ time," *Journal of Algorithms*, vol. 37, no. 1, pp. 2–36, 2000.

[82] H. Nagamochi and T. Ibaraki, "Graph connectivity and its augmentation: applications of MA orderings," *Discrete Applied Mathematics*, vol. 123, pp. 447–472, 2002.

[83] Z. Nutov, "Approximating connectivity augmentation problems," *ACM Transactions on Algorithms*, vol. 6, no. 1, article 5, 2009.

[84] J. Plesník, "Minimum block containing a given graph," *Archiv der Mathematik*, vol. 27, no. 1, pp. 668–672, 1976.

[85] S. Khuller and R. Thurimella, "Approximation algorithms for graph augmentation," *Journal of Algorithms*, vol. 14, no. 2, pp. 214–225, 1993.

[86] S. Taoka, T. Watanabe, and T. Mashima, "Maximum weight matching-based algorithms for k-edge-connectivity augmentation of a graph," in *Proceedings of the IEEE International Symposium on Circuits and Systems (ISCAS '05)*, pp. 2231–2234, May 2005.

[87] A. Rosenthal and A. Goldner, "Smallest augmentation to biconnect a graph," *SIAM Journal on Computing*, vol. 6, no. 1, pp. 55–66, 1977.

[88] T. S. Hsu and V. Ramachandran, "Finding a smallest augmentation to biconnect a graph," *SIAM Journal on Computing*, vol. 22, no. 5, pp. 889–912, 1993.

[89] T. Watanabe and A. Nakamura, "A minimum 3-connectivity augmentation of a graph," *Journal of Computer and System Sciences*, vol. 46, no. 1, pp. 91–128, 1993.

[90] T. Jordán, "On the optimal vertex-connectivity augmentation," *Journal of Combinatorial Theory B*, vol. 63, no. 1, pp. 8–20, 1995.

[91] T. Hsu, "On four-connecting a triconnected graph," in *Proceedings of the 33rd Annual Symposium on Foundations of Computer Science (FOCS '92)*, pp. 70–79, IEEE Computer Society, Washington, DC, USA, October 1992.

[92] T. Jordán, "A note on the vertex-connectivity augmentation problem," *Journal of Combinatorial Theory B*, vol. 71, no. 2, pp. 294–301, 1997.

[93] B. Jackson and T. Jordán, "A near optimal algorithm for vertex-connectivity augmentation," in *Proceedings of the 11th International Conference on Algorithms and Computation (ISAAC '00)*, pp. 312–325, Springer, London, UK, December 2000.

[94] B. Jackson and T. Jordán, "Independence free graphs and vertex connectivity augmentation," *Journal of Combinatorial Theory B*, vol. 94, no. 1, pp. 31–77, 2005.

[95] G. Kortsarz and Z. Nutov, "Approximating minimum-cost connectivity problems," in *Handbook of Approximation Algorithms and Metaheuristics*, Chapter 58, Chapman & Hall/CRC, 2007.

[96] G. Liberman and Z. Nutov, "On shredders and vertex connectivity augmentation," *Journal of Discrete Algorithms*, vol. 5, no. 1, pp. 91–101, 2007.

[97] J. Cheriyan and R. Thurimella, "Fast algorithms for *k*-shredders and *k*-node connectivity augmentation," *Journal of Algorithms*, vol. 33, no. 1, pp. 15–50, 1999.

[98] L. A. Végh, "Augmenting undirected node-connectivity by one," *SIAM Journal on Discrete Mathematics*, vol. 25, no. 2, pp. 695–718, 2011.

[99] A. Frank and T. Jordán, "Minimal edge-coverings of pairs of sets," *Journal of Combinatorial Theory, Series B*, vol. 65, no. 1, pp. 73–110, 1995.

[100] A. Frank and L. A. Végh, "An algorithm to increase the node-connectivity of a digraph by one," *Discrete Optimization*, vol. 5, no. 4, pp. 677–684, 2008.

[101] A. Frank, "Connectivity augmentation problems in network design," in *Mathematical Programming: State of the Art 1994*, J. R. Bridge and K. G. Murty, Eds., University of Michigan, Ann Arbor, Mich, USA, 1994.

[102] M. Grötschel, C. L. Monma, and M. Stoer, "Design of survivable networks," in *Handbooks in Operations Research and Management Science*, vol. 7, pp. 617–672, 1995.

[103] M. Penn and H. Shasha-Krupnik, "Improved approximation algorithms for weighted 2- and 3-vertex connectivity augmentation problems," *Journal of Algorithms*, vol. 22, no. 1, pp. 187–196, 1997.

[104] S. Khuller, "Approximation algorithms for finding highly connected subgraphs," in *Approximation Algorithms for NP-Hard Problems*, D. S. Hochbaum, Ed., pp. 236–265, PWS Publishing, Boston, Mass, USA, 1997.

[105] S. Khuller and B. Raghavachari, "Improved approximation algorithms for uniform connectivity problems," *Journal of Algorithms*, vol. 21, no. 2, pp. 434–450, 1996.

[106] R. Ravi and D. P. Williamson, "An approximation algorithm for minimum-cost vertex-connectivity problems," *Algorithmica*, vol. 18, no. 1, pp. 21–43, 1997.

[107] G. N. Frederickson and J. JáJá, "On the relationship between the biconnectivity augmentation and travelling salesman problems," *Theoretical Computer Science*, vol. 19, no. 2, pp. 189–201, 1982.

[108] C.-L. Li, S. T. Mccormick, and D. Simchi-Levi, "The complexity of finding two disjoint paths with min-max objective function," *Discrete Applied Mathematics*, vol. 26, no. 1, pp. 105–115, 1990.

[109] B. Yang, S. Q. Zheng, and S. Katukam, "Finding two disjoint paths in a network with min-min objective function," in *Proceedings of the 15th IASTED International Conference on Parallel and Distributed Computing and Systems*, November 2003.

[110] A. Itai, Y. Perl, and Y. Shiloach, "The complexity of finding maximum disjoint paths with length constraints," *Networks*, vol. 12, no. 3, pp. 277–286, 1982.

[111] A. Bley, "On the complexity of vertex-disjoint length-restricted path problems," *Computational Complexity*, vol. 12, no. 3-4, pp. 131–149, 2003.

[112] C.-L. Li, S. T. Mccormick, and D. Simchi-Levi, "Finding disjoint paths with different path costs: complexity and algorithms," *Networks*, vol. 22, no. 7, pp. 653–667, 1992.

[113] D. Xu, Y. Chen, Y. Xiong, C. Qiao, and X. He, "On finding disjoint paths in single and dual link cost networks," in *Proceedings of the IEEE INFOCOM*, March 2004.

[114] Q. She, X. Huang, and J. P. Jue, "How reliable can two-path protection be?" *IEEE/ACM Transactions on Networking*, vol. 18, no. 3, pp. 922–933, 2010.

[115] B. H. Shen, B. Hao, and A. Sen, "On multipath routing using widest pair of disjoint paths," in *Proceedings of the High Perfomance Switching and Routing (HPSR '04)*, pp. 134–140, April 2004.

[116] A. A. Beshir and F. A. Kuipers, "Variants of the min-sum link-disjoint paths problem," in *Proceedings of the 16th Annual IEEE Symposium on Communications and Vehicular Technology (IEEE SCVT '09)*, IEEE/SCVT, Louvain-la-Neuve, Belgium, November 2009.

[117] R. Bhatia, M. Kodialam, and T. V. Lakshman, "Finding disjoint paths with related path costs," *Journal of Combinatorial Optimization*, vol. 12, no. 1-2, pp. 83–96, 2006.

[118] H. D. Sherali, K. Ozbay, and S. Subramanian, "The time-dependent shortest pair of disjoint paths problem: complexity, models, and algorithms," *Networks*, vol. 31, no. 4, pp. 259–272, 1998.

[119] J. W. Suurballe, "Disjoint paths in a network," *Networks*, vol. 4, no. 2, pp. 125–145, 1974.

[120] J. W. Suurballe and R. E. Tarjan, "A quick method for finding shortest pairs of disjoint paths," *Networks*, vol. 14, pp. 325–336, 1984.

[121] N. Taft-Plotkin, B. Bellur, and R. Ogier, "Quality-of-service routing using maximally disjoint paths," in *Proceedings of the 7th International Workshop on Quality of Service (IWQoS)*, pp. 119–128, London, UK, May 1999.

[122] R. G. Ogier, V. Rutenburg, and N. Shacham, "Distributed algorithms for computing shortest pairs of disjoint paths," *IEEE Transactions on Information Theory*, vol. 39, no. 2, pp. 443–455, 1993.

[123] D. Sidhu, R. Nair, and S. Abdallah, "Finding disjoint paths in networks," *ACM SIGCOMM Computer Communication Review*, vol. 21, no. 4, pp. 43–51, 1991.

[124] J. Roskind and R. E. Tarjan, "Note on finding minimum-cost edge-disjoint spanning trees," *Mathematics of Operations Research*, vol. 10, no. 4, pp. 701–708, 1985.

[125] G. Xue, L. Chen, and K. Thulasiraman, "Quality-of-service and quality-of-protection issues in preplanned recovery schemes using redundant trees," *IEEE Journal on Selected Areas in Communications*, vol. 21, no. 8, pp. 1332–1345, 2003.

[126] W. Zhang, G. Xue, J. Tang, and K. Thulasiraman, "Faster algorithms for construction of recovery trees enhancing QoP and QoS," *IEEE/ACM Transactions on Networking*, vol. 16, no. 3, pp. 642–655, 2008.

[127] P. Cholda, A. Mykkeltveit, B. E. Helvik, O. J. Wittner, and A. Jajszczyk, "A survey of resilience differentiation frameworks in communication networks," *IEEE Communications Surveys & Tutorials*, vol. 9, no. 4, pp. 32–55, 2007.

[128] S. Ramasubramanian, M. Harkara, and M. Krunz, "Linear time distributed construction of colored trees for disjoint multipath routing," *Computer Networks*, vol. 51, no. 10, pp. 2854–2866, 2007.

[129] Y. Guo, F. A. Kuipers, and P. Van Mieghem, "A link-disjoint paths algorithm for reliable QoS routing," *International Journal of Communication Systems*, vol. 16, no. 9, pp. 779–798, 2003.

[130] R. Banner and A. Orda, "The power of tuning: a novel approach for the efficient design of survivable networks," *IEEE/ACM Transactions on Networking*, vol. 15, no. 4, pp. 737–749, 2007.

[131] O. Gerstel and G. Sasaki, "Quality of protection (QoP): a quantitative unifying paradigm to protection service grades," *Optical Networks Magazine*, vol. 3, no. 3, pp. 40–49, 2002.

[132] A. V. Goldberg and R. E. Tarjan, "Finding minimum-cost circulations by canceling negative cycles," *Journal of the ACM*, vol. 36, no. 4, pp. 873–886, 1989.

[133] H. Luo, L. Li, and H. Yu, "Routing connections with differentiated reliability requirements in WDM mesh networks," *IEEE/ACM Transactions on Networking*, vol. 17, no. 1, pp. 253–266, 2009.

[134] F. A. Kuipers, A. Orda, D. Raz, and P. Van Mieghem, "A comparison of exact and ε-approximation algorithms for constrained routing," in *Proceedings of the 5th IFIP Networking Conference*, Coimbra, Portugal, May 2006.

[135] A. Chakrabarti and G. Manimaran, "Reliability constrained routing in QoS networks," *IEEE/ACM Transactions on Networking*, vol. 13, no. 3, pp. 662–675, 2005.

[136] D. Coudert, P. Datta, S. Perennes, H. Rivano, and M. E. Voge, "Shared risk resource group: complexity and approximability issues," *Parallel Processing Letters*, vol. 17, no. 2, pp. 169–184, 2007.

[137] J. Q. Hu, "Diverse routing in optical mesh networks," *IEEE Transactions on Communications*, vol. 51, no. 3, pp. 489–494, 2003.

[138] R. Bhandari, *Survivable Networks: Algorithms for Diverse Routing*, Kluwer Academic Publishers, New York, NY, USA, 1999.

[139] P. Datta and A. K. Somani, "Graph transformation approaches for diverse routing in shared risk resource group (SRRG) failures," *Computer Networks*, vol. 52, no. 12, pp. 2381–2394, 2008.

[140] X. Luo and B. Wang, "Diverse routing in WDM optical networks with shared risk link group (SRLG) failures," in *Proceedings of the 5th IEE International Workshop on Design of Reliable Communication Networks (DRCN '05)*, Island of Ischia, Naples, Italy, October 2005.

[141] H. W. Lee, E. Modiano, and K. Lee, "Diverse routing in networks with probabilistic failures," *IEEE/ACM Transactions on Networking*, vol. 18, no. 6, pp. 1895–1907, 2010.

[142] W. D. Grover, *Mesh-Based Survivable Transport Networks: Options and Strategies for Optical, MPLS, SONET and ATM Networking*, Prentice Hall PTR, London, UK, 2003.

[143] D. Xu, Y. Xiong, C. Qiao, and G. Li, "Trap avoidance and protection schemes in networks with shared risk link groups," *Journal of Lightwave Technology*, vol. 21, no. 11, pp. 2683–2693, 2003.

[144] H. Zang, C. S. Ou, and B. Mukherjee, "Path-protection routing and wavelength assignment (RWA) in WDM mesh networks under duct-layer constraints," *IEEE/ACM Transactions on Networking*, vol. 11, no. 2, pp. 248–258, 2003.

[145] A. Sen, S. Murthy, and S. Banerjee, "Region-based connectivity—a new paradigm for design of fault-tolerant networks," in *Proceedings of the 15st International Conference on High Performance Switching and Routing (HPSR '09)*, Paris, France, June 2009.

[146] P. K. Agarwal, A. Efrat, S. Ganjugunte, D. Hay, S. Sankararaman, and G. Zussman, "The resilience of WDM networks to probabilistic geographical failures," in *Proceedings of the IEEE INFOCOM*, pp. 1521–1529, Shanghai, China, April 2011.

[147] S. Neumayer, A. Efrat, and E. Modiano, "Geographic max-flow and mincut under a circular disk failure model," in *Proceedings of the 31st Annual IEEE International Conference on Computer Communications (INFOCOM '12)*, March 2012.

[148] S. Trajanovski, F. A. Kuipers, P. Van Mieghem, A. Ilić, and J. Crowcroft, "Critical regions and region-disjoint paths in a network".

[149] A. A. Beshir, F. A. Kuipers, P. Van Mieghem, and A. Orda, "On-line survivable routing in WDM networks," in *Proceedings of the 21st International Teletraffic Congress (ITC '21)*, Paris, France, September 2009.

[150] A. A. Beshir, F. A. Kuipers, A. Orda, and P. Van Mieghem, "Survivable impairment-aware traffic grooming in WDM rings," in *Proceedings of the 23rd International Teletraffic Congress*, San Francisco, Calif, USA, September 2011.

[151] A. A. Beshir, F. A. Kuipers, A. Orda, and P. Van Mieghem, "Survivable routing and regenerator placement in optical networks," in *Proceedings of the 4th International Workshop on Reliable Networks Design and Modeling (RNDM '12)*, Petersburg, Russia, October 2012.

[152] A. A. Beshir, R. Nuijts, R. Malhotra, and F. A. Kuipers, "Survivable impairment-aware traffic grooming," in *Proceedings of the 16th European Conference on Networks and Optical Communications (NOC '11)*, Northumbria University, Newcastle upon Tyne, UK, July 2011.

11

Gain Improvement of Dual Band Antenna Based on Complementary Rectangular Split-Ring Resonator

Noelia Ortiz, Francisco Falcone, and Mario Sorolla

Millimeter Wave Laboratory, Electrical and Electronic Engineering Department, Public University of Navarra, Arrosadía Campus, 31006 Pamplona, Spain

Correspondence should be addressed to Mario Sorolla, mario@unavarra.es

Academic Editors: C. Luxey and J. K. Muppala

A simple and successful dual band patch linear polarized rectangular antenna design is presented. The dual band antenna is designed etching a complementary rectangular split-ring resonator in the patch of a conventional rectangular patch antenna. Furthermore, a parametric study shows the influence of the location of the CSRR particle on the radiation characteristics of the dual band antenna. Going further, a miniaturization of the conventional rectangular patch antenna and an enhancement of the complementary split-ring resonator resonance gain versus the location of the CSRR on the patch are achieved. The dual band antenna design has been made feasible due to the quasistatic resonance property of the complementary split-ring resonators. The simulated results are compared with measured data and good agreement is reported.

1. Introduction

The possibility of obtaining media with simultaneously negative permeability and permittivity was hypothesized by Veselago in the late 1960s [1]. In spite of the interesting properties presented by such media, it was not until 2000 that the first experimental evidence of a medium with simultaneously negative permeability and permittivity was demonstrated [2]. The original medium proposed in [2] consists of a bulky combination of metal wires and split-ring resonators (SRRs) [3].

The SRR electromagnetic properties have been already analyzed in [4, 5]. This analysis shows that the SRR behaves as an LC resonant tank that can be excited by an external time-varying magnetic field applied parallel to the particle axis, thus producing a quasi-static resonant effect [4]. Therefore, the SRR has subwavelength dimensions at its quasi-static resonance, allowing very compact device designs. Up to now, these self-resonant particles have been used in the design of microwave filters in planar technology [6, 7]. However, in this paper, we have taken advantage of the complementary split-ring resonator (CSRR) concept [8] to design a miniaturized dual band patch antenna with vertical polarization, also studying how to improve radiation efficiency for

the resonance produced by the CSRR in this kind of antennas. The CSRR is inspired on Babinet principle [9], and, as occurs with the SRR, it also exhibits a quasi-static resonance, which enables the particle to be electrically small [8, 9].

Up to now, the use of metamaterial concepts in practical miniaturized antennas is a very challenging research topic [10–16] and the achieved results based on self-resonance particles as SRRs or CSRRs [16] exhibit low radiation efficiencies driving to low-gain antennas comparing to the results of the parametric study presented in this paper. In this sense, the excitation of a CSRR etched in the patch of a conventional patch antenna allows us to design dual band patch antennas. Going further, the presence of the CSRR etched in some positions of the path also produces a miniaturization of both patch antenna resonances, leading to miniaturized dual band antennas. Replacing the CSRR within a slot of its same external dimensions, the slot does not exhibit a resonance at the same frequency of the CSRR, but at higher frequencies and more than one slot should be placed in the patch depending on their position in order to achieve a dual band response. The resonance frequency of a rectangular slot on a dielectric is approximately given by $c_{light}/(a + b) \cdot \sqrt{\varepsilon_r}$, where c_{light}, ε_r, a, and b are the speed of light in vacuum, dielectric relative permittivity, and the external dimensions of the rectangular iris, respectively. In opposition to the resonance frequency of a rectangular slot, the resonant frequency of the CSRR is much lower for the same physical size. Hence, it can be designed to exhibit a resonance at lower frequencies comparing to different shapes of slots that can also be etched in a conventional patch. The design presented in this paper gives an alternative solution to the existing dual band antenna designs [17], as the ones carried out by loading a rectangular patch antenna with a pair of bent slots or embedded step slots close to the patch nonradiating edges, or the ones done by spur lines or shorted microstrip antenna with rectangular patch. Overall, as it can be shown in this paper, the properties of the CSRR allow us to design dual band miniaturized antennas based on the anisotropic properties of the CSRR as indicated by the measurements of a fabricated prototype and the parametric studies of the presented design in opposition to dual band antennas produced by the radiation of slots, whose resonances are dependent on their physical length. The prototype has been designed to exhibit a dual band behaviour in two frequency bands in the range from 4 GHz to 5 GHz for wireless applications. Nowadays, there is a growing trend to integrate different wireless communication systems in one single user terminal as long as to reduce the overall size. Since all these systems work at different frequency bands, dual and multiband antennas with frequency ratios around 1.2 between different bands are desirable. For this application, the type of antennas presented in this paper are a good alternative as introducing different CSRRs on the patch multiband antennas can be obtained very easily taking as a starting point the dual band antennas presented in this paper. The dual band antenna design presented has been validated, and a parametric study of the CSRR location and its influence on antenna radiating characteristics is presented and analyzed.

2. CSRR Excitation in a Rectangular Patch

The excitation of CSRRs has been usually driven by an incident electric field normal to the particle plane. In order to understand the excitation of these particles, let us consider the CSRR presented in Figures 1(b) and 1(c). Comparing the excitation of an SRR with a CSRR, the CSRR particle should be rotated 90° from the position of the SRR particle, as it is shown in Figure 1(a). Following the theoretical discussion shown in [4, 5], the operation of the SRR near its first resonance frequency obeys the effect of resonant polarizabilities, which gives the resonant magnetic and electric dipolar moments m_z, p_x, and p_y as a function of the exciting field components B_z^{inc}, E_x^{inc}, and E_y^{inc}. Complementarily, using the Babinet principle [9], the CSRR can be excited by the incident complementary fields E^{incc} and B^{incc}, which are related to E^{inc} and B^{inc} by $E^{incc} = c \cdot B^{inc}$ and $B^{incc} = -(1/c) \cdot E^{inc}$ by means of another set of resonant polarizabilities, thus given an electric dipole p_z^c and magnetic dipoles m_x^c and m_y^c. Then, as seen in Figures 1(b) and 1(c), depending on the CSRR position inside the patch, it will be excited by incident electric field normal to the particle plane (E_z) and by incident magnetic field tangent to the particle plane (B_x). For the excitation of the CSRR by the magnetic field (B_x), the

CSRR should be rotated 90° in the patch as it is shown in Figure 1(c) comparing to the orientation of the CSRR in Figure 1(b).

In order to show graphically the excitation of the CSRR by the existing fields inside a rectangular patch antenna, Figures 2 and 3 show the electric fields and surface current distributions at the resonance frequency of the CSRR for the locations of this particle according to the layouts of Figures 2(a) and 3(a). In Figure 2, the CSRR particle has been located for its proper excitation by E_z electric field component, placed in one position inside the area where E field distributions are higher. Otherwise, in Figure 3, the CSRR particle has been located where magnetic field distributions are more concentrated, for the best suitable CSRR excitation by B_x magnetic field component. Though, for this case, the CSRR is also excited by E_z. The simulations of the structures presented in this paper have been performed with the commercial finite-integration time-domain CST Microwave Studio Code.

3. Parametric Study

The parametric study carried out in this work shows how the position of the CSRR (without changing its dimensions) has influence on the radiation efficiency of both antenna resonances for the orientation of the particle as it is in Figure 1(b). On this way, for some locations of the CSRR in the patch, radiation efficiencies up to 50% are achieved for both resonances. These results together with the measurement results of the prototype comparing to the simulated results show the usefulness of this kind of dual band patch antennas. The simulated antenna in the parametric study has the same dimensions as the fabricated one, excluding the placement of the CSRR inside the patch, which varies from Pos = −9 mm to Pos = 9 mm in the y-axis direction and from u = 1 mm to u = 13 mm in the x-axis direction. In Figure 1(b), the references of both Pos and u parameters are specified. The substrate employed in the simulated and fabricated prototype is the commercially available Arlon 250-LX-0193-43-11 (ε_r = 2.43 and thickness h = 0.49 mm). The physical width and length of the rectangular patch antenna are 18.43 mm and 23.68 mm, respectively [18]. Then, its resonance has been set around 5 GHz. The width of the micro strip line is 1.34 mm, corresponding to a characteristic impedance of 50 Ω. This line exhibits an offset from the centre of the patch antenna in order to match its reflection coefficient at its working frequency. The offset is ($X1$ = −13.37 mm and $Y1$ = 0 mm) (see Figure 1(b)).

The CSRR particle has been designed to exhibit its quasi-static resonance frequency below the resonance frequency of the patch, obtaining more compact devices highlighting the advantages of the resonance properties of anisotropic particles comparing to other slots already used for dual band antenna designs. The radiation produced by conventional slots does not have the same origin comparing to the radiation produced by a CSRR particle, and their electric length should be longer comparing to the electric length of the CSRR. The necessary physical dimensions of the CSRR to achieve a radiation frequency below the resonant frequency

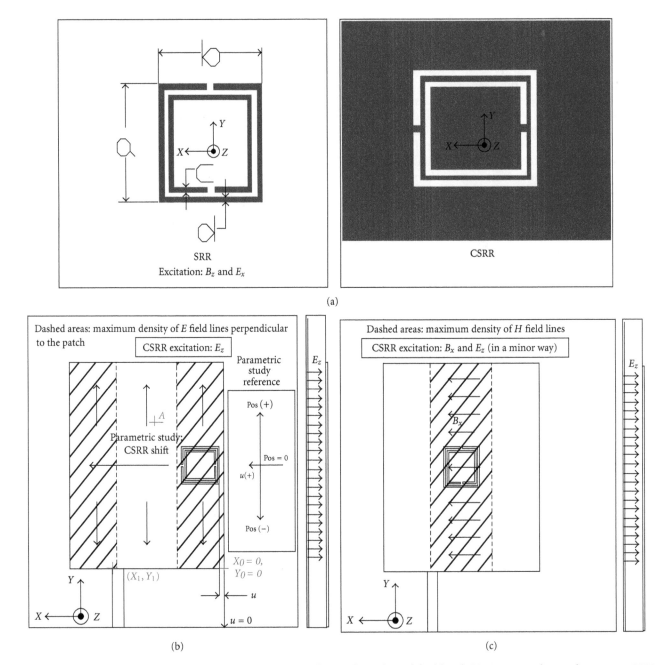

FIGURE 1: (a) SRR and CSRR topologies relevant dimensions. (b) Configuration of dual band CSRR-rectangular patch antenna. CSRR excitation by incident electric field normal to the particle plane, E_z. (c) Configuration of dual band CSRR-rectangular patch antenna. CSRR excitation by magnetic field tangent to the particle plane, B_x, and by electric field normal to the particle plane, E_z.

of the designed rectangular patch have been calculated using the design formulas for SRR reported in [4], resulting in this case in $a = 4.6$ mm, $b = 4.2$ mm, and $c = d = 0.2$ mm. In all the results presented in this paper, the first resonance of the dual band antenna is the one produced by the excitation of the CSRR, while the second resonance is produced by the conventional patch itself.

In Figures 4(a) and 4(b) radiation efficiencies as results from the parametric study are shown for both resonances. Figure 4(a) shows how the radiation efficiency of the resonance produced by the excitation of the CSRR increases while

the anisotropic particle is placed at the radiating edges of the rectangular patch (*Pos parameter* values of -9 mm and 9 mm). However, there are some positions for the CSRR inside the patch where the radiation due to the CSRR is cancelled. These positions correspond to values around *Pos parameter of 0* mm and values around this value. This means that when the CSRR is etched in the centre of the rectangular patch its resonance is cancelled leading to a single resonance antenna.

Figure 4(b) shows how the radiation efficiency of the resonance produced by the patch decreases for some

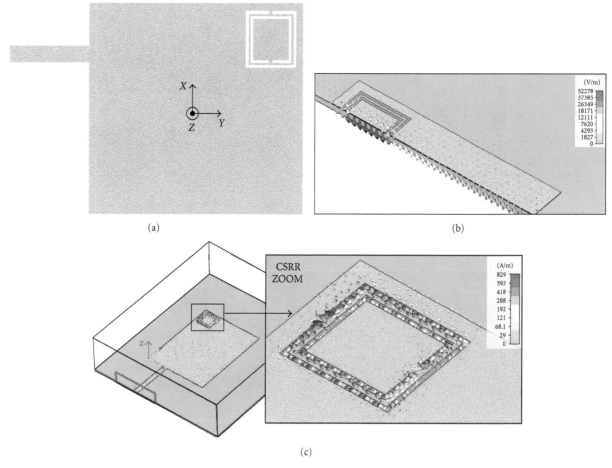

FIGURE 2: (a) Top view of the layout for E field and current distributions analysis in reference with Figure 1(b). (b) Simulated E_z field distribution in the CSRR at its resonant frequency. (c) Simulated current distributions in the CSRR at its resonant frequency.

u positions when the CSRR is placed at the radiating edges of the conventional patch antenna. However, there are other u positions at these edges where both resonances exhibit radiation efficiencies up to 50%. The position values where radiation efficiency has been set to zero mean that the resonance produced by the CSRR particle or by the patch has been cancelled as explained before. The results of the parametric study for radiation efficiencies of both resonances show that the results are not symmetric, these differences are due to the asymmetric microstrip line excitation of the rectangular patch.

In Figures 5(a) and 5(b) gain values for u parameter values ($u = 3, 4, 11, 12$, and 13), which drive to the highest radiation efficiencies for both resonances, are depicted. The discontinuities with no values in the curves of Figures 5(a), 6(a), and 6(b) are because there is no resonance of the CSRR for those positions.

For the locations where the CSRR is etched around the centre of the rectangular patch, $u = 6$ mm, $u = 7$ mm, and $u = 8$ mm, both resonances, the one produced by the CSRR and the one produced by the patch, are shifted to lower frequencies, resulting in a miniaturization of both frequency bands of dual band patch antenna comparing to a conventional rectangular patch antenna of the same dimensions.

By contrast, as the CSRR moves away from the centre of the patch towards the nonradiating edges (in u direction for all its *Pos parameter* values), the resonance produced by the rectangular patch shifts to higher frequencies comparing to the resonant frequency of the conventional rectangular patch itself. In Figures 6(a) and 6(b) the resonant frequencies for the first and second resonances versus *Pos parameter* and $f2/f1$ ratio are shown for $u = 1$, $u = 6$, and $u = 13$ parameter values, where $f1$ and $f2$ are the resonance produced by the CSRR and the one produced by the rectangular patch, respectively. The miniaturization ratio of this type of antennas based on this design is around 1.2, but it also depends on the position of the CSRR on the patch, as the resonance frequencies are shifted. This behaviour is clearly shown in Figures 6(a) and 6(b).

From Figures 6(a) and 6(b) the miniaturization factor has been calculated for two different positions of the CSRR on the patch. In the first case, for particle location parameters of $u = 13$ mm and Pos $= -9$ mm the miniaturization factor is 1.16, corresponding to a radiation efficiency of 45.37% and gain of 3.59%. For the second case, the position parameters values are $u = 6$ mm and Pos $= 0$ mm. In this case the resonance produced by the CSRR has been cancelled and a single-band antenna is achieved. The miniaturization factor

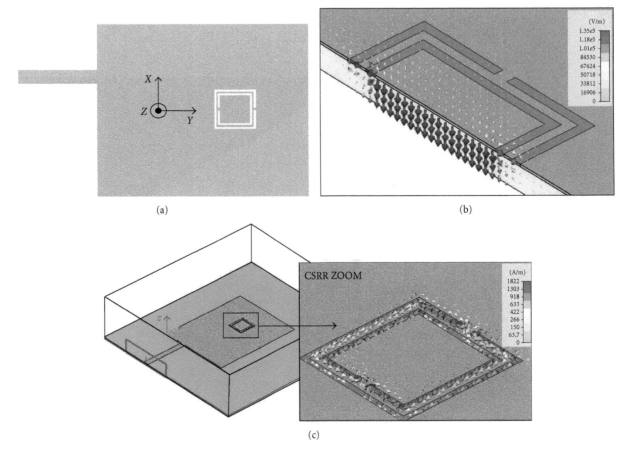

FIGURE 3: (a) Top view of the layout for E field and current distributions analysis in reference with Figure 1(c). (b) Simulated E_z field distribution in the CSRR at its resonant frequency. (c) Simulated current distributions in the CSRR at its resonant frequency.

is 1.1, corresponding to a radiation efficiency of 84.36% and gain of 6.56 dB.

4. Experimental Results

In order to demonstrate the usefulness of this dual band antenna design, a prototype has been fabricated. The fabricated prototype has been chosen from the parametric study in a case where the radiation efficiency is low comparing to the highest values obtained of this parameter. This case has been chosen to validate the usefulness of this design in a worst case condition. The prototype has been fabricated using a laser drilling machine. The design parameters of the CSRR particle are $a = 4.6$ mm, $b = 4.2$ mm, and $c = d = 0.2$ mm (the same ones of those of the CSRR used in the parametric study). In the fabricated prototype the CSRR has been placed at A point (see Figure 1(b)) being the coordinates of this point (X = −9.3 mm, Y = 15.54 mm).

In Figure 7 simulated and measured reflection coefficient results of the fabricated prototype are shown. For matching measurements data has been collected by using an HP8510 network analyzer. As it can be seen in Figure 7, there is a frequency shift of 162 MHz to lower frequencies for the lower resonance. The upper resonance presents a frequency shift of 84 MHz, shifted to lower frequencies. Although

there is a frequency shift between simulated and measured results, the matching values achieved are properly predicted by simulations. The discrepancies between simulated and measured results are due to the manufacturing process as the CSRR manufacturing tolerances are critical, changing slightly its frequency resonance. In simulations, materials have been simulated considering their corresponding finite conductance and substrate has been simulated considering its dielectric losses. In Figure 8 a picture of the fabricated prototype is shown.

In Figures 9(a) and 9(b) measured results for normalized gain radiation patterns for 0° and 90° phi cut planes for both resonant frequencies are shown. Besides, simulated results just for 90° phi cut are shown. No more simulated cuts are introduced to maintain the figures legible. These frequencies are $F1 = 4.19$ GHz and $F2 = 4.808$ GHz, the resonant frequencies produced by the CSRR particle and conventional patch, respectively. The radiation pattern measured results show the feasibility of this type of dual band antenna design. Both resonances show cross-polar levels around −20 dB for theta 0°.

Table 1 shows a comparison between simulated and measured results of the fabricated prototype from impedance matching and radiation point of views. This table shows that both resonances have similar characteristics. From matching

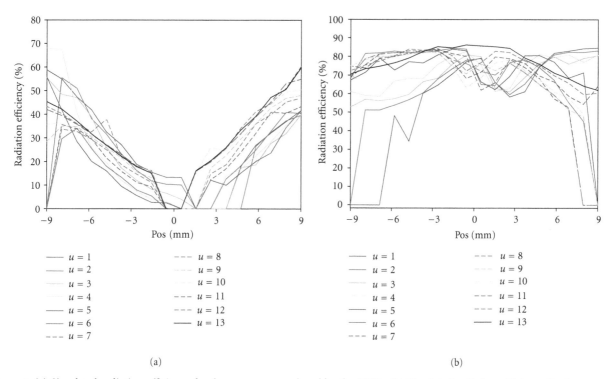

Figure 4: (a) Simulated radiation efficiency for the resonance produced by the CSRR. (b) Simulated radiation efficiency for the resonance produced by the rectangular patch antenna.

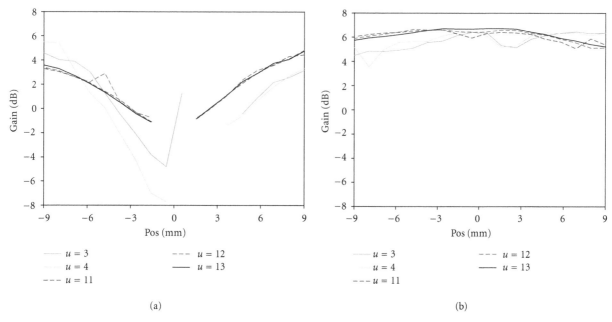

Figure 5: (a) Simulated gain values for the resonance produced by the CSRR. (b) Simulated gain values for the resonance produced by the rectangular patch antenna.

point of view, the parameters shown in Table 1 are reflection coefficient values for both resonant frequencies. From radiation point of view, parameters shown in Table 1 are peak directivity, peak gain, and radiation efficiency. Directivity values have been calculated [18] from measured gain radiation patterns for both resonances in order to calculate efficiency and verify the good agreement between simulated

and measured data. Within the fabricated prototype the parametric study made in this work has been validated due to the good agreement between simulations and measured results. Although gain and radiation efficiency obtained by the resonance produced by the CSRR is low comparing to the second resonance in the fabricated prototype, these values are in accordance with the simulated results. Furthermore,

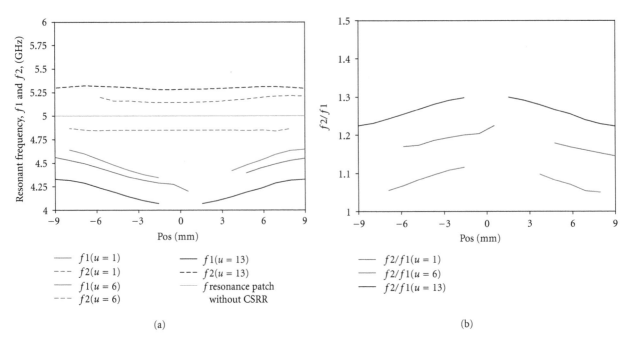

(a)   (b)

FIGURE 6: (a) Parametric study results. $f1$ and $f2$ resonant frequencies. (b) Parametric study results. $f2/f1$ ratio.

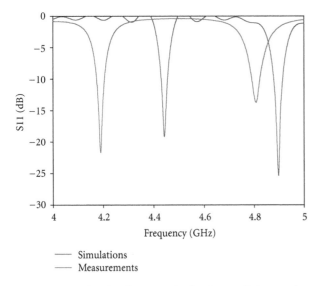

FIGURE 7: Simulated and measured reflection coefficient results.

FIGURE 8: Fabricated prototype.

TABLE 1

Parameters	Simulated results	Measured results
Matching characteristics		
First resonance ($F1$)		
$F1$, (GHz)	4.352	4.19
Reflection coefficient, (dB)	-16.75	-21.25
Effective bandwidth at -5 dB (%)	1.60	1.52
Second resonance ($F2$)		
$F2$, (GHz)	4.892	4.808
Reflection coefficient, (dB)	-15.15	-13.86
Effective bandwidth at -5 dB (%)	1.79	1.72
Radiation characteristics		
First resonance ($F1$)		
Peak directivity, (dBi)	7.16	7.36
Peak gain, (dB)	-0.97	-0.11
Radiation efficiency (%)	15.38	17.92
Second resonance ($F2$)		
Peak directivity, (dBi)	7.243	7.74
Peak gain, (dB)	5.946	5.85
Radiation efficiency, (%)	74.18	64.83

it is remarkable that gain values obtained for the positions of the CSRR in the patch studied in this work are higher compared to previous works [16].

Up to this point, in order to compare the performances of the dual band antenna topology presented in this paper with those of the same conventional patch antenna without a CSRR etched in its centre, in Table 2 measured data of the conventional rectangular patch antenna is shown.

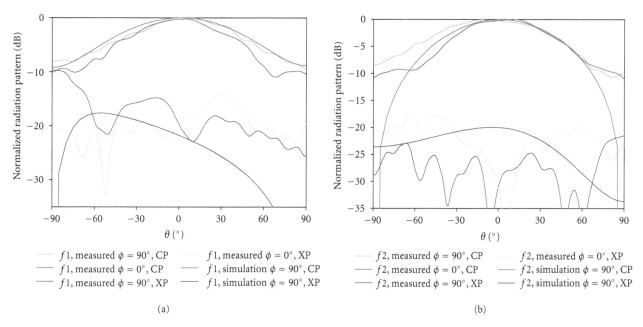

FIGURE 9: (a) Measured normalized copolar and cross-polar gain radiation patterns for 0° and 90° phi cuts. Simulated normalized copular and cross-polar gain radiation pattern for 90° phi cut at $F1 = 4.19$ GHz. (b) Measured normalized copolar and cross-polar gain radiation patterns for 0° and 90° phi cuts. Simulated normalized copular and cross-polar gain radiation pattern for 90° phi cut at $F2 = 4.808$ GHz.

TABLE 2

Parameters	Measured results
Patch antenna	
Matching characteristics	
Frequency, (GHz)	5.16
Reflection coefficient, (dB)	−22.3
Effective bandwidth at −5 dB (%)	1.9
Radiation characteristics	
Peak directivity, (dBi)	7.55
Peak gain, (dB)	6.08
Radiation efficiency (%)	71.3

Comparing Tables 1 and 2, the designed prototype presents similar performances to those of the conventional patch antenna from matching point of view (effective bandwidth and reflection coefficient values). On the other side, from radiation point of view, the designed and fabricated dual band antenna resonances show lower radiation efficiencies as it has been mentioned before.

Finally, to understand in an oversimplified way the radiation mechanism of the proposed antenna, one needs to consider the pair of electric dipoles that are described in [9] and the effect of the finite ground plane. In a recent work a refined equivalent circuit model for the CSRR which explains more accurately the physical interpretation of the influence of reactive parameters [19] is presented. This circuit model will be developed in further works in order to take into account the radiation resistance and the internal coupling to the patch and ground plane.

5. Conclusions

In this work a dual band patch antenna based on a CSRR has been proposed, studied, and successfully tested, demonstrating the feasibility of this type of dual band antennas, adding a miniaturization of patch dimensions for some locations of the CSRR inside the patch. A good agreement between simulated and measured results is shown. The parametric study shows the influence of the location of the CSRR on the patch on the radiation characteristics. The design of the dual patch antenna is simple as the only design parameters comparing to a conventional path antenna are the ones of the CSRR particle design parameters. Also, multiband antennas can be designed in a similar way by simply adding different CSRRs on the patch.

Acknowledgments

This work has been supported by the Spanish Government and EU Feder by the Contracts Consolider "Engineering Metamaterials" CSD2008-00066 and TEC2008-06871-C02-01.

References

[1] V. G. Veselago, "The electrodynamics of substances with simultaneously negative values of ε and μ," *Soviet Physics Uspekhi*, vol. 10, pp. 509–514, 1968.

[2] D. R. Smith, W. J. Padilla, D. C. Vier, S. C. Nemat-Nasser, and S. Schultz, "Composite medium with simultaneously negative permeability and permittivity," *Physical Review Letters*, vol. 84, no. 18, pp. 4184–4187, 2000.

[3] J. B. Pendry, A. J. Holden, D. J. Robbins, and W. J. Stewart, "Magnetism from conductors and enhanced nonlinear

phenomena," *IEEE Transactions on Microwave Theory and Techniques*, vol. 47, no. 11, pp. 2075–2084, 1999.

[4] R. Marqués, F. Mesa, J. Martel, and F. Medina, "Comparative analysis of edge- and broadside-coupled split ring resonators for metamaterial design—theory and experiments," *IEEE Transactions on Antennas and Propagation*, vol. 51, no. 10, pp. 2572–2581, 2003.

[5] R. Marqués, F. Medina, and R. Rafii-El-Idrissi, "Role of bianisotropy in negative, permeability and left-handed metamaterials," *Physical Review B*, vol. 65, no. 14, pp. 1444401–1444406, 2002.

[6] F. Martín, F. Falcone, J. Bonache, T. Lopetegi, R. Marqués, and M. Sorolla, "Miniaturized coplanar waveguide stopband filters based on multiple tuned split rin resonators," *IEEE Microwave and Wireless Components Letters*, vol. 13, no. 12, pp. 511–513, 2003.

[7] F. Falcone, F. Martín, J. Bonache, R. Marqués, T. Lopetegi, and M. Sorolla, "Left handed coplanar waveguide band pass filters based on Bi-layer split ring resonators," *IEEE Microwave and Wireless Components Letters*, vol. 14, no. 1, pp. 10–12, 2004.

[8] F. Falcone, T. Lopetegi, J. D. Baena, R. Marqués, F. Martín, and M. Sorolla, "Effective negative-ε stopband microstrip lines based on complementary split ring resonators," *IEEE Microwave and Wireless Components Letters*, vol. 14, no. 6, pp. 280–282, 2004.

[9] F. Falcone, T. Lopetegi, M. A. G. Laso et al., "Babinet principle applied to metasurface and metamaterial design," *Physical Review Letters*. In press.

[10] R. W. Ziolkowski and A. D. Kipple, "Application of double negative materials to increase the power radiated by electrically small antennas," *IEEE Transactions on Antennas and Propagation*, vol. 51, no. 10, pp. 2626–2640, 2003.

[11] F. Qureshi, M. A. Antoniades, and G. V. Eleftheriades, "A compact and low-profile metamaterial ring antenna with vertical polarization," *IEEE Antennas and Wireless Propagation Letters*, vol. 4, no. 1, pp. 333–336, 2005.

[12] R. K. Baee, G. Dadashzadeh, and F. G. Kharakhili, "Using of CSRR and its equivalent circuit model in size reduction of microstrip antenna," in *Proceedings of the Asia-Pacific Microwave Conference (APMC '07)*, pp. 1–4, 2007.

[13] Y. Lee, S. Tse, Y. Hao, and C. G. Parini, "A compact microstrip antenna with improved bandwidth using complementary split-ring resonator (CSRR) loading," in *Proceedings of the IEEE Antennas and Propagation Society International Symposium*, pp. 5431–5434, June 2007.

[14] L. Meng, L. Mingzhi, and J. C. Tie, "Novel miniaturized dual band antenna design using complementary metamaterial," in *Proceedings of the International Workshop on Metamaterials (META '08)*, pp. 374–376, November 2008.

[15] J. Liu, S. Gong, Y. Xu, X. Zhang, C. Feng, and N. Qi, "Compact printed ultra-wideband monopole antenna with dual band-notched characteristics," *Electronics Letters*, vol. 44, no. 12, pp. 710–711, 2008.

[16] H. Zhang, Y. Q. Li, X. Chen, Y. Q. Fu, and N. C. Yuan, "Design of circular/dual-frequency linear polarization antennas based on the anisotropic complementary split ring resonator," *IEEE Transactions on Antennas and Propagation*, vol. 57, no. 10, Article ID 5196779, pp. 3352–3355, 2009.

[17] K.-L. Wong, *Compact and Broadband Microstrip Antennas*, John Wiley & Sons, New York, NY, USA, 2002.

[18] J. D. Kraus and R.J. Marhefka, *Antennas for all Applications*, McGraw-Hill, New York, NY, USA, 3rd edition, 2002.

[19] F. Aznar, M. Gil, J. Bonache, and F. Martín, "Revising the equivalent circuit models of resonant-type metamaterial transmission lines," in *Proceedings of the IEEE MTT-S International Microwave Symposium Digest (MTT '08)*, pp. 323–326, June 2008.

12

Experimental Performance Evaluation of POBICOS Middleware for Wireless Sensor Networks

Jouni Hiltunen, Mikko Ala-Louko, and Markus Taumberger

Converging Networks Laboratory, VTT Technical Research Centre of Finland, Kaitoväylä 1, 90590 Oulu, Finland

Correspondence should be addressed to Jouni Hiltunen, jouni.hiltunen@vtt.fi

Academic Editors: N. Abu-Ghazaleh, Y. Jiang, R. Montemanni, and S. Weller

The advances in the theory of wireless sensor networks have been remarkable during the past decades, but there is a lack of extensive experimental evaluations. In this paper we present performance-evaluation methods and results for POBICOS (platform for opportunistic behaviour in incompletely specified, heterogeneous object communities), which is an advanced middleware for wireless sensor networks (WSNs). The measurements concern energy consumption, duty cycle, and OS task profiling as well as communication characteristics such as round trip time (RTT) and throughput. In addition, a bandwidth analysis during a long-term experiment of fully functional POBICOS network and application is studied. Based on the evaluation results, power mode and data cache improvements are presented as well as CPU clock frequency optimizations.

1. Introduction

The research done in the field of WSNs has advanced a lot in the past decades. The achieved performance of a WSN implementation is inevitably tied to the characteristics of the used platform, and therefore, the performance evaluation cannot rely solely on the theoretical background. Our study presents an experimental performance evaluation of POBICOS which is an advanced opportunistic WSN middleware implemented on TinyOS operating system and Imote2 hardware platform.

The performance evaluation methods and results are related to energy consumption, duty cycle, and OS task profiling as well as communication characteristics such as round trip time and throughput. In addition, a bandwidth analysis during a long-term experiment of fully functional POBICOS network and application is included. Based on the evaluation results, power mode and data cache improvements are presented as well as CPU clock frequency optimizations.

Energy consumption of battery-powered sensor motes is a very crucial implementation issue which affects the operational costs of the WSN. The energy consumption is mainly affected by the achieved duty cycle and power modes of the motes. The overall operational energy consumption of the motes may be obtained through online energy consumption monitoring or through a hybrid method, in which the results of offline energy consumption measurements and online duty cycle monitoring are combined.

The duty cycle investigation is based on CPU usage monitoring which, in case of the Imote2 platform, can be implemented through performance monitoring unit (PMU) events. The duty cycle optimization can be achieved through monitoring the CPU usage of each running task with a task profiler. This usually requires modifications to the OS source code, but in the case of TinyOS the implementation of the task profiler is straightforward because of TinyOS's simple concurrency model which is based on a single thread and nonpreemptive tasks.

The communication performance of WSN middleware depends on the underlying physical and media access control layers. IEEE 802.15.4 is such a standard widely used in WSNs. The current implementation of the POBICOS supports ZigBee which adds tree topology routing on top of the 802.15.4. Since POBICOS implements services such as reliable transport and packet fragmentation the RTT and throughput measurements were conducted to find out how much additional delay and overhead the POBICOS middleware adds to those of ZigBee.

The middleware internal protocols perform tasks, such as network management, that require control messages to be sent amongst the nodes. Therefore, bandwidth analysis is an important performance metric when comparing different middleware solutions. We have done a network-wide bandwidth analysis to determine the bandwidth usage of the middleware when running a typical application.

2. Middleware Description

Opportunistic applications are developed without knowledge of the resources that will be present at deployment environment. They use the resources that happen to be available in an environment to achieve the application goals. In POBICOS, such applications are built of collections of microagents that work in an event-driven manner. Microagents can be created and released dynamically, and they can communicate with each other according to the application logic. The microagents are arranged in a tree-based hierarchy, where each microagent has a parent and optionally one or more children. Microagents can only communicate with their parent and children. In case a microagent becomes orphan, for example when the network gets partitioned, it releases itself to ensure a consistent state of the application.

The open-source POBICOS middleware [1] offers mechanisms to host microagents on different hardware platforms by executing them in a virtual machine [2]. It automatically handles the placement of microagents onto the actual hardware according to their resource requirements. A resource discovery is performed each time a microagent is created by the application. The middleware can also migrate microagents to other nodes depending on parameters, for example, to reduce their communication distance [3]. A middleware-level heartbeat protocol detects the disappearance of microagents and propagates this event to its parent and children. Other main features of the middleware are transparent inter-agent communication, security mechanisms [4], and multi-faceted resource access.

The middleware is fully decentralized and each node is running its own instance of it, which makes performance aspects very critical.

3. Performance Evaluation Methods

3.1. Energy Consumption Measurements. The measurement setup for the energy consumption measurements is depicted in Figure 1, and the used hardware is listed in Table 1. A nonintrusive method for measuring the current is achieved by using a probe that measures the current in a conductor through inductive coupling with no electrical contact. The output signal of the probe is amplified by the current probe amplifier, and the amplified signal is displayed in the oscilloscope. Power consumption is then calculated by multiplying the measured current with the 3.3 V operating voltage.

3.2. Task Profiler. The implemented task profiler enables online monitoring of the middleware, see Figure 2. The task profiler collects and stores the CPU PMU events for each running task and timer interrupt. Each record contains

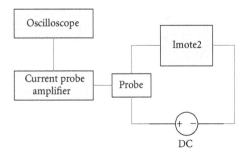

Figure 1: Energy measurement setup.

Table 1: List of the used hardware.

Imote2 battery board	IBB2400
Imote2 processor board	IPR2400
Imote2 radio board	CC2480 board based on TI's Z-Accel Demonstration Kit
Imote2 sensor board	ITS400
Oscilloscope	Tektronix TDS3052 500 MHz/ 5GS/s
Current probe amplifier	Tektronix AM503B
Current probe	Tektronix A6302

only the prevailing PMU counter values and the task/timer IDs which are stored in sequential order. Most of the task monitoring processing is done in the aggregator which is connected to the mote through UART. The task profiler data is requested from the mote on demand to the aggregator which calculates absolute PMU values and converts the task and timer IDs to descriptive names. The names are derived from app.c file which is produced by the nesC compiler from the application code. The presented system provides a lightweight solution for performance monitoring.

3.3. Communication Measurements

3.3.1. RTT. RTTs were measured on two different levels of the POBICOS communications stack:

(i) PoHWCommM—a low-level communication component using the ZigBee subsystem that gives a reference point for comparison.

(ii) PoCommM—the main POBICOS communication component responsible of implementing the reliable transport service with fragmentation of messages.

In both cases, RTT was measured over one hop using two Imote2 motes with empty and full payload lengths. When node A sends a message to node B a timestamp is taken. Upon receiving the message, node B responds by sending the exact same message back to node A. Another timestamp is taken when node A receives the message from node B. RTT is calculated by subtracting the two timestamps. The time accuracy of the measurement was 1 ms so each payload length was tested 10 times and the RTT's averaged.

3.3.2. Throughput. Imote2 network of two nodes over one hop is used in the measurements. Node A sends maximum

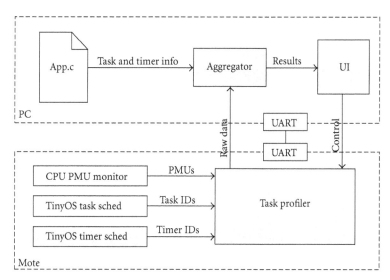

Figure 2: Task profiler block diagram.

length packets of 51 B to node B. The throughput is then calculated every 1 second for ZigBee and for the POBICOS best-effort mode. For POBICOS reliable mode, which introduces acknowledgments and retransmission in case of lost packets, the throughput calculation was done every 1 minute.

3.3.3. Bandwidth Analysis. The bandwidth analysis data was obtained directly from the main communication component (PoCommM) of the middleware through which all the traffic of the higher-level protocols of the middleware traverses. PoCommM provides a parameterized TinyOS interface to the higher-level protocols which means that each protocol is assigned a unique ID that can be used to identify the active protocol for each message sent. PoCommM logs the message lengths, interface IDs, and the transmission mode (unreliable versus reliable) with timestamps. This log can then be used to derive the perprotocol bandwidth usage. The time interval for the bandwidth calculation was chosen to be one minute. The layered architecture of the POBICOS communication components is illustrated in Figure 3. The middleware internal protocols wire to PoCommM which utilizes PoHWCommM to gain access to the ZigBee subsystem. PoCommM logs the communication service usage statistics.

4. Measurement Results

4.1. Energy Consumption Measurements. The energy consumption measurements were conducted with and without the middleware, using different power modes and CPU clock frequencies. To investigate the energy consumption of different power modes extensively, support for the standby power mode was implemented since the used TinyOS platform supported only active and idle power modes. Figure 4 presents the power consumption measurements with Imote2 battery, processor, and sensor boards as well as additional ZigBee radio board included.

In the power consumption measurements presented above, the active mode means running a processor-bound TinyOS task (an empty for-loop). The memory-bound task is an exception where the Imote2 internal memory is continuously accessed. Both the active and nonactive modes were measured within the same test run using periodic duty cycle where 1 s activity was followed by 1 s of inactivity. The measured current consumption multiplied with the operating voltage equals the momentary power consumption of the mote. The total energy consumption is then obtained by integrating the measured power-consumption curve over time.

The comparison of 13 MHz and 104 MHz CPU clock frequency modes shows that energy efficiency is better with 104 MHz mode if the standby mode is in use. Although the 13 MHz mode consumes ∼100 mW less in the active mode, the same processor-bound task takes eight-times longer to complete. In the standby mode, the power consumption does not depend on the operating frequency. Without the standby mode, the 13 MHz should be preferred since the middleware is expected to be in idle state most of the time and the idle mode energy efficiency is poorer at the higher CPU clock frequency. However, the implementation of standby mode is essential since it saves 55 mW in 13 MHz mode and 110 mW in 104 MHz mode compared to the idle mode.

For the middleware energy efficiency it is important that the mote remains in nonactive mode most of the time since all middleware tasks consume ∼180 mW more than in the standby mode. The radio reception, radio transmission, LEDs and light sensor reading consume additional ∼16 mW compared to the processor-bound task. The memory-bound task consumes 13 mW less than the processor bound task.

The ZigBee radio board is a significant energy sink of the POBICOS node since it constitutes over 20% of the total energy consumption. The middleware initializes the ZigBee radio to the active mode, but without the middleware the radio remains in the idle state. The radio consumes 33 mW

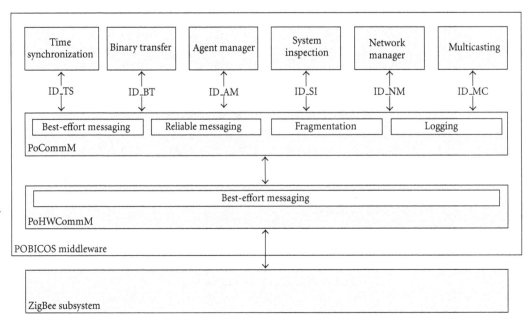

FIGURE 3: POBICOS communication components.

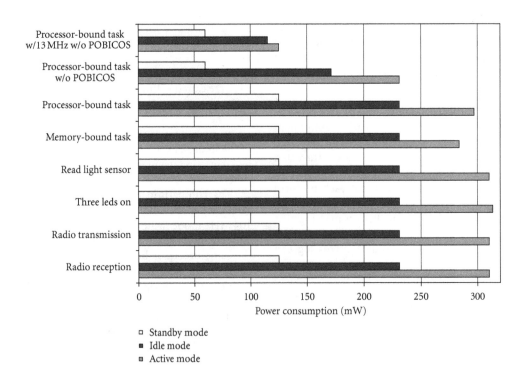

FIGURE 4: Power consumption with middleware, CPU clock frequency 104 MHz.

when not initialized, 100 mW in listening state, and 110 mW in transmitting and reception states.

The worst case energy profile concerning the initialization sequence of a node in an empty network is presented in Figure 5. The initialization energy consumption is dominated by the radio board especially when the node is a ZigBee coordinator since it consumes 17 s while the total initialization duration is 21 s. However, the radio initialization sequence is faster if there are other nodes

in network. The TinyOS initialization lasts 2 seconds and POBICOS initialization duration is < 0.5 second.

Real-world data regarding the duty cycle of a POBICOS node was gathered from an experiment of running a POBICOS system in an office building continuously for four days. In the experiment, temperature and light sensing nodes were used that periodically poll the sensor values and send them via the radio channel to be processed. The CPU loads of the nodes were obtained using the methods presented in

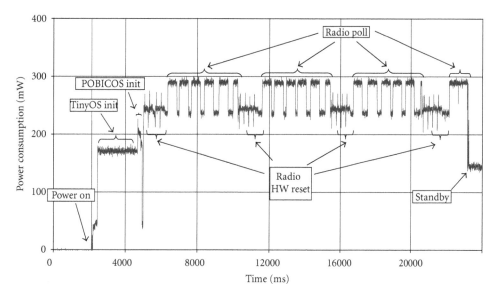

FIGURE 5: Worst case initialization sequence energy profile of a ZigBee coordinator.

Section 3. The locally measured load values of each node were sent every 10 seconds over the air to a monitoring node that was connected to a POBICOS administration and monitoring tool (PAM). PAM was used to create a log file of the reported load values.

Analysis of the log file of one node revealed that the CPU load during the experiment was close to constant except for the first load report that includes the execution of the initialization sequence of the middleware. The CPU load value of the first report was 44.100% after which, it stabilized to 0.040%. The average CPU load during the whole experiment was 0.057%. The results obtained from other nodes were observed to be similar.

We are now able to estimate the energy consumption of a POBICOS node during the experiment when we combine the online measurements of the duty cycle of a node with the offline measurements of the power consumption presented in Figure 4. If we assume the respective power consumptions during active and standby modes to be constant, the total energy consumption can be calculated with the following equation:

$$E(t) = \int P(t) \cdot dt = (\mathrm{DC} \cdot P_A + (1 - \mathrm{DC}) \cdot P_S) \cdot t, \quad (1)$$

where $E(t)$ is the energy consumption at time t, $P(t)$ is the power consumption at time t, DC is the duty cycle, P_A is the constant power consumption in active mode, and P_S is the constant power consumption in standby mode.

From the measurement data (Figure 4) we can obtain a P_A of 310.2 mW and a P_S of 125.4 mW. Furthermore, we use the abovementioned value of 0.00057 for DC. This yields us a daily energy consumption of 10.844 kJ per one POBICOS node. In one year this adds up to a consumption of 3.958 MJ which corresponds to 1.099 kWh.

4.2. Task Profiler. The results obtained with the task profiler in a two-node network without an application running are

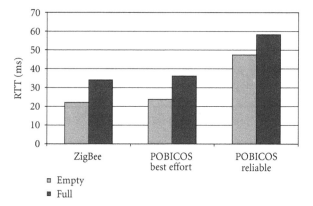

FIGURE 6: Results of the RTT measurements.

presented in Table 2 and the task descriptions in Table 3. In this case the duty cycle is less than 1%. The results indicate that a significant number of the used CPU cycles are wasted by dependency stalls because the data cache is not supported by the TinyOS platform. The support for the data cache was implemented later, and the results of the data cache measurements with TinyOS Blink application are presented in Table 4. The data cache was observed to save a significant number of CPU clock cycles.

4.3. Communication Measurements

4.3.1. RTT. The results of the RTT measurements are presented in Figure 6. It depicts the RTT values for the ZigBee subsystem and for the POBICOS best-effort and reliable modes. Whereas in the first two tests the RTT constitutes solely of two messages, the reliable mode includes also the acknowledgment messages sent automatically for each received message.

TABLE 2: 1.5 second Task Profiler sample run in a two-node network without an application running.

Task name	Data cache accesses	Dependency stall (cycles)	Run time (ms)	CPU instructions	CPU clock cycles
McuSleep.sleep	0	0	458.4375	0	0
PoPerfInspM$CpuUsageMilliTimer$fired	N/A	N/A	0.1250	N/A	N/A
McuSleep.sleep	0	0	0.0312	0	0
VirtualizeTimerC0updateFromTimer	68	3492	0.1250	943	11557
McuSleep.sleep	0	0	15.0938	0	0
PoCommTimersM$BaseTimer$fired	176	6239	0.2188	1647	22157
McuSleep.sleep	0	0	0.0312	0	0
VirtualizeTimerC0updateFromTimer	68	3492	0.1250	943	11481
McuSleep.sleep	0	0	69.2500	0	0
PoReliableTransportIstub$Timer$fired	11005	234337	6.0312	78984	610469
VirtualizeTimerC0updateFromTimer	68	3493	0.1250	943	11665
McuSleep.sleep	0	0	8.1875	0	0
CC2480P$sendDoneTask	22	1674	0.0938	594	8577
McuSleep.sleep	0	0	13.0312	0	0
CC2480P$receiveTask	10794	222670	4.3750	65291	443417
McuSleep.sleep	0	0	8.4688	0	0
CC2480P$sendDoneTask	23	1646	0.0938	599	8525
McuSleep.sleep	0	0	13.0312	0	0
CC2480P$receiveTask	3175	65010	1.8750	20568	190225
McuSleep.sleep	0	0	126.9688	0	0
PoNetworkMngrM$MilliTimer$fired	126	5162	0.1875	1281	19181
McuSleep.sleep	0	0	0.0312	0	0
VirtualizeTimerC0updateFromTimer	68	3493	0.1250	943	11549
McuSleep.sleep	0	0	846.4688	0	0

TABLE 3: Middleware and TinyOS task descriptions from the sample run.

Task name	Source	Description
McuSleep.sleep	TinyOS	Command called in task scheduler when there is no tasks to be run.
PoPerfInspM$CpuUsageMilliTimer$fired	POBICOS	Timer task to measure CPU load periodically. Default measurement period is 3 seconds. Because this task resets the performance counters details of the profiler cannot measure all metrics.
VirtualizeTimerC0updateFromTimer	TinyOS	Task to manage TinyOS timers.
PoCommTimersM$BaseTimer$fired	POBICOS	Task to manage reliable transport timers. Default period is 4 seconds.
PoReliableTransportIstub$Timer$fired	POBICOS	Timer task to manage reliable transport transmissions.
CC2480P$sendDoneTask	POBICOS	Radio transmission task.
CC2480P$receiveTask	POBICOS	Radio reception task.
PoNetworkMngrM$MilliTimer$fired	POBICOS	Task for network management. Default period is 1 second.

We can see that the RTTs of ZigBee and POBICOS best-effort mode are very closely equal with a minor increase observable in the POBICOS best-effort mode. The overhead introduced by the POBICOS reliable mode can be mainly explained by the acknowledgment mechanism of the reliable transport service. The transmissions of the acknowledgments from node B to node A precede the transmission of the response message, therefore increasing the RTT.

4.3.2. Throughput. The results of the throughput tests are presented in Figure 7. Again, we compare ZigBee with the two POBICOS transport modes.

From the figure we immediately observe that the POBICOS best-effort mode seemingly outperforms ZigBee, while both achieve a throughput around 42 kbps. Obviously, this must be considered as measurement inaccuracy, and we can conclude that the overhead introduced by the POBICOS

TABLE 4: Data cache measurement results with TinyOS Blink application.

	Data cache off	Data cache on	Improvement (%)
Data cache accesses	58062	58062	N/A
Total CPU cycles	536046	137423	74.364
Data dependency stall cycles	395451	36	99.991
Data cache miss cycles	58054	2	99.997

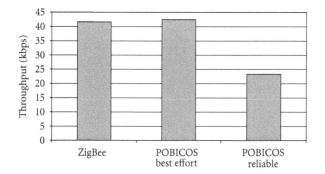

FIGURE 7: Results of the throughput tests.

best-effort mode is negligible. The POBICOS reliable mode achieves a noticeably lower throughput of 23.2 kbps which can be explained by the occasional packet loss during the measurements and the relatively long resending timeout of 7 seconds.

4.3.3. Bandwidth Analysis. Similarly as the duty-cycle measurements, the results presented in this section are extracted from the real-world experiment. In the experiment, a total of 61 POBICOS nodes were used to run an example application. This bandwidth analysis is performed at the network level, that is, we present the bandwidth usage of the whole network instead of individual nodes. The node bandwidth usages were calculated with one minute intervals and summed together to form the network-level bandwidth usage. It must be noted that the results do not include the automatic retransmissions of the POBICOS reliable transport protocol. Figure 8 presents the bandwidth usage during the whole experiment which lasted four days.

As seen from the figure, the bandwidth usage is close to constant with the exception of the peak at the application start-up phase where most of the microagent creations and resource probings take place. The reduction in the bandwidth usage at approximately 5 : 30 on the second night is merely a statistical anomaly. It is caused by resource probing multicasts distributing over two measurement periods whereas in the start of the experiment all the multicast messages are sent within one measurement period.

Next, we will take a closer look at the bandwidth usage in the system start-up phase, which is depicted in Figure 9. The figure shows the individual bandwidth usages of the middleware's internal protocols with different colours

stacked on top of each other while the envelope of the curve corresponds to the total bandwidth usage.

The small system inspection and multicasting load between 15 : 24 and 15 : 27 is caused by the PAM tool upon its start-up phase where it collects information from the nodes of the network. After that, we can see that the middleware idles as there is no application running. The application is started at 16 : 08 which introduces a bandwidth peak that reaches its peak around 850 Bps. The peak is mostly caused by the microagent host probing messages, sent via the multicasting protocol, and microagent binary transfers from the application pill to the host nodes. The application deployment finishes at 16 : 33 after which we see small agent-manager traffic that encompasses the application-level messages.

The bandwidth usage during one hour of normal operation is plotted in Figure 10. Again, the plot is stacked so the envelope of the curve corresponds to the total bandwidth usage.

The bandwidth during normal operation comprises agent manager messages that originate from the application. The multicast peaks are also caused by the application logic, which polls for new temperature and brightness sensor microagent-candidate hosts every 10 minutes.

The results of the experiment startup and the normal operation suggest that there would be room for optimization in the multicast-based host-probing protocol as it dominates the bandwidth usage compared to the application traffic which averages below 10 Bps. Another major bandwidth user is the microagent binary transfer protocol. This is expected as all the microagent binaries are transmitted at runtime over the air from the application pill.

5. Related Work

The research done in overall performance evaluation of WSN middleware implementations is rather limited. The most relevant scientific overall study to our best knowledge is the work by Ribeiro et al. [5] in which the performance of SensorBus is studied. SensorBus is a message-oriented adaptive middleware running on Crossbow's MICAz motes with TinyOS. The measured metrics include throughput, packet delivery fraction, motes' energy consumption, and policy initialization response time in case of an external service request. The throughput and packet delivery fraction results can be used to compare the performances of different multihop routing protocols while response time and energy consumption results provide comparable results with our study.

Santos et al. and Bertocco et al. [6, 7] provide measurement results from simple WSN experiments without a middleware layer. The setup in [6] consists of Crossbow's TelosB motes with Contiki OS. The results obtained in the study provide basic reference to one-hop data-gathering WSN application without advanced self-adaptation functionalities. The experimental evaluation conducted in [7] is based on Moteiv's Tmote Sky motes running custom high-layer, single-hop, master-slave, industrial-monitoring

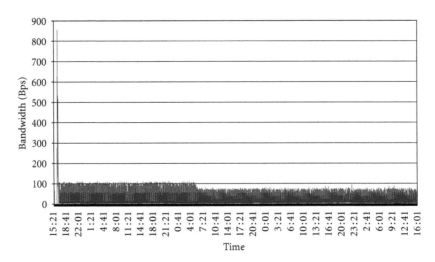

FIGURE 8: Bandwidth usage during the whole experiment.

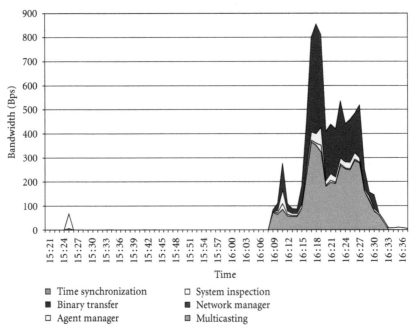

FIGURE 9: Bandwidth usage during the experiment start-up phase.

protocol which performs two types of tasks: periodical slave polling for receiving sensor data and asynchronous alarm transmissions. The results can be used to estimate the effect of radio interference on both types of tasks.

The performance of the underlying physical and MAC layers under real-world conditions has a dramatic effect on the WSN overall performance. Therefore, the studies performed in [8, 9] provide valuable resources to analyze our measurements. The testbed used in [8] consists of MICAz motes with TinyOS. It was shown that applying the testbed to practical environments is feasible, and the guidelines for the placement of the motes were given. Woon and Wan [9] present realistic experiments on both one-hop

and multihop topologies with Freescale MC13193 Evaluation Kit. It presents comparable performance metrics such as throughput, packet delivery ratio, and delay, and it also shows that experimental results are valuable compared to normal simulated environments.

There are some published WSN performance measurement and verification tools such as [10–12]. Rost and Balakrishnan and Ramanathan et al. [10, 11] introduce online network management tools but their main focus is on failure detection. On the other hand, Zheng [12] proposes to apply formal verification techniques to ensure the correctness of the implementation using model checking techniques. These techniques provide valuable knowledge

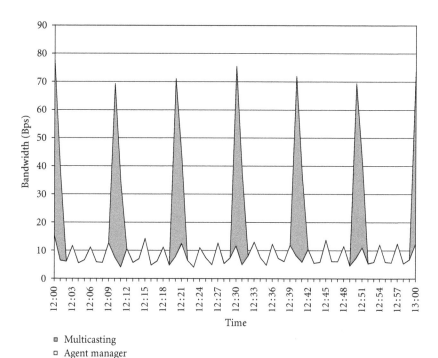

FIGURE 10: Bandwidth usage during 1 hour of normal operation.

on real-time behavior details of the system, but we are more interested in performance of the distributed WSN application as a whole.

The duty cycle of the motes is an important aspect of the WSN performance. Profilers can be used to obtain the details of the processor usage such as in [13] where the OS is interrupted frequently to collect the currently running task and in [14] where activity tracking across the network is monitored. The perceived duty cycle combined with offline energy measurements can be used to estimate the overall WSN energy consumption. Also real-time energy measurements can be achieved by utilizing hardware built-in switching regulators as in [15] and by using XScale PMU events as in [16]. The reference results for offline measurement with Mica2 motes can be obtained from [17].

6. Conclusions

The full performance evaluation of a WSN middleware implementation requires an extensive set of methods and tools which are able to measure low-level operations such as PMU events and high-level effects such as communication overheads. In addition, the measurements should not interfere with the operation of the running middleware. Distributed methods were found to be efficient when combined with offline measurements such as the presented energy measurements.

The preferred CPU clock frequency in terms of energy efficiency was found to be dependent on the available power modes. The influence of the data cache to the CPU usage

performance was found to be dramatic. Our implementation shows also some deficiencies in terms of energy efficiency and initialization sequence duration that can be caused by the usage of separate ZigBee radio board.

The communication measurements suggest that the most crucial target for optimization would be the multicasting protocol which is used by the binary transfer and host object probing services of the middleware. In addition, it was observed that the underlying ZigBee network may induce heavy packet loss which severely affects the throughput of the reliable transport mode of POBICOS due to a long resending timeout.

The future work includes improvements in energy efficiency. For energy-efficient operation of POBICOS the radio board power-saving modes should be taken into use. Currently, all the motes are acting as ZigBee routers and for the routing purposes they are in continuous listening state. Energy savings would be achieved if some of the motes were ZigBee end devices or if the ZigBee routers had their power-saving modes enabled with synchronized sleeping periods.

Acknowledgments

The authors would like to thank the POBICOS consortium partners involved in the middleware design and implementation, Warsaw University of Technology (Poland), and Center for Research and Technology Thessaly (Greece). This work was done in the framework of the EU FP7 Project POBICOS supported by European Commission and VTT Technical Research Centre of Finland.

References

[1] http://www.ict-pobicos.eu/.

[2] A. Pruszkowski, T. Paczesny, and J. Domaszewicz, "From C to VM-targeted executables: techniques for heterogeneous sensor/actuator networks," in *8th IEEE Workshop on Intelligent Solutions in Embedded Systems (WISES '10)*, pp. 61–66, July 2010.

[3] N. Tziritas, T. Loukopoulos, S. Lalis, and P. Lampsas, "Agent placement in wireless embedded systems: memory space and energy optimizations," in *IEEE International Symposium on Parallel and Distributed Processing, Workshops and Phd Forum (IPDPSW '10)*, 2010.

[4] P. Tarvainen, M. Ala-Louko, M. Jaakola et al., "Towards a lightweight security solution for user-friendly management of distributed sensor networks," in *9th International Conference on Next Generation Wired/Wireless Networking, and 2nd Conference on Smart Spaces*, S. Balandin, D. Moltchnov, and Y. Koucheryavy, Eds., vol. 5764 of *Lecture Notes in Computer Science*, pp. 97–109, September 2009.

[5] A. R. L. Ribeiro, L. C. Freitas, C. R. L. Francês, and J. C. W. A. Costa, "Middleware performance evaluation in wireless sensor networks," in *International Telecommunications Symposium (ITS '06)*, pp. 207–212, September 2006.

[6] A. Santos, A. Cardoso, and P. Gil, "Poster abstract: a case study on performance enhancement in WSN using Contiki OS," in *European Conference on Wireless Sensor Networks (EWSN '10)*, 2010.

[7] M. Bertocco, G. Gamba, A. Sona, and S. Vitturi, "Experimental characterization of wireless sensor networks for industrial applications," *IEEE Transactions on Instrumentation and Measurement*, vol. 57, no. 8, pp. 1537–1546, 2008.

[8] K. E. Tepe, P. R. Casey, and N. Kar, "Design and implementation of a testbed for IEEE 802.15.4 (Zigbee) performance measurements," *EURASIP Journal on Wireless Communications and Networking*, vol. 2010, Article ID 103406, 2010.

[9] W. T. H. Woon and T.-C. Wan, "Performance evaluation of IEEE 802.15.4 wireless multi-hop networks," *International Journal of Ad Hoc and Ubiquitous Computing*, vol. 3, no. 1, pp. 57–66, 2008.

[10] S. Rost and H. Balakrishnan, "Memento: a health monitoring system for wireless sensor networks," in *3rd Annual IEEE Communications Society on Sensor and Ad hoc Communications and Networks (SECON '06)*, pp. 575–584, September 2006.

[11] N. Ramanathan, K. Chang, R. Kapur, L. Girod, E. Kohler, and D. Estrin, "Sympathy for the Sensor Network Debugger," in *3rd International Conference on Embedded Networked Sensor Systems (SenSys '05)*, 2005.

[12] M. C. Zheng, "An automatic approach to verify sensor network systems," in *4th IEEE International Conference on Secure Software Integration and Reliability Improvement Companion (SSIRI-C '10)*, pp. 7–12, June 2010.

[13] M. K. Watfa and M. Moubarak, "Building performance measurement tools for wireless sensor network operating systems," in *7th International Conference on Advances in Mobile Computing and Multimedia (MoMM '09)*, pp. 599–604, December 2009.

[14] R. Fonseca, P. Dutta, P. Levis, and I. Stoica, "Quanto: tracking energy in networked embedded systems," in *8th USENIX conference on Operating systems design and implementation (OSDI '08)*, 2008.

[15] P. Dutta, M. Feldmeier, J. Paradiso, and D. Culler, "Energy metering for free: augmenting switching regulators for real-time monitoring," in *International Conference on Information Processing in Sensor Networks (IPSN '08)*, pp. 283–294, April 2008.

[16] G. Contreras and M. Martonosi, "Power prediction for intel XScale® processors using performance monitoring unit events," in *International Symposium on Low Power Electronics and Design (ISLPED '05)*, pp. 221–226, August 2005.

[17] M. Calle and J. Kabara, "Measuring energy consumption in wireless sensor networks using GSP," in *17th International Symposium on Personal, Indoor and Mobile Radio Communications (PIMRC '06)*, September 2006.

13

A Reliable and Efficient Highway Multihop Vehicular Broadcast Model

Deng Chuan[1] and Wang Jian[2]

[1] Institute of Communication Engineering, PLA University of Science and Technology,
  Nanjing 210007, China
[2] National KeyLaboratory of Automotive Dynamic Simulation, College of Automotive Engineering,
  Jilin University, Changchum 130025, China

Correspondence should be addressed to Wang Jian, wangjian591@gmail.com

Academic Editors: M. Listanti and Y. M. Tseng

A reliable and efficient highway broadcast model based on gain prediction is proposed to solve excessive information retransmission and channel conflict that often happen to flooding broadcast in vehicular ad hoc network. We take accountof the relative speeds, the intervehicle distance, and the coverage difference of the neighboring vehicles into predicting the gain of every neighbor, and further select the neighbor with the maximum gain as the next hop on the every direction of road. Simulations show that the proposed model is clearly superior to the original flooding model and a recent variant based on mobility prediction in packet arrival rate, average delay, forwarding count, and throughput.

1. Introduction

Vehicular ad hoc network (VANET) is a temporary autonomous system composed by a group of vehicles equipped with transceivers and global positioning system (GPS). VANET is specifically designed to communicate among vehicles so that drivers can acquire the information about other vehicles (e.g., speed, direction, and location) as well as real-time traffic information beyond visual range. The current main goal of VANET is providing safety and comfort for passengers [1]. With this stream of research, highway safety has attracted more attentions, such as active accident warning, icy patch alarm, and others. Whether a successive collision can be effectively avoided is mainly dependent on transmitting warning information reliably and efficiently on multipaths. Due to limited transmission range of nodes, each mobile vehicle in VANET acts as router, for transmitting information to destination. Broadcast is a common means to disseminate messages. Among various broadcast approaches, flooding is the first one. Each node rebroadcasts the received message exactly once, which results

in broadcast storm problems [2]. Although [2] proposes mechanisms to improve flooding, they are not effective for all range of node density and packet loads in VANET [3]. Therefore, multihop broadcast in VANET is faced with many challenges [4].

This work proposes a *reliable broadcast routing based on gain prediction* (RB-GP) in which the relative speeds and coverage differences of the neighboring vehicles are calculated, and the intervehicle distance is also considered, and thus the neighbor under consideration with gain and reliability is selected as the next hop on the every direction. Moreover, RB-GP switches to the storage and forwarding when there are not proper next hop temporarily, weakening the negative impacts caused by the serious topological segmentation in VANET [5].

The remainder of this paper is organized as follows. Section 2 introduces the background, including some standards and related work. The RB-GP model is explained in details in Section 3. The simulations are provided in Section 4. Finally, in Section 5, some conclusions are drawn, and suggestions for future work are made.

2. Background

2.1. IEEE 802.11p/IEEE 1609 Standards. IEEE 802.11a/b/g/ has been extensively used in the wireless network but is not adaptive to vehicular networks because this standard is designed only for little mobility. Recently, IEEE 802.11-based solutions for vehicular networks are also investigated by IEEE 802.11p. IEEE 802.11p wireless access in the vehicular environment (WAVE) defines amendments to IEEE 802.11 to support intelligent transportation system (ITS) applications in the area of traffic safety and efficiency, as, for instance, *green-light optimal speed advisory* or *traffic jam ahead warning*. Its protocol stack is shown in Figure 1. The IEEE 1609 family of standards for WAVE consists of four trail use standards [7]: (1) *resource manager* (IEEE 1609.1) describes the data and management services offered within the WAVE architecture, defines command message formats and the appropriate responses to those messages, data storage formats that must be used by applications to communicate between architecture components, and status and request message formats; (2) *security services for applications and management messages* (IEEE 1609.2) defines the circumstances for using secure message exchanges and how those messages should be processed based upon the purpose of the exchange; (3) *networking services* (IEEE 1609.3) defines network and transport layer services, including addressing and routing, in support of secure WAVE data exchange; (4) *multi-channel operations* (IEEE 1609.4) provides enhancements to the IEEE 802.11 media access control (MAC) to support WAVE operations. As a whole, the IEEE 1609 family of standards defines the architecture, communications model, management structure, security mechanisms, and physical access for high-speed (up to 27 Mb/s) short-range (up to 1000 m) low-latency wireless communications in the vehicular environment. We employ IEEE 802.11p as the lower layers' (PHY and MAC) communication protocol in order to simulate more real scene.

2.2. Related Work. Much of the literature [8, 9] on inter-vehicle communications (IVCs) is navigation safety related. At the network layer, the most common way to broadcast safety messages is via reliable, robust flooding. However, the efficiency of flooding quickly decreases with the number of nodes. For scalable delivery, researchers have proposed georouting and further have focused on exploiting innate characteristics of vehicular networks such as high speed, but restricted, mobility. Recently, there have been many literatures for alleviating broadcast storms [10, 11]. For example, urban multihop broadcast (UMB) [12] features a form of redundant flood suppression scheme where the furthest node in the broadcast direction from a sender is selected to forward and acknowledge the packet. The scheme alleviates broadcast storm and hidden terminal problems. However, according to the contention resolution scheme, the potential relay nodes wait the longest time before retransmission. UMB may lead to a large delay, especially in high-mobility scenarios. Segment-oriented data abstraction and dissemination (SODAD) [13] collects only the information relative to a given locality (i.e., a road segment) to create a scalable decentralized information system. But SODAD is specially designed for the provision of comfort applications. Movement prediction-based routing (MOPR) [14] predicts future positions of vehicles and estimates the time needed for the transmission of data to decide whether a route is likely to be broken or not during the transmission time. The performance of the scheme largely depends on the prediction accuracy and the estimate of the transmission time that depends, in turn, on several factors such as network congestion status, driver's behavior, and the used transmission protocols. Distributed movement-based routing algorithm (MORA) [15] exploits the position and direction of movement of vehicles. The metric used in this protocol is a linear combination of the number of hops and a target functional, which can be independently calculated by each node. This function depends on the distance of the forwarding car from the line connecting the source and destination and on the vehicle's movement direction. Each vehicle needs to be able to implement this in a distributed manner. Preferred group broadcasting (PGB) [16] aims to reduce control messages overhead by eliminating redundant transmissions and to obtain stable routes with the ability to autocorrect. PGB classifies each node that receives a broadcast packet (e.g., route request) into one of the three groups based on the sensed signal level: preferred group, IN group, and OUT group. PGB enhancements are bound to ad hoc on-demand distance vector (AODV), however. Vector-based tracking detection (V-TRADE) and history-enhanced V-TRADE (HV-TRADE) [17] classify the neighbors into different forwarding groups each of which only selects a small subset of vehicles with high speed to rebroadcast the message. But they still select the fastest nodes which is not suitable for the highly dynamic vehicular topology. Recently, reliable broadcast routing scheme based on mobility prediction (RB-MP) [18] selects the node with the maximum speed on the every direction as the next hop according to the prediction holding time provided by position and relative velocity, which can effectively avoid the problems in the earlier discussed work. But the coverage of the node with the maximum speed may be very small in the next rebroadcasting because the maximum speed is affected by the relative speed and the intervehicle distance. One consideration in selecting a proper rebroadcast node is that the node with a short distance may increase transmission hops, but the node with a long away trip often causes connection instability. Therefore, for a suitable tradeoff between reliability and efficiency, the work in this paper is partially motivated from the aforementioned work and aims to a reliable and efficient broadcasting scheme for highway scenario.

3. RB-GP Model

3.1. Definitions. We list necessary definitions as follows for clear presentation.

Neighbor nodes set $N(i)$ is composed of node i's of all neighbors. $|(N_i)|$ is the total number of members in $N(i)$.

Two-hop node communicates with node i only by one forwarder.

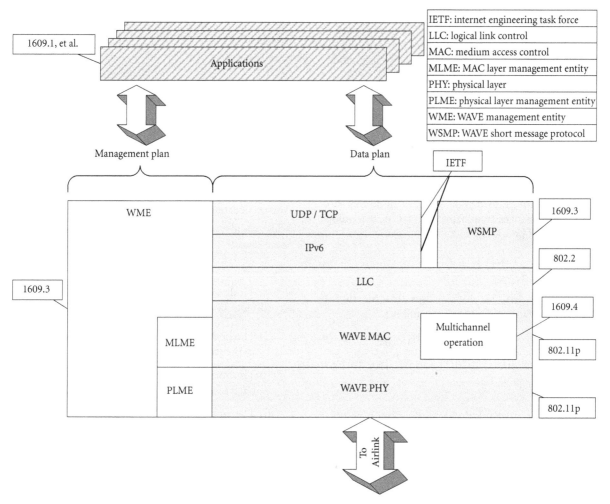

FIGURE 1: Protocol stack [6].

Two-hop node set $T(i)$ is composed of node i's all two-hop nodes. $|T(i)|$ denotes the total number of members in $T(i)$. $T(i)$ is defined as

$$T(i) = \bigcup_{j \in N(i)} T^j(i), \tag{1}$$

where $T^j(i)$ is the two-hop set connected by the neighbor j; that is, $T^j(i) = N(j)$.

Forwarding nodes set $R(i)$ is composed of the nodes; node i supposes which will forward the packets from it.

Neighbor information table records neighbor information, such as location, speed, and direction.

Position updating period μ is regular periodic interval by which the node's location is evaluated.

Prediction holding time of the connection λ_{ij} is the time that node i may stay in the transmission range of node j [18]. Without loss of generality, it is assumed that node i and node j are on a straight road, so λ_{ij} can be calculated by

$$\lambda_{ij} = \begin{cases} \left| \dfrac{\max\{0, \ \Delta D_{ij}\} \times R - D_{ij}}{\Delta v_{ij}} \right|, & \Delta v_{ij} \neq 0, \\ 2 \times \mu, & \Delta v_{ij} = 0, \end{cases} \tag{2}$$

$$D_{ij} = \sqrt{\left(x_i - x_j\right)^2 + \left(y_i - y_j\right)^2}, \tag{3}$$

$$\Delta D_{ij} = \begin{cases} \text{sign}(D - D_0), & \text{if } D_0 \text{ exists}, \\ 0, & \text{otherwise}, \end{cases} \tag{4}$$

$$\Delta v_{ij} = v_i^2 + v_j^2 - 2 \times v_i \times v_i \times \cos\left(\theta_i - \theta_j\right), \tag{5}$$

$$\theta_i = \begin{cases} \left(2\pi + \arctan \dfrac{y_i - y_{i0}}{x_i - x_{i0}}\right) \% 2\pi, & x_i > x_{i0}, \\ \pi + \arctan \dfrac{y_i - y_{i0}}{x_i - x_{i0}}, & x_i < x_{i0}, \\ \dfrac{\pi}{2} \times \max\{0, \ \text{sign}(y_i - y_{i0})\}, & \\ \quad - \dfrac{3\pi}{2} \times \min\{0, \ \text{sign}(y_i - y_{i0})\}, & x_i = x_{i0}, \end{cases} \tag{6}$$

where i and j are the ID of the receiver and the sender, respectively. (x_{i0}, y_{i0}) and (x_{j0}, y_{j0}) are the previous position while (x_i, y_i) and (x_j, y_j) are the current. When the distance between node i and node j increases, the function sign() returns $+1$, otherwise returns -1.

Direct gain $E(i, j)$ is the ratio of the coverage difference of the neighboring nodes i, j to node i's two-hop node set $T(i)$. The precondition for calculating $E(i, j)$ is ensuring that the neighbor node j can receive the packets from node i successfully; that is, $\lambda_{ij} > \mu$. $E(i, j)$ is calculated by

$$E(i, j) = \frac{|N(j)| - |N(i)|}{|T(i)|}. \quad (7)$$

Indirect gain $I(i, j)$ is the benefit possibly brought by the assumption that node i selects node j as the next hop, and also its precondition is that node j can receive node i's packets. In detail, if $\lambda_{ij} > \mu$ and λ_{ij} is close to μ, it means that node j will leave the transmission range of node i in short time, and some changes may happen to its local topology. $I(i, j)$ is calculated by

$$I(i, j) = \frac{\mu}{\lambda_{ij}}. \quad (8)$$

Gain function $G(i, j)$. node i uses this function to calculate the gain value of neighbor j as follows:

$$G(i, j) = \alpha E(i, j) + (1 - \alpha)I(i, j), \quad (9)$$

where $\alpha \in [0, 1]$, as $E(i, j) \in [0, 1]$ and $I(i, j) \in (0, 1)$; so the range of $G(i, j)$ is $[0, 1]$.

3.2. Specific Process.
In RB-GP model, node information is assumed to be available for each node which can be acquired through beacon or periodical short message exchanging, including ID (node identity), position (x, y is the GPS coordinate), speed (the average relative speed Δv_{ij}), and direction (direction of the relative speed ΔD_{ij} defined by an angle with x-axis). Each node establishes its own neighbor information table through exchanging node information with each other. The neighbor information table is exchanged only between one-hop neighbors and is not forwarded to other far away nodes.

The design goal of RB-GP model is to maximize the range of every rebroadcasting and to minimize transmission delay through selecting the proper next hop on every direction and meanwhile ensures the neighbor node can receive the packets from the upstream node. In detail, RB-GP model tries to find the neighbor node with the biggest gain on the every direction. We take Figure 2, for example, to explain the working process of RB-GP model. The current forwarding node records the identities of the next hops on all directions into packet header in order that the next hop can decide whether or not it needs to rebroadcast the received packets. Node A's working process is as follows when receiving a broadcasting packet p.

Step 1. Node A judges whether it has received p before. If so, it will drop p directly and exit.

Step 2. Node A judges whether it is indeed the forwarding node selected by the upstream node through analyzing the packet header. If not, it exits; otherwise node A continues the next step or stores p temporarily when the network is not connected.

TABLE 1: Simulation parameters.

Description	Value
Simulated area	1200 m × 600 m
Simulated scenarios	Six crossed roads with two ways and two lanes
MAC protocol	802.11 p
Data rate	1 Mbps
Transmitting range	250 m
Packet size	1024 Bytes
Simulation time	100 s
Beacon interval	1 s
Position updating period μ	1 s
Vehicle number	100
Speed range	40 km/h~80 km/h

Step 3. Node A classifies the neighbors into three groups according to node A's neighbor information table.

  (i) The nodes locate in the same road as node A and are in the front of A, as node F in Figure 2.

  (ii) The nodes locate in the same road as A and are in the back of A, as node B.

  (iii) The nodes locate in the different road from A, as nodes C, D, and G.

Step 4. Node A calculates the gain value G of every neighbor node using (9) and, further, selects the node with the maximum gain in each group as the next hop, records its ID into the header of p, and finally sends packet p.

Node A will start the store-and-forward mechanism [19] when it does not find any proper node in Step 3. Node A stores the broadcasting packet in memory temporarily and then continues forwarding to other appropriate nodes within its communication range at some time.

4. Simulations

We adopt NS2.34 [20] to evaluate the RB-GP, the RB-MP, and the flooding models and use VanetMobiSim [21] to create highway scenario.

4.1. Settings.
Table 1 lists the simulation parameters, and Figure 3 shows the simulated scenario we used in this work. We mainly focus on highway scenario, so traffic lights and roadblocks are neglected. Vehicles randomly decide to keep going ahead, to turn left, or to turn right when arriving at a crossroad (blind intersection).

4.2. Results.
We used the following metrics to compare the performances of the RB-GP, the RB-MP, and the flooding: packet arrival rate, average delay, forwarding count, and throughput. Each simulation result corresponds to an average over 50 independent of experiments.

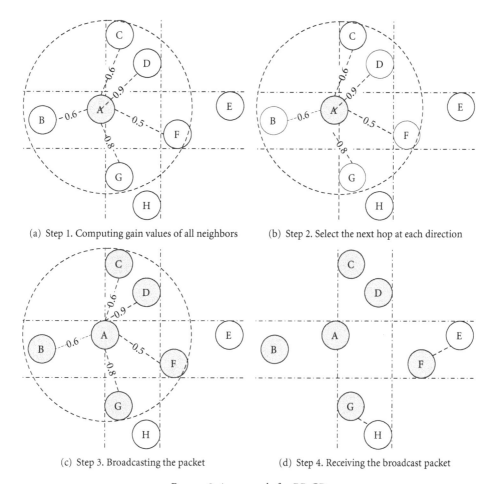

(a) Step 1. Computing gain values of all neighbors

(b) Step 2. Select the next hop at each direction

(c) Step 3. Broadcasting the packet

(d) Step 4. Receiving the broadcast packet

FIGURE 2: An example for RB-GP.

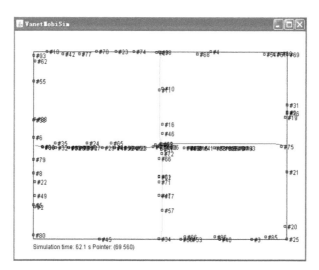

FIGURE 3: An example for highway scenario.

We first investigate the performances of different models, and the results are shown in Figure 4. In Figure 4(a), RB-GP model is superior to the other two models in packet arrival rate. This is because RB-GP model chooses the node with the maximum gain as the next hop on the every direction so that each selected node can cover most nodes and receive the broadcasting packet successfully, resulting in a high packet arrival rate. Although the flooding model has a high packet arrival rate at initial simulation because it requires all nodes to rebroadcast the received packets again, the packet arrival rate is quickly decreasing because of a large number of redundant information and channel conflict

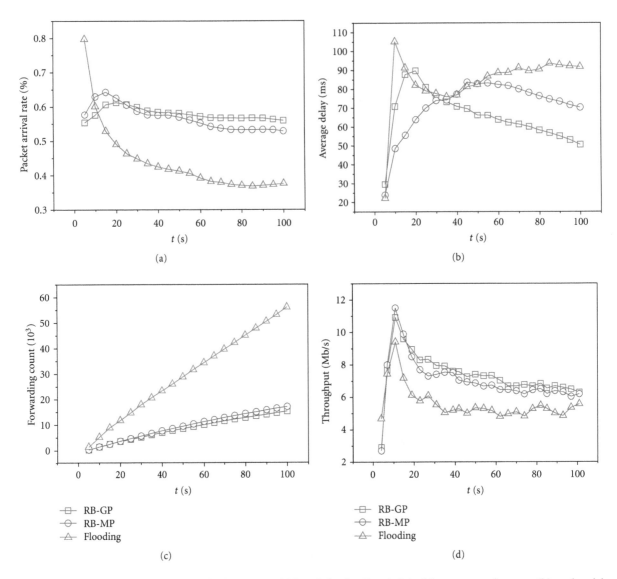

FIGURE 4: The comparisons of the RB-GP (□), the RB-MP (○) and the flooding (△) in (a) average packet rate, (b) packet delay, (c) forwarding count, and (d) throughput with parameter $\alpha = 0.5$.

as system running. The RB-MP model selects the node with the maximum speed as the next hop, so the coverage difference of the neighboring vehicles may be small, resulting in lower packet arrival rate than that of the RB-GP model. In Figure 4(b), RB-GP model shows a slightly higher average delay than RB-MP model at initial simulation because of the incompleteness of node information, but the average delay is gradually decreasing with information exchange and finally has the smallest average delay in three models. Figure 4(c) illustrates the forwarding count of three models. As aforementioned, selecting a node in the short range as the next hop will increase the forwarding count, but, in the converse case, the selected link may become instable because of quick movement and signal interference. RB-GP model balances the link reliability and the transmission distance and reduces the unnecessary information retransmission and the probability of channel conflict, so resulting in the smallest

forwarding counts. Figure 4(d) reflects the changing trend of end-to-end throughput. The curves of all the models reach the peak at initial simulation due to network instability, but the throughputs begin to fall back and steady with system running; RB-GP model behaves better than the other two models because of a high packet arrival rate.

We now turn to explore the impacts of only introduced parameter α on RB-GP model, and the results are shown in Figure 5. The parameter α represents the weight that the direct gain and the indirect gain contribute to calculating the total gain of a given node. $\alpha = 0$ means that the selection of forwarding nodes is determined entirely by the indirect gain, and $\alpha = 1$ expresses the opposite selecting rule. From Figure 5, one can conclude that the packet arrival rate gets to the maximum when $\alpha = 0.7$; the average delay arrives at minimum when $\alpha = 0.3$; the parameter α has little effects on the forwarding count and the throughout.

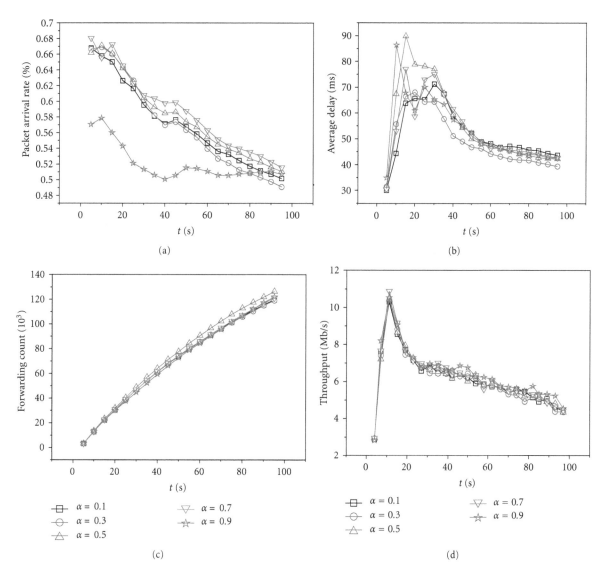

FIGURE 5: Effects of parameter α on the RB-GP model in (a) average packet rate, (b) packet delay, (c) forwarding count, and (d) throughput when α = 0.1 ($\square$), 0.3 ($\bigcirc$), 0.5 ($\triangle$), 0.7 ($\triangledown$), and 0.9 (star).

5. Conclusions

Due to the limited transmission range in vehicular networks, single-hop transmission usually cannot cover all destination nodes, so designing a reliable and efficient multihop broadcast model is one of the fundamental tasks in VANET. We propose a novel multihop broadcast model RB-GP for highway scenario through introducing the concept of gain prediction. The gain value is related with the relative speed, the intervehicle distance, and the coverage difference of the neighboring vehicles. RB-GP model selects the node with the biggest gain as the next hop on the every direction and meanwhile ensures that the selected node can receive the packets successfully, thus achieves decreasing channel conflict and unnecessary information retransmission. The results show that RB-GP is superior to the RB-MP and the flooding models in packet arrival rate, average delay, forwarding count, and throughput.

The future work will focus on multihop broadcast model in other road scenarios, such as urban, and, further, consider the possible broadcast pattern in hybrid networks, that is, synchronously communicating with cellular and ad hoc technologies.

Acknowledgment

This project work was sponsored by the National High-Tech R&D Program of China (863 Program), under Grant no. 2009aa01z426.

References

[1] C. Y. Chang, Y. Xiang, and M. L. Shi, "Development and status of vehicular ad hoc networks," *Journal on Communications*, vol. 28, no. 11, pp. 116–126, 2007.

[2] S. Y. Ni, Y. C. Tseng, and Y. S. Chen, "The broadcast storm problem in a mobile ad hoc network," in *Proceedings of the 5th Annual ACM/IEEE International Conference on Mobile Computing and Networking*, pp. 151–162, Seattle, Wash, USA, 1999.

[3] L. Da, H. Huang, X. Li, and F. Tang, "A distance-based directional broadcast protocol for urban vehicular ad hoc network," in *Proceedings of the International Conference on Wireless Communications, Networking and Mobile Computing*, vol. Shanghai, China, pp. 1520–1523, Shanghai, China, 2007.

[4] L. J. Chen, H. Jiang, J. Wu, C. C. Guo, W. P. Xu, and P. L. An, "Research on transmission control on vehicle ad-hoc network," *Journal of Software*, vol. 18, no. 6, pp. 1477–1490, 2007.

[5] Y. Z. Li, J. X. Liao, T. H. Li, and X. M. Zhu, "A contention-based forwarding routing protocol for vehicular ad hoc networks in city scenarios," *Acta Electronica Sinica*, vol. 37, no. 12, pp. 2639–2645, 2009.

[6] "P1609.0 IEEE Trial-Use Standard for Wireless Access in Vehicular Environments (WAVE)- Architecture".

[7] I. W. Group, "IEEE P 802.11p/D3.0, Draft Amendament for Wireless Access in Vehicular Environments (WAVE)," 2007.

[8] T. M. Marc, "Inter-vehicle communications: assessing information dissemination under safety constraints," in *Proceedings of the 4th Annual IEEE/IFIP Conference on Wireless On Demand Network Systems and Services*, pp. 59–64, Obergurgl, Austria, 2007.

[9] C. Suthaputchakun, "Priority-based inter-vehicle communication for highway safety messaging using IEEE 802.11e," *International Journal of Vehicular Technology*, vol. 2009, Article ID 423141, 12 pages, 2009.

[10] R. Chen, W. Jin, and A. Regan, "Multi-hop broadcasting in vehicular Ad Hoc networks with shockwave traffic," in *Proceedings of the 2nd IEEE Intelligent Vehicular Communications System Workshop*, pp. 1–5, Las Vegas, Nev, USA, 2010.

[11] J. R. Francisco, M. R. Pedro, and S. Ivan, "Reliable and efficient broadcasting in vehicular Ad Hoc networks," in *Proceedings of the IEEE Vehicular Technology Conference*, pp. 1–5, Barcelona, Spain, 2009.

[12] G. Korkmaz, F. Ekici, F. Ozgoner, and O. Ozgoner, "Urban multi-hop broadcast protocol for inter-vehicle communication systems," in *Proceedings of the 1st ACM International Workshop on Vehicular Ad Hoc Networks*, pp. 76–85, Philadelphia, Pa, USA, October 2004.

[13] L. Wischhof, A. Ebner, and H. Rohling, "Information dissemination in self-organizing intervehicle networks," *IEEE Transactions on Intelligent Transportation Systems*, vol. 6, no. 1, pp. 90–101, 2005.

[14] H. Menouar, M. Lenardi, and F. Filali, "A movement prediction based routing protocol for vehicle-to-vehicle communications," in *Proceedings of the International Workshop on Vehicle-to-Vehicle Communications*, pp. 1–8, San Diego, Calif, USA, 2005.

[15] F. Granelli, G. Boato, and D. Kliazovich, "MORA: a movement-based routing algorithm for vehicle Ad Hoc networks," in *Proceedings of the IEEE Workshop on Automotive Networking and Applications*, pp. 256–265, San Francisco, Calif, USA, 2006.

[16] V. Naumov, R. Baumann, and T. Gross, "An evaluation of inter-vehicle ad hoc networks based on realistic vehicular traces," in *Proceedings of the 7th ACM International Symposium on Mobile Ad Hoc Networking and Computing (MOBIHOC '06)*, pp. 108–119, Florence, Italy, May 2006.

[17] M. Sun, W. Feng, T. H. Lai, K. Yamada, H. Okada, and K. Fujimura, "GPS-based message broadcasting for inter-vehicle communication," in *Proceedings of the International Conference on Parallel Processing*, pp. 279–286, Toronto, Canada, 2000.

[18] P. Lai, X. Wang, N. Lu, and F. Liu, "A reliable broadcast routing scheme based on mobility prediction for VANET," in *Proceedings of the IEEE Intelligent Vehicles Symposium*, pp. 1083–1087, Xi'an, China, June 2009.

[19] M. Chuan, Y. Peng, B. Davison, and L. Cheng, "Store-and-Forward Performance in a DTN," in *Proceedings of the IEEE Vehicular Technology Conference*, pp. 187–191, Melbourne, Australia, 2006.

[20] NS2, http://www.isi.edu/nsnam/ns.

[21] VanetMobiSim, http://vanet.eurecom.fr.

14

A Radon Slantlet Transforms Based OFDM System Design and Performance Simulation under Different Channel Conditions

Abbas Hasan Kattoush

EE Department, Tafila Technical University, Tafila 66110, Jordan

Correspondence should be addressed to Abbas Hasan Kattoush, akattoush@yahoo.ca

Academic Editor: K. Teh

Due to its good orthogonality, slantlet transform (SLT) is used in orthogonal frequency division multiplexing (OFDM) systems to reduce intersymbol interference (ISI) and intercarrier interference (ICI). This eliminates the need for cyclic prefix (CP) and increases the spectral efficiency of the design. Finite Radon transform (FRAT) mapper has the ability to increase orthogonality of subcarriers, is nonsensitive to channel parameters variations, and has a small constellation energy compared with conventional fast-Fourier-transform- (FFT-) based OFDM. It is also able to work as a good interleaver, which significantly reduces the bit error rate (BER). In this paper both FRAT mapping technique and SLT modulator are implemented in a new design of an OFDM system. The new structure was tested and compared with conventional FFT-based OFDM, Radon transform-based OFDM, and SLT-based OFDM for additive white Gaussian noise (AWGN) channel, flat fading channel (FFC), and multipath selective fading channel (SFC). Simulation tests were generated for different channel parameters values. The obtained results showed that the proposed system has increased the spectral efficiency, reduced ISI and ICI, and improved BER performance compared with other systems.

1. Introduction

Orthogonal frequency division multiplexing system is one of the most promising technologies for current and future wireless communications. It is a form of multicarrier modulation technologies where data bits are encoded to multiple subcarriers, while being sent simultaneously [1]. Each subcarrier in an OFDM system is modulated in amplitude and phase by the data bits. Modulation techniques typically used are binary phase shift keying, quadrature phase shift keying (QPSK), quadrature amplitude modulation (QAM), 16-QAM, 64-QAM, and so forth. The process of combining different subcarriers to form a composite time-domain signal is achieved using FFT and inverse FFT (IFFT) operations [2].

The main problem in the design of a communications system over a wireless link is to deal with multipath fading, which causes a significant degradation in terms of both the reliability of the link and the data rate [3]. Multipath fading channels have a severe effect on the performance of wireless communication systems even those systems that exhibit efficient bandwidth, like OFDM. There is always a need for

developments in the realization of these systems as well as efficient channel estimation and equalization methods to enable these systems to reach their maximum performance [4]. The OFDM receiver structure allows relatively straightforward signal processing to combat channel delay spreads, which was a prime motivation to use OFDM modulation methods in several standards [5–8].

In transmissions over a radio channel, the orthogonality of the signals is maintained only if the channel is flat and time-invariant and channels with a Doppler spread and the corresponding time variations corrupt the orthogonality of the OFDM subcarrier waveforms [9]. In a dispersive channel, self-interference occurs among successive symbols at the same subcarrier casing ISI, as well as among signals at different subcarriers casing ICI. For a time-invariant but frequency-selective channel, ICI, as well as ISI, can effectively be avoided by inserting a cyclic prefix before each block of parallel data symbols at the cost of power loss and bandwidth expansion [2].

Conventional OFDM/QAM systems are robust for multipath channels due to the cyclically prefixed guard interval that is inserted between consequent symbols to cancel ISI. However, this guard interval decreases the spectral efficiency of the OFDM system as the corresponding amount [10]. Thus, there have been approaches of wavelet-based OFDM that do not require the use of the guard interval [11–16]. It is found that OFDM based on Haar orthonormal wavelets is capable of reducing the ISI and ICI, which are caused by the loss in orthogonality between the carriers.

Recently, Selesnick [17] has constructed a new orthogonal discrete wavelet transform, the slantlet transform, with two zero moments and improved time localization [18]. SLT transform found important applications in signal and image processing; it has been successfully applied in image compression and denoising. Also, SLT found a new application in communications, it was used as a main building block in designing an improved spectral efficiency OFDM system where the SLT modulator replaces the FFT modulator.

The Radon transform (RT) was first introduced by Radon [19, 20] and the theory, basic aspects, and applications of this transform are studied in [21, 22] while the finite Radon transform (FRAT) was first studied by Beylkin [23]. RT is the underlying fundamental concept used for computerized tomography scanning, as well as for a wide range of other disciplines, including radar imaging, geophysical imaging, nondestructive testing, and medical imaging [21]. Recently, FRAT was proposed as a mapping technique in OFDM system [24–26].

In this paper the idea of one-dimensional serial Radon transform-based OFDM proposed in [25] is developed farther towards increasing spectral efficiency and reducing BER. Further performance gains and higher spectral efficiency were made by combining both FRAT and SLT in the design of OFDM system. Simulation results show that the proposed system has better performance than Fourier, Radon, and SLT transform-based OFDM under different channel conditions.

2. Slantlet Transform-Based OFDM System

The slantlet transform was first proposed by Selesnick [17]. It is an orthogonal discrete wavelet transform (DWT) with two zero moments and with improved time localization. It uses a special case of a class of bases described by Alpert et al. in [27], the construction of which relies on Gram-Schmidt orthogonalization. SLT is based on the principle of designing different filters for different scales unlike iterated filter-bank approaches for the DWT. Selesnick described the basis from a filter-bank viewpoint, gave explicit solutions for the filter coefficients, and described an efficient algorithm for the transform.

The usual iterated DWT filter-bank and its equivalent form are shown in Figure 1. The "slantlet" filter-bank is based on the equivalent structure that is occupied by different filters that are not products. With this extra degree of freedom obtained by giving up the product form, filters of shorter length are designed satisfying orthogonality and zero moment conditions.

For the two-channel case the Daubechies filter [28] is the shortest filter, which makes the filter-bank orthogonal and

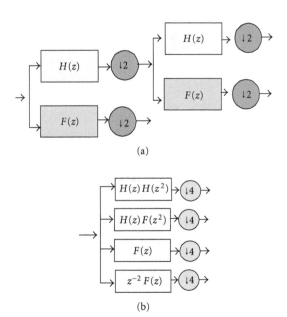

FIGURE 1: Two-scale iterated filter-bank and its equivalent form using the DWT.

has K zero moments. For $K = 2$ zero moments, filters $H(z)$ and $F(z)$ are of length 4. For this system, the iterated filters in Figure 1 are of length 10 and 4. Without the constraint that the filters are products, an orthogonal filter-bank with $K = 2$ zero moments can be obtained where the filter lengths are 8 and 4, as shown in Figure 2. That is a reduction by two samples, which is a difference that grows with the number of stages. This reduction in length, while maintaining desirable orthogonality and moment properties, is possible because these filters are not constrained by the product form arising in the case of iterated filter-banks.

The filters coefficients used in the SLT filter-bank as derived in [17] are given by

$$G_1(z) = \left(-\frac{\sqrt{10}}{20} - \frac{\sqrt{2}}{4}\right) + \left(\frac{3\sqrt{10}}{20} + \frac{\sqrt{2}}{4}\right)z^{-1}$$

$$+ \left(-\frac{3\sqrt{10}}{20} + \frac{\sqrt{2}}{4}\right)z^{-2} + \left(\frac{\sqrt{10}}{20} - \frac{\sqrt{2}}{4}\right)z^{-3},$$

$$F_2(z) = \left(\frac{7\sqrt{5}}{80} - \frac{3\sqrt{55}}{80}\right) + \left(-\frac{\sqrt{5}}{80} - \frac{\sqrt{55}}{80}\right)z^{-1}$$

$$+ \left(-\frac{9\sqrt{5}}{80} + \frac{\sqrt{55}}{80}\right)z^{-2} + \left(-\frac{17\sqrt{5}}{80} + \frac{3\sqrt{55}}{80}\right)z^{-3}$$

$$+ \left(\frac{7\sqrt{5}}{80} + \frac{3\sqrt{55}}{80}\right)z^{-4} + \left(\frac{9\sqrt{5}}{80} + \frac{\sqrt{55}}{80}\right)z^{-5}$$

$$+ \left(\frac{\sqrt{5}}{80} - \frac{\sqrt{55}}{80}\right)z^{-6} + \left(-\frac{7\sqrt{5}}{80} - \frac{3\sqrt{55}}{80}\right)z^{-7},$$

$$H_2(z) = \left(\frac{1}{16} + \frac{\sqrt{11}}{16}\right) + \left(\frac{3}{16} + \frac{\sqrt{11}}{16}\right)z^{-1}$$

$$+ \left(\frac{5}{16} + \frac{\sqrt{11}}{16}\right)z^{-2} + \left(\frac{7}{16} + \frac{\sqrt{11}}{16}\right)z^{-3}$$

$$+ \left(\frac{7}{16} - \frac{\sqrt{11}}{16}\right)z^{-4} + \left(\frac{5}{16} - \frac{\sqrt{11}}{16}\right)z^{-5}$$

$$+ \left(\frac{3}{16} - \frac{\sqrt{11}}{16}\right)z^{-6} + \left(\frac{1}{16} - \frac{\sqrt{11}}{16}\right)z^{-7}.$$

$$(1)$$

Some characteristic features of the SLT filter-bank are being orthogonal and having two zero moments, and it also has octave-band characteristic. Each filter-bank has a scale dilation factor of two and provides a multiresolution decomposition. The slantlet filters are piecewise linear. Even though there is no tree structure for SLT, it can be efficiently implemented like an iterated DWT filter-bank [17]. Therefore, a computational complexity of the SLT is of the same order as that of the DWT.

The block diagram of the SLT-OFDM system is depicted in Figure 2. It is very similar to that of FFT-OFDM; the only differences are in the OFDM modulator-demodulator blocks. The processes of serial to parallel (S/P) conversion, signal demapping, and insertion of training sequence are the same as in the FFT-OFDM system. The SLT-based OFDM modulator consists of zero padding and inverse SLT (ISLT) blocks while the SLT-based OFDM demodulator consists of SLT and zero-pad removal blocks as shown in Figure 2. The main difference between FFT-OFDM and SLT-OFDM is that in SLT-OFDM there is no need for adding a cyclic prefix to OFDM symbols as shown in Figure 3; therefore, the spectral efficiency and the data rate of SLT-OFDM are better than those of FFT-OFDM.

3. The Radon Mapping Technique

Radon transform-based OFDM was recently proposed [24, 25]; it was found that, as a result of applying FRAT, the bit error rate (BER) performance was improved significantly, especially in the existence of multipath fading channels. Also, it was found that Radon transform-based OFDM structure is less sensitive to channel parameters variation, like maximum delay, path gain, and maximum Doppler shift in selective fading channels, as compared with the standard OFDM structure.

In Radon transform-based OFDM system, FRAT mapping is used instead of QAM mapping [25, 26]. The other processing parts of the system remain the same as in the conventional QAM OFDM system. It is known that FFT based OFDM obtain the required orthogonality between subcarriers from the suitability of IFFT algorithm [2]. Using FRAT mapping with the OFDM structure increases the orthogonality between subcarriers since FRAT computation uses one-dimensional (1D) IFFT algorithm. Also, FRAT is designed to increase the spectral efficiency of the OFDM system through increasing the bit per Hertz of the mapping.

Subcarriers are generated using N points discrete Fourier transform (DFT), and guard interval (GI) inserted at the start of each symbol is used to reduce ISI.

The procedure steps of using the serial Radon transform-based OFDM mapping are as follows [25].

Step 1. Suppose $d(k)$ is the serial data stream to be transmitted using OFDM modulation scheme. Converting $d(k)$ from serial form to parallel form will construct a one-dimensional vector containing the data symbols to be transmitted:

$$d(k) = \begin{pmatrix} d_0 & d_1 & d_2 & \cdots & d_n \end{pmatrix}^T, \quad (2)$$

where k and n are the time index and the vector length, respectively.

Step 2. Convert the data packet represented by the vector $d(k)$ from one-dimensional vector to a $p \times p$ two-dimensional matrix $D(k)$, where p should be a prime number according to the matrix resizing operation.

Step 3. Take the two-dimensional (2D) FFT of the matrix $D(k)$ to obtain the matrix, $F(r,s)$. For simplicity it will be labeled by F:

$$F(r,s) = \sum_{m=0}^{p-1} \sum_{n=0}^{p-1} D(m,n)e^{-j(2\pi/p)rm}e^{-j(2\pi/p)ns}. \quad (3)$$

Step 4. Redistribute the elements of the matrix $\mathcal{F}$ according to the following optimum ordering algorithm first described in [29]. The optimum number of FRAT projections is one projection for each column, and the best ordering of the 2D FFT coefficients in these projections can be achieved if the normal vectors are determined as [29]

$$(a_k, b_k) = \arg\min \left| \left(C_p(a_k), C_p(b_k) \right) \right|,$$

$$(a_k, b_k) \in \{nu_k : 1 \le n \le p-1\}, \quad (4)$$

$$\text{st. } C_p(b_k) \ge 0.$$

Here, $C_p(x)$ denotes the centralized function of period p; $C_p(x) = x - p \cdot \text{round}(x/p)$. Hence, $\|(C_p(a_k), C_p(b_k))\|$ represents the distance from the origin to the point (a_k, b_k) on the Fourier plane. The constraint $C_p(b_k) \ge 0$ is imposed in order to remove the ambiguity in deciding between (a, b) and $(-a, -b)$ as the normal vector for the projection. As a result the optimal normal vectors are restricted to having angles in $[0, \pi)$. So, the dimensions of the resultant matrix will be $p \times (p+1)$ and will be denoted by the symbol $\mathcal{F}_{\text{opt}}$.

Step 5. Take the 1D IFFT for each column of the matrix $\mathcal{F}_{\text{opt}}$ to obtain the matrix of Radon coefficients, R:

$$R = \frac{1}{p} \sum_{k=0}^{N-1} \mathcal{F}_{\text{opt}} e^{j2\pi kn/p}. \quad (5)$$

Step 6. Construct the complex matrix $\overline{R}$ from the real matrix R such that its dimensions will be $p \times (p+1)/2$ according to

$$\overline{r_{l,m}} = r_{i,j} + jr_{i,j+1}, \quad 0 \le i \le p, \ 0 \le j \le p, \quad (6)$$

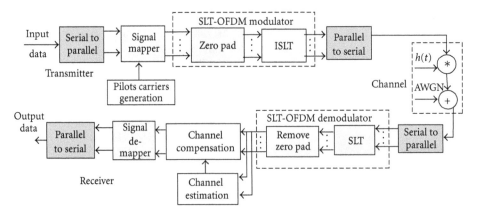

FIGURE 2: Block diagram of SLT-OFDM system.

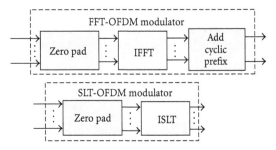

FIGURE 3: FFT-OFDM and SLT-OFDM modulators.

where $\overline{r_{l,m}}$ refers to the elements of the matrix $\overline{R}$, while $r_{i,j}$ refers to the elements of the matrix R. Matrixes R and $\overline{R}$ are given by

$$
R = \begin{bmatrix}
r_{1,1} & r_{1,2} & r_{1,3} & \cdots & r_{1,p+1} \\
r_{2,1} & r_{2,2} & r_{2,3} & \cdots & r_{2,p+1} \\
\vdots & \vdots & \vdots & \cdots & \vdots \\
\vdots & \vdots & \vdots & \cdots & \vdots \\
r_{p-1,1} & r_{p-1,2} & \cdots & \cdots & r_{p-1,p+1} \\
r_{p,1} & r_{p,2} & r_{p,3} & \cdots & r_{p,p+1}
\end{bmatrix},
$$

$$
\overline{R} = \begin{bmatrix}
r_{1,1} + jr_{1,2} & r_{1,3} + jr_{1,4} & \cdots & r_{1,p} + jr_{1,p+1} \\
r_{2,1} + jr_{2,2} & r_{2,3} + jr_{2,4} & \cdots & r_{2,p} + jr_{2,p+1} \\
\vdots & \vdots & \cdots & \vdots \\
\vdots & \vdots & \cdots & \vdots \\
r_{p-1,1} + jr_{p-1,2} & \cdots & \cdots & r_{p-1,p} + jr_{p-1,p+1} \\
r_{p,1} + jr_{p,2} & \cdots & & r_{p,p} + jr_{p,p+1}
\end{bmatrix}.
$$

(7)

Complex matrix construction is made for a purpose of increasing the bit per Hertz of mapping before resizing the mapped data.

Step 7. Resize the matrix $\overline{R}$ to a one-dimensional vector $r(k)$ of length $p \times (p+1)/2$:

$$
r(k) = \begin{pmatrix} r_0 & r_1 & r_2 & \cdots & r_{p(p+1)/2} \end{pmatrix}^T. \tag{8}
$$

Step 8. Take the 1D IFFT for the vector $r(k)$ to obtain the subchannel modulation:

$$
s(k) = \frac{1}{p(p+1)/2} \sum_{k=0}^{N_C-1} r(k)e^{j2\pi kn/(p(p+1)/2)}, \tag{9}
$$

where N_C referes to number of carriers.

Step 9. Finally, convert the vector $s(k)$ to serial data symbols: $s_0, s_1, s_2, \ldots, s_n$.

4. Proposed System for Radon-SLT-Based OFDM Transceiver

Due to good orthogonality of both SLT and FRAT, which reduce ISI and ICI, in the proposed system there is no need of using cyclic prefix (CP). The block diagram of the proposed Radon-SLT-based OFDM system is depicted in Figure 4 and the ISLT modulator and SLT demodulator are also shown in the same figure.

The processes of serial to parallel conversion, signal demapping, and insertion of training sequence are the same as in the system of FFT-OFDM. Also, the zeros are added as in the FFT-based case and for the same reasons. After that the ISLT is applied to the signal. The main and important difference between FFT-based OFDM and SLT-based OFDM is that in SLT-based OFDM the cyclic prefix is not added to OFDM symbols. Therefore, the data rates in SLT-based OFDM are higher than those of the FFT-based OFDM. At the receiver, the zeros padded at the transmitter are removed, and the other operations of channel estimation, channel compensation, signal demapping, and parallel to serial (P/S) conversion are performed in the same manner as in FFT-based OFDM.

In the conventional OFDM system, the length of input data frame is 60 symbols, and after S/P conversion and QAM mapping the length becomes 30 symbols. Zero padding

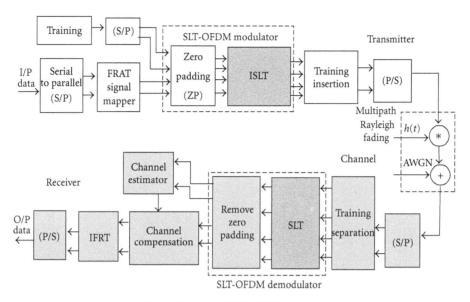

FIGURE 4: Block diagram of FRAT-SLT-based OFDM system.

operation makes the length 64 symbols, which are the input to IFFT (subcarrier modulation). After adding CP (usually 40% of the length of the frame), the frame length becomes 90 symbols. Since OFDM operations applied to the training symbols are the same as those applied to the transmitted data (except the mapping operation), the length of the training symbols is also 90 symbols. The training and data frames are transmitted as one frame starts with training, so the length of transmitted frame is 180 symbols [30]. In the proposed system, the length of the input data frame must be $(p \times p)$, where p is a prime number. The closest number to 60 is (7×7), which makes the frame length 49 symbols. This is because the input of FRAT must be a two-dimensional matrix with size $(p \times p)$.

5. Simulation Results of Proposed System

Four types of OFDM systems were simulated: FFT-OFDM, Radon-OFDM, SLT-OFDM, and proposed Radon-SLT-based OFDM systems using MATLAB version 7. The BER performances of the four systems were found for different channel models: AWGN channel, flat fading channel, and selective fading channel. System parameters used through the simulations are $T_S = 0.1\,\mu\text{sec}$, FRAT window: 7 by 7, and DWT bins $N = 64$.

5.1. Performance of Proposed OFDM System in AWGN Channel. Figure 5 shows the results of simulation of the proposed system compared with other systems in AWGN channel. It is clearly seen that FRAT-SLT-based OFDM has better performance than the other three systems: FFT-OFDM, SLT-OFDM, and FRAT-OFDM. This is due to the high orthogonality of the proposed system. To have BER = 10^{-4}, FFT-OFDM requires 28 dB, FRAT-OFDM requires 25.5 dB, SLT-OFDM requires 21.5 dB, and FRAT-SLT-based OFDM requires 17 dB. And to have BER = 10^{-5}, FFT-OFDM requires 31.5 dB, FRAT-OFDM requires 28 dB, SLT-OFDM

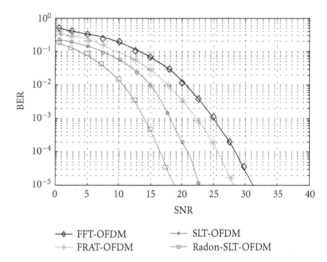

FIGURE 5: BER performance of FRAT-SLT-based OFDM in AWGN channel.

requires 23 dB, and FRAT-SLT-based OFDM requires 19 dB. From the results it can be noted that the proposed system has 12 dB advantage over FFT-OFDM, 9.5 dB over FRAT-OFDM, and 5 dB over SLT-OFDM.

5.2. Performance of Proposed OFDM System in Flat Fading Channel with AWGN. In this channel, all signal frequency components are affected by a constant attenuation and linear phase distortion, in addition to an AWGN. The channel was selected to be multipath and Rayleigh distributed. Doppler frequency used in simulation is calculated as follows: $c = 300 \times 10^6$ m/sec, in GSM system $f_c = 900$ MHz so,

$$f_d = f_c \times \frac{v}{c} = 900 \times 10^6 \times \frac{1}{\text{sec}} \times \frac{v}{300 \times 10^8 \text{ m/sec}},$$
$$f_d = \frac{3}{(1\,\text{m})} \times v. \tag{10}$$

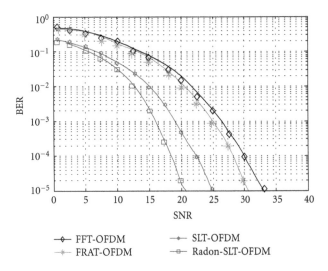

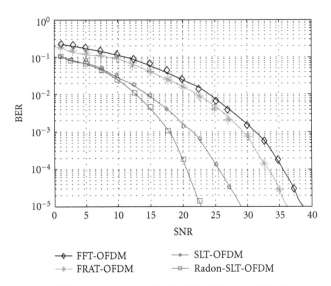

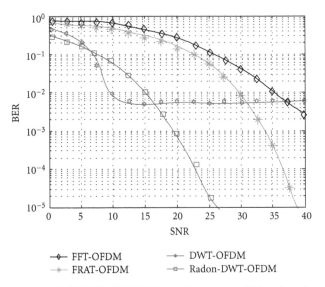

FIGURE 6: BER performance of FRAT-SLT-OFDM in FFC at Doppler frequency 4 Hz.

FIGURE 7: BER performance of FRAT-SLT-OFDM in SFC at Doppler frequency 4 Hz.

The Doppler frequency used is that corresponding to a walking speed (4.8 km/hour), and it has a value $f_d = (3/1 \, \text{m}) \times (4.8 \times 1000 \, \text{m}/3600 \, \text{sec}) = 4 \, \text{Hz}$.

The results of simulations for 4 Hz Doppler frequency are shown in Figure 6. From Figure 6 it can be seen that to have BER = 10^{-5}, FFT-OFDM requires 33 dB, FRAT-OFDM requires 31 dB, SLT-OFDM requires 25 dB, and FRAT-SLT-based OFDM requires 20.5 dB. So the proposed system offers 12.5 dB SNR improvement compared with FFT-OFDM, 10.5 dB compared with FRAT-OFDM, and 4.5 dB compared with SLT-OFDM for this channel model. Other Doppler-Shift frequencies were used for proposed system simulation over the flat fading Rayleigh channel; the values used are 80 Hz corresponding to car speed (96 km/hour), 300 Hz corresponding to helicopter speed (360 km/hour), and 500 Hz corresponding to airplane speed (600 km/hour), and the same results were obtained for these frequencies. The reason for best performance results of FRAT-SLT-based OFDM is the good orthogonality of Radon transform and the excellent orthogonality of SLT.

5.3. BER Performance of Proposed OFDM System in SFC with AWGN.
In this section, the channel model is assumed to be selective fading channel. A second ray Raleigh-distributed multipath fading channel is assumed, where the parameters of the multipaths channel are path gain equal to −8 dB and path delay $\tau_{\text{max}} = 0.1 \, \mu\text{sec}$.

The BER performance of the proposed system and the other OFDM systems over a selective fading channel with Doppler frequency of 4 Hz is shown in Figure 7. It can be seen that to have BER = 10^{-5}, FFT-OFDM requires 37.5 dB, FRAT-OFDM requires 35.5 dB, SLT-OFDM requires 29 dB, and FRAT-SLT-based OFDM requires 22.5 dB. So the proposed system offers great SNR improvement compared with FFT-OFDM, FRAT-OFDM, and SLT-OFDM for this channel model.

FIGURE 8: FRAT-SLT-OFDM BER performance in SFC at Doppler frequency 300 Hz.

The same performance characteristics of the systems over selective fading channel with Doppler frequencies 80 Hz, 300 Hz, and 500 Hz were simulated. Figure 8 shows the BER performance of FRAT-SLT-based OFDM in selective fading channel with Doppler frequency of 300 Hz. From Figure 8, it is clearly seen that FFT-based OFDM needs more than 40 dB of SNR to have BER = 10^{-4}, while FRAT-based OFDM needs around 39 dB of SNR to reach BER = 10^{-5}, SLT-based OFDM BER performance does not exceed 0.002425 with increasing SNR, whereas the proposed FRAT-SLT based OFDM has much better performance than the other three systems, and it reaches BER = 10^{-5} at SNR = 26.5 dB.

Figure 9 shows the BER performance of FRAT-SLT-based OFDM in selective fading channel with Doppler frequency of 500 Hz. From Figure 9, the following conclusion can

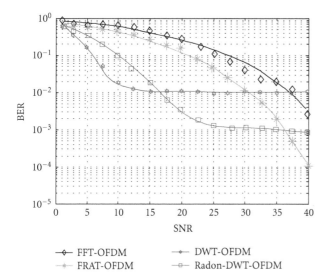

FIGURE 9: BER performance of FRAT-SLT-OFDM in SFC at Doppler frequency 500 Hz.

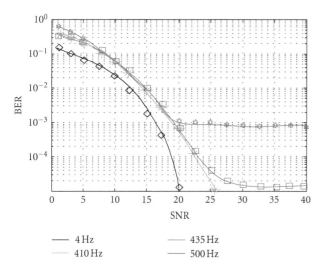

FIGURE 10: FRAT-SLT-OFDM BER performance in SFC at different Doppler frequencies.

be stated: when Doppler frequency exceeds 500 Hz, the proposed system suffers from the same problem that SLT-based OFDM system suffers from, and the performance of the proposed system does not increase with increasing SNR when the Doppler frequency exceeds 500 Hz. It is seen that OFDM systems are very sensitive systems to the variation of Doppler frequency in selective fading channel.

The effect of Doppler frequency value on BER performance for the proposed system is provided in Figure 10. It can be seen from Figure 10 that the critical value of Doppler frequency for the proposed system is around 435 Hz.

6. Conclusions

In this paper a novel OFDM generation method is proposed, simulated, and tested. The proposed system uses Radon-SLT mapping instead of QAM mapping, which increases the

orthogonality. The optimal ordering (best direction) in the Radon mapper can be considered as a good interleaver, which serves in error spreading. In the proposed system there is no need for using CP because of excellent orthogonality offered by FRAT and SLT, which in its order reduces the system complexity, increases the transmission rate, and increases spectral efficiency. Simulation results of the proposed Radon-SLT-based OFDM show a very good SNR gain improvement and a BER performance as compared with SLT-OFDM, FRAT-OFDM, and FFT-OFDM in an AWGN, a flat fading, and a selective fading channels. It offers more than 15 dB SNR improvement compared with FFT-OFDM for selective fading channel at Doppler frequency 4 Hz. From the simulation results, it can be seen that the proposed Radon-SLT-based OFDM has the smallest sensitivity to variations of the channel parameters.

References

[1] N. Al-Dhahir, "Optimum finite-length equalization for multicamer transceivers," *IEEE Transactions on Communications*, vol. 44, no. 1, pp. 56–64, 1996.

[2] S. B. Weinstein and P. M. Ebert, "Data transmission by frequency-division multiplexing using the discrete Fourier transform," *IEEE Transactions on Communications*, vol. 19, no. 5, pp. 628–634, 1971.

[3] N. H. Tran, H. H. Nguyen, and T. Le-Ngoc, "Bit-interleaved coded OFDM with signal space diversity: subcarrier grouping and rotation matrix design," *IEEE Transactions on Signal Processing*, vol. 55, no. 3, pp. 1137–1149, 2007.

[4] W. G. Jeon, K. H. Chang, and Y. S. Cho, "An equalization technique for orthogonal frequency-division multiplexing systems in time-variant multipath channels," *IEEE Transactions on Communications*, vol. 47, no. 1, pp. 27–32, 1999.

[5] R. V. Nee and R. Prasad, *OFDM for Wireless Multimedia Communications*, Artech-House, London, UK, 2000.

[6] I. Koffman and V. Roman, "Broadband wireless access solutions based on OFDM access in IEEE 802.16," *IEEE Communications Magazine*, vol. 40, no. 4, pp. 96–103, 2002.

[7] R. Prasad, *OFDM for Wireless Communications Systems*, Artech-House, 2004.

[8] I. Lee, J. S. Chow, and J. M. Cioffi, "Performance evaluation of a fast computation algorithm for the DMT in high speed subscriber loop," *IEEE Journal on Selected Areas in Communications*, vol. 13, no. 9, pp. 1564–1570, 1995.

[9] L. J. Cimini Jr., "Analysis and simulation of a digital mobile channel using orthogonal frequency division multiplexing," *IEEE Transactions on Communications*, vol. 33, no. 7, pp. 665–675, 1985.

[10] S. Kang and K. Chang, "A novel channel estimation scheme for OFDM/OQAM-IOTA system," *ETRI Journal*, vol. 29, no. 4, pp. 430–436, 2007.

[11] A. R. Lindsey, "Wavelet packet modulation for orthogonally multiplexed communication," *IEEE Transactions on Signal Processing*, vol. 45, no. 5, pp. 1336–1339, 1997.

[12] S. Mallat, *A Wavelet Tour of Signal Processing*, Academic Press, New York, NY, USA, 2nd edition, 1999.

[13] IEEE Std., *IEEE Proposal for 802.16.3, RM Wavelet Based (WOFDM) PHY Proposal for 802.16.3*, Rainmaker Technologies, Inc., 2001.

[14] X. D. Zhang, P. P. Xu, G. A. Zhang, and G. G. Bi, "Study on complex wavelet packet based OFDM modulation (CWP-OFDM)," *Tien Tzu Hsueh Pao/Acta Electronica Sinica*, vol. 30, no. 4, pp. 477–479, 2002.

[15] H. Zhang, D. Yuan, and M. Pätzold, "Novel study on PAPRs reduction in wavelet-based multicarrier modulation systems," *Digital Signal Processing*, vol. 17, no. 1, pp. 272–279, 2007.

[16] A. H. Kattoush, W. A. Mahmoud, and S. Nihad, "The performance of multiwavelets based OFDM system under different channel conditions," *Digital Signal Processing*, vol. 20, no. 2, pp. 472–482, 2010.

[17] I. W. Selesnick, "The slantlet transform," *IEEE Transactions on Signal Processing*, vol. 47, no. 5, pp. 1304–1313, 1999.

[18] E. R. Dougherty, J. T. Astola, and K. O. Egiazarian, "The fast parametric slantlet transform with applications," in *Image Processing: Algorithms and Systems III*, vol. 5298 of *Proceedings of SPIE*, San Jose, Calif, USA, January 2004.

[19] J. Radon, "Über die Bestimmung von Funktionen durch ihre Integralwerte längs gewisser Mannigfaltigkeiten. Berichte über die Verhandlungen der Königlich Sächsischen Gesellshaft der Wissenschaften zu Luipzig," *Mathematisch-Physikalische Klasse*, vol. 69, pp. 262–277, 1917.

[20] J. Radon, "On the determination of functions from their integral values along certain manifolds," *IEEE Transactions on Image Processing*, vol. 5, pp. 170–176, 1986.

[21] S. R. Deans, *The Radon Transform and Some of Its Applications*, John Wiley & Sons, New York, NY, USA, 1983.

[22] E. D. Bolker, "The finite radon transform," *Integral Geometry, Contemporary Mathematics*, vol. 63, pp. 27–50, 1987.

[23] G. Beylkin, "Discrete radon transforms," *IEEE Transactions on Acoustics, Speech, and Signal Processing*, vol. 35, no. 2, pp. 162–172, 1987.

[24] W. Al-Jawhar, A. H. Kattoush, S. M. Abbas, and A. T. Shaheen, "A high performance parallel Radon based OFDM transceiver design and simulation," *Digital Signal Processing*, vol. 18, no. 6, pp. 907–918, 2008.

[25] A. H. Kattoush, W. A. Mahmoud, A. Shaheen, and A. Ghodayyah, "The performance of proposed one dimensional serial radon based OFDM system under different channel conditions," *The International Journal of Computers, Systems and Signals*, vol. 9, no. 2, pp. 3–16, 2008.

[26] A. H. Kattoush, W. A. M. Al-Jawher, S. M. Abbas, and A. T. Shaheen, "A n-radon based OFDM trasceivers design and performance simulation over different channel models," *Wireless Personal Communications*, vol. 58, no. 4, pp. 695–711, 2009.

[27] B. Alpert, G. Beylkin, R. Coifman, and V. Rokhlin, "Wavelet-like bases for the fast solution of second-kind integral equations," *SIAM Journal on Scientific Computing*, vol. 14, pp. 159–184, 1993.

[28] I. Daubechies, *Ten Lectures on Wavelets*, SIAM, Philadelphia, Pa, USA, 1992.

[29] M. N. Do and M. Vetterli, "The finite ridgelet transform for image representation," *IEEE Transactions on Image Processing*, vol. 12, no. 1, pp. 16–28, 2003.

[30] J. G. Proakis, *Digital Communications*, McGraw-Hill, 4ht edition, 2001.

15

Antenna Optimization Using Multiobjective Algorithms

X. L. Travassos,[1] D. A. G. Vieira,[2] and A. C. Lisboa[2]

[1] *Electromagnetic Devices Laboratory, SENAI-Integrated Centre of Manufacture and Technology, 41650-050 Salvador, BA, Brazil*
[2] *ENACOM-Handcrafted Technologies, 31310-260 Belo Horizonte, MG, Brazil*

Correspondence should be addressed to D. A. G. Vieira, douglas.vieira@enacom.com.br

Academic Editors: I.-S. Koh and B.-H. Soong

This paper presents several applications of multiobjective optimization to antenna design, emphasizing the main general steps in this process. Specifications of antennas usually involve many conflicting objectives related to directivity, impedance matching, cross-polarization, and frequency range. These requirements induce multiobjective problems, which are formulated, solved, and analyzed here for three distinct antenna designs: a bowtie antenna for ground-penetrating radars, a reflector antenna for satellite broadcast systems, and a meander-line antenna for radio-frequency identification tags. Both stochastic and deterministic methods are considered in the analysis.

1. Introduction

Antenna optimization aims at creating advanced and complex electromagnetic devices that must be competitive in terms of performance, serviceability, and cost effectiveness. This process involves selection of appropriate objective functions (usually conflicting), design variables, parameters, and constraints. In most antenna optimization problems, several goals must be satisfied simultaneously in order to obtain an optimal solution. As these objectives are often conflicting, no single solution may exist that is best regarding all considered goals. In many situations, antenna optimization can be viewed as a multidisciplinary engineered problem. However, most of the problems can be divided into search for optimal solutions and approximate solution of Maxwell's equations using numerical methods.

Important features regarding antenna optimization have to be considered: the objective function might have several local minima and its evaluation can be expensive. Of course, trying to find the global minimum can be prohibitive; therefore, using a suitable method for the given problem is fundamental for a proper engineering solution.

For instance, some problems have well-established engineering solutions that were achieved after several years of tests and experiments. In such a situation, it may be desired to find a novel design which improves the known standard result, even though it may not be a global minimum. When the gradient or at least one subgradient is known, there are a couple of deterministic methods which can guarantee improvement (if an improved solution exists) of a given result [1].

Nevertheless, conditions where deterministic methods work well may not be achieved and, thus, stochastic methods may become a good alternative. In fact, stochastic methods such as genetic algorithms, particle swarm optimization, and immune systems are known to be very robust and capable of finding good results. However, they are also known to have slow convergence; that is, they require a high number of oracle queries. Solving antenna optimization problems is, therefore, a conflicting problem where fast methods only carry local guarantees while robust methods are prone to have very slow convergence. The aim of this paper is to present some antenna optimization problems and clarify some of the main issues related to the choice of optimization algorithms for antenna design.

Multiobjective optimization and its application to antennas for ground penetrating radar (GPR), satellite broadcast communications, and RFID tags are the subject of this work.

2. Antenna Designs with Multiple-Objective Optimization

A trial and error process is often used for antenna design, where the designer must have considerable experience and intuition. This type of design has been subject to fundamental changes. Modern antenna systems are no longer designed on a simple desk using tables and calculators with inevitable design errors. Today, the design is computer aided, and both highly complex antennas and complete electronic systems are simulated together. In this context, optimization comes naturally as a designer's tool to produce an efficient and automatic "trial and error" process.

In order to formulate an optimization problem, degrees of freedom in the design must be properly identified and parameterized, and objectives and constraints for the design must be quantified given a set of parameters. A canonical query form for optimization problems is the extremum of quantities (e.g., maximum directivity, minimum standing-wave ratio) given some bounds in quantities (e.g., upper bound on size, lower bound on amplitude gap between polarizations).

For problems with more than one objective, the concept of optimum becomes more complex, and it is qualified as Pareto optimum [2]. In this concept, for instance, the set of parameters where the directivity is maximum is not necessarily where the standing-wave ratio is minimum, so that tradeoffs between them become also an optimum in the sense that no point in the Pareto set has both objectives better than another point in it.

An antenna design usually involves specifications related to directivity, impedance matching, cross-polarization, and frequency range, which can be formulated as both objective or constraint functions. The types of these functions define the class of the optimization problem. In antenna design, evaluations of the computational model used in the optimization problem (i.e., evaluations of a black box problem, also called oracle queries) are, most of the time, expensive since they are based on numerical methods to approximate solutions of Maxwell's equations. Hence, the optimization speed is closely related to the number of oracle queries. Furthermore, there are theoretical guarantees of reaching global optima only for a few classes of problems, like linear and convex ones.

It is important to point out that the designer experience and intuition are still fundamental, and that optimization is only a tool. Good designers can define meaningful optimization problems, reduce the search space, and provide good starting points. Reducing search space not only speeds up the optimization but also potentially leads to problems with global optimality guarantees of solution. The design instances given hereinafter highlight and illustrate each one of these aspects.

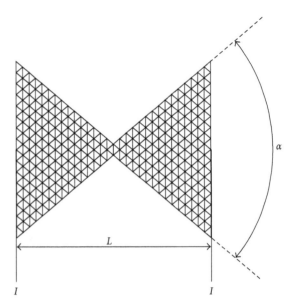

FIGURE 1: Geometry of the bowtie antenna.

3. Design Instances

3.1. Bowtie Antenna Design for Ground-Penetrating Radar. Most antennas for commercial ground-penetrating radar (GPR) are bowtie dipoles because of their light weight, low cost, and broadband characteristics. However, bowtie antennas have dipole-like omnidirectional patterns with broad main beams perpendicular to the plane of the antenna. Consequently, the image created by a GPR assessment could not correspond to the actual target, and closely spaced objects cannot be detected separately.

A multiobjective optimization problem to design more efficient bowtie dipole antennas can be formulated as [3, 4]

$$\text{minimize} \quad f(x) = \begin{bmatrix} -G_{\max}(x, v) \\ A(x) \end{bmatrix}$$
$$\text{subject to} \quad g(x) = A_{\min} - A(x) \leq 0, \quad (1)$$
$$x_{\min} \leq x \leq x_{\max},$$

where $x \in \mathbb{R}^n$ is the vector of design variables, v is the frequency, $G_{\max}$ is the antenna gain, and $A(x)$ is the metal area. The objective of this problem is to minimize the metal area and to maximize the gain in the plane perpendicular to the antenna, with also a lower bound on metal area.

The bowtie antenna geometry (see Figure 1 and Table 1) was parameterized by length L, flare angle α, and presence/absence of triangular elements $b \in \{0, 1\}^{c^2-1}$, where $c \in \{2, 3, \ldots\}$ is the triangular grid density. All these parameters are design variables. The binary variable b behaves like a topological geometric degree of freedom for the problem. It also introduces integer constraints to the problem. These constraints cannot be relaxed (i.e., $b \in \{0, 1\}^{c^2-1}$ cannot be simulated), which makes stochastic algorithms more suitable than deterministic ones to solve the problem.

The optimal antenna suggested by a multiobjective genetic algorithm (MGA) for $v = 1\,\text{GHz}$, $A_{\min} = 0.8A_{\max}$

TABLE 1: Optimization problem variables.

	Parameter		
	$L(\lambda)$	α (°)	R (%)
Min	0.10	30	0
Max	1.00	120	20
Opt	0.87	79	11

(i.e., $R = 20\%$), and $c = 16$ was $\alpha = 79°$, $L = 26$ cm, and $R = 11\%$ ($A_{\min}$, $A_{\max}$, c, L, R) of elements removed (see Table 1). The gain obtained in the plane normal to the antenna was 6.37 dB against 3.40 dB of the respective standard bowtie antenna (i.e., $b = 1$), with an improvement of the half-power beam width from 57.6° to 43.2°. This result is the one whose metal area is maximal among a Pareto set with about 80 elements. Other solutions can be used according to the designer's needs. This approximate Pareto optimal set took about 2,500 oracle queries within 50 iterations of the MGA. A notable feature of stochastic algorithms is their ability to naturally provide a Pareto set as a result, instead of a single point.

During optimization, the method of moments (MoMs) was used to analyze the bowtie antenna. To validate the optimization result, a near field calculation was performed with the finite element method (FEM). FEM is slower and less accurate than MoM for far field, but it can handle complex geometries and material inhomogeneities accurately in the near field [3]. Therefore, FEM was chosen to perform an investigation considering the coupling effects of a geometrically complex antenna over an inhomogeneous dielectric. Moreover, a conductor shield was added to the antenna to improve directivity. The goal was to verify the behavior of a nondestructive assessment to detect the presence of a conducting bar buried 15 cm in the concrete and located parallel to the direction of the antenna. The changes in the antenna's input impedance were studied for three different scenarios.

3.2. Reflector Antenna Design for Satellite Coverage. Satellite coverage problems query for an antenna whose radiation pattern is as close as possible to a given specification. Many requirements can be specified other than maximum directivity inside the target area, like broadband operation, low cross-polarization, or maximum energy confinement inside the target area. They can be formulated as objective functions or constraint functions.

To formulate optimization problems, sample points are uniformly spread all over the target, so that good measures of coverage (mean gain inside target, G_{av}) and energy confinement (energy ratio inside target E_{in}) can be taken. These measures are distinct for each sample frequency. Ideally, coverage also means energy confinement since illuminating a target implicitly means only that target is covered. However, due to physical constraints, transition to outside regions is not discontinuous and energy confinement has to be formulated separately. A multiobjective optimization

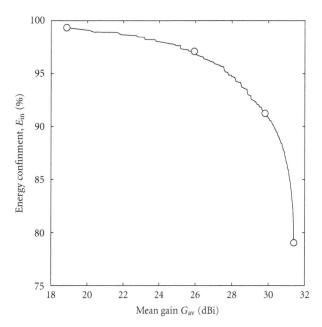

FIGURE 2: Pareto front for coverage and energy confinement. Radiation patterns for marked points are given in Figure 3.

problem formulation for satellite coverage with requirements on frequency range, coverage and energy confinement can be written as [1, 5, 6]

$$\text{minimize} \quad f(x) = \begin{bmatrix} -G_{\mathrm{av}}(x, v) \\ -E_{\mathrm{in}}(x, v) \end{bmatrix} \qquad (2)$$

$$\text{subject to} \quad x_{\min} \leq x \leq x_{\max}, \qquad (3)$$

where $x \in \mathbb{R}^n$ is the vector of design variables, and $v \in \mathbb{R}^o$ is the vector of sample frequencies. The set of objective functions is considered for each sample frequency. For example, 3 sample frequencies for coverage and energy confinement lead to an optimization problem with 6 objective functions.

Figure 2 shows the Pareto front of the coverage problem (2) for $o = 1$ and $n = 38$ [6], where the radiation patterns of points marked are shown in Figure 3. Each Pareto optimal point took about 295 oracle queries within 5 iterations of the cone of efficient directions algorithm (CEDA). The results consider a single-reflector single-feed offset reflector antenna with circular aperture, parameterized by 35 degrees of freedom on four cubic triangular Bézier patches [1] representing the reflector shape, and 3 parameters relative to feed rotation and position on the $x = 0$ plane, as shown in Figure 4. This parameterization considers, as reference, a parabolic antenna with circular aperture of radius $R = 0.762$ m, focal distance $F = 1.506$ m, and offset $H = 1.245$ m [5] (see respective radiation pattern in Figure 5).

Due to distance from target and power supply constraints, reflector antennas are the best choice since they can be highly directive and efficient. For a single reflector antenna, the expected shape is nearly parabolic, convex, and smooth. The parameterization used in the aforementioned results [1] tries to encompass all these features, but it is

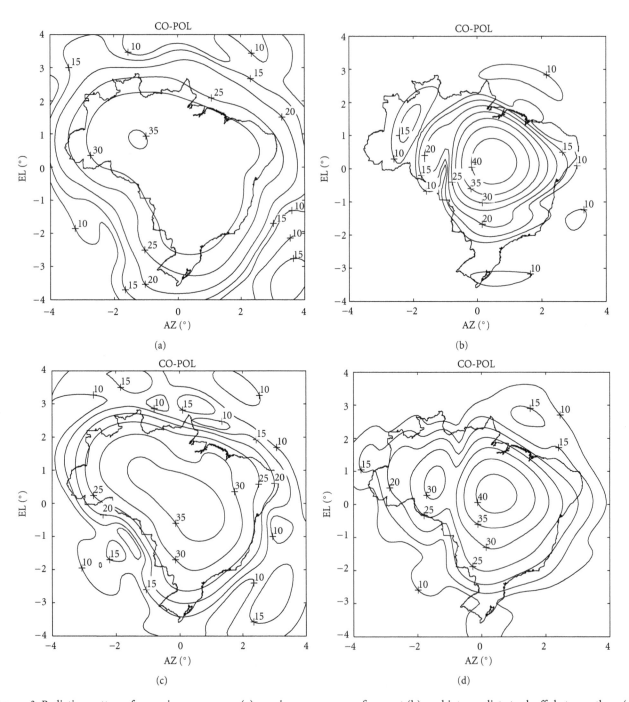

FIGURE 3: Radiation patterns for maximum coverage (a), maximum energy confinement (b), and intermediate tradeoffs between them (c, d).

quite extensive. A more elegant parameterization was used by Duan and Rahmat-Samii [5], but its truncated basis functions with trigonometric functions make the optimization problem harder to solve, especially because of higher multimodality in the objective functions, and the expected convex shape is more difficult to guarantee. A better choice would be orthogonal basis functions for convex functions.

Since the expected optimal antenna is smooth and greater than a few wavelengths, it can be quickly and accurately analyzed using physical optics (PO) approximation [7] applied to far field evaluations. The far-field integral for

the current source from PO is solved using Gauss-Legendre numerical integration method.

One last point to consider is that CEDA presents a monotonic convergence, which means that all objectives are improved after every iteration. This notable ability implies a fast and robust convergence in practice and can be used to seed starting points for stochastic algorithms. Stochastic algorithms are in turn well suited to map Pareto sets and skip bad local minima, which makes them suitable for seeding starting points for deterministic algorithms. This cyclic relationship suggests a hybrid approach, which has

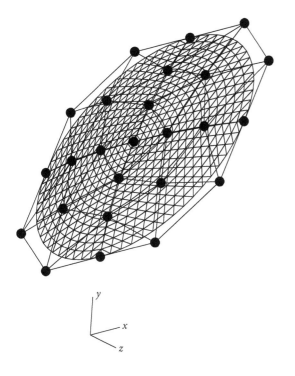

Figure 4: The reflector antenna is parameterized by reflector shape and feed position and rotation on plane $x = 0$. The reflector shape is defined by a Bézier surface whose parameters are the 25 control points (shown in dark dots) of a triangular control mesh.

already been used in literature, especially under the recent concept of memetic algorithms.

3.3. Optimal Design of Meander-Line Antennas for Radio-Frequency Identification. The low cost of electronic microcircuits and their low power consumption have made the development of identification systems through radio frequency practical, especially since the decade of the 1990s. Radio frequency identification (RFID) has been applied for tracking of products, luggage, books, animals, and other items where the tags can be attached to the objects, injected under the skin or embedded within items [8].

The RFID total market value in 2009 grew to $5.56 billion, of which $2.18 billion was spent only on passive tags alone [9]. Therefore, optimizing radio frequency identification systems has become crucial in improving the productivity and lowering costs in industry and supply chains. An RFID system consists basically in a receiver (tag), an emitter (reader), and a computational system (direct link). The tags have two main structures: the microchip, which provides the necessary power to transmit and receive information, and the antenna. The tags can be active, passive, or semiactive, depending on the mechanism of powering the microchip and transmitting information. Active tags have a local power source and electronics for performing

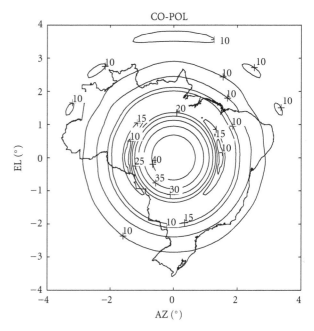

Figure 5: Radiation patterns for the reference parabolic reflector antenna.

specialized tasks [10]. The type of RFID tags chosen is based on the specific application. For low-cost tags and relatively short read ranges (around 3 m [11]), passive tags are most appropriate.

Due to the diversity of materials and packages that need to be identified, tag antennas development for passive UHF RFID systems has become challenging. The performance of the tag antennas is very dependent on the properties of the objects which the tags are attached to. The material of the objects can influence the capacitive characteristics of the tag antenna as well as modify its radiation pattern. Many studies have been carried out in order to investigate these effects in tags attached to metallic surfaces and water [12, 13] and to dielectrics [14, 15]. An effort to find the best optimized tag antenna for a given application improves the performance of the entire RFID system, because it can increase the power transfer coefficient and the read range.

The design in this paper was motivated by an application in the coffee industry. In this business, the product is stored in sacks in the producers' farms and needs to be transported to the local cooperatives. Each cooperative receives coffee sacks from different producers, normally using treadmills, and the receiving process demands time and labor force and is usually inefficient. In addition, the origin of the coffee must be traced until it reaches the final consumer and the material flow must be controlled in real time. In this context, RFID systems can be used to improve the productivity and competitiveness and reduce costs.

Meander-line antennas are one of the most commonly used in UHF RFID tags, mainly because of their tunability and size. Several papers have been published on RFID meander-line antenna design. Some articles have sought improved antenna gains and small size by using different configurations of meander-line antennas for passive RFID, which were explored applying genetic algorithm

TABLE 2: Optimization problem variables for multiobjective formulation.

				Parameter (mm)						
	w	b	a_1	a_2	a_3	a_4	s_1	s_2	s_3	s_4
Max	0.50	12.60	1.00	1.00	1.00	1.00	1.00	1.00	1.00	1.00
Min	0.80	21.00	7.00	7.00	7.00	7.00	7.00	7.00	7.00	7.00
Opt	0.78	15.11	4.70	3.98	6.42	5.66	3.80	1.42	6.00	3.77

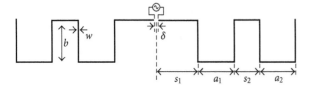

FIGURE 6: Geometry of the meander antenna for $c = 2$.

TABLE 3: Specifications and optimal antenna profile.

Parameter	Value
L_{min} (mm)	10
L_{max} (mm)	100
v_{min} (MHz)	902
v_{max} (MHz)	928
Zs (Ω)	27.4–200.9i

(GA) optimization and the method of moments (MoMs) [16, 17]. In [15], a loaded meander-line tag antenna was designed focusing on a specific application: box tracking in warehouses; the box content and the sensitivity to fabrication process were also considered.

Some methods have been used to characterize impedances and design meander-line antennas [18], including multiobjective optimization [19], and GA has been shown to be an efficient optimization tool for selecting globally optimal parameters of the antenna [20]. This paper introduces design techniques using optimization in order to cope with operation inside a frequency range.

3.3.1. Model and Parametrization. The meander-line antenna geometry (see Figure 6) is parameterized by the number of meanders c on each side, feed gap, trace width w, height b, meander step length a_i, and spacing between meanders s_i, $i = 1, \ldots, c$.

The antenna is discretized into regular quasiregular triangles and analyzed using a method of moments with a voltage gap feed assuming that $\delta = 0$. The implementation was validated with classical antenna simulation software.

The parameters other than δ that compose the design variables are

$$x = \begin{bmatrix} w \\ b \\ a_1 \\ \vdots \\ a_c \\ s_1 \\ \vdots \\ s_c \end{bmatrix}, \tag{4}$$

which are variables (degrees of freedom) to be optimized in order to attend some given objectives.

3.3.2. Optimization Problem. A meander-line antenna cannot provide high directivity. This is a desired behavior considering that isotropic radiation would not be ideal for the application. The remaining features of interest are input impedance and size, which are used in the multiobjective optimization problem formulation:

$$\text{minimize} \quad f(x) = \text{SWR}(x, v) \tag{5}$$

$$\text{subject to} \quad g(x) = \begin{bmatrix} L_{min} - L(x) \\ L(x) - L_{max} \end{bmatrix} \leq 0, \tag{6}$$

$$x_{min} \leq x \leq x_{max},$$

where $x \in \mathbb{R}^n$ is the vector of design variables (4), $n = 2 + 2c$, SWR is the standing wave ratio, L is the antenna length, and $v \in \mathbb{R}^o$ is the vector of sample frequencies. There is one objective function for each sample frequency, hence a total of o objective functions. The optimization problem (5) queries for antennas with minimum SWR in each sample frequency and whose overall length and design variables lie inside an interval.

To optimize the worst case SWR inside the frequency range, the mono-objective optimization problem formulation

$$\text{minimize} \quad f(x, t) = t \tag{7}$$

$$\text{subject to} \quad g(x, t) = \begin{bmatrix} \text{SWR}(x, v) - t \\ L_{min} - L(x) \\ L(x) - L_{max} \end{bmatrix} \leq 0 \tag{8}$$

$$x_{min} \leq x \leq x_{max}$$

can be derived, where t is the worst case SWR.

3.3.3. Optimization Results. The optimal variable results of (5) for $c = 4$ and $o = 5$ sample frequencies inside the frequency range are shown in Table 2. The target impedance, frequency range and length constraints are given in Table 3. The length was 71.51 mm and the worst standing wave ratio (SWR) was 4.04 for the optimal antenna. SWR behavior inside the frequency range is shown in Figure 7. The result took 395 problem oracle queries within 9 iterations of the multiobjective deterministic algorithm with monotonic convergence [21].

In order to compare the two formulations (multiobjective and worst case), the CEDA algorithm was limited to 395 oracle queries to optimize (8) for $c = 4$, $o = 5$, and settings in Table 3, whose optimal results are shown in Table 4. The length was 62.67 mm and the worst standing wave ratio (SWR) was 3.99 for the optimal antenna. SWR behavior inside the frequency range is shown in Figure 8.

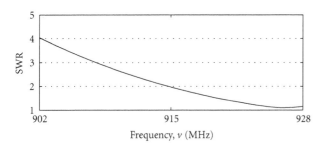

FIGURE 7: Standing wave ratio behavior inside frequency range.

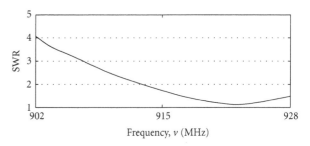

FIGURE 8: Optimal standing wave ratio behavior inside frequency range for worst case formulation.

TABLE 4: Optimization problem variables for worst case formulation.

	w	b	a_1	a_2	a_3	a_4	s_1	s_2	s_3	s_4
Max	0.50	12.60	1.00	1.00	1.00	1.00	1.00	1.00	1.00	1.00
Min	0.80	21.00	7.00	7.00	7.00	7.00	7.00	7.00	7.00	7.00
Opt	0.60	15.81	5.95	2.26	3.82	1.94	4.39	3.13	4.25	6.09

The best SWR of about 1 was verified inside a frequency range of 1.75% for optimal 4-meander antennas, even though the worst SWR is about 4. More degrees of freedom could be considered in order to improve worst cases (e.g., increasing the number of meanders or parametrizing each meander height individually).

The multiobjective formulation converges faster than the worst-case formulation. Furthermore, the theoretical guarantee of always improving all objective functions after each iteration may be very suitable in real world applications. However, considering that SWRs at sample frequencies of 1 and 40 could be considered Pareto optimal for the former formulation, results for the worst case formulation may be regarded more meaningful.

4. Conclusion

Multiobjective design of antennas is an important and active field of inquiry. Many important problems, such as those presented in this paper, have been considered in the last few years. The approaches discussed in this paper are conceptually different. Evolutionary optimization relies on global search for the best solution. Even though they are robust techniques, they depend on some user's defined parameters and the convergence may be slow. Deterministic methods have asymptotic fast convergence. However, they are prone to getting trapped in local minima. In practice, the choice of the optimization algorithm will depend on the nature of the problem and the designer's experience.

Acknowledgments

This work was supported by the National Counsel of Technological and Scientific Development (CNPq), Minas Gerais State Research Foundation (FAPEMIG), and Bahia State Research Foundation (FAPESB).

References

[1] A. C. Lisboa, D. A. G. Vieira, J. A. Vasconcelos, R. R. Saldanha, and R. H. C. Takahashi, "Multiobjective shape optimization of broad-band reflector antennas using the cone of efficient directions algorithm," *IEEE Transactions on Magnetics*, vol. 42, no. 4, pp. 1223–1226, 2006.

[2] K. Deb, *Multi-Objective Optimization Using Evolutionary Algorithms*, John Wiley & Sons, New York, NY, USA, 2002.

[3] X. L. Travassos, N. Ida, C. Vollaire, and A. Nicolas, "Solution of Maxwell's equations for the simulation and optimization of the radar assessment of concrete structures," *Research in Nondestructive Evaluation*, vol. 18, no. 3, pp. 151–161, 2007.

[4] X. L. Travassos, *Modélisation numérique pour l'évaluation non destructive électromagnétique: application au contrôle non destructif des structures en béton*, Ph.D. thesis, L'École Centrale de Lyon, Ecully, France, June 2007.

[5] D.-W. Duan and Y. Rahmat-Samii, "Generalized diffraction synthesis technique for high performance reflector antennas," *IEEE Transactions on Antennas and Propagation*, vol. 43, no. 1, pp. 27–40, 1995.

[6] A. C. Lisboa, D. A. G. Vieira, J. A. Vansconcelos, R. R. Saldanha, and R. H. C. Takahashi, "Decreasing interference in satellite broadband communication systems using modeled reflector antennas," *IEEE Transactions on Magnetics*, vol. 44, no. 6, pp. 958–961, 2008.

[7] C. A. Balanis, *Advanced Engineering Electromagnetics*, John Wiley & Sons, 1989.

[8] S. Polniak, "The RFID case study book: RFID application stories from around the globe," Tech. Rep., Abhisam Software, 2007.

[9] P. Harrop, "Printed RFID in 2010," IDTechEx, 2010.

[10] Z. N. Chen, *Antennas for Portable Devices*, John Wiley & Sons, 2007.

[11] D. M. Dobkin, *The RF in RFID: Passive UHF RFID in Practice*, Elsevier, 2008.

[12] N. A. Mohammed, M. Sivakumar, and D. D. Deavours, "An RFID tag capable of free-space and on-metal operation," type, Information and Telecommunications Technology Center, 2008.

[13] J. Y. Park and J. M. Woo, "Miniaturised dual-band S-shaped RFID tag antenna mountable on metallic surface," *Electronics Letters*, vol. 44, no. 23, pp. 1339–1341, 2008.

[14] J. D. Griffin and G. D. Durgin, "Radio link budgets for 915MHz RFID antennas placed on various objetcs," in *Texas Wireless Symposium*, vol. 44, Atlanta, Ga, USA, 2005.

[15] K. V. S. Rao, P. V. Nikitin, and S. F. Lam, "Antenna design for UHF RFID tags: a review and a practical application," *IEEE Transactions on Antennas and Propagation*, vol. 53, no. 12, pp. 3870–3876, 2005.

[16] G. Marrocco, A. Fonte, and F. Bardati, "Evolutionary design of miniaturized meander-line antennas for RFID applications," in *Proceedings of the IEEE Antennas and Propagation Society International Symposium*, pp. 362–365, June 2002.

[17] G. Marrocco, "Gain-optimized self-resonant meander line antennas for RFID applications," *IEEE Antennas and Wireless Propagation Letters*, vol. 2, pp. 302–305, 2003.

[18] X. Qing, C. K. Goh, and Z. N. Chen, "Impedance characterization of rfid tag antennas and application in tag co-design," *IEEE Transactions on Microwave Theory and Techniques*, vol. 57, no. 5, pp. 1268–1274, 2009.

[19] X. L. Travassos, D. A. G. Vieira, A. C. Lisboa, M. M. B. Lima, and N. Ida, "Antenna optimization using multi-objective algorithms," in *Proceedings of the 4th European Conference on Antennas and Propagation (EuCAP '10)*, April 2010.

[20] D. Zhou, R. A. Abd-Alhameed, and C. H. See, "Meanderline antenna design for UHF RFID tag using a genetic algorithm," in *Proceedings of the Progress in Eletromagnetics Research Symposium*, pp. 1253–1257, March 2009.

[21] D. A. G. Vieira, R. H. C. Takahashi, and R. R. Saldanha, "Multicriteria optimization with a multiobjective golden section line search," *Mathematical Programming*, vol. 131, no. 1-2, pp. 131–161, 2012.

16

Project and Realization of a Wide-Range High-Frequency RFID Gate Allowing Omnidirectional Detection of Transponders

Giuliano Benelli, Stefano Parrino, and Alessandro Pozzebon

Department of Information Engineering, University of Siena, Via Roma 56, 53100 Siena, Italy

Correspondence should be addressed to Alessandro Pozzebon, alessandro.pozzebon@unisi.it

Academic Editor: M. S. Hwang

We describe the study and development of a 2-meter-wide HF RFID gate providing omnidirectional detection of transponders. Common commercial HF RFID gate structures provide a maximum reading range around 150 cm. Moreover, this value is in most cases guaranteed only for the maximum coupling direction, with lower values for the other 2 orientations. The proposed structure raises the value of the reading range up to 200 cm for every orientation of the transponder, with even better results (220 cm) when the transponder is in the position of maximum coupling. This result has been achieved through numerical simulations, focused on the study of the geometry of the antenna system and on the realization of the matching circuit and then confirmed with the physical implementation of the system.

1. Introduction

With the term RFID (Radio Frequency Identification) are indicated all the technologies that allow the contactless identification (i.e., the unambiguous recognition) of an item, an animal, or a person using the electromagnetic fields as the mean of communication [1, 2].

Obviously the term RFID encompasses several different technological devices, with different operating frequencies and different electronic features. Due to this fact, every time that RFID is chosen as the right technology to be used for a particular application, specific studies have to be done in order to identify the adequate technical solution offering the best ratio among costs and performances.

In addition, the use of electromagnetic fields in particular environments such as hospitals or any other public building can have several limitations due to the presence of people and the interaction with other electronic devices.

While the historical applicative fields of RFID have always been the access control, the industrial tracking, and the surveillance systems, in the last years new scenarios are emerging: one of the most significant is, for example, the field of the Healthcare. The integration of automatic identification techniques with the technological frameworks of hospitals, emergency rooms, or nursing homes can increase the efficiency of all the assistance operations improving the mobility and the accessibility to the informative systems.

The paper is organized as follows. In Section 2, the basic concepts concerning the antennas for HF RFID systems are described, focusing on the materials to be used, on the factors influencing the final performances, and on the matching of the antenna. Section 3 describes the possible configuration of antenna gate structures. In Section 4, the simulations necessary to project a standard gate structure are described, while in Section 5 the simulations carried on to develop the wide-range structure are analyzed. Section 6 describes the physical implementation of the gate structure emerged from the simulations. Finally, Section 7 provides some concluding remarks and future works.

2. Antennas for HF RFID Systems

An RFID system is basically composed by the transponders, or tags, which are the smart devices located on the item to be identified, and the reader, which performs the effective identification operations. The project of the antenna structure of the reader is especially important because it can notably affect the performances of the system and its installation in the final destination [3–8].

In general, the reading distance of a tag depends mainly on the physical dimensions of the antenna system adopted, because the intensity of the magnetic field increases with the growth of these dimensions.

On the other hand, if the dimensions come through a certain limit the following problems can occur:

(i) Signal-noise ratio (SNR) decreases;

(ii) law values of electromagnetic emissions can be surpassed;

(iii) "holes" can be generated in the emitted magnetic field, creating shade zones where the tag cannot be read;

(iv) the inductance can grow up to a level that makes the matching of the system extremely difficult if not totally impossible.

2.1. The Materials and the Design. An antenna can be ideally built with every kind of conductive material, but in practice the most common solutions are based on the use of

(i) hollow copper tubes (also aluminium is a good option, but is less malleable), with the diameter going from 1/2 inch (i.e., 15 mm) for smaller loops (e.g., 500 mm ∗ 500 mm) up to 3/4 inch (i.e., 22 mm) for bigger loops;

(ii) copper strips usually from 10 mm to 50 mm wide.

During the realization of an antenna or a system of more antennas, many factors can influence the final performances. Among the most significant the following can be listed.

(i) For the solutions described before the following rule applies: the bigger the antenna is, the wider the diameter of the tube or the width of the strip should be. This fact reduces the inductance of the antenna; a good alternative can be offered by the interconnection of two parallel antennas, in order to obtain the same inductance of a single antenna.

With larger antennas wider reading ranges are achievable, but there is a limit due to the equivalent inductance of the antenna: over $5\,\mu$Henry the matching of the antenna becomes virtually impossible.

(ii) The presence of metal in the proximities of the system can reduce the performances of the antennas. In particular the most part of the negative effect simply derives from the detuning of the antenna and can be resolved readapting the matching circuit. Anyway if the metal is too close it can absorb a great part of the emitted power: for this fact the tuning of an antenna should be made only when the antenna is positioned in its final destination.

(iii) The presence of other antennas next to the system can alter the performances due to the mutual coupling phenomenon: anyway in some cases, for example, in the case of the studied system, this effect is

deliberately wanted because it can increase the performances. This fact will be specifically examined in the next sections.

(iv) The activation of the transponders depends directly on the power transmitted from the antenna through the magnetic coupling, but the energy that they can receive is the highest only when they are in the position of maximum coupling, that is, when the antenna loop is parallel to the transponder and the lines of the generated magnetic field are perpendicular to the transponder.

Due to this fact only in this position the reading distance is maximum: when the corner among the transponder and the lines of the field is less than 90° the coupling decreases lowering the read distance.

2.2. The Matching of the Antenna. Antennas used for inductively coupled passive RFID systems are designed as loops, allowing the magnetic field component in close field conditions, which is the one that enables the reading of the tag, to be prevalent over the electric field component; therefore the input impedance of a loop is essentially reactive (in particular inductive) [9].

The antenna is linked to the reader through a coaxial cable with a characteristic impedance of 50 Ω and it is evident that with a direct link the most part of the input power would be reflected due to the mismatching.

For this fact the antenna too should have a 50 Ω characteristic impedance, and this can be done adding a matching circuit between the coaxial cable and the antenna [10].

Among the various matching techniques the most important are the Gamma matching, the T-matching, the use of balun, and the Capacitive matching. We will consider this last option even if it is perhaps the most complex because small variations of the capacity (in the order of picoFarad) can make a great difference in the matching operation.

The idea is to use a parallel capacitive RC matching network, in order to make the LC parallel circuit resound and to match the real part of the obtained impedance.

This configuration is quite simple to be realized and the values of the components can be adjusted in order to obtain the best matching possible.

The circuit is divided into two parts: the first one, directly linked to the terminals of the antenna, is formed by a resonant circuit at the frequency $f_0 = 13.56$ MHz. This is composed by the loop inductance, a parallel capacity, and a resistance in order to define the quality factor Q of the circuit.

The second part of the matching circuit is composed by a network which has the task to match the input impedance, now exclusively real, seen at the terminals of the matching resonance circuit.

3. Antenna Configurations

3.1. Gate Configurations. One of the most common technical solutions for the tracking operations is the realization of gate structures: in this kind of solutions more antennas, connected to a single reader, create a sort of "Tunnel" through

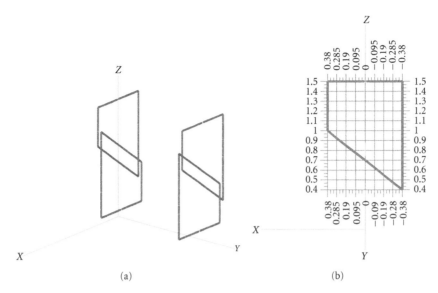

FIGURE 1: Gate geometry (a); a single antenna (b).

which the tagged items are carried and at the same time recognized.

Gates can be single, double, or multiple and they can be composed by up to 8 antennas.

Typical applications include solutions integrated in conveyor belts, structures located at the doors of warehouses or at the exits of shops to check the items bought by customers.

The simplest configuration foresees the use of two antennas, typically rectangular, located one in front of the other and linked to a reader through a multiplexer: obviously this kind of configuration covers an overall area approximately twice the one covered by a single antenna.

Two different cases can be studied. In the first one only one antenna is powered, while the second one is only matched and located in front of the other: in this case the performances of the powered antenna increase due to the phenomenon of mutual coupling.

In the second case the both antennas are connected through a "Splitter", and both are powered: in this situation the reading distance can be even more than doubled, due to the fact that each antenna emits its own magnetic field. Anyway a phenomenon of field cancellation can occur in this case deriving from the perspective and the distance of the antennas.

4. Project and Realization of a Standard Gate

4.1. Standard Gate Simulations. The first simulations have been carried out on a 1.30 m wide gate structure: this width represents a good starting point because it is the width covered by common RFID gates.

The proposed geometry is shown in Figure 1(a) and foresees the use of two overlapped antennas on both sides of the gate.

Due to the phenomenon of mutual inductance, the matching of the antenna is different from the case of a single

powered antenna and the case of the 4 powered antennas, and an adequate model has been realized [11].

In the first case we have a single powered antenna with the other three put at open circuit and described as mutually coupled inductances with coupling coefficient equal to

$$K_{i,j} = \frac{M_{i,j}}{\sqrt{L_i L_j}}. \tag{1}$$

With four identical antennas we have

$$L_i = L_j \Longrightarrow L_1 = L_2 = L_3 = L_4 = L,$$

$$K_{i,j} = K_{j,i} = \left(\frac{M_{i,j}}{\sqrt{L_i L_j}} \right) \Bigg|_{L_i = L_j = L} = \left(\frac{M_{i,j}}{L} \right). \tag{2}$$

This representation is justified by the fact that when we calculate $M_{1,2}$ in practice we consider a two-port network where each port is powered by a current generator, and we calculate its Z parameters

$$V_1 = Z_{11} \cdot I_1 + Z_{12} \cdot I_2 \Longrightarrow V_1 = j\omega L \cdot I_1 + j\omega M_{12} \cdot I_2,$$
$$V_2 = Z_{21} \cdot I_1 + Z_{22} \cdot I_2 \Longrightarrow V_2 = j\omega M_{21} \cdot I_1 + j\omega L \cdot I_2. \tag{3}$$

With both the ports powered with the same current $I = I_1 = I_2$ from the first equation we have $V_1 = j\omega L \cdot I_1 + j\omega M_{12} \cdot I_1$ and we calculate the input impedance

$$L'_{\text{tot}} = L + M_{21} \tag{4}$$

and then

$$M_{21} = L'_{\text{tot}} - L, \tag{5}$$

where L'_{tot} is the inductance of the system when the antennas 1 and 2 are powered with the same current while the other

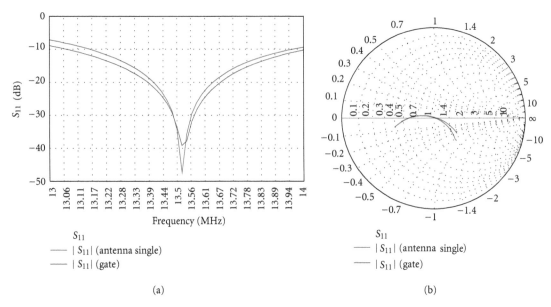

FIGURE 2: Reflection coefficient on the cartesian graphic (a) and on the Smith Chart (b).

two are put at open circuit, and L is the inductance of a single loop when the other three are put at open circuit. Simulating the system with POSTFEKO and calling 1 and 2 the antennas on one side and 3 and 4 the other two we calculated then the following parameters:

(i) L, with only one antenna powered and the others put at open circuit: $\omega L = 222.1\,\Omega \Rightarrow L = 222.1\,\Omega/2\pi f|_{f=13.56\,\mathrm{MHz}} \simeq 2.608\,\mu\mathrm{H} = 2608\,\mathrm{nH}$;

(ii) M_{12} with only antennas 1 and 2 powered: $\omega L'_{\mathrm{tot}} = 252.67\,\Omega \Rightarrow M_{12} = L'_{\mathrm{tot}} - L = 252.67\,\Omega/\omega - 2608\,\mathrm{nH} \simeq 358\,\mathrm{nH}$;

(iii) M_{13} with only antennas 1 and 3 powered: $\omega L'_{\mathrm{tot}} = 224.7\,\Omega \Rightarrow M_{13} = L'_{\mathrm{tot}} - L = 224.7\,\Omega/\omega - 2608\,\mathrm{nH} \simeq 30.53\,\mathrm{nH}$;

(iv) M_{14} with only antennas 1 and 4 powered: $\omega L'_{\mathrm{tot}} = 224.0377\,\Omega \Rightarrow M_{14} = L'_{\mathrm{tot}} - L = 224.037\,\Omega/\omega - 2608\,\mathrm{nH} \simeq 22.74\,\mathrm{nH}$;

(v) M_{23} with only antennas 2 and 3 powered: $\omega L'_{\mathrm{tot}} = 224.039\,\Omega \Rightarrow M_{23} = L'_{\mathrm{tot}} - L = 224.039\,\Omega/\omega - 2608\,\mathrm{nH} \simeq 25.1\,\mathrm{nH}$;

(vi) M_{24} with only antennas 2 and 4 powered: $\omega L'_{\mathrm{tot}} = 224.99\,\Omega \Rightarrow M_{24} = L'_{\mathrm{tot}} - L = 224.99\,\Omega/\omega - 2608\,\mathrm{nH} \simeq 33.93\,\mathrm{nH}$;

(vii) M_{34} with only antennas 3 and 4 powered: $\omega L'_{\mathrm{tot}} = 252.92\,\Omega \Rightarrow M_{34} = L'_{\mathrm{tot}} - L = 252.92\,\Omega/\omega - 2608\,\mathrm{nH} \simeq 361.97\,\mathrm{nH}$.

Analyzing these coefficients we can see that M_{12} and M_{34} present the highest values (ten times higher than the others), which is obvious because this is the mutual induction among the overlapped antennas. Moreover we can see that the values of the couples M_{13}-M_{24}, M_{14}-M_{23} and M_{12}-M_{34} are very similar and in fact they should be identical due to

symmetry reasons: they are a bit different due to numerical approximations. Finally we can see that M_{13} and M_{24} are slightly higher than M_{14} and M_{23} because antenna couples 1-3 and 2-4 are faced and the concatenated magnetic flux is greater.

It is interesting to see the differences in the performances from the case of a single antenna to the case of the gate. From Figure 2 we can see that both the antenna and the gate have a good matching, even if slightly moved (40 kHz) from the operative frequency, but in the case of the gate the band is evidently wider.

4.2. The Magnetic Field. Figure 3(a) shows the representation of the near field $|H_y|$ on the y-z plan with $x = 0$, and we can see that the gate presents along the y direction a higher reading distance than the single antenna on the maximum coupling direction of the transponder. The z coordinate has been chosen in order to maximize the field configuration for both the structures, and this is verified approximately at the center of the loop ($x = 0$, $z = 1.10$ m and y variable) for a single antenna and at the center of the overlapping area for the gate ($x = 0$, $z = 0.9$ m and y variable).

A more accurate analysis shows that for $x = 0$ the gates has $|H_y| \geq 60$ mA/m (the minimum value for the tag reading) in the 0.10 m $\leq$ for all $z \leq 1.5$ m range (the total height of the gate) and for all $y \in [0, 1.3\,\mathrm{m}]$ (the distance from the two sides of the gate). The single antenna presents instead $|H_y| \geq 60$ mA/m in the best case, with $x = 0$ and $z = 1.10$ in the 0 m $\leq$ for all $y \leq 1.09$ m range, and in the worst case, with $x = 0$ and $z = 0.4$ in the 0 m $\leq$ for all $y \leq 0.25$ m range.

Figure 3(b), 3(c) show $|H_x|$ along y at the variation of z, respectively, for the gate and for the single antenna: in the first case we can see that in the best case ($z = 0.7$ m) $|H_x| \geq 60$ mA/m up to $y \simeq 0.47$ m while with the single antenna, in the best case ($z = 0.6$ m), we reach the value of $y \simeq 0.37$ m.

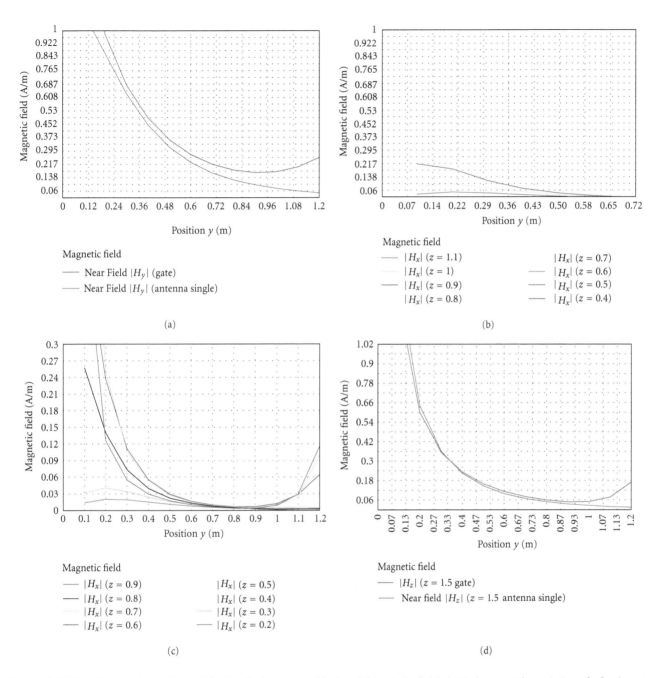

FIGURE 3: $|H_y|$ on the y-z plain with $x = 0$ for the single antenna (blue) and the gate (red) (a); $|H_x|$ along y at the variation of z for the gate (b) the single antenna (c); $|H_z|$ for $x = 0$, y variable and $z = 1.5$ m for the single antenna (blue) and the gate (red) (d).

Finally Figure 3(d) shows the values of $|H_z|$ for $x = 0$, y variable and $z = 1.5$ m (the value at which both the antenna and the gate present maximum $|H_z|$). While in the case of the gate, performances seem to be worse than in the case of the single antenna, we can notice the rise of an interesting phenomenon: first of all, due to mutual coupling, an induced magnetic field is created also in correspondence to the not powered antenna for $x = 0$; next to this, two field lobes appear exactly in correspondence to the overlapping, where mutual coupling plays an important role; finally we can notice an increase of the field also in correspondence to the overlapping area of the two facing antennas, underlining also in this case the presence of a remarkable mutual induction.

Moreover we also have to consider that the single antenna presents higher values first of all thanks to the limited dimensions of its geometry, and then because the regions where the tag is detectable are thinner than the ones provided by the gate.

This is also argued by the fact that, with the same powering, the current flowing through the powered antenna of the gate is lower than the current flowing through the single antenna, even if the performances are higher.

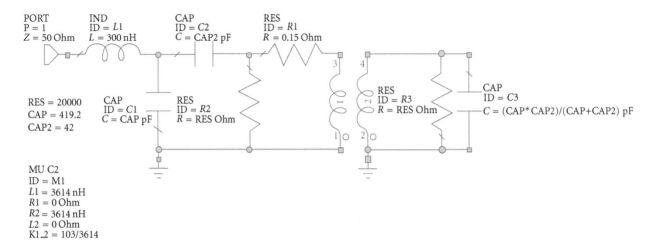

FIGURE 4: Matching circuit with AWR.

5. Project of the Wide-Range Gate: Simulations

5.1. The Geometry. The first simulations have focused on the search of the right geometry: at the end of the study the width of overlapping surface has been fixed at 22 cm. This has proved to be the best result because on equal current flow the generated field is the highest in the three dimensions.

The four antennas obviously present the same dimensions and their perimeter is equal to $(55 + 90 + 145 + 90\sqrt{2})$ cm $\simeq 4.173$ m; in our case wavelength is equal to $\lambda = c/f = 22.12$ m: we can then affirm that every loop is around $\lambda/5$ wide. The system composed by two overlapped antennas is 1.78 m high and 0.90 m wide. In the final disposition the system will be raised 12 cm above the floor: if we consider the system as placed on the x-z plan we have 0.12 m $\leq z \leq$ 1.90 m, $x = 0$ and $y = 0$ (while for the other half of the gate we have $y = 2$ m), with the center of the system located at $z \simeq 1$ m.

The geometry has been realized with CADFEKO simulation environment, while with POSTFEKO we calculated the values of the impedance of each loop and the mutual inductance between the overlapped antennas:

$$(\omega L_1)|_{f=13.56\,\text{MHz}}$$
$$= 307.76\,\Omega \implies L_1 = L_2 = L_3 = L_4 = 3614\,\text{nH},$$
$$\omega L_{12} = L_{21} = 316.53\,\Omega, \tag{6}$$
$$M_{12} = M_{21} = \frac{\omega L_{12} - \omega L_1}{\omega} = 103\,\text{nH}.$$

We can finally calculate the quality factor of the antenna $Q = 20000/316.53 \simeq 60$.

5.2. The Matching. The calculated values have been introduced in the AWR circuit simulator: the matching circuit is shown in Figure 4; the reflection coefficient (Figure 5(a)) is extremely interesting because the cartesian graphic presents two resonance peaks, on the left (13.48 MHz) and on the right (13.62 MHz) of the operative frequency (13.56 MHz):

the coupling phenomenon is used to enlarge the band using the two close resonances.

The values of CAP, CAP2, and RES provided by AWR have been introduced in POSTFEKO: the resulting matching is shown in Figures 5(c) and 5(d).

5.3. The Generated Field. In this section we analyze the configuration of the magnetic field generated by the system, assuming only the upper antenna to be powered.

(i) $|H_x|$: the H_x field presents two lobes in correspondence to the vertical segments of the system: in particular (considering a x-z plan with $y = 1$ m) we have a maximum of the field for the negative x at $x = -0.56$ m, where $H_x > 60$ mA/m in the range 0.076 m $\leq$ for all $z \leq 1.22$ m, and another one for the positive x at $x = 0.64$ m, where $H_x > 60$ mA/m in the range 0.09 m $\leq$ for all $z \leq 1.28$ m.

We can suppose that when we power the lower antenna the section covered by the field will be the mirror of the one covered by the upper: in this case the section covered will belong to the range 0.80 m $\leq$ $z \leq 1.99$ m. Joining the two antennas we will cover all the z in the range between 0.09 m and 1.99 m. If we consider an y-z plan at $x = -0.56$ m and we power both the antennas at the distance of few milliseconds we can see that $|H_x| > 60$ mA/m for all z and for all y.

(ii) $|H_y|$: the considerations on $|H_y|$ are notably easier because the structure covers all the operative volume with enough strength to read a tag, even reaching a distance up to 1.40 m.

(iii) $|H_z|$: on the x-z plan for $y = 1$ m and $x = 0.14$ m we have that $|H_z| \geq 60$ mA/m 0.66 m $\leq$ for all $z \leq$ 1.80 m and $0 \leq$ for all $z \leq 0.15$ m. In these intervals $|H_z| \geq 60$ mA/m for all $y \in (0, 1\,\text{m})$.

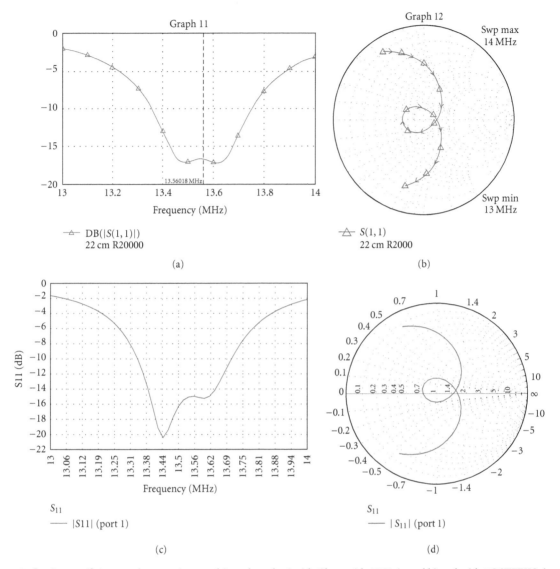

FIGURE 5: Reflection coefficient on the cartesian graphic and on the Smith Chart with AWR (a and b) and with POSTFEKO (c and d).

Finally, from the dimensions of the system we can assume that when we power the second antenna we have $|H_z| \geq$ 60 mA/m for all $y \in (0, 1 \, m)$, $0.22 \, m \leq$ for all $z \leq 1.36 \, m$ and $1.87 \leq$ for all $z \leq 2.02 \, m$, having then the volume belonging to half gate fully covered.

5.4. Varying the Antenna Factor Q.

We saw that in the matching circuit of each antenna, simulated with AWR, we put the value of $R = 20 \, K\Omega$; in reality we could also have reached the matching with lower values of R: in particular we studied the cases with $R = 15 \, K\Omega$, $R = 10 \, K\Omega$ and $R = 5 \, K\Omega$. Evidently, using these values also the values of the capacities vary, but it is important to underline that the antenna factor Q decreases, due to the relation of direct proportionality between Q and R.

In Figure 6 we can see $|S_{11}|_{dB}$ in cartesian coordinates and on the Smith chart in relation to the studied cases: the red graph represents the $R = 20 \, k\Omega$ case, the blue graph

represents the $R = 15 \, k\Omega$ case, the violet graph represents the $R = 10 \, k\Omega$ case, and the brown graph represents the $R = 5 \, k\Omega$ case. We can thus observe that the band at $-10 \, dB$ is obviously wider with a decrease of R, but we can see that with $R = 5 \, K\Omega$, even if we have the widest band (700 KHz), the phenomenon of the double peak does not appear, and the covering of the operative volume is definitely the worst.

We can then conclude that the double resonance is extremely useful because with the two peaks, in correspondence to the frequencies of the subcarriers, the band is wide enough to transmit and at the same time Q is high enough to allow the existence of a sufficiently high irradiated magnetic field.

The analysis of the generated fields with POSTFEKO produced the following results.

(i) $R = 5 \, K\Omega$: considering the maximum plan for $x = 0.35 \, m$ and $0.12 \, m \leq$ for all $z \leq 1.90 \, m$, $|H_x| > 60 \, mA/m$ only up to $y = 0.8 \, m$; considering the maximum plan for $x = 0$ and $0.12 \, m \leq$ for all $z \leq 1.90 \, m$,

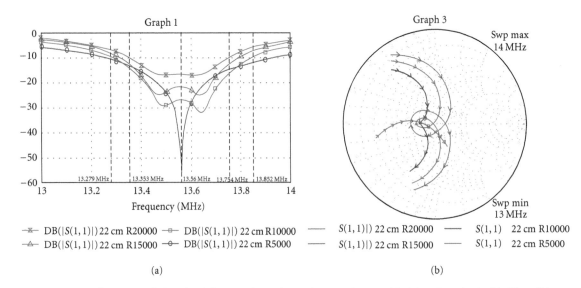

(a)   (b)

FIGURE 6: Reflection coefficient for different values of R on the cartesian graphic (a) and on the Smith Chart (b).

$|H_y| > 60\,\text{mA/m}$ up to $y = 1.20\,\text{m}$; considering the maximum plan for $x = 0$ and $0.12\,\text{m} \leq$ for all $z \leq 1.90\,\text{m}$, $|H_z| > 60\,\text{mA/m}$ up to $y = 0.8\,\text{m}$.

(ii) $R = 10\,\text{K}\Omega$: considering the plans described above, $|H_x| > 60\,\text{mA/m}$ up to $y = 0.8\,\text{m}$; $|H_y| > 60\,\text{mA/m}$ up to $y = 1.2\,\text{m}$; $|H_z| > 60\,\text{mA/m}$ up to $y = 0.8\,\text{m}$.

(iii) $R = 15\,\text{K}\Omega$: considering the plans described above, $|H_x| > 60\,\text{mA/m}$ up to $y = 0.9\,\text{m}$; $|H_y| > 60\,\text{mA/m}$ up to $y = 1.3\,\text{m}$; $|H_z| > 60\,\text{mA/m}$ up to $y = 0.9\,\text{m}$.

We can see that in none of these case we can have a reading of the tags up to 1 m in every direction: in the first and in the second case we have a homogeneous reading up to 0.8 m, while in the third we arrive at 0.9 m.

5.5. Varying the Geometry of the Gate. Simulations have been made also with different lengths of the overlapping section. In particular we considered 3 different alternative overlapping lengths (12 cm, 18 cm, and 44 cm) and the case with no overlapping (with a 2 cm distance between the antennas).

Figure 7 shows the reflection coefficient $|S_{11}|_{\text{dB}}$ in the cases considered together with the final 22 cm solution (red graph in Figure 7).

In these four cases we had the following results.

(i) In the 12 cm case (Blue graph in Figure 7) we had a homogeneous reading up to 0.7 cm

(ii) In the 18 cm case (Violet graph in Figure 7) we had a homogeneous reading up to 0.6 cm.

(iii) In the 44 cm case (Brown graph in Figure 7) we had a homogeneous reading up to 0.6 cm.

(iv) In the not overlapped case (Green graph in Figure 7) we had a homogeneous reading up to 0.7 cm.

In none of these cases we reached satisfying results.

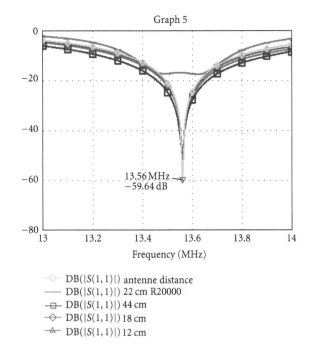

FIGURE 7: Reflection coefficient for different values of the overlapping surface on the cartesian graphic.

6. Hardware Implementation

Following the positive results of the simulations we went on with the realization of a prototype. The following materials were used:

(i) copper tubes for the antennas (16 mm diameter);

(ii) passive electronic elements (inductances, resistors, etc.) for the matching circuit;

(iii) wooden structures to hold the antennas.

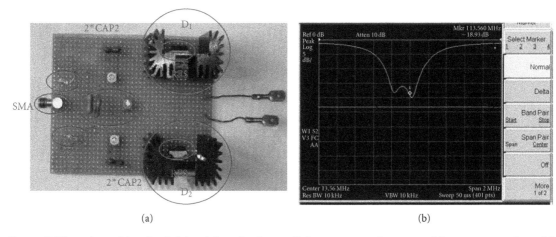

(a)   (b)

FIGURE 8: The real matching circuit (a) and the reflection coefficient as seen on the screen of the spectrum analyzer (b).

The wide diameter of the tubes has been necessary because simulations showed that we had better results for what concerned the strength and the shape of the magnetic field, while with a thinner tube the equivalent inductance of the antenna would have been higher (over 6 μHenry) making the matching circuit unstable due to the very low capacities required.

6.1. The Real Matching Circuit. After the realization of the antenna structure we went on with the implementation of the matching circuit for both the antennas, paying attention to use the same components with the same values, with the exception of the trimmers that have been regulated by hand during the matching phase.

The matching circuit realized for each antenna includes the components shown in Figure 8(a), where L, CAP, and CAP2 e RES correspond to the components seen in the simulated circuit while D_1 and D_2 are heat sinks. The lateral symmetric capacities (CAP2) and the central capacities (CAP) are formed by capacitors with constant capacity and capacitors with variable capacity (trimmers) in parallel. Once realized the circuit the following step focused on the matching of each antenna: this has been done linking, through a coaxial cable, the SMA connector of the circuit with a E4403B spectrum analyzer. In order to avoid the detuning phenomenon for the 4 antennas system the following prescriptions concerning the coaxial cables have been taken in account the following.

(i) To reduce the noise effects, a ferrite core has to be positioned, with at least three loops of the cable, at each end of the coaxial cable.

(ii) The coaxial cable linking the multiplexer and the reader has to be at most 50 cm long.

(iii) The coaxial cables connecting the antennas must have the same length ($\lambda/2$ is the best choice to simplify the matching).

(iv) The matching has to be made separately for each half of the gate keeping in mind that while a cable is linked to the spectrum analyzer, the other cable must have

an unlinked end and the other end connected to the second circuit, because this will be the configuration that the reader will find when the antennas will be powered one by one at a distance of few milliseconds.

Once the analyzer has been calibrated and connected the antenna, the trimmers have been regulated watching the waveform on the analyzer screen (Figure 8(b)), in order to obtain a matching similar to the one of the simulations. Initially the trimmers have been chosen with wide ranges of capacitive values (6–50 pF). Subsequently, once found a good matching, they have been replaced with other trimmers providing lower range values (increasing also CAP and CAP2 if necessary). Once reached the final matching, it has been found that the band at -10 dB was 680 kHz, then wider than the estimated one ($\sim$400 kHz). A following test has shown that some of transponders crossing the gate were not read: this means that the irradiated magnetic field was not strong enough to allow the identification of the tags in every orientation. This fact is probably due to capacitive phenomenons that make the equivalent inductance of the real antenna different from the one of the simulated antenna: as a consequence the antenna factor Q is lower than the estimated one and then also the field strength is reduced. This fact also justifies the difference in the bandwidth.

For this reason it has been necessary to double the value of the resistances RES (from 20 KΩ to 40 KΩ) in order to increase Q and the emitted field strength, and to vary all the values of the capacities to obtain the identification of the tags on the whole crossing.

The final circuit for every antenna is implemented with the following components:

$$\begin{aligned}
\text{RES} &= 40 \text{ K}\Omega, \\
\text{CAP} &= 334\text{–}342 \text{ pF}, \\
2 \cdot \text{CAP2} &= 48.3\text{–}51.8 \text{ pF}, \\
L &= 360 \text{ nH}.
\end{aligned} \tag{7}$$

The double resonance peak appears on the cartesian graph of the reflection coefficient provided by the spectrum analyzer, proving the fact that both the antennas are matched and resonant at two different, but very close frequencies: the mutual coupling phenomenon among the loops is used to widen the band using the two close resonances.

6.2. Measures of the Reading Distance. Once the matching of the system was achieved we moved to the test of the reading distances. The measures have been made using a FEIG ID ISC.LR2000 reader, ISO15693 compliant: its ID ISOStart configuration software has been used to test the functionalities of the reader, the reading range, and the communication with the tags. The measure of the maximum reading distance has been carried out using the Test-ISO Inventory procedure, provided with the control software, which performs a continuous scanning of the operative volume of the antenna reading, in case of detection, the serial number of the tag. The tags used for the measures are manufactured by Texas Instrument (I-Code 1 Tags), they are ISO15693 compliant and they present a $85 * 44$ mm surface.

Studying only half gate (two antennas) we verified that a tag was correctly read in all the volume up to 1 m of distance. In particular for each orientation of the tag we found the following results:

(i) a tag, whose surface was oriented along the y direction and crossing the gate along the x direction was read at distance up to 1.10 m;

(ii) a tag, whose surface was oriented along the x direction and crossing the gate along the x direction was read at distance up to 1.03 m;

(iii) a tag, whose surface was oriented along the z direction and crossing the gate along the x direction was read at distance up to 1.00 m.

This means that a tag is detectable in all the three orientation across a 2 m wide and 2 m high gate.

The testing of the system with all the four antennas has confirmed these results, leaving the matching parameters practically unchanged.

6.3. Interaction with Other Materials. Another set of tests has been performed in order to measure the probability of error in the reading of tags in presence of not electromagnetically transparent materials.

We saw that the impact on the transmission of metallic materials and polar liquids is obviously extremely harmful (reduction of $\simeq 60\%$ in the first case and $\simeq 30\%$ in the second) when the distance between the tag and these materials is less than 10 cm. In contrast, with transparent materials (e.g., paper materials) the system works with excellent performances ($\simeq 100\%$). It has also been proved that the presence of two or more tags in the same area compromises the reading only when the tags are perfectly overlapped and their distance is lower than 4 cm.

In particular the tests have been carried out positioning the tags on the following items and moving them across the gate in the middle of the crossing section (the worst case):

(i) empty paper packages;

(ii) plastic bottles filled with water;

(iii) aluminium cans;

(iv) human body.

For what concerns non interfering materials (paper), the reading rate was around 100%. In particular

(i) with 5 tags put randomly inside a paper box, performing 20 crossings of the gate the rate was 5/5 for all the crossings;

(ii) with 8 tags put randomly, on 20 crossing we had the following rates: 8/8 in 18 crossings and 7/8 in 2 crossings;

(iii) with 8 tags, 5 of which oriented in the position of worst coupling, on 20 crossings we had the following rates: 6/8 in 2 cases, 7/8 in 12 cases and 8/8 in 6 cases.

In the case of plastic bottles two tests were undertaken.

(i) 20 crossings were made with three bottles equipped with a transponder, put randomly inside a paper box: in this case the reading rate was always 3/3.

(ii) Positioning the three bottles with the transponders in position of worst coupling the rate decreased at 2/3 in all the 20 crossings.

In the case of metallic materials is evident that no reading is possible when the tag is in contact with metal. In particular, in the case of aluminum cans the transponder was identified with a 100% rate only when the distance from the can is higher than 10 cm. Anyway, with a distance from 5 to 10 cm the results were still satisfying, with a rate around 60%.

A final test was carried out to analyze the interaction with the human body. No problems (100% successful readings) were noticed when the transponder was positioned inside a pocket of a man crossing the gate.

6.4. Law Requirements. Every time that a technological system is studied to be utilized in public environments, it has to be compliant with all the regulations concerning the safety of the final users. In the case of RFID systems European regulation is developed on two different levels:

(i) CEPT recommendations, whose decisions are not binding for the member countries;

(ii) European Commission directives, whose decisions are binding for the EU member countries and its lack of actuation is subject to the infraction procedure with the following economic sanctions.

In general these organizations set the operative band or frequency, the emitting power and the maximum time of communication between tags and readers. For what concerns the RF power, this term can generate confusion because there are some different methods of coupling between transponder and reader, depending on the operative frequency.

For frequencies up to 13.56 MHz we have inductive coupling (the system operates in close field conditions) and we can speak of maximum field strength (H-field), expressed in dBμA/m. The CEPT ERC/REC 70-03 recommendation determines the technical requirements for the use of Short Range Devices (SRD) for the CEPT countries [12].

The recommendation is divided in 13 annexes: number 9 and 11 are the ones concerning the RFID technology. Annex 9 covers the bands and regulates the parameters for the inductive applications, including, for example, animal identification, alarm systems, access control, and items tracking.

Key points of CEPT ERC/REC 70-03 a.9 are

(1) frequency: 13.553–13.567 MHz for RFID and EAS (Electronic Article Surveillance) only;

(2) intensity of magnetic field: 60 dBμA/m at 10 m;

(3) duty cycle: no Restriction;

(4) channel spacing: no spacing.

Annex 11 does not concern instead our case because it specifies the limitations for the other three RFID frequency bands. In conclusion, we have to comply with annex 9, in particular with the second point concerning the maximum magnetic field strength.

6.5. The Project and the Laws. The first step towards the check of the requirements has been made once again with the simulations: we saw that the maximum value of magnetic field strength at 10 m of distance is $9.421 \cdot 10^{-4}$ A/m. The requirements recommend a 60 dBμA/m magnetic field strength at 10 m distance. $60 = 20 \lg_{10} x \Rightarrow x = 10^3$ so this value can be expressed in linear measurement as $10^3 \, \mu$A/m = 10^{-3} A/m: therefore the values of the simulations are under this threshold.

The second phase of the requirements check has been realized directly in laboratory on the final structure: the system has been powered with 8 W and the magnetic field has been measured with a probe linked to a spectrum analyzer. The obtained values have confirmed the positive results of the simulations.

7. Conclusions

In this paper we have shown how to realize an RFID gate detecting tags in every orientation across a 2 m wide and 2.15 m high section. This solution has been achieved through numerical simulations of the structure, through which the ideal geometry of the system and the adapted configuration of the matching circuit as been identified.

Following the simulations, a prototype of the structure has been realized and tested in laboratory: while some parameters (mainly for what concerns the matching circuit) required some adjustments, the results of the simulations were substantially confirmed. Tests concerning the performances of the system have involved the reading timing, the interaction with critical materials, the reading of overlapped transponders, and the total number of transponders readable simultaneously. All these tests have provided positive results, encouraging the prosecution of the research activities.

Additional work is going on in order to realize a structure to be adapted in a better way to the real destination environments. In particular future work is mainly focused on the realization of a system with reduced dimensions, in order to employ it in the highest number of possible different scenarios.

References

[1] K. Finkenzeller, *RFID Handbook: Fundamentals and Applications in Contactless Smart Cards, Radio Frequency Identification and Near-Field Communication*, John Wiley and Sons, 3rd edition, 2010.

[2] D. E. Brown, *RFID Implementation*, McGraw-Hill Professional, 2007.

[3] A. Goulbourne, "HF antenna design notes, technical application report," Tech. Rep. 11-08-26-003, Texas Instruments, Radio Frequency Identification Systems, 2003.

[4] C. A. Balanis, *Antenna Theory. Analysis and Design*, Harper & Row, 1982.

[5] H. Lehpamer, *RFID Design Principles.*, Artech House, Norwood, Mass, USA, 2008.

[6] S. Kawdungta, C. Phongcharoenpanich, and D. Torrungrueng, "Design of flat spiral rectangular loop gate antenna for HF-RFID systems," in *Proceedings of the Asia Pacific Microwave Conference (APMC '08)*, Hong Kong, December 2008.

[7] N. C. Karmakar, *Handbook of Smart Antennas for RFID Systems*, John Wiley and Sons, 2010.

[8] J. M. Rathod and Y. P. Kosta, "Low cost development of RFID antenna," in *Proceedings of the Asia Pacific Microwave Conference (APMC '09)*, pp. 1060–1063, Singapore, December 2009.

[9] C. Reinhold, P. Scholz, W. John, and U. Hilleringman, "Efficient antenna design of inductive coupled RFID-systems with high power demand," *Journal of Communications*, vol. 2, no. 6, 2007.

[10] B. Jiang, J. R. Smith, M. Philipose, S. Roy, K. Sundara-Rajan, and A. V. Mamishev, "Energy scavenging for inductively coupled passive RFID systems," in *Proceedings of the IEEE Instrumentation and Measurement Technology Conference*, vol. 10, pp. 984–989, Ontario, Canada, May 2005.

[11] C. M. Zierhofer and E. S. Hochmair, "Geometric approach for coupling enhancement of magnetically coupled coils," *IEEE Transactions on Biomedical Engineering*, vol. 43, no. 7, pp. 708–714, 1996.

[12] *European Standard (Telecommunications series)*. ETSI EN 300-330, *Part 1: technical characteristic and test methods*, 1999.

17

A Transmission Power Self-Optimization Technique for Wireless Sensor Networks

F. Lavratti,[1] **A. Ceratti,**[1] **D. Prestes,**[1] **A. R. Pinto,**[2] **L. Bolzani,**[1] **F. Vargas,**[1] **C. Montez,**[3] **F. Hernandez,**[4] **E. Gatti,**[5] **and C. Silva**[6]

[1] *Signals & Systems for Computing Group (SiSC), Catholic University of Rio Grande do Sul (PUCRS), 90619-900 Porto Alegre, RS, Brazil*
[2] *DCCE, Universidade Estadual Paulista (UNESP), 15054-000 São José do Rio Preto, SP, Brazil*
[3] *PGEAS, Universidade Federal de Santa Catarina (UFSC), 88040-900 Florianópolis, SC, Brazil*
[4] *Unidad Reguladora de Servicios de Comunicaciones (URSEC), Universidad ORT, 11300 Montevideo, Uruguay*
[5] *Instituto Nacional de Tecnologia Industrial (INTI), C1001AAF Buenos Aires, Argentina*
[6] *Pontificia Universidad Católica del Perú (PUCP), Lima 32, Peru*

Correspondence should be addressed to L. Bolzani, leticia@poehls.com

Academic Editor: F. Vasques

Wireless sensor networks (WSNs) are generally used to monitor hazardous events in inaccessible areas. Thus, on one hand, it is preferable to assure the adoption of the minimum transmission power in order to extend as much as possible the WSNs lifetime. On the other hand, it is crucial to guarantee that the transmitted data is correctly received by the other nodes. Thus, trading off power optimization and reliability insurance has become one of the most important concerns when dealing with modern systems based on WSN. In this context, we present a transmission power self-optimization (TPSO) technique for WSNs. The TPSO technique consists of an algorithm able to guarantee the connectivity as well as an equally high quality of service (QoS), concentrating on the WSNs efficiency (Ef), while optimizing the transmission power necessary for data communication. Thus, the main idea behind the proposed approach is to trade off WSNs Ef against energy consumption in an environment with inherent noise. Experimental results with different types of noise and electromagnetic interference (EMI) have been explored in order to demonstrate the effectiveness of the TPSO technique.

1. Introduction

Recent advancements in wireless communication and electronic technology have made possible the development of small, low-cost, low-power, and multifunctional sensor nodes [1, 2]. Wireless sensor networks (WSNs) are composed of communication nodes, which contain sensing, data processing, and communication components as well as power supply, typically a battery. In more detail, these nodes are able to collect different types of data and to communicate with each other. Nowadays, WSNs have been increasingly deployed for both civil and military applications which typically work in harsh environments. Considering sensor nodes, resources like processor, memory, and battery are generally restricted, since their replacement is considered

prohibitive due to the hazardous and inaccessible places where they are supposed to operate [3]. In this scenario, where nodes are likely to operate on limited battery life, power conservation can be considered one of the most important issues [4]. Transmitting at unnecessary high power not only reduces the lifetime of the WSNs nodes but also introduces excessive interference. Thus, transmitting at the lowest possible power while preserving the network connectivity and reliability has become crucial points related to WSNs [4, 5]. In this paper, Ef is defined as the number of received messages by the master node (MN) in relation to the estimated number of sent messages by the slave nodes (SNs).

It is important to point out that communication reliability in WSNs can be degraded by different interference sources, such as WLAN, Bluetooth, or any other device that shares the 2.4 GHz bandwidth. In addition to this bandwidth, the always increasing population of AM/FM radio devices is also responsible for increasing the environment noise hostility [6]. This evokes some concerns about the robustness of sensor network communications and can limit the wide adoption of WSN technology by the industry.

In this paper, we present a transmission power self-optimization (TPSO) technique able to adjust individually the transmission power of each sensor node that composes the WSN, in order to guarantee a predefined efficiency (Ef) for the network [7, 8]. The TPSO technique aims at guaranteeing the lowest possible transmission power while maintaining the connectivity of the WSN as well as the reliability of the transmitted data. Thus, the main idea behind the self-optimization algorithm is to assure the trade-off between WSNs Ef and data transmission energy consumption. The proposed approach trades off the longest WSNs lifetime against the highest possible efficiency, and vice versa. To do so, this work presents a complete evaluation of the TPSO technique's effectiveness in different scenarios that exploit three types of noise considered inherent to the environment: (1) it exploits the distance variation between network nodes, (2) it exploits conducted EMI noise affecting the WSN, and (3) it exploits radiated EMI noise affecting the WSN. The effectiveness of the proposed technique has been evaluated using a suitable developed case study composed of eight SNs that communicate with one MN in a star-topology network. The main goals of this paper are.

(1) To provide experimental results showing the impact of the previously mentioned sources of noise on the WSNs communication. In more detail, to demonstrate that the distance variation between the nodes composing the WSN as well as the conducted and irradiated EMI do degrade the WSNs Ef. Consequently, the presence of any of these types of noise or any combination of them increases the necessity to communicate using a higher transmission power level in order to maintain the connectivity of the WSN as well as the WSNs Ef under expected values.

(2) To demonstrate the effectiveness of the TPSO technique, by showing that it can guarantee the targeted WSNs Ef in a time-variant noise environment, while decreasing the energy necessary for data transmission between nodes.

The obtained results during the experiments quantified the impact of the previously mentioned interference sources in WSNs and demonstrate the effectiveness of the proposed solution. In this sense, the experimental results show that the TPSO technique significantly reduces the energy consumption with respect to the data transmission, while maintaining the targeted WSNs Ef.

This paper has been organized as follows. Section 2 summarizes the background related to WSN concerns. Section 3 presents the TPSO technique, detailing the communication model as well as the self-optimization algorithm. Section 4 presents the case study adopted for experiments. This section also details the three different scenarios used for noise

injection on the WSN and summarizes the obtained results. Finally, Section 5 draws the conclusions.

2. Background

Nowadays, the adoption of WSNs in several civil and military scenarios has become a highly viable solution when aiming at the transmission of collected data in inaccessible places. However, the sensor nodes are usually powered by battery and consequently its preservation in order to increase the WSNs lifetime is considered crucial. Thus, the fact that WSNs are applied in locations where the access is difficult and replacing the battery would often not be feasible defines the goal of long battery life as essential to such networks [3]. Moreover, the reliability of the data collected, processed, and delivered has to be assured. As a result, high reliability and low energy consumption have become important issues when dealing with WSNs. In this context, several techniques have been proposed in order to deal with the previously mentioned concerns.

Concerning reliability, WSNs are required to collect, process, and deliver information interacting with the environment where they are placed. Thus, due to uncontrolled environment inherent noise, it does not surprise that WSNs frequently show low connectivity levels demonstrating poor quality of service (QoS) [9]. One strategy to cope with the QoS requirements is to adopt data fusion techniques. In dense networks, they are used in order to increase the sensor's reading dependability to achieve a more accurate estimation of the environment and finally to assure a longer network lifetime [3]. In these approaches, sensed scalars are sent to master nodes (MNs) which themselves fuse the data with the objective to extract useful information from a set of readings.

Another factor that interferes with the QoS is the increasing number of nodes that compose WSNs. This fact leads to a high complexity of the systems and the impossibility of human administration. Facing these problems, the development of computing systems that do not need human intervention to operate correctly has emerged. Thus, systems with so-called self-management characteristics, computer systems that are able to manage themselves based on high-level objectives given by the administrators before the beginning of the WSNs operation have been developed to cope with the increasing complexity [10]. The approach described in this work is considered to regulate the transmission power level and, therefore, manage a part of the administration itself.

Due to the fact that all sensor nodes composing the network are battery powered, the above, mentioned reliability concerns are desired to be developed with strategies that also aim at the minimization of the transmission power. In other words, power conservation strategies can help to prolong the lifetime of the sensor nodes and consequently of the WSN as a whole. Higher transmission power enhances the connectivity among the entire network and improves its capacity, but leads to faster exhaustion of the batteries. Indeed, transmitting at unnecessary high power not only reduces the lifetime of the WSN but also introduces excessive interference. It is in the network designer's best interest to have each node transmit at the lowest possible power while preserving network connectivity. It is a desirable characteristic, but it is difficult to modify the transmission power after the system's deployment. However, transmitting at low transmission power can compromise the connectivity and consequently the reliability of the transmitted data. As a result, the development of such systems has to deal with a trade-off between the WSNs lifetime and its reliability. In other words, a high transmission power would guarantee a high reliable system but lead to shorter system lifetime. A low transmission power is able to make the component's battery last for a longer period, but the system may not work properly or without a satisfying reliability.

Finally, the reliability and the energy consumption represent decisive factors for the choice of the transmission power of the WSN. Indeed, different factors can affect the definition of the optimal transmission power. The number and the distances between the sensor nodes deployed can interfere drastically in the obtained reliability of the network. In more detail, an increased density of the network deployed requires a lower transmission power.

Thus, as a result of the previously mentioned concerns, choosing the optimal transmission power has become an important issue for WSNs. In [4], a suitable criterion for a optimal transmission power has been introduced. One of the goals of forming a network is to have connectivity, in other words, each node should be able to communicate with the other ones. The connectivity level of the ad hoc wireless network depends on the transmission power of the nodes. If the transmission power is too small, the network might be disconnected. However, transmitting at excessively high power is inefficient due to mutual interferences in the shared radio channel and the decreased battery lifetime. Thus, it is intuitively clear that the optimal transmission power is the minimum power sufficient to guarantee the network's connectivity. Ideally, the transmission power of a node should be adjusted on a link-by-link basis to achieve the maximum possible power savings [4]. Nonetheless, due to the absence of a central controller in a pure ad hoc network with flat architecture, performing power control on a link-by-link basis is a complicated task. A more feasible solution for the implementation of the WSN is to have all the nodes use the same transmission power.

To conclude, it is important to highlight that none of the above-mentioned approaches is able to adjust the transmission power level of the operating WSN. By choosing the transmission power level before inserting the nodes into an unpredictable environment, these techniques are not able to guarantee the trade-off between QoS and battery life.

3. The Proposed Technique

The transmission power self-optimization (TPSO) technique basically deals with the trade-off between WSNs Ef and energy consumption. In what follows, we will describe the communication model adopted and the self-optimization algorithm.

((•))
![Master node icon] Master node

((•))
![Slave node icon] Slave node

FIGURE 1: WSN model.

3.1. *Communication Model.* The adopted model considers one master node (MN), also called base station, and n Slave nodes (SNs) according to Figure 1. In more detail, the data collected by the SNs is sent to the MN that performs data fusion. All the SNs reach the master using just one hop.

In this work, the concept of session monitoring is adopted. A session S is composed of t session time (ST) rounds with the length R. Therefore, S is composed of $ST_0, ST_1, ST_2, \ldots, ST_{(t-1)}$. The round concept is used to synchronize nodes, and it also represents the periodicity of the data fusion task [3].

Regarding the MN, it performs the data fusion considering only the messages that arrived on time. In this particular work, the MN only fuses data that arrived within the same session. Thus, the number of required messages, the round time, (RT) and the session time (ST) parameters are sent by the MN at the beginning of each session, forming the so-called checkpoint [3]. Moreover, the MN computes the performance metrics during the checkpoint round in order to adjust the WSN.

In the communication model adopted in this work, we considered the efficiency (Ef) metric. In more detail, Ef is measured considering the number of received messages by the MN before finishing the session in execution in relation to the estimated number of sent messages by the SNs. Thus, Ef is calculated according to the following equation:

$$Ef = \frac{\sum_{i=1}^{N} Mr_i}{E_{Ms}}, \tag{1}$$

where N is the number of rounds, Mr is the number of received messages, and E_{Ms} is the estimative of the sent messages by the SNs. In more detail, E_{Ms} is given by (2) where K represents the number of required messages by the MN and De is the SN's density in the considered WSN. Thus, this

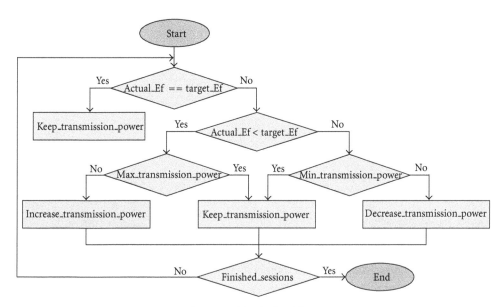

FIGURE 2: TPSO algorithm.

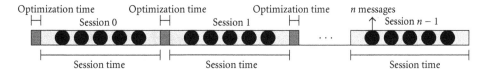

FIGURE 3: Conceptual idea of the proposed technique.

metric indicates how many messages are used during data fusion task:

$$E_{Ms} = K \times De \times N. \qquad (2)$$

3.2. The Transmission Power Self-Optimization Technique. The TPSO technique is based on a simple and decentralized algorithm that runs on the application layer of the WSN [7, 8]. The main idea behind the TPSO technique is to adjust the transmission power taking into consideration the entire WSNs *Ef*. To do so, the TPSO technique uses the *Ef* associated to each SN to compute the WSNs *Ef*. In more detail, the MN is responsible to compute the WSNs *Ef* as well as the *Ef* associated to each SN and to send the specific *Ef* to each SN. Finally, the SNs are in charge of adjusting their own transmission power levels based on their *Ef* by performing the TPSO algorithm. Figure 2 depicts the block diagram of the self-optimization algorithm.

Observing the block diagram shown in Figure 2, it is possible to note that the transmission power is adjusted by comparing the *actual_Ef*, computed at the end of each session, and the *target_Ef*, set at the beginning of the communication. In more detail, the *actual_Ef* is computed using the data collected during the ST, that is, while the set of messages that composes the considered session are sent. Regarding the *target_Ef*, it is important to note that the value set at the beginning of the communication has a tolerance of 5%, which means setting a *target_Ef* of 90%, this value oscillates from 85% to 95%. Moreover, it is important to highlight

that the sensor nodes have a predefined minimum and maximum transmission power, which cannot be exchanged or overwritten by the algorithm. Thus, the TPSO technique increases or decreases the transmission power step-by-step passing through all the transmission power levels available for each node. Finally, the self-optimization algorithm is performed by the SNs that compose the WSN and it can be adopted in WSNs that do not provide any type of transmission power optimization.

Figure 3 shows the conceptual idea of the TPSO technique related to the temporal execution of the self-optimization algorithm. Observing Figure 3, it is possible to see between two consecutive sessions that the adjustment of the transmission power is performed during the so-called *optimization time*. In detail, the MN computes the *Ef* associated to each SN during the *optimization time* and sends these values to them. The algorithm running on the SN then adjusts the transmission power level according to the *actual_Ef* when it is necessary.

4. Experimental Results

This section evaluates the effectiveness of the TPSO technique using different types of interference mechanisms. The experiments have been performed considering three different scenarios divided as follows: *Scenario 1* evaluates the impact of the distance variation between the MN and SNs on the communication efficiency. *Scenario 2* exploits the use

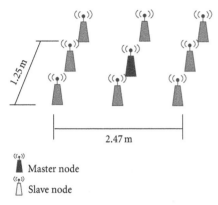

FIGURE 4: Case study adopted.

TABLE 1: Transmission power levels.

Level	XBee PRO [dBm]
0	10
1	12
2	14
3	16
4	18

FIGURE 5: PCB of the WSNs nodes.

of conducted EMI to generate power supply disturbances (PSDs) able to degrade the WSNs communication. Finally, *Scenario 3* uses irradiated EMI based on AM/FM or WiFi noise to affect the WSN. Thus, the main goals of these experiments have been twofold: (1) to demonstrate the impact of the different types of interference on the WSNs *Ef* and (2) to demonstrate the effectiveness of the TPSO technique in order to maintain the *target_Ef* when different types of interferences affect the WSN.

4.1. Case Study. In order to demonstrate the TPSO technique's effectiveness with respect to the three scenarios mentioned above, we developed a case study composed of nine sensor nodes as shown in Figure 4.

Observing Figure 4, it is possible to see that the case study adopted is composed of one master node (MN) and eight slave nodes (SNs) performing the following tasks.

(i) *Master node (MN)*: it starts the communication with the SNs and performs the fusion of the received data. It is also in charge of computing the *Ef* of each SN and sending them the parameters necessary to perform the transmission power optimization.

(ii) *Slave node (SN)*: it sends data messages to the MN and executes the TPSO algorithm in order to optimize the transmission power based on the parameters sent by the MN.

It is important to point out that both MN and SNs are XBee PRO modules, which use the IEEE 802.15.4 networking protocol for fast point-to-multipoint or peer-to-peer networking [11]. The IEEE 802.15.4 is a standard that specifies the lower two layers of the wireless communication protocol: (1) the physical layer (PHY) and (2) the media access control (MAC). Indeed, the IEEE 802.15.4 supports the unique needs of low-cost, low-power, and low-rate WSN. The PHY layer can operate with 250 Kbps of maximum transmission rate. Regarding the MAC, it supports two types of operating modes: (1) *beaconless mode,* a nonslotted carrier sense multiple access collision avoidance (CSMA/CA) and (2) *beacon mode*, where beacons are sent periodically by a PAN coordinator [12]. In the latter case, nodes are synchronized by a superframe structure. Finally, the XBee PRO modules can be

configured to operate using five different transmission power levels that range from 0 to 4. Table 1 summarizes the transmission power levels of the XBee PRO module and their respective communication power in dBm. Observing this table, it is possible to see that the minimum transmission power level corresponds to 10 dBm and the maximum to 18 dBm.

Figure 5 shows the printed circuit board (PCB) of a wireless sensor (MN or SN). This board was designed by the Computing Signals and Systems Group (SiSC) of the Catholic University (PUCRS) and was used during all the experiments. It is basically built around two major components: the XBee PRO module and the ARM 7 microprocessor, which runs the self-optimization algorithm.

4.2. Scenario 1. Scenario 1 aims to analyze the impact of distance variation between SNs and the MN on the WSNs *Ef* as well as to demonstrate the effectiveness of the proposed approach in order to maintain a *target_Ef* by automatically increasing the transmission power of SNs when necessary. Thus, first of all, the case study described previously has been analyzed in an environment exposed to real noise where one of the SNs has been moved from an initial position with respect to the MN to a different final position further away from the MN. In more detail, the distance between one of the SNs and the MN has been increased step-by-step and the behavior of the WSN has been analyzed in terms of *Ef* and energy consumption of the WSN. In this scenario, an "experiment" was defined as a set of 72 sessions, each

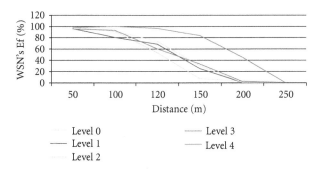

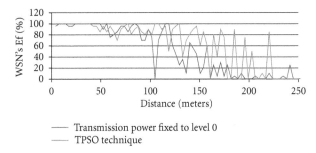

FIGURE 6: *Scenario 1*. Distance impact on WSNs *Ef* and energy consumption considering the five different transmission power levels of the XBee PRO module.

FIGURE 8: *Scenario 1*. Comparison between the WSNs *Ef* obtained using transmission power level fixed to 0 and the one associated to the TPSO algorithm.

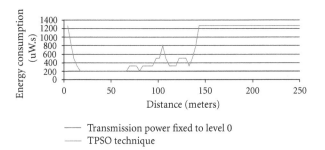

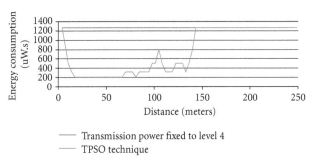

FIGURE 7: *Scenario 1*. Comparison of energy consumption obtained using transmission power level fixed to 0 and the TPSO algorithm.

FIGURE 9: *Scenario 1*. Comparison of energy consumption obtained using transmission power level fixed to 4 and the TPSO algorithm.

one composed of 20 messages. The *session time* has been configured to be of 10 s and the *optimization time* to be 0.5s.

Figure 6 depicts results for one SN moving far away from the MN considering six steps of the distance variation. In this sense, Figure 6 analyzes the WSNs *Ef* considering distances of 50, 100, 120, 150, 200, and 250 meters with respect to the original position of the SN. For each previously mentioned distance, we considered the five different transmission power levels for the XBee PRO module ranging from 0 to 4.

Observing Figure 6, we can see that the WSNs *Ef* decreases when the distance between the MN and the SN increases demonstrating the negative impact of the increasing distance on the WSNs *Ef*.

For the following graphs, we considered *Scenario 1* as described earlier. In more detail, the distances assumed values from 0 to 250 meters, the *target_Ef* was set to 90% and the transmission power level was fixed to 0 or to 4. It is important to highlight that setting *target_Ef* to 90% means that a tolerance of 5% is allowed. Figures 7 and 8 depict the results obtained by setting the transmission power level to 0. Figure 7 compares the energy consumed as a function of distance comparing the fixed 0-level transmission power with the one associated to the TPSO technique. Figure 8 compares the WSNs *Ef* while using a fixed 0-level transmission power and while adopting the TPSO algorithm.

The average *Ef* of the WSN using the 0-level fixed transmission power was measured to be 49.59%, while using the TPSO algorithm such value increased to 62.81%. This corresponds to an increase of 13.21%. At the same time,

the power consumption of the proposed technique is about 285% higher than the power consumed by the WSN to transmit at fixed 0-level. Therefore, observing Figures 7 and 8, one can conclude that the TPSO achieves a higher *Ef* consuming more power. For applications where efficiency is a key-requirement and must be guaranteed even consuming more energy, the proposed TPSO technique is a good alternative.

It should also be observed that neither of the two configurations achieved the aimed efficiency level of 90%. This is attributed to the fact that when the distance between the MN and the SN increased beyond 150 meters, there was almost no connectivity between them. Therefore, even transmitting at the highest power level (4), the TPSO is not able to compensate the impact of the distance (even though the communication efficiency is higher with TPSO technique than without it). This is a typical case of transmission power saturation. Thus, the high energy consumption increase of the WSN with the TPSO technique can be attributed to the fact that the maximum transmission power is maintained until the end of the experiment, even if the WSNs *Ef* could not be further improved due to the high distance between MN and SN.

Figures 9 and 10 are similar to Figures 7 and 8, except for the fact that instead of using the lowest transmission level (0), Figures 9 and 10 depict results for the highest transmission level (4). Figure 9 compares the energy consumption associated to WSN using the proposed technique and WSN using the transmission power fixed to level (4). Figure 10

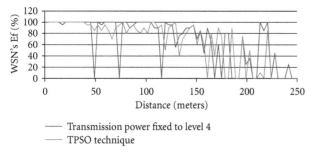

FIGURE 10: *Scenario 1*. Comparison of WSNs *Ef* obtained using transmission power level fixed to 4 and the TPSO algorithm.

demonstrates the WSNs *Ef* while adopting the proposed algorithm and while using the fixed transmission power level.

The results depicted in Figures 9 and 10 clearly demonstrate the efficiency of the TPSO technique. When the distance between the SN and MN increases, it is possible to observe that the energy consumption increases in order to maintain the target WSNs *Ef*. It is worth noting that the energy consumption is associated with the transmission power level adopted during the communication between the MN and SNs. In more detail, the WSNs *Ef* with the fixed transmission power level 4 is 65.68% whereas the TPSO yields 62.81%, or of 2.87% less than the one using the maximum transmission power level. In addition, it should be noted that the energy consumption of the proposed approach is 38.87% lower when compared to the fixed transmission power level 4. Thus, one can conclude that the TPSO technique saves more than a third in energy while loosing less than 3% of efficiency to communicate.

4.3. Scenario 2. Scenario 2 exploits the use of power supply disturbances (PSD) in order to generate conducted EMI on the WSN. During this phase, we used suitable developed equipment able to generate PSD according to the IEC 61000-4-29 standard [13]. This IEC standard defines rules for immunity testing to voltage dips, short interruptions, and voltage variations on d.c. input power port of integrated circuits and systems. Due to the large possible range, the voltage dips' percentage that can be assumed during the experiments, an initial experiment has been performed in order to find the maximum variation supported by the WSN nodes. The results obtained showed that the WSN nodes are able to maintain the connectivity between MN and SN up to the limit of 16% of voltage dip with respect to nominal *Vdd* of 3.3 V. During the experiments, the PSD's frequency has been set to 500 Hz.

Finally, it is important to point out that an experiment is defined as a set of 50 sessions, each one composed of the same 10 messages. These 10 messages are sent during each session by the SNs to the MN. Indeed, the *session time* has been configured to be of 10 s and the *optimization time* to be of 0.5 s. Figure 11 depicts the equipment used to generate noise in the form of voltage dips at the *Vdd* input pins of the nodes composing the WSN. This waveform was captured with an oscilloscope. It is important to underline that no noise was

FIGURE 11: *Scenario 2*. (a) IEC 61000-4-29 compliant noise injected at the *Vdd* input port of the WSN nodes; (b) Noise generator developed by the SiSC-PUCRS Group [14].

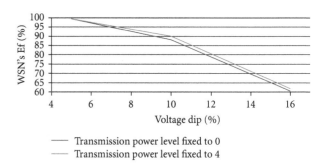

FIGURE 12: *Scenario 2*. Conducted EMI impact on WSNs *Ef* and energy consumption considering the five different transmission power levels of the Xbee PRO module.

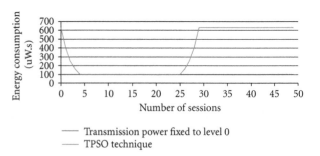

FIGURE 13: *Scenario 2*. Comparison of energy consumption considering the transmission power fixed at level 0 and the WSN with the TPSO technique.

injected during the first 25 sessions, whereas voltage dips have been injected during the execution of the sessions 25 to 49.

Figure 12 shows the impact of the PSD on the WSNs *Ef*. Observing this figure, it is possible to conclude that increasing the percentage of voltage dip decreases significantly the WSNs *Ef*.

The results obtained with respect to PSD in *Scenario 2* have been summarized in Figures 13–16. Figure 13 compares the energy consumption and Figure 14 compares the *Ef* of

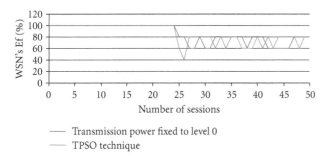

FIGURE 14: *Scenario 2*. Comparison of WSNs *Ef* considering the transmission power fixed at level 0 and the WSN with the TPSO technique.

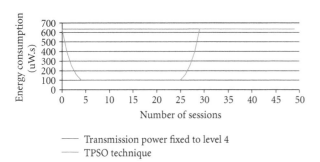

FIGURE 15: *Scenario 2*. Comparison of energy consumption considering the transmission power fixed at level 4 and the WSN with the TPSO technique.

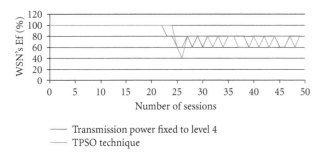

FIGURE 16: *Scenario 2*. Comparison of WSNs *Ef* considering the transmission power fixed at level 4 and the WSN with the TPSO technique.

WSNs with and without the TPSO technique. The WSN without the proposed self-optimization algorithm has been set to ensure communication between nodes using the fixed minimum transmission power level, level 0 in Table 1, and the WSN with TPSO assumed the target *Ef* = 90%. Observing these figures, it is possible to conclude that the average WSNs *Ef* guaranteed by the WSN with and without the TPSO technique was of 85% and 84%, respectively. Note that the energy consumed by the WSN with the TPSO technique was higher than the one consumed by the WSN communicating at the minimum transmission power level. This can be justified by the fact that the WSN with the proposed approach increases the transmission power level in order to guarantee the *target_Ef* of 90%. It can also be observed in Figure 14 that with voltage dips set to maximum allowed value of 16%, the noise is so strong that a saturation

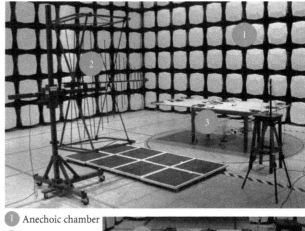

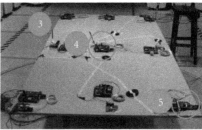

1 Anechoic chamber
2 Antenna
3 WSN
4 Master node (MN)
5 Slave node (SN)

FIGURE 17: EMI environment adopted.

of the transmission power can be observed from session 28 onwards. Here even the transmission power level set to its maximum is not able to raise the WSNs *Ef* above a level of about 70%.

Now looking at Figure 15, the graph is showing the comparison of the energy consumption of a WSN with the transmission power level fixed to the maximum value and an WSN with the proposed technique applied. The graph of Figure 16 shows the comparison of the same two WSN in respect to their *Ef*. In media, the *Ef* of the maximum transmission level WSN is of 86% and the WSN using the proposed approach is reaching 85.5%. Thus, we can conclude that the TPSO technique is practically maintaining the same reliability, while it is saving more than 55% of energy consumption.

4.4. Scenario 3. The main goal of the experiments performed in *Scenario 3* was to demonstrate the impact of irradiated EMI on the WSNs *Ef*. The experiments have been performed using an anechoic chamber and an antenna which irradiates noise over the WSN. Figure 17 depicts the EMI environment adopted where it is possible to see the antenna and the WSN placed on the table inside the anechoic chamber according to the case study's diagram presented in Figure 4. In more detail, the WSN has been exposed to two different types of irradiated EMI. The first type concerns AM/FM noise that has been irradiated over the WSN according to the following characteristics:

(i) carrier frequency of 2.4093 GHz (channel 11 of 802.15.4),

(ii) AM/FM simultaneous modulation,

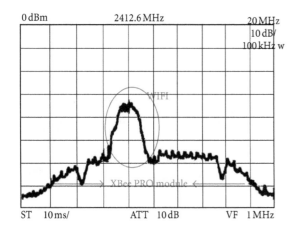

FIGURE 18: Frequency spectrum.

(iii) signal bandwidth: 40 kHz,

(iv) AM modulated signal frequency: 20 kHz,

(v) power generator from −20 dBm to −10 dBm.

The second type of noise is WiFi signal irradiated over the WSN with a power level of +14 dBm. The noise was transmitted through channel 1 of the WiFi frequency spectrum. Figure 18 depicts the frequency spectrum used by the XBee PRO module to communicate and the one of WiFi noise. Observing this figure, it is possible to see the superposition of the two spectrums.

In the following, experiments aiming to evaluate the TPSO technique's efficiency in the presence of noise have been performed. It is worth noting that noise was applied only during the second half of the 50 sessions that compose an experiment. In more detail, during the sessions numbered 0 to 24 the noise generator was switched off, and during the sessions numbered 25 to 49 the noise generator was switched on and applied different levels of AM/FM noise as well as WiFi.

5. Experiments Using AM/FM Noise

Figure 19 shows the impact of the AM/FM noise of −10d BM on the WSNs *Ef*. In more detail, each point in the graph represents a specific XBee PRO module transmission power level from 0 to 4 during the 50 sessions (axis *x*) against the WSNs average *Ef* (axis *y*). For instance, when the XBee PRO modules are transmitting with level 0 (10 dBm), the whole WSN consumed 6.33 mW.s, which resulted in a WSN efficiency of 36.80% without EMI. Similarly, the efficiency rises to 93.96% for the WSN operating in a noise-free environment.

The WSNs average *Ef* mentioned above has been calculated as arithmetic average of the values of the WSNs *Ef* during the 50 performed sessions. Regarding the WSNs energy consumption value, it has been obtained throughout the sum of the energy consumed during the 50 sessions. Thus, considering the transmission power level 0, it is possible to see that the noise drastically affects the WSNs *Ef*, since the average has been reduced from about 93.96% to 36.8% when

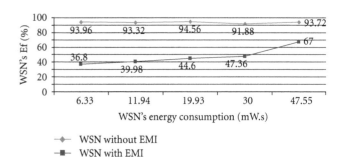

FIGURE 19: *Scenario 3*. EMI influence on WSNs *Ef* applying AM/FM noise of −10 dBm.

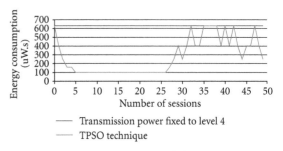

FIGURE 20: *Scenario 3*. Comparison of the energy consumption yielded by the TPSO technique with respect to WSN operating with transmission power fixed to level 4.

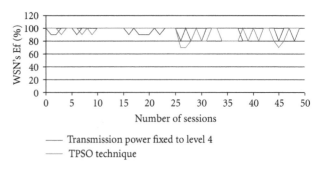

FIGURE 21: *Scenario 3*. Comparison of the WSNs *Ef* of the TPSO technique with respect to WSN operating with the transmission power fixed to level 4.

exposed to EMI. Indeed, we can observe that the reduction of the WSNs *Ef* is smaller when the WSN is configured to transmit at the transmission power level 4 (18 dBm, which represents the maximum transmission power level that the WSN can adopt). In this case, the reduction of the WSNs *Ef* has been from 93.72% to 67.00%.

In order to better illustrate the effectiveness of the proposed self-optimization algorithm, Figures 20 and 21 depict the WSNs *Ef* and the WSNs total energy consumption considering the following characteristics: (1) the WSN has been set to communicate the transmission power level fixed to 4 and (2) the WSN adopting the TPSO algorithm has been configured to target 90% of WSNs *Ef*. In this case, the effectiveness of the TPSO technique is clearly visible since the self-optimization algorithm is able to guarantee

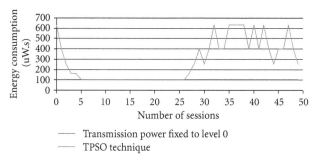

FIGURE 22: *Scenario 3*. Comparison of the energy consumption of the TPSO technique with respect to WSN operating with the transmission power fixed to level 0.

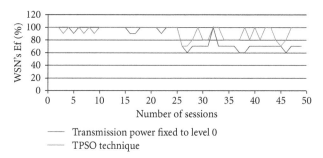

FIGURE 23: *Scenario 3*. Comparison of the WSNs *Ef* of the TPSO technique with respect to WSN operating with the transmission power fixed to level 0.

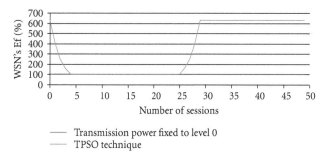

FIGURE 24: *Scenario 3*. Comparison of the energy consumption of the TPSO technique with respect to WSN operating with the transmission power fixed to level 0.

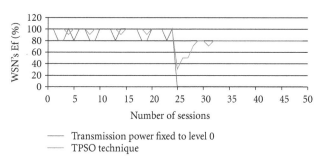

FIGURE 25: *Scenario 3*. Comparison between the WSNs *Ef* obtained using transmission power level fixed to 0 and the TPSO algorithm.

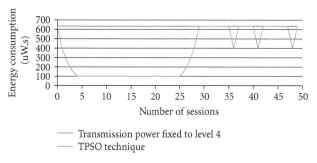

FIGURE 26: *Scenario 3*. Comparison of the energy consumption of the TPSO technique with respect to WSN operating with the transmission power fixed to level 0.

the WSN' *Ef* as defined by the *target_Ef* (90%) while reducing the energy consumption by 55.6%. In other words, the TPSO algorithm increases the transmission power level in order to compensate for the decrease of the WSNs *Ef* as response to the high AM/FM noise applied on the system (starting from session 25), so that to assure the *target_Ef*. In this scenario, the WSN' *Ef* for transmission power level 4 is 94.6% (with an average energy consumption per session equal to 631 uW.s), whereas for the TPSO technique, the WSN' *Ef* rendered 93.2% (with an average consumption of 279.7 uW.s).

Figures 22 and 23 show that the self-optimization algorithm increases transmission power level (starting from session 25) in order to guarantee the WSNs *Ef* at 90%. Thereby, it is demonstrated the effectiveness of the proposed technique. These figures depict the WSNs *Ef* and energy consumption between the WSN configured to transmit with the minimum transmission power level and the WSN implemented with the proposed approach. Observing such figures, it is possible to conclude that WSNs *Ef* associated to the network with the TPSO approach achieves an *Ef* of 93.2% while the WSN without the self-optimization algorithm reaches an *Ef* of 84%. Indeed, the higher WSNs *Ef* seen in Figure 23 has been achieved with an increase of about 170% of energy consumption.

6. Experiments Using WiFi Noise

Figures 24–27 demonstrate how the WSNs efficiency changes in the presence of WiFi noise. Figure 24 compares the energy consumed by a WSN in two different moments: (1) configured to transmit at the lowest power level available in the XBee PRO modules; and (2) with the WSN making use of the TPSO technique.

Figure 25 depicts the *Ef* of the WSN at two moments, one with the transmission power level fixed to 0, and one based on the TPSO technique. The WSN with the fixed transmission level reaches an average *Ef* of 46.4%, while the network based on the TPSO technique achieves 86.6%. In order to reach higher communication efficiency for the WSN, the TPSO technique switches to higher transmission power levels to cope with the introduced noise. This yields a 253% more energy consumed.

In Figures 26 and 27, we observe the results of the energy consumption and the efficiency of a WSN with a

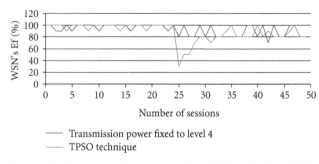

FIGURE 27: *Scenario 3*. Comparison of the WSNs *Ef* of the TPSO technique with respect to WSN operating with the transmission power fixed to level 4.

transmission power fixed to the maximum level in comparison with a network adopting the TPSO approach. In more detail, Figure 26 shows the power consumed by the WSN to communicate, while Figure 27 shows the WSNs *Ef*.

Observing Figure 26, we can clearly observe that the proposed approach reduces the transmission power level during the noise-free period (between sessions 0 and 25) and, thereby, dramatically reduces the overall WSN energy consumption. In detail, the technique is able to reduce the energy consumption by 46.12% along with the execution of the 50 sessions. The obtained results depicted in Figure 27 show that the average *Ef* drops from 92% to 89% when comparing the fixed transmission power level with the TPSO technique. Therefore, the proposed approach is able to reduce the power consumption to almost a half while reducing the WSNs *Ef* by only 3%. Indeed, it is important to underline that the WSNs *Ef* is still in between the tolerance interval predefined for these experiments, which is 5% higher or 5% lower than the WSNs *target_Ef*.

7. Final Considerations

In this paper, we present a transmission power self-optimization technique that aims at guaranteeing a given WSNs *Ef* while trying to reduce the energy consumption required to transmit data between nodes. Thus, the main idea behind the proposed algorithm is to optimize energy consumption when the environment inherent noise is low and to guarantee the connectivity and reliability of the transmitted data when the noise is high. In more detail, the self-optimization algorithm uses the information computed by the MN to adjust the transmission power level associated to each SN. Consequently, the self-optimization algorithm assures the compromise between WSNs *Ef* and energy consumption. In this scenario, the adoption of the TPSO technique increases the lifetime of WSNs in noisy environments without affecting their QoS.

Experimental results demonstrated the convenience of using the self-optimization algorithm instead of setting a fixed transmission power level available in the XBee PRO modules. When a WSN without the TPSO technique is considered, the transmission power is set at the beginning of the communication and remains the same during its entire

network lifetime. This characteristic can be negative considering a WSN in a real environment where the inherent noise is not constant.

Due to the fact that the inherent environment noise is completely variable and random, the TPSO technique will always guarantee the lowest possible transmission power during the communication, while ensuring the *target_Ef* when it is feasible. In this sense, if the noise is too high, the self-optimization algorithm will try to increase the transmission power level until reaching the targeted *Ef* or the transmission power's saturation. Reversely, if the noise is low, the TPSO technique adjusts the transmission power to the lowest possible level that guarantees the WSNs *target_Ef*. For battery-powered systems, the use of the proposed technique is very rewarding and, sometimes, the unique possible solution to ensure network's lifetime beyond minimum boundaries.

Acknowledgment

This work has been partially supported by the Brazilian National Science Foundation (CNPq) under contract number 490547/2007–2009.

References

[1] I. F. Akyildiz, W. Su, Y. Sankarasubramaniam, and E. Cayirci, "A survey on sensor networks," *IEEE Communications Magazine*, vol. 40, no. 8, pp. 102–105, 2002.

[2] A. Bhrathidasan and V. A. S. Ponduru, "Sensor networks: an overview," *IEEE Potentials*, vol. 22, no. 2, pp. 20–23, 2003.

[3] A. R. Pinto, M. Camada, M. A. R. Dantas, C. Montez, P. Portugal, and F. Vasques, "Genetic machine learning algorithms in the optimization of communication efficiency in wireless sensor networks," in *Proceedings of the 35th Annual Conference of the IEEE Industrial Electronics Society (IECON '09)*, pp. 2448–2453, November 2009.

[4] S. Panichpapiboon, G. Ferrari, and O. K. Tonguz, "Optimal transmit power in wireless sensor networks," *IEEE Transactions on Mobile Computing*, vol. 5, no. 10, Article ID 1683791, pp. 1432–1446, 2006.

[5] F. Wang, M. T. Thai, Y. Li, X. Cheng, and D. Z. Du, "Fault-tolerant topology control for all-to-one and one-to-all communication in wireless networks," *IEEE Transactions on Mobile Computing*, vol. 7, no. 3, pp. 322–331, 2008.

[6] C. A. Boano, Z. He, Y. Li, T. Voigt, M. Zuniga, and A. Willig, "Controllable radio interference for experimental and testing purposes in wireless sensor networks," in *Proceedings of the 4th International Worshop on Pratical Issues in Building Sensor Network Applications (SenseApp '09)*, 2009.

[7] F. Lavratti, A. R. Pinto, D. Prestes, L. Bolzani, F. Vargas, and C. Montez, "Towards a transmission power self-optimization in reliable wireless sensor networks," in *Proceedings of the 11th Latin-American Test Workshop (LATW '10)*, March 2010.

[8] F. Lavratti, A. R. Pinto, L. Bolzani et al., "Evaluating a transmission power self-optimization technique for WSN in EMI environments," in *Proceedings of the 13th Euromicro Conference on Digital System Design: Architectures, Methods and Tools (DSD '10)*, pp. 509–515, September 2010.

[9] J. A. Stankovic, T. F. Abdelzaher, C. Lu, L. Sha, and J. C. Hou, "Real-time communication and coordination in embedded

sensor networks," *Proceedings of the IEEE*, vol. 91, no. 7, pp. 1002–1022, 2003.

[10] J. O. Kephart and D. M. Chess, "The vision of autonomic computing," *Computer*, vol. 36, no. 1, pp. 41–50, 2003.

[11] XBee/XBee-PRO OEM RF Modules, http://www.digi.com.

[12] IEEE 802.15.4 Standard Specification, 2009, http://www .ieee802.org/15/pub/TG4.html.

[13] Electromagnetic Compatibility (EMC)—part 4-29: Testing and measurement techniques—Voltage dips, short interruptions and voltage variations on d.c. input power port immunity tests (1st Edition) Normative, 2000–2008, http://www.iec .ch.

[14] F. Vargas and D. P. Prestes, "Conducted electromagnetic noise generator for testing integrated circuits," Patent INPI number PI0705324-0 INPI, 2007, http://www.inpi.gov.br.

Permissions

The contributors of this book come from diverse backgrounds, making this book a truly international effort. This book will bring forth new frontiers with its revolutionizing research information and detailed analysis of the nascent developments around the world.

We would like to thank all the contributing authors for lending their expertise to make the book truly unique. They have played a crucial role in the development of this book. Without their invaluable contributions this book wouldn't have been possible. They have made vital efforts to compile up to date information on the varied aspects of this subject to make this book a valuable addition to the collection of many professionals and students.

This book was conceptualized with the vision of imparting up-to-date information and advanced data in this field. To ensure the same, a matchless editorial board was set up. Every individual on the board went through rigorous rounds of assessment to prove their worth. After which they invested a large part of their time researching and compiling the most relevant data for our readers. Conferences and sessions were held from time to time between the editorial board and the contributing authors to present the data in the most comprehensible form. The editorial team has worked tirelessly to provide valuable and valid information to help people across the globe.

Every chapter published in this book has been scrutinized by our experts. Their significance has been extensively debated. The topics covered herein carry significant findings which will fuel the growth of the discipline. They may even be implemented as practical applications or may be referred to as a beginning point for another development. Chapters in this book were first published by Hindawi Publishing Corporation; hereby published with permission under the Creative Commons Attribution License or equivalent.

The editorial board has been involved in producing this book since its inception. They have spent rigorous hours researching and exploring the diverse topics which have resulted in the successful publishing of this book. They have passed on their knowledge of decades through this book. To expedite this challenging task, the publisher supported the team at every step. A small team of assistant editors was also appointed to further simplify the editing procedure and attain best results for the readers.

Our editorial team has been hand-picked from every corner of the world. Their multi-ethnicity adds dynamic inputs to the discussions which result in innovative outcomes. These outcomes are then further discussed with the researchers and contributors who give their valuable feedback and opinion regarding the same. The feedback is then collaborated with the researches and they are edited in a comprehensive manner to aid the understanding of the subject.

Apart from the editorial board, the designing team has also invested a significant amount of their time in understanding the subject and creating the most relevant covers. They scrutinized every image to scout for the most suitable representation of the subject and create an appropriate cover for the book.

The publishing team has been involved in this book since its early stages. They were actively engaged in every process, be it collecting the data, connecting with the contributors or procuring relevant information. The team has been an ardent support to the editorial, designing and production team. Their endless efforts to recruit the best for this project, has resulted in the accomplishment of this book. They are a veteran in the field of academics and their pool of knowledge is as vast as their experience in printing. Their expertise and guidance has proved useful at every step. Their uncompromising quality standards have made this book an exceptional effort. Their encouragement from time to time has been an inspiration for everyone.

The publisher and the editorial board hope that this book will prove to be a valuable piece of knowledge for researchers, students, practitioners and scholars across the globe.

List of Contributors

Manju Mathew, A. B. Premkumar and A. S. Madhukumar
Centre for Multimedia and Network Technology, School of Computer Engineering, Nanyang Technological University, 50 Nanyang Avenue, Singapore

Shirook M. Ali, Huanhuan Gu, Kelce Wilson and James Warden
Advanced Technology, Research In Motion Limited, 560 Westmount Rd. N., Waterloo, ON, Canada

Jin Nakazawa and Hideyuki Tokuda
Faculty of Environment and Information Studies, Keio University, 5322 Endo, Fujisawa-shi, Kanagawa 252-0882, Japan

Jialing Li, Enoch Lu and I-Tai Lu
Department of ECE, Polytechnic Institute of NYU, 6 Metrotech Center, Brooklyn, NY 11201, USA

Jasmina Barakovic Husic
BH Telecom, Joint Stock Company, Sarajevo, Directorate BH Mobile, Obala Kulina bana 8, 71000 Sarajevo, Bosnia and Herzegovina

Himzo Bajric
BH Telecom, Joint Stock Company, Sarajevo, Executive Directorate for Technology and Service Development, Obala Kulina bana 8, 71000 Sarajevo, Trg BiH 1, 71000 Sarajevo, Bosnia and Herzegovina

Sabina Barakovic
Department for Informatics and Telecommunication Systems, Ministry of Security of Bosnia and Herzegovina, Trg BiH 1, 71000 Sarajevo, Bosnia and Herzegovina

Joao Paulo R. Pereira
School of Technology and Management, Polytechnic Institute of Braganca (IPB), 5301-857 Braganca, Portugal

Pedro Ferreira
Institute for Systems and Robotics, Technical University of Lisbon (IST), 1049-001 Lisbon, Portugal

Tafzeel ur Rehman Ahsin and Slimane Ben Slimane
Department of Communication Systems (CoS), School of Information and Communication Technology, KTH Royal Institute of Technology, 16440 Stockholm, Sweden

Saman Zonouz
University of Miami, Coral Gables, FL, USA

Parisa Haghani
University of Illinois, Champaign, IL, USA

Hongbing Lian and Andras Farago
Erik Jonsson School of Engineering and Computer Science, University of Texas at Dallas, Richardson, TX 75083, USA

F. A. Kuipers
Faculty of Electrical Engineering, Mathematics and Computer Science, Delft University of Technology, P.O. Box 5031, 2600 GA Delft, The Netherlands

Noelia Ortiz, Francisco Falcone and Mario Sorolla
Millimeter Wave Laboratory, Electrical and Electronic Engineering Department, Public University of Navarra, Arrosadia Campus, 31006 Pamplona, Spain

Jouni Hiltunen, Mikko Ala-Louko and Markus Taumberger
Converging Networks Laboratory, VTT Technical Research Centre of Finland, Kaitovayla 1, 90590 Oulu, Finland

Deng Chuan
Institute of Communication Engineering, PLA University of Science and Technology, Nanjing 210007, China

Wang Jian
National Key Laboratory of Automotive Dynamic Simulation, College of Automotive Engineering, Jilin University, Changchum 130025, China

Abbas Hasan Kattoush
EE Department, Tafila Technical University, Tafila 66110, Jordan

X. L. Travassos
Electromagnetic Devices Laboratory, SENAI-Integrated Centre of Manufacture and Technology, 41650-050 Salvador, BA, Brazil

D. A. G. Vieira and A. C. Lisboa
ENACOM-Handcrafted Technologies, 31310-260 Belo Horizonte, MG, Brazil

Giuliano Benelli, Stefano Parrino and Alessandro Pozzebon
Department of Information Engineering, University of Siena, Via Roma 56, 53100 Siena, Italy

F. Lavratti, A. Ceratti, D. Prestes, L. Bolzani and F. Vargas
Signals & Systems for Computing Group (SiSC), Catholic University of Rio Grande do Sul (PUCRS), 90619-900 Porto Alegre, RS, Brazil

A. R. Pinto
DCCE, Universidade Estadual Paulista (UNESP), 15054-000 Sao Jose do Rio Preto, SP, Brazil

C. Montez
PGEAS, Universidade Federal de Santa Catarina (UFSC), 88040-900 Florianopolis, SC, Brazil

F. Hernandez
Unidad Reguladora de Servicios de Comunicaciones (URSEC), Universidad ORT, 11300 Montevideo, Uruguay

E. Gatti
Instituto Nacional de Tecnologia Industrial (INTI), C1001AAF Buenos Aires, Argentina

C. Silva
Pontificia Universidad Catolica del Peru (PUCP), Lima 32, Peru

Printed in the USA
CPSIA information can be obtained
at www.ICGtesting.com
JSHW051444221024
72173JS00006B/1575

9 781632 401342